Sorrow AND Comfort

 A Devotional Study of Isaiah

WARREN HENDERSON

All Scripture quotations are from the New King James Version of the Bible, unless otherwise noted. Copyright © 1982 by Thomas Nelson, Inc. Nashville, TN

Sorrow and Comfort – A Devotional Study of Isaiah
By Warren Henderson
Copyright © 2017

Cover Design by Benjamin Bredeweg

Published by Warren A. Henderson
3769 Indiana Road
Pomona, KS 66076

Editing/Proofreading:
  Marilyn MacMullen, Dan Macy, David Lindstrom, and William Yuille

Perfect Bound ISBN 978-1-939770-42-4
eBook ISBN 978-1-939770-43-1

Available through many on-line retailers.

Other Books by the Author

Afterlife – What Will It Be Like?
Answer the Call – Finding Life's Purpose
Be Holy and Come Near – A Devotional Study of Leviticus
Behold the Saviour
Be Angry and Sin Not
Conquest and the Life of Rest – A Devotional Study of Joshua
Exploring the Pauline Epistles
Forsaken, Forgotten, and Forgiven – A Devotional Study of Jeremiah
Glories Seen & Unseen
Hallowed Be Thy Name – Revering Christ in a Casual World
Hiding God – The Ambition of World Religion
In Search of God – A Quest for Truth
Infidelity and Loyalty – A Devotional Study of Ezekiel and Daniel
Knowing the All-Knowing
Managing Anger God's Way
Mind Frames – Where Life's Battle Is Won or Lost
Out of Egypt – A Devotional Study of Exodus
Overcoming Your Bully
Passing the Torch – Mentoring the Next Generation For Christ
Relativity and Redemption – A Devotional Study of Judges and Ruth
Revive Us Again – A Devotional Study of Ezra and Nehemiah
Seeds of Destiny – A Devotional Study of Genesis
The Beginning of Wisdom – A Devotional Study of Job, Psalms, Proverbs, Ecclesiastes, and Song of Solomon
The Bible: Myth or Divine Truth?
The Evil Nexus – Are You Aiding the Enemy?
The Fruitful Bough – Affirming Biblical Manhood
The Fruitful Vine – Celebrating Biblical Womanhood
The Hope of Glory – A Preview of Things to Come
The Olive Plants – Raising Spiritual Children
Your Home the Birthing Place of Heaven

Table of Contents

Preface 1
Overview of Isaiah.. 3
Devotions in Isaiah 11
Endnotes 427

Preface

Our English word "comfort" is derived from two Latin roots, *con*, "to be with," and *fortis*, "strong." Literally "comfort" means "to strengthen by companionship."[1] A child facing a lonely trek down a dark road would naturally be filled with fear, but if his father comes alongside and holds his hand as they walk together, all fear is gone. Likewise, God wants His people to realize the blessed reality of His presence when facing life's trials in the ever-shifting valley of shadows: *"Yea, though I walk through the valley of the shadow of death, I will fear no evil; for You are with me; Your rod and Your staff, they comfort me"* (Ps. 23:4). "Comfort" in times of distress is one of the principal benefits of walking with God.

Therefore, Isaiah implores his countrymen who have suffered severe chastening to seek God's forgiveness and comfort through genuine repentance and humility. Comfort is a key component of Isaiah's overall message in his book. He desires the Jewish nation to experience *the Lord's salvation* (the meaning of Isaiah's name). It is not surprising then that the English word "comfort" (from the Hebrew *nacham*) appears more times in Isaiah than in any other book in the Bible. Godly comfort is the sole lasting solution for life's sorrows. Additionally, no other book in the Bible has more occurrences of the word "sorrow." Plainly, *sorrow and comfort* are intertwined qualities of the prophet's messages to God's covenant people:

> *The ransomed of the Lord shall return, and come to Zion with singing, with everlasting joy on their heads. They shall obtain joy and gladness; sorrow and sighing shall flee away. "I, even I, am He who comforts you. Who are you that you should be afraid?"* (51:11-12).

Isaiah reveals how God can righteously forgive repentant sinners and share with them His glory through the finished work of His faithful Servant, the Lord Jesus Christ – Israel's Messiah. We, in the Church Age, do well to consider all that Isaiah reveals about God's means of forgiveness, extending salvation, comfort, blessing, and the fullness of joy to the repentant.

Sorrow and Comfort is a "commentary-style" devotional which upholds the glories of Christ while exploring the book of Isaiah within the context of the whole of Scripture. I have endeavored to include in this book some principal gleanings from other writers. The short devotional format allows the reader to use the book either as a daily devotional or as a reference for deeper study.

— Warren Henderson

Overview of Isaiah

The Author

Isaiah is the author of the book which bears his name. His name means "Jehovah is salvation." We are informed that Isaiah was the son of Amoz (1:1). Jewish tradition holds that Isaiah was related to King Uzziah, but there is nothing in Scripture to suggest that. His prophetic ministry spanned the reigns of four Judean kings: Uzziah, Jotham, Ahaz, and Hezekiah (1:1). Isaiah likely died during Manasseh's rule. He lived in Jerusalem, was married, and had at least two sons, Shear-Jashub and Maher-Shalal-Hash-Baz, whose names, as we will see, have prophetic meanings (7:3, 8:3). Isaiah personally delivered God's messages to Ahaz (7:3) and Hezekiah (38:1). Isaiah's ministry began in the year that King Uzziah died (740 B.C.; 6:1, 14:28) and continued until after Sennacherib's death in 681 B.C. for a minimum of 58 years.

Some critics have suggested that chapters 40-66 were penned centuries later by a different author, who introduced Jewish history into Isaiah's writings as yet-unfulfilled prophecy. This would then explain how Isaiah was able to so precisely foretell future events, because in reality, these had already occurred. Sceptics often resort to this line of thinking, but the fact that the New Testament credits Isaiah with the authorship of the latter portion of his book should silence anyone who believes in the inerrancy of Scripture (Matt. 8:17; Luke 4:17-19).

The Date

As Isaiah wrote the biography of Hezekiah (2 Chron. 32:32) and recorded Sennacherib's death (37:38) it is likely that he died early in Manasseh's reign. Second-century church writer Justin Martyr states that Isaiah was sawn in half by Manasseh (he suggests that Hebrews 11:37 refers to Isaiah's martyrdom). Manasseh gained the throne of Judah in 686 B.C. It seems likely that the book was penned sometime between 687 and 681 B.C.; Isaiah would have been in his eighties.

Outline

The book of Isaiah divides readily into three main sections. The first section, dealing with various judgments (chps. 1-35) can be divided into three groupings of prophetic pronouncements: to Israel (chps. 1-12), to the Gentile nations (chps. 13-23), and to the entire world (chps. 24-27). The second section (chps. 36-39) is a historical record of God's intervention to save the Jewish nation from Assyrian invaders during the days of Hezekiah. The third section (chps. 40-66) is occupied with comfort for the faithful oppressed Jewish Remnant.

This final section of twenty-seven chapters can be further divided into three nine-chapter groups, which are separated by the phrase: *"There is no peace for the wicked"* (48:22, 57:21). The first nine-chapter section pertains to promises of Israel's future deliverance from Babylon and eventually from all Gentile oppression. The second division of nine chapters relates to prophecies of God's Messiah who will serve and suffer to secure a righteous means of satisfying God's wrath for Israel's sin. Chapter 53, speaking of Messiah's crucifixion, is the centerpiece of this section. The final nine chapters foretell the wonderful blessings available to the nation of Israel and to repentant Gentiles through Christ in the Kingdom Age, a time when Israel will be refined and restored to God, and Christ will rule the nations with a rod of iron.

The Theme

Two great themes are contrasted throughout Isaiah's book: God's chastening of the wayward, or punishment of the wicked, is compared with His comfort and blessing to the faithful. Despite Israel's infidelity, Isaiah declares God's determination to honor all His promises to their patriarchs. Paul explains that this was made possible through Christ.

> *For all the promises of God in Him are Yes, and in Him Amen, to the glory of God through us. Now He who establishes us with you in Christ and has anointed us is God, who also has sealed us and given us the Spirit in our hearts as a guarantee* (2 Cor. 1:20-22).

God's faithfulness and love was fully demonstrated to His covenant people by sending His only begotten Son to be their Messiah and Savior. Isaiah then foretells that Israel would initially despise and reject the One who was the solution to all their problems. Additionally, he

Overview of Isaiah

also prophesied that through Messiah's death and resurrection, Israel would later be forgiven and then restored to a position of honor and blessing among the nations under His rule. It is not surprising, then, that the glory of the kingdom, in some form, is found at the close of each of Isaiah's challenges against Jewish corruption and threats of judgment. To this end, J. G. Bellett suggests that there are five distinct and successive subjects addressed by the prophet:

1. Evil times, days of corruption in Israel, whether in the prophet's own time or otherwise.
2. Judgment of this corruption, whether by the Assyrian, the Chaldean, or others.
3. The present age, "the times of the Gentiles," the interval during which Israel is disclaimed.
4. The crisis, as it is sometimes called, "the times of the end," the last of the seventy weeks of Daniel, when God deals with Israel again, and enters on the closing judgment of the earth and the nations.
5. The glory of the kingdom which follows this crisis or judgment, commonly known by the name of the millennium. (These last two seasons or eras are called, as I may say, by all the prophets, "the day of the Lord.").[2]

In all these matters, God's steadfast faithfulness to Israel is demonstrated despite their rebellious ways. Though His covenant people would suffer much despair, God would be faithful to honor all His promises to them. This evangelical prophet confirms that God's comfort and salvation was available to them then, and is still available today through the Lord Jesus Christ!

Style

The prophetic content, vivid imagery, beautiful poetry, literary construction, use of metaphor, and overall brilliance of style make Isaiah a standout among Old Testament prophetic books. Merrill F. Unger said that "Isaiah is the greatest of the Hebrew prophets and orators. ... Correctly he has been called the 'Prince of Old Testament Prophets'"[3] Alfred Martin nicely summarizes the literary style of Isaiah:

> In extent and variety of vocabulary Isaiah excels; this is occasioned, no doubt, by the length of the book and by its unusual variety in subject matter. Figures of speech abound. Personification, metaphor,

simile follow one another in rapid succession. There is paronomasia, or play on words, [and alliterations] which in not usually evident in the English translation. There are actual songs in the book [e.g., chps. 5, 12, 35, 54 among others]. Another characteristic mark of Isaiah's style is his use of satire. Where could one find a more scathing denunciation of idolatry than in Isaiah's mocking comments about the man who cuts down a tree, uses part of it to make a fire to warm himself and to cook his food, and makes another part of it into a god (44:13-20)?[4]

New Testament Quotations

The Christ-enriched text of Isaiah is frequently referenced throughout the New Testament. In all there are 66 direct quotations and 348 allusions to Isaiah's writings in the New Testament. The only Old Testament book with more references in the New Testament is Psalms with 79 quotations and 333 allusions.[5] J. G. Bellett outlines the book of Isaiah as follows and then observes that revelation from each segment (excluding the historical section of chapters 36-39) is quoted in the New Testament to ensure prophetic continuity in revealing the Lord Jesus as the Jewish Messiah:

Subjects:
1. The Preface, Isa. 1
2. The Day of the Lord, Isa. 2-4
3. The Vineyard, Isa. 5
4. The Throne of Judicial Glory, Isa. 6
5. The Confederacy; or, Emmanuel and the Children, Isa. 7-9:7
6. The Assyrians, Isa. 9:8-12
7. The Threshing of Nations, Isa. 13-27
8. The Five [Six] Woes, Isa. 28-35
9. The Historic Interlude, Isa. 36-39
10. Israel in Babylon, Isa. 40-48
11. Jesus and Jerusalem, Isa. 49
12. The Risen Jesus and the Remnant, Isa. 50-52:12
13. The Cross and its Virtues, Isa. 52:13-55
14. The Remnant Manifested, Isa. 56-57
15. Israel Trained for the Kingdom, Isa. 58-60
16. The Two Advents, Isa. 61-63:6
17. Israel's Prayer and Messiah's Answer, Isa. 63:7-65
18. The Conclusion, Isa. 66[6]

The developing theme of God's faithfulness despite Israel's moral and spiritual failure becomes most evident at chapter 40, with the disclosure of prophetic details pertaining to Christ's first advent. This section could be prefaced by Paul's declaration to the Galatians: *"But when the fullness of the time had come, God sent forth His Son, born of a woman, born under the law, to redeem those who were under the law, that we might receive the adoption as sons"* (Gal. 4:4-5). Isaiah supplies more prophetic references to the coming Messiah than any other Old Testament prophet. It should be no surprise, then, that during His earthly sojourn the Lord Jesus quoted Isaiah more than any other prophet.

The Holy One of Israel

Forty-two times in the Old Testament God is spoken of as "the Holy One"; thirty of these references are in Isaiah. The more specific title "the Holy One of Israel" is found thirty-one times in the Old Testament, with twenty-five of these references occurring in Isaiah. "The Holy One of Israel" is clearly the characteristic title of God throughout the book of Isaiah and speaks of the distinct and unique relationship that the Creator has with the Jewish nation.

A Mini-Bible

It is understood that chapter and verse delineations were not assigned to Isaiah until the mid-sixteenth century, about two millennia after the book was written. However, its organization of sixty-six chapters is a remarkable reflection of the whole Bible which consists of sixty-six books. The first thirty-nine chapters of Isaiah are a volume of judgments against wayward Israel and the surrounding pagan nations. This section aligns well with the thirty-nine books of the Old Testament as the Jews were under the Law, which demanded judgment for disobedience. God is holy; blatant Jewish transgression and the wickedness of the nations must be punished.

The final twenty-seven chapters of Isaiah reflect the central message of the New Testament – comfort and renewal to repentant sinners through the New Covenant sealed with Christ's own blood (Heb. 8:8). Isaiah foretells that the Messiah, God incarnate, is coming to the earth to be nailed to the cross and be judged for humanity's sin. Then He will be exalted to His throne to rule the entire planet.

Sorrow and Comfort

The correlations of Isaiah's chapter structure and New Testament books are many. For example, Matthew, the fortieth book of the Bible, quotes from Isaiah chapter forty and verse 3:

> *In those days John the Baptist came preaching in the wilderness of Judea, and saying, "Repent, for the kingdom of heaven is at hand!" For this is he who was spoken of by the prophet Isaiah, saying: "The voice of one crying in the wilderness: 'Prepare the way of the Lord; make His paths straight'"* (Matt. 3:1-3).

Besides announcing the ministry of John the Baptist to prepare the way for the Lord's messianic ministry (40:3), Isaiah also reveals the essence of the One John would later be speaking of:

> **The glory of the Lord shall be revealed, and all flesh shall see** *it together; for the mouth of the Lord has spoken* (40:5).

> *O Zion, you who bring good tidings, get up into the high mountain; O Jerusalem, you who bring good tidings, lift up your voice with strength, lift it up, be not afraid; say to the cities of Judah,* **"Behold your God!"** (40:9).

The Son of God descended from the heights of heaven and came to earth to be born of a lowly virgin: *"Behold, the virgin shall conceive and bear a Son, and shall call His name Immanuel"* (7:14). Indeed, phrases such as *"the glory of the Lord shall be revealed," "all flesh shall see,"* and *"behold your God"* tell us that the Messiah would be God incarnate. The writer of Hebrews expresses the matter this way:

> *In these last days spoken to us by His Son, whom He has appointed heir of all things, through whom also He made the worlds; who being the brightness of His glory and the express image of His person, and upholding all things by the word of His power, when He had by Himself purged our sins, sat down at the right hand of the Majesty on high, having become so much better than the angels, as He has by inheritance obtained a more excellent name than they* (Heb. 1:2-4).

Messiah would be the brightness of God's glory and the express image of His person (Heb. 1:2-4). This revelation is first presented in Matthew in the New Testament (the fortieth book of the Bible) by quoting the fortieth chapter of Isaiah. To ensure that everyone understands who Messiah really is, Matthew quotes Isaiah 7:14, but then adds the meaning of *Immanuel* – *"God with us"* (Matt. 1:23). This is why the Lord Jesus declared, *"He who has seen Me has seen the Father"* (John 14:9).

The organization of Isaiah, its vivid poetic imagery, its many specific predictions of Christ and the consummation of God's salvation for Israel, cause this book to be a standout among all other prophetic books. May the Lord refresh our hearts as we contemplate its vast revelation concerning both advents of the Savior and the overall faithfulness of God to accomplish all that He says He will do.

> Isaiah ... is the greatest of the Hebrew prophets and orators. For splendor of diction, brilliance of imagery, versatility and beauty of style, he is unequalled. Correctly he has been called the "Prince of Old Testament Prophets."
>
> — Merrill F. Unger

Devotions in Isaiah

God's Hatred
Isaiah 1:1-17

The book commences with these words, *"The vision of Isaiah the son of Amoz"* (v. 1). The prophetic books of Obadiah, Micah, and Nahum begin in a similar fashion. Moses foretold that Jehovah would speak to the Jewish nation through prophets. Additionally, God would communicate with His prophets through supernatural means, such as visions: *"If there is a prophet among you, I, the Lord, make Myself known to him in a vision"* (Num. 12:6). Isaiah, the son of Amoz, was such a prophet. Old Testament prophets not only heard the Lord, but often saw the very messages they were to convey to God's people.

Isaiah's ministry was to the southern kingdom, and it extended through the reigns of four kings: Uzziah, Jotham, Ahaz, and Hezekiah (v. 1). From a political, economic, and military standpoint, all these kings fared well. Three of the kings did largely what was morally right, Hezekiah especially so, but Ahaz did much evil, including offering his own children as burnt sacrifices to Baal (2 Chron. 28:2-3). Some historical evidence suggests that Isaiah continued his prophetic ministry until being executed by King Manasseh. Manasseh reigned longer and did more evil than any other monarch of the Southern Kingdom.

Speaking for the Lord, Isaiah summons the heavens and the earth to hear God's indictment against Israel: *"Hear, O heavens, and give ear, O earth!"* (v. 2). The Hebrew word for *"hear"* means "to consider intelligently" while the latter Hebrew verb rendered *"give ear"* simply means, "listen." The idea then is to thoroughly listen to God's case against His people and then to render an intelligent decision. This literary device was employed by the prophet to undeniably affirm that all creation would agree with God on the validity of His accusations.

As compared to the remainder of the book, this opening message, in which God charges His covenant people and their capital city with flagrant ingratitude, has a more general character than any other chapter. Indeed, the second message, detailing crimes and judicial penalties (2:1-4:6) and the woe message of chapter 5, reads more like a preface for the book. Perhaps this is why Isaiah organized his book so that his calling in chapter 6 follows his introductory remarks in the first five chapters.

God Hates Israel's Sin

God had labored to create and build up a special people for His good pleasure, but the Jewish nation had rebelled against His intentions and care for them (v. 2). Isaiah then describes the deplorable spiritual state of the Jewish nation as one of insensibility and indifference to the things of God. The Jewish nation did not even display the instinctive awareness and respect that an ox possesses for its owner, or a donkey (known proverbially as a stupid animal) for its master's crib (v. 3).

> The brutes obey their God,
> And bow their necks to men;
> But we more base, more brutish things,
> Reject His easy reign.
>
> — Isaac Watts

Israel superficially identified with the Lord, but did not know Him, and worse, did not want to know Him, nor did they recognize the Lord's claims upon them; hence Isaiah's harsh indictment:

Alas, sinful nation, a people laden with iniquity, a brood of evildoers, children who are corrupters! They have forsaken the Lord, they have provoked to anger the Holy One of Israel, they have turned away backward (v. 4).

Let us not pass over this injunction without challenging our own hearts. To what extent do we really know our Owner, the Lord Jesus Christ, and to what measure are we satisfied with Him? The crib speaks of where we rest and are fed – where we are refreshed. How well do we know God's Word and character? How willing are we to rest in Him, trust His promises, and honor His commands? The prophet's message is timeless: Those redeemed by the crucified One owe Him their full allegiance and devotion, not a superficial religious nod.

As mentioned in the *Overview* section, the title "the Holy One of Israel" is found twenty-five times in Isaiah and speaks of God's awesome purity in relationship to Israel. "The Holy One of Israel" was intimately aware that the spiritual disposition of His people was deplorable. Even with God-fearing kings ruling over them, they were full of iniquity, evil-doings, and corruption. Then writing as if the future had already taken place, Isaiah said that Judah had experienced God's chastening hand through natural disasters and merciless invaders, but without a transforming effect (vv. 5-7). Their open sores and untreated wounds pictured their wretched spiritual condition, but though badly beaten and bruised, they were still oblivious as to why they were suffering.

Militarily speaking, Judah was like a makeshift shelter for laborers in the melon patch – an easy target for conquest, but for the sake of His covenant, God protected His people from extinction (v. 8). He chose to maintain a remnant of them in the land and not to annihilate them as He did the wicked inhabitants of Sodom and Gomorrah (v. 9). Paul informs us in the Epistle to the Romans that God has always maintained a faithful Jewish remnant through the ages. Paul quotes verse 9 to affirm that even in Israel's final restoration, only a remnant will be saved; most will not trust in Christ for salvation (Rom. 9:29). This understanding is important, as it better identifies the audience that Isaiah is mainly addressing throughout his book – the loyal Jewish remnant and not apostate Israel.

God Hates Israel's Religion

Having just spoken of the wicked cities God destroyed centuries earlier, Isaiah then likens the civil and religious leaders of his day to the rulers of Sodom and Gomorrah (v. 10). Yet, Israel had greater guilt than the heathen, for Israel had more divine light to walk in. Consequently, the prophet does more than just condemn the wicked; he calls Israel's vain religiosity an abomination to God:

> *"To what purpose is the multitude of your sacrifices to Me?" says the Lord. "I have had enough of burnt offerings of rams and the fat of fed cattle. I do not delight in the blood of bulls, or of lambs or goats. When you come to appear before Me, who has required this from your hand, to trample My courts? Bring no more futile sacrifices; incense is an abomination to Me. The New Moons, the Sabbaths, and the calling of assemblies – I cannot endure iniquity and the sacred*

meeting. Your New Moons and your appointed feasts My soul hates; they are a trouble to Me, I am weary of bearing them. When you spread out your hands, I will hide My eyes from you; even though you make many prayers, I will not hear. Your hands are full of blood" (vv. 11-15).

The Lord was fed up with Israel's vain religiosity: *"Wickedness and the solemn meeting I cannot bear"* (v. 13; JND). He utterly despised their sacrifices, offerings, prayers, and observances! The seriousness of Israel's offense is bluntly expressed by the phrase *"My soul hates"* in verse 14, which literally means, "I hate with all my heart!" The Jews were a morally corrupt and spiritually bankrupt people that were using religion as a cloak to cover their sin. The nation was superficially observing the Law without understanding the real purpose of what they were doing. William Kelly observes that the Jews in Isaiah's day had sacred form without the power of divine truth:

> Divine privileges only rendered their moral state more portentous and intolerable. If they approached the doom of Sodom but for Jehovah's mercy, morally they were already Sodom, and, therefore, their sacrifices, feasts, and assemblies all the more odious to Jehovah, who felt His courts to be profaned by their tread, and refused to hear their multiplied prayers. There was no real repentance, no trembling at His word, but a religious veil over utter and shameless iniquity.[7]

Truth is a prominent moral and personal attribute of God: He is *"the God of truth"* (65:16), thus all that God says and commands is founded in truth (Ps. 119:142, 151). The Psalmist declares, *"the entirety of Your word is truth"* (119:160). God's perfect nature ensures that nothing less than absolute truth will be evident in all His words and deeds; He cannot lie or act contrary to His holy character (1 Sam. 15:29; Heb. 6:18). Therefore, if man truly desires to lay hold of deep truth (i.e. those unfathomable mysteries beyond natural explanation), he must venture beyond humanism, religiosity, and pride to humbly beseech Him who is the embodiment of all truth.

The Jews had religious movement, but no spiritual direction. The temple was bustling with pious activity, but true worshippers must approach God in revealed truth, and with pure hearts and clean hands to refresh His heart. To do otherwise, as Solomon proclaims, provokes the Lord to jealous anger: *"One who turns away his ear from hearing the law, even his prayer is an abomination"* (Prov. 28:9). Though the Jews offered up *"many prayers"* to Jehovah, He ignored their irritating gestures of piety because of their deplorable spiritual and moral state. They lifted up their hands in prayer, but failed to notice that their hands were stained with innocent blood (v. 15). Actions speak louder than words, especially when the One who is listening and watching is omniscient. Their hearts were far from the Lord; their actions were offending the Lord, and hence, their prayers were loathed by Him.

Much of the vain religiosity of Judaism is alive and well in Christendom today. Sadly, many professing Christians have become dull to the Word of God, deaf to the conviction of the Holy Spirit, and seared in their conscience such that they can mindlessly practice their religion while continuing in sin. Isaiah's rebuke of Judah is no less applicable today. Dear believer, are you appreciating the joyful presence of a holy God? Do you feel that the Lord is hearing and acting on your prayers? If not, it is time to take action. The following are several reasons why God may choose to ignore or not act on our prayers with favor:

1. Rejecting or not yielding to God's Word (Prov. 28:9; 1 Jn. 3:22).
2. Husbands not properly caring for and respecting their wives (1 Pet. 3:7).
3. Fostering selfish motives (Jas. 4:3).
4. Having an unforgiving heart (Mark 11:25).
5. Doubting God's faithfulness (Jas. 1:6-7; Mark 11:24).
6. Praying with unconfessed sin (Ps. 66:18).
7. Praying for what is contrary to God's will (1 Jn. 5:14-15).

The Church would do well to heed Isaiah's warning to Israel. It is human nature to traditionalize that which has no importance to God to displace what does. If Isaiah were before us today, he would affirm that the Lord hates check-the-box Christianity with the same fervor as He hates vain Judaism. That which displaces true devotion to and appreciation for Christ with meaningless religious trinkets and habitual routines is loathsome to God.

When our awe of God is supplanted by stained-glass windows, huge pipe organs, gold crucifixes, burning candles, smoking incense, fancifully robed clergymen; or when meetings of the church become social gatherings; or when the study of God's Word is replaced by

Sorrow and Comfort

friendly chit-chat, storytelling, and entertaining spoofs; or when praising God becomes the occupation of professionals instead of the delight of all God's people; or when family activities trump meetings of the church; or when the lack of creature comforts hinders us from engaging in worship, we are no less guilty of snubbing God than Israel was in Isaiah's day. Would not such behavior then provoke God's chastening hand? Lord, we ask you to do whatever it takes to awaken the pampered Church from her lethargic, semi-comatose spiritual condition, for You must have the preeminence in all things, especially in Your Church (Col. 1:18)!

Meditation

> Nothing exposes religion more to the reproach of its enemies than the worldliness and hard-heartedness of its professors.
>
> — Matthew Henry

> I consider that the chief dangers which confront the coming century will be religion without the Holy Ghost; Christianity without Christ; forgiveness without repentance; salvation without regeneration; politics without God; and Heaven without Hell.
>
> — William Booth

Let Us Reason Together
Isaiah 1:18-31

Israel's Options

The only solution to the spiritual travesty that Isaiah has just described is wholesale and heartfelt repentance. Israel needed to abandon the old life and to adopt new patterns of thinking which would prompt godly conduct (vv. 16-17). God's people must be washed through repentance, then cease from evil, seek justice, do what is good and proper, and assist those in need. One cannot pursue righteousness without first choosing to be cleansed of corruption. James also affirms this to be the solution to spiritual lethargy in the Church Age:

> But he who looks into the perfect law of liberty and continues in it, and is not a forgetful hearer but a doer of the work, this one will be blessed in what he does. If anyone among you thinks he is religious, and does not bridle his tongue but deceives his own heart, this one's religion is useless. Pure and undefiled religion before God and the Father is this: to visit orphans and widows in their trouble, and to keep oneself unspotted from the world (Jas. 1:25-27).

Christianity is not a religion, but Christian doctrine lived out produces the right kind of religion that pleases God. When one comes into a right relationship with God through the Lord Jesus Christ, then, and only then, is he or she able to please God by doing sincere and God-enabled deeds. World religion is an exhaustive system of *doings* apart from God's truth and God's enablement. The doing of good things does not define what true Christianity is, but Spirit-filled Christians do prove that Christianity is real. God is not impressed by religious ritual, developed church tradition, sanctimonious form, and denominational smugness, but rather with personal living that conforms to divine truth (Col. 2:20-23).

After confronting Israel about their vain religiosity and telling them what they needed to do to please God, He then informs them how to do it – truly seek the Lord and receive cleansing and forgiveness:

> *"Come now, and let us reason together," says the Lord, "though your sins are like scarlet, they shall be as white as snow; though they are red like crimson, they shall be as wool. If you are willing and obedient, you shall eat the good of the land; but if you refuse and rebel, you shall be devoured by the sword"; for the mouth of the Lord has spoken* (vv. 18-20).

The scene pictures a courtroom where two parties present their arguments in a particular case. Israel does not speak, but the Lord does: *"Come now, and let us reason together"* (v. 18). This statement cannot be separated from the previous rebuke: *"Wash yourselves, make yourselves clean; put away the evil of your doings from before My eyes. Cease to do evil, learn to do good"* (vv. 16-17). Willful obedience verifies that the Word of God was effectual in changing the heart and conscience. This means that the hearer received and acted upon Scripture in genuine faith. God's grace is not contingent on doing good deeds or on self-advancement in righteousness; rather His promises of blessings are received by those who trust and obey His Word. Divine blessing follows our repentance and cleansing. This is the type of reasoning which ultimately leads to receiving God's gift of salvation. Approaching God any other way than through faith in His Word leaves the debt of sin (Rom. 4:3-4).

Scripture repeatedly offers man an opportunity to search out and commune with God if man will yield to what God wants him to understand: *"You will seek Me and find Me, when you search for Me with all your heart"* (Jer. 29:13). *"Now set your heart and your soul to seek the Lord your God"* (1 Chron. 22:19). *"The Lord is near to all who call upon Him, to all who call upon Him in truth"* (Ps. 145:18). God is *reason-able*, and He invites man to explore truth with Him. King Solomon wisely instructed, *"Consider the work of God"* (Eccl. 7:13). Man is to ponder God's nature, character, Word, and works, but must include Him in the exercise, or else humanly-derived conclusions will lack reliability. We must reason together with God. Why? Because without God's help man cannot understand or reason out what God has purposely concealed: *"The secret things belong to the Lord our God, but those things which are revealed belong to us and to our children"* (Deut. 29:29). Because God alone holds absolute truth, He will always transcend human reasoning and religion.

William MacDonald summarizes what Isaiah is saying to his countrymen:

> Divine reasoning, accepted by faith, teaches that there is cleansing from sin, that this cleansing is totally apart from human merit or effort, and that it is only through the redemption which the Lord Jesus accomplished by the shedding of His blood on the cross.[8]

This divine reasoning and admonition spans all dispensations of God's working with humanity – those who humble themselves before the Lord and come to Him on His terms will be forgiven. "Willing" and "obedient" in verse 19 and "refuse" and "rebel" in verse 20 are paired words relating to the human will and its choices. God is always ready to extend grace and forgiveness to those who will agree with Him on the matter of sin, and will act in faith to stand with Him against themselves. F. B. Hole explains how these words of grace and forgiveness are a foreshadowing of the gospel message today:

> The "all have sinned" of Romans 3 is followed by justification, freely offered through "His grace." Only the cleansing, offered in verse 18, was in its nature a "passing over" of sins "through the forbearance of God," as stated in Romans 3:25, since the only basis for a cleansing full and eternal lay in the sacrifice of Christ, centuries ahead. Notice too how "if" occurs in verses 19 and 20. The cleansing and blessing offered hinge upon obedience. To refuse and rebel brings judgment. Both blessing and judgment are concerned with matters of this life, since what is involved in the life to come appears but little in the Old Testament. When the Gospel preacher of today happily and appropriately uses these verses, he of course refers to the eternal consequences of receiving or rejecting the offer, basing what he says on New Testament scripture.[9]

Whether to the Jews, the Church, or the lost, God is calling and pleading with individuals to trust Him, but He does not force anyone heavenward against his or her will. Because reason and free choice are required to approach God, man is required to weigh out the evidence, grapple over the possibilities, consider God's Word, and come to a logical conclusion which will cause him to act in good faith. God assists a true seeker every step of the way. Reasoning without God leads us nowhere (Prov. 1:7, 9:10)! Unfortunately, Israel rejected the messages of God's prophets. The nation would not reason together with

Sorrow and Comfort

the Lord. May the Church learn from their mistake: right morality and spiritualty are far more important to God than ceremonial exactness and religious form.

Israel's Judgment

Originally, God considered Jerusalem a faithful city (probably speaking of her initial condition under David's and Solomon's reigns), but now she is adulterous, exemplifying all the evil that afflicted the land (v. 21). Jeremiah, Ezekiel, and Hosea also invoke the imagery of the virgin wife of Jehovah (Israel) becoming a lascivious harlot to speak of her moral filth and idolatrous ways. Previously, God had greatly valued her purity, but now the Jewish nation was as repugnant as watered-down wine and worthless as dross metal (vv. 22-23). Alfred Barnes notes:

> Wine was regarded as the most pure and valuable drink among the ancients. It is used, therefore, to express that which should have been most valued and esteemed among them – that is to say, their rulers.[10]

Watered-down wine was distasteful to the palate and dross has no value; likewise Israel had been intermingled with those things which weakened their purity and destroyed their virtue. As a result, God promised to exile His people. This punitive act would cause them to realize how intolerable they were to Him in their degenerate state (v. 24). It is a somber thing to hear God refer to His people as His enemies and adversaries; however, the terminology conveys the heartache, jealousy, and anger God feels when His people disparage Him and misplace their devotion. From God's perspective, Israel's behavior was adulterous!

The New Testament contains a similar warning for believers. God hates worldliness in the Church today as He did in Israel in Isaiah's day (Jas. 4:4). It is vitally important to realize that lusting in our hearts for what God hates is no less offensive to Him than actually engaging in it. The Lord Jesus taught that adultery in the heart is disloyalty from God's perspective; unfortunately, we are all guilty of this form of infidelity (Matt. 5:28)!

> Passion is the evil in adultery. If a man has no opportunity of living with another man's wife, but if it is obvious for some reason that he

would like to do so, and would do so if he could, he is no less guilty than if he was caught in the act.

— Augustine

Consecration to God demands purity in thought and deed because He is worthy of such contemplations and behavior. We must keep ourselves clean from worldliness (Jas. 4:4), humanism (Col. 2:8), unlawful lusting (Gal. 5:16-17), and the deeds of the flesh (Col. 3:5). A holy life is essential for dedicated service to the Lord and it is our affection and appreciation for Christ, the Head of the Church, that motivates us to be holy. The loss of love for Christ and of enjoying His presence results in unholy living and apostasy, which then prompts His displeasure.

The second and third chapters of Revelation contain an important example of what happens when the Church's affection for Christ wanes. In order of digression, the church at Ephesus left its first love – Christ (Rev. 2:4), as a result *"the deeds of the Nicolaitans"* (Rev. 2:6) developed in that church, which then led to *"the doctrine of the Nicolaitans"* in the church at Pergamos (Rev. 2:15). With Christ supplanted as head by a clergy system, the next compromise was that a woman named Jezebel was being allowed to teach and lead the church at Thyatira (Rev. 2:20). Next is the church at Sardis, to whom the Lord says, *"thou hast a name that thou livest,* **and art dead***"* (Rev. 3:1; KJV). The Church engages in dead works when Christ is not the center and head of its gathering. Hence six times the Lord demands that these four churches repent of their wicked ways. Not only is the Lord worthy of our affection, but undefiled love for Him will also safeguard us against worldliness and engaging in false doctrine.

Having reviewed Jerusalem's past faithfulness (v. 21) and her present putrid condition (vv. 22-23), the prophet now foretells Jerusalem's future (vv. 24-31). God's judgments on the Jewish nation will purge the dross and reestablish a faithful remnant in Israel (v. 25), honorable judges and rulers over His people (v. 26), and Jerusalem as a righteous city: *"Zion shall be redeemed with justice, and her penitents with righteousness"* (v. 27). Then God's justice will rule over the land.

God's purifying judgment will destroy the wicked; all those with pagan garden shrines or who had embraced idols under the terebinth (sacred oak) trees will be ashamed (vv. 28-30). They and their works shall be burned with unquenchable fire (v. 31). This may refer to Babylon's destruction of Jerusalem, but more specifically, Isaiah is speaking of the eternal judgment of the wicked in the Lake of Fire (Rev. 20:11-15).

In summary, the outcome of God's litigation against the Jewish nation is that the repentant will be purified, restored, and blessed, but the rebellious will be punished forever. Ultimately, God will have a holy people solely for Himself and be fully vindicated of the wicked. God's indignation will be satisfied and then peace, righteousness, and prosperity will govern man's habitation with God.

Meditation

> A true revival means nothing less than a revolution, casting out the spirit of worldliness and selfishness, and making God and His love triumph in the heart and life.
>
> — Andrew Murray

Jerusalem's Restoration
Isaiah 2

The first chapter was introduced as a "vision" that Isaiah saw, but in this chapter the prophet speaks of "the word" that he had witnessed (v. 1). This indicates the delivery of a second message (chps. 2-4) which was distinct from the first in timing and content. J. M. Riddle describes the complementary organization of the two distinct sections of this message, both of which describe the coming glory of Jerusalem.

> The unit begins and ends with a description of Jerusalem's coming glory, but the emphases are different. The unit commences by describing her *administrative glory* (2:1-5), and concludes by describing her ultimate *moral glory* (4:2-6). The intervening verses describe the way in which her moral glory will be achieved. Jerusalem's coming glory, described in 2:1-5, will only be attained after sin has been thoroughly judged. There must be purging before blessing. ... [The section addressing Jerusalem's moral glory] may be considered as follows: The conditions necessitating divine judgment (2:6-9); the chastening necessary before blessing (2:10-4:1); the coming moral glory of God's people (4:2-6).[11]

The prophet speaks of Jerusalem's future prominence in the Millennial Kingdom in order to post a warning against Israel's present worldliness and idolatry. The previous chapter concluded with God's promise to judge the wicked with unquenchable fire and to eternally bless the righteous. Isaiah continues the latter thought by further explaining the good things that would come to Israel *"in the latter days"* when the house of Jehovah will be established. When God has His rightful place among men, divine blessings flow from His temple and the *"nations shall flow to it"* (v. 2).

The Mountain

This future era of bliss will occur *"when the mountain of the Lord's house"* (v. 2) will be above all mountains of the earth (i.e., God's

Sorrow and Comfort

kingdom will have worldwide acknowledgment and rule). Isaiah and Micah were contemporaries, and both prophets foretold God's glorious mountain on earth, speaking of Messiah's future earthly kingdom (Micah 4:1-3).

When applied metaphorically in Scripture, mountains symbolize governmental authorities or kingdoms (e.g., Micah 4:1; Rev. 17:9-10). There was one instance during the latter days of the Lord's ministry in Decapolis that a brilliant outshining of His glory was witnessed by three of His disciples. The event is what we commonly call the "transfiguration" of the Lord and foretells what Isaiah is alluding to in verses 2-5. Matthew describes the scene:

> *Now after six days Jesus took Peter, James, and John his brother, led them up on a high mountain by themselves; and He was transfigured before them. His face shone like the sun, and His clothes became as white as the light* (Matt. 17:1-2).

One can only imagine the dazzling glory of the Lord on this high mountain in a remote region and apparently at night (Luke 9:32-37). In the preceding verse, the Lord Jesus had said, *"Assuredly, I say to you, there are some standing here who shall not taste death till they see the Son of Man coming in His kingdom"* (Matt. 16:28). Years later, Peter confirmed what was represented by this incident: *"the power and coming of our Lord Jesus Christ"* – the revealing of *"His majesty"* (2 Pet. 1:16). For a brief moment the disciples were given a foretaste of the coming kingdom.

While Christ was transfigured a bright cloud overshadowed the mount and God the Father declared, *"This is My beloved Son, in whom I am well pleased. Hear Him!"* (Matt. 17:5). There is a glorious earthly kingdom coming in which Jesus Christ will be wonderfully recognized as Son by the Father. He will rule the earth with the full glory, honor, and authority of who He is as the faithful Son of God.

In summary, the transfiguration foretells a future day when Christ will return to judge the nations and His glory will be seen throughout the earth (vv. 10, 19, 21). When that kingdom is established, the word of God will go forth from Jerusalem and the righteous from all nations will come to *"the house of the God of Jacob"* and be taught by Christ (v. 3). No injustice, violence, and warring will be permitted in Christ's kingdom; it will be characterized by peace, prosperity, and righteousness (v. 4).

Walking in the Light

Not only will all nations seek Israel's God, "the house of Jacob," speaking of Israel, will enjoy communion with Him also. The entire Jewish nation will *"walk in the light of the Lord"* (v. 5). Isaiah employs the term "the house of Jacob" eight times in his book to speak of Israel. In chapter 4, Isaiah tells us that the Jews who live through the Tribulation will gaze upon Christ (the Branch of the Lord) and appreciate His splendor, glory, fruitfulness, and beauty (4:2-4). Given Isaiah's revelation it would be sensible for Israel to walk with God in the light now. They should not wait until the kingdom to obey God's Law. Isaiah then identifies the infractions of God's people against His Law (vv. 6-11) and the consequences of their disobedience if they did not repent (2:12-4:1).

Why had God chosen not to commune with His people and instead was poised to punish them? Isaiah rehearses Israel's sins:

- They were following the religious practices of the East, probably referring to the Assyrians (v. 6).
- They were engaging in soothsaying like the Philistines (v. 6).
- They were forging alliances with heathen nations, thus undermining the consecration of their children (v. 6).
- They were trusting in their great wealth and horses/chariots (i.e., military strength) instead of the Lord (v. 7).
- They were worshiping idols they had made with their own hands (vv. 8-9).

Matthew Henry derives a prudent application for the Church to consider given God's charges against Israel in verse 7:

> It is not having silver and gold, horses and chariots, that displeases God, but depending upon them, as if we could not be safe, and easy, and happy without them, and could not but be so with them. Sin is a disgrace to the poorest and the lowest. And though lands called Christian are not full of idols, in the literal sense, are they not full of idolized riches? And are not men so busy about their gains and indulgences, that the Lord, his truths, and precepts, are forgotten or despised?[12]

Although God had not rendered His sentence yet, the above indictments explain why Isaiah exclaims: *"Jerusalem is ruined, and*

Judah is fallen" (3:8). The Jews, and no one else, were responsible for pulling God's judgment down on their heads. The sickening depravity of the nation caused the indignant prophet to ask the Lord not to forgive those bowing down to idols (v. 9). Obviously, the prophet loved his countrymen, but this literary ploy emphasizes the utter travesty of Israel's spiritual condition – they did not deserve God's mercy! J. A. Motyer refers to verses 6-9 as the most rhythmic and compelling piece that Isaiah ever wrote; he then adds, "it opens with *abandoned* and ends with *do not forgive* – an iron band of hopelessness gripping the apostates."[13] He further notes what self-sufficient nations, like Israel, pride themselves in:

> Verses 6-8 contain things on which nations pride themselves: Broad-minded tolerance (v. 6), financial reserves (v. 7a), military potential (v. 7b), and religious interest (v. 8). These are not matters of pride, says Isaiah, but things which have brought low and humbled all alike. … When human beings depart from the Lord – no matter what they depart to – they progressively lose their true humanity. Their dignity, the image of God, is humiliated.[14]

There are at least two applications from the prophet's indictment against Israel which are pertinent for the Church to heed today. First, where there is much gold and silver, general affluence and self-sufficiency (pictured in the horses and chariots), idols will abound as there is no reason to seek, know, or yield to God. It is natural for men, in times of plenty, to worship the works of their hands and to esteem their own doings, but during a season of need, or desperation, they cry out for help to One they perceive to be more powerful. No wonder the Lord continues to challenge and test our faith with various trials; it is His means of drawing us near to Him while we learn the sufficiency of His grace.

The Lord wants all believers to learn what Paul learned through hardship, *"My grace is sufficient for you, for My strength is made perfect in weakness"* (2 Cor. 12:9). This is why the Lord said: *"Blessed are the poor in spirit, for theirs is the kingdom of heaven. Blessed are those who mourn, for they shall be comforted. Blessed are the meek, for they shall inherit the earth"* (Matt. 5:3-5). The Lord does not need our wealth or religious feats; He simply wants our hearts soft, pliable, and beating for Him.

Second, many nations which the world thinks of as "Christian" are *"filled with eastern ways."* The growth of the New Age cults, the influx of Eastern Religions, the following of fortunetellers, horoscopes, and other forms of divinations and necromancy indicate an invasion of Eastern mysticism in the Western world, in place of wide acceptance of the gospel of Jesus Christ.

The abundance of wealth, a powerful military, and the pursuit of Eastern religions translates to being high on self and having no need for God. If God promised to judge His covenant people harshly for similar offenses, what chastening awaits those nations founded on Christian ethics and gospel truth?

The Day of the Lord

Isaiah speaks of "the Day of the Lord" in verse 12, the first of three references in his book. To summarize, the Day of the Lord is an Old Testament term that speaks of those times when Jehovah intervened in a visible and powerful way to judge the wicked on earth. This meaning continues into the New Testament and speaks of the Tribulation Period and the Millennial Kingdom of Christ.

Peter tells us that *the Day of the Lord* and the Millennial Kingdom conclude with destruction of the earth (2 Pet. 3:10), and will be followed by *the Day of God*, often referred to as *the eternal state* (2 Pet. 3:12). Isaiah states that *"all the host of heaven shall be dissolved, and the heavens shall be rolled up like a scroll"* (34:4). He later foretells that after the Millennial Kingdom, God will create a new heaven and new earth (65:17) – a matter which John says occurs right after the 1000-year reign of Christ and the Great White Throne judgment of the wicked (Rev. 20:7-21:1).

Isaiah introduced us to the Kingdom Age in verses 1-5; he reveals more on this subject throughout his prophetic ministry. Jerusalem will be the religious center of the world. Christ will reign from there and all the nations will come there to praise, worship, and learn of Him. There will be no war or violence, only peace. All the earth will see the glory of the Lord Jesus (60:18-20) and any nation opposing the Lord will be laid waste (60:12). The Day of the Lord speaks of the era in which God will bring all this about.

Ultimately, it will be God alone who will be exalted on earth. When the Lord comes to establish His kingdom, the wicked will seek to escape *"the terror of the Lord, and the glory of His majesty"* by hiding under rocks or in caves (vv. 10-11). John alludes to this same scene in the book of Revelation.

> *Then the sky receded as a scroll when it is rolled up, and every mountain and island was moved out of its place. And the kings of the earth, the great men, the rich men, the commanders, the mighty men, every slave and every free man, hid themselves in the caves and in the rocks of the mountains, and said to the mountains and rocks, "Fall on us and hide us from the face of Him who sits on the throne and from the wrath of the Lamb! For the great day of His wrath has come, and who is able to stand?"* (Rev. 6:14-17).

There is a coming day when all those blinded by arrogance and pride will see the glory and power of the Lord Jesus Christ and realize too late that they cannot escape His judgment. All shall be humbled before Him, for *"the Lord alone shall be exalted in that day"* (vv. 11, 17). Isaiah then jumps forward to describe the particular judgments of God which will precede the establishment of Christ's kingdom (vv. 12-18). William MacDonald summarizes these judgments:

> The Lord of hosts will deal with all human arrogance, whether of individuals (cedars and oaks), governments (high mountains and hills), military might (tower and wall), or commerce (ships and beautiful sloops). Man's loftiness will be leveled and the Lord alone will be exalted. Idols will be abandoned.[15]

The Lord's penetrating glorious presence ensures that no wicked person will be able to hide from His scrutiny in the Day of the Lord (v. 19). The wicked will lose confidence in their wealth and idols and will seek shelter from the Lord Jesus Christ (v. 20). But they will find no place to hide *"from the terror of the Lord, and the glory of His majesty when He arises to shake the earth mightily"* (vv. 19, 21). At that time, the Lord's people will understand that those fleeing from His presence are under judgment and are not creditable – only the Lord is worthy of His people's full confidence (v. 22).

Israel did not heed Isaiah's warning to relinquish their idolatry and their worldly ways to obtain divine approval and blessing – and to this day the Jewish nation is still under God's chastening hand. The New Testament repeatedly applies two complementary means to call the believer's heart out of the world. The first is to set one's mind on things above (Col. 3:1-2), and the second is to come to realize what Isaiah said is true – the things of the earth are temporary and shakable.

As the writer of Hebrews reminds us, in a coming day, all that is not of the Lord will be removed: *"... removing of those things that are shaken, as of things that are made, that those things which cannot be shaken may remain. Wherefore, we receiving a kingdom which cannot be moved, let us have grace, whereby we may serve God acceptably with reverence and godly fear; for our God is a consuming fire"* (Heb. 12:27-29). The world is a nasty and temporal place, but heaven is the wonderful and eternal abode of God. This is why believers should devote themselves and all their resources to the Lord. All that is not dedicated to Him will ultimately burn up, without securing for us any eternal benefit. Unfortunately, the nation of Israel will not realize this certainty until the Day of the Lord. May the Church reckon it true today.

Meditation

> If you don't see the greatness of God, then all the things that money can buy become very exciting. If you can't see the sun, you will be impressed with a street light. If you've never felt thunder and lightning, you'll be impressed with fireworks. And if you turn your back on the greatness and majesty of God, you'll fall in love with a world of shadows and short-lived pleasures.
>
> — John Piper

The Wages of Sin
Isaiah 3

Isaiah continues from the last chapter itemizing Judah's sins deserving of divine retribution and the chaos that would result when Nebuchadnezzar's armies destroyed Jerusalem. The agonizing scene foretold in chapter 3 is then contrasted in the next chapter with Jerusalem's glory in the Kingdom Age. What message is the prophet conveying by this specific organization? He is warning future generations that the same rancid attitudes that marked Israel when God summoned Babylon to destroy Jerusalem will be prevalent again when the Antichrist is permitted to capture the city and ransack houses just prior to Christ's second advent (Zech. 14:2).

Liquidation of Resources

God will liquidate all that Israel was counting on for security, including their wealth, livestock, and stores of food. Even fresh drinking water would become scarce (v. 1). He further promised to remove (i.e., through death or captivity) Israel's elders, judges, counselors, craftsmen, and mighty warriors (vv. 2-3). Why did Isaiah include the diviner and enchanter in this list of those the Lord would purge from Israel? John A. Martin answers this question:

> The fact that Isaiah included the soothsayer (v. 2) and the clever enchanter (v. 3) in this list does not mean he was endorsing them. He was merely noting those on whom the nation was depending for survival and security. The Mosaic Covenant prohibited involvement in soothsaying and enchanting (Deut. 18:10-14).[16]

All that the Jewish nation relied on to feel secure would be stripped away, including their pagan soothsayers. Speaking of the future Babylonian conquest, Isaiah was foretelling that the nation's self-confidence, idolatry, and immorality would result in widespread death and destruction. Afterwards, Jewish survivors would be led by the foolish and the weak (vv. 4-7). Everyone would be looking for someone to show them where to find their basic necessities: food, water, and shelter. Relating to this desperate situation, F. C. Jennings observes: "The result of a government that does not command respect is the subversion of all natural order."[17] The situation in Jerusalem will be so bleak that inexperienced children or anyone possessing a cloak could be put in charge of the survivors. Foolishness and injustice will guide the Jewish remnant into further misery.

Isaiah carefully explains why such disaster should befall Israel:

For Jerusalem stumbled, and Judah is fallen, because their tongue and their doings are against the Lord, to provoke the eyes of His glory. The look on their countenance witnesses against them, and they declare their sin as Sodom; they do not hide it. Woe to their soul! For they have brought evil upon themselves (vv. 8-9).

Verse 9 contains the first of twenty-one "woes" employed by Isaiah in his book. The Hebrew word *howy* is used nineteen times to convey a passionate lament, usually an expression of despair which anticipates imminent disaster. For the two "woes" Isaiah levies on himself (6:5, 24:16), he uses the related Hebrew word *'owy* as a cry of interjection (i.e., he is not pronouncing prophetic judgment on himself). No book in the Bible has more "woes" than Isaiah.

Today, people often blurt out, "Oh my God," to express grief or shock in regard to imminent peril or a sudden catastrophe. This is the somber tone of Isaiah's proclamation. The nation was emboldened to do evil, and like the wicked city of Sodom, the Jews did not even try to conceal their sin (vv. 8-9). Regrettably they had provoked God to anger and instigated their own calamity.

Isaiah then reminds the righteous that God is a fair judge and that they need not fear His judgment; rather they will be rewarded for their good works (v. 10). On the other hand, *the wages of sin is death* (Rom. 6:23), so the wicked should be anxious about God recompensing their evil deeds (v. 11).

Accountability for Those Responsible

Israel's leaders lacked spiritual vigor and were permitting the nation to err from the path of righteousness (v. 12). Apparently, they were being influenced to do so by naïve youths, manipulating women (perhaps the wives of various leaders), and self-seeking deceivers.

Sorrow and Comfort

Isaiah then supplies two more reasons why God was ready to pass judgment on the leaders of Israel (v. 13): *"For you have eaten up the vineyard; the plunder of the poor is in your houses"* (v. 14). The prophet likens the Jewish leadership to a husbandman charged by God to care for His vineyard (the Jewish nation) to ensure its productivity.

However, the leaders had oppressed the people and profited from the poor, which caused those in their care to err from the path of righteousness. The *"Lord God of hosts"* was deeply offended by this and personally rebuked Judah's leaders: *"What do you mean by crushing My people and grinding the faces of the poor"* (v. 15)? Instead of leading the people heavenward, Judah's leaders were grinding the people into the ground. How true that the corruption of the best things is the worst kind of corruption! Isaiah's indictment against Israel's shepherds is similar to Ezekiel's scathing reprimand recorded in Ezekiel 34.

Isaiah then used satire to portray Jerusalem's condition before and after judgment by mocking Jerusalem's high-society women (3:17-4:1). The women of Judah were proud, their faces were pasted with cosmetics, they engaged in suggestive mannerisms, and were adorned with expensive clothing and jewelry (vv. 16-23). Why would God notice the makeup, apparel, and adornments of the Jewish women? He disapproved of their behavior because it was evidence of inward carnality. Making one's appearance more attractive than it really was to impress those who should not care was the mindset that was ruining the nation spiritually. The Jews cared more about influencing the opinions of others through outward show than having any kind of legitimate interaction with God inwardly.

Both Paul and Peter admonished Christian women not to fall into the same trap of externalism that the Jews were suffering from. The apostles describe the type of feminine adorning that God does and does not appreciate:

> *That the women adorn themselves in modest apparel, with propriety and moderation, not with braided hair or gold or pearls or costly clothing, but, which is proper for women professing godliness, with good works* (1 Tim. 2:9-10).

> *Do not let your adornment be merely outward – arranging the hair, wearing gold, or putting on fine apparel, rather let it be the hidden*

person of the heart, with the incorruptible beauty of a gentle and quiet spirit, which is very precious in the sight of God (1 Pet. 3:3-4).

A wife should seek to please her husband by giving him her best, but she has no business being a social distraction or seductive menace. Vivacious speech, flirtatious gestures, or enhancing one's feminine features to astound others does not impress God. William Kelly observes:

> When women live for display in apparel, no further proof is needed to bring to their door the charge that the sanctity of the home is tainted, and that there is no real heart for the relations God has set up. Such finery is assuredly not for a husband or the family, but, small as it is, it escapes not the withering notice of the Judge of all. Dress, gait, glances, are all noticed by the Spirit of God.[18]

While all this application is profitable to consider, we must be careful not to miss Isaiah's point: The conduct of these Jewish women merely typified what the entire nation was doing. As a people, the Jews were appearing to be something they were not – genuinely spiritual. They sought to amaze others, but not to please the Lord.

Having condemned their distasteful and pompous mannerism, God describes how the women of Judah will behave after the nation is chastened (vv. 24-25): The Jewesses' skin previously covered with expensive cosmetics would be encrusted with scabs. They would be stripped naked of their fine attire and only the fortunate ones would have sackcloth for clothing. Their beautiful and well-kept hair would be shaved off. E. J. Young summarizes that these flaunting Jewish women will suffer the appropriate outcome that their sensual behavior demanded: "Those who delight in immodest exposure will be rewarded with immodest exposure at the hands of vile men."[19] Instead of having clout and respect in society, they would be tied up with ropes, branded, and led away like cattle. Branding may refer to the literal marking of slaves or figuratively of long exposure to the hot sun as a slave (e.g., Song 1:6).

The women of Judah who are not slaughtered by the Babylonians will suffer social desolation. Their high-minded chitchat will be replaced with mourning and their preoccupation with frivolous glamor and wealth will be displaced by survival yearnings (v. 26). As Isaiah had already put it, they would *"eat the fruit of their doings"* (v. 10).

Israel's brazen wickedness could not be tolerated by their holy God; their phony religious doings would result in much suffering.

There are several types of death spoken of in Scripture, but there are three deaths, or literal "separations," that are most significant to all mankind. We are all born *spiritually dead*; we are spiritually separated from God. Then, when *physical death* occurs, our soul separates from our body. If physical death occurs while a person is still spiritually dead, *eternal death* (judgment in hell) is assured. Hebrews 9:27 proclaims, *"It is appointed unto men once to die, but after this the judgment."* At this juncture, the nation of Israel is spiritually dead, separated from God. The Jewish people have chosen the heathen and frivolous things of the world instead of communing with their God who longs for their devotion. Isaiah was prophesying the tremendous cost of their stubborn and foolish rebellion. Thankfully, the physical death of the entire nation will never occur. The way for future spiritual restoration and divine blessing, as discussed in chapter 4, is still open.

Meditation

> There hath not one tear dropped from thy tender eye against thy lusts, the love of this world, or for more communion with Jesus Christ, but as it is now in the bottle of God; so then it shall bring forth such plenty of reward, that it shall return upon thee with abundance of increase.
>
> — John Bunyan

> Carnal Christians tend to show off their differences and superiorities in clothing, speech or deeds. They desire to shock people into recognizing all their undertakings.
>
> — Watchman Nee

The Branch of the Lord
Isaiah 4

God's indictment against Israel was levied in chapter 1. Then the prophet briefly foretold Israel's future restoration to God (in a general sense) during the Kingdom Age (2:1-5) before describing the divine judgment they would experience for their idolatry and worldliness (2:6-4:1). Verse 1 closes the long section detailing Israel's future severe chastening by Babylon. So many men will die in that invasion that surviving women will compete with each other to obtain a husband (i.e., there will be seven women for every surviving man). These women even promise to support themselves as long as they could carry their husband's name to escape the reproach of being unmarried and childless (v. 1).

Some commentators, such as Albert Barnes, believe that the verse is describing polygamy: "It means that so great should be the calamity, so many 'men' would fall in battle, that many women would, contrary to their natural modesty, become suitors to a single man, to obtain him as a husband and protector."[20] Given the context, this does seem to be Isaiah's meaning: women will be so desperate that they will be willing to marry even if it means a polygamous relationship.

Although polygamy was not God's design for marriage, we do see Jewish kings taking several wives. Sometimes a Jewish man might marry a second wife, if his first wife was unable to bear children (e.g., Hannah in 1 Sam. 1). Whether Isaiah is referring to polygamy or just an intense competition to obtain a husband in the aftermath of judgment is uncertain. However, the prophet's point is that those women in the previous chapter obsessed with personal vanity will be disappointed; in the end they will have only shame and no one will notice them in the way they desired. Neither should we be surprised that God does not bless our hollow pursuits – He sees the heart and all the makeup in the world will not change who we are.

The Kingdom

Having bludgeoned his countrymen over the head with oracles forecasting impending doom, Isaiah breaks to provide them a message of hope. We also pause to consider an obvious question spawned from Isaiah's stern message: How might God's displeasure for a particular society be displayed today? The answer is, in much the same way it was shown towards Jerusalem in Isaiah's day. J. A. Motyer identifies six signs from chapter 3 of a society not experiencing God's blessing (i.e., in decline):

> (1) The disappearance of solid leadership (3:1-3). (2) The appearance of immature, capricious leaders (3:4). (3) Society becomes divided (3:5a). (4) The age-gap opens up (3:5b). (5) Values are at a discount and those who should be despised take the initiative (3:5c). (6) An air of despair dominates elections (3:6-7). All this arises from moral and spiritual causes. It is not the result of failures of policy but of speaking and acting against the Lord and provoking Him; blatant sin inviting its just reward (3:8-11).[21]

One can hardly deny that these same characteristics are already evident in many Western countries which once held to a Christian heritage, but now have a growing population which is provoking the Lord to anger through willful sin and rebellion.

The prophet then shares a conciliatory message – the Jewish people would eventually be restored to God, speaking of the Kingdom Age (vv. 2-5). The Babylonian conquest of Jerusalem foreshadows an even more horrific event in Israel's future. Ezekiel tells us that at the beginning of the Tribulation Period, the Jews will be back in the land of Israel and resting from warfare (Ezek. 38:8). Not long after this event, Daniel tells us, Israel will sign a seven-year peace treaty with the Antichrist (Dan. 9:27). Just as the false prophets in Jeremiah's day preached a false message of "peace, peace" right before their Babylonian oppressors arrived to decimate them (Jer. 4:10), the Jewish people will enjoy a short season of false peace just before suffering a holocaust in the last half of the Tribulation Period.

Before the Tribulation Period is over, two-thirds of the Jews in the world will be slaughtered (Zech. 13:7-8). Zechariah mentions that Jerusalem will be captured by the Antichrist before the Lord returns to liberate His covenant people by destroying him and his armies (Zech. 14). In this sense, the events surrounding the Babylonian invasion are a precursor to the more devastating period for Israel yet to occur during the Tribulation Period (Matt. 24:15-29).

The Branch of the Lord

The term "in that day" (v. 2) is often used by the prophets to foretell a new era of judgment or blessing. Isaiah applies the phrase forty-three times – significantly more than any other prophet. The context of the passage assists us in determining the proper implication of the expression. For example, sometimes "in that day" is tied with the Assyrian's invasion of Judah (22:1-14), or with the Babylonian captivity (Jer. 39:16-17). At other times the phrase speaks of the end of the Tribulation Period and the commencement of the Kingdom Age (27:12-13; Jer. 30:8).

It is evident that verses 2-6 have the latter meaning in mind because an era of blessing arrives by the establishment of *the Branch of the Lord* in Jerusalem, speaking of the second advent of Christ. The faithful Jews who survive the Tribulation Period will see the full beauty and glory of their Messiah and the entire earth shall be abundantly productive. This suggests the lifting of curses placed on the earth after humanity's fall in Eden. Paul explains that the revelation of the Son of God and the restoration of man to God is what the entire planet is waiting for.

> *For the earnest expectation of the creation eagerly waits for the revealing of the sons of God. For the creation was subjected to futility, not willingly, but because of Him who subjected it in hope; because the creation itself also will be delivered from the bondage of corruption into the glorious liberty of the children of God. For we know that the whole creation groans and labors with birth pangs together until now* (Rom. 8:19-22).

When the Branch of the Lord appears, the redeemed will be established at His side. The devastation caused by sin will be reversed. Originally, man was created to rule over the earth so as to represent the image and likeness of God (Gen. 1:26; Heb. 2:6-8). When man sinned, God could not have an imperfect head ruling over a perfect creation, so God cursed the earth and made it a fitting habitation for a condemned race to suffer in their sin. Yet, in a coming day, the Branch of the Lord will completely repair the damage that resulted from sin and then everyone on the earth and creation itself will rejoice!

Sorrow and Comfort

The Four Branches

Jeremiah states that the Messiah will sprout from David's line and thus "the branch" is a fitting depiction of Him. In the Old Testament, God speaks prophetically of His Son being a Branch in four ways, which align with the unique vantage points of Christ in the four Gospels:

> *"Behold, the days are coming," says the Lord, "That I will raise to David **a Branch of righteousness; a King** shall reign and prosper, and execute judgment and righteousness in the earth"* (Jer. 23:5; also see Isa. 11:1).

> *Hear, O Joshua, the high priest, you and your companions who sit before you, for they are a wondrous sign;*
> *for behold, I am bringing forth **My Servant the Branch*** (Zech. 3:8).

> *Then speak to him, saying, "Thus says the Lord of hosts, saying: 'Behold, **the Man whose name is the Branch**! From His place He shall branch out, and He shall build the temple of the Lord'"* (Zech. 6:12).

> *In that day **the Branch of the Lord** shall be beautiful and glorious; and the fruit of the earth shall be excellent and appealing for those of Israel who have escaped* (v. 2).

The four divine titles of the Lord perfectly align with the four Gospel presentations of Christ:

    Unto David a Branch ... a King – Gospel of Matthew
    My Servant, the Branch – Gospel of Mark
    The Man ... the Branch – Gospel of Luke
    The Branch of the Lord – Gospel of John

F. B. Hole summarizes the wonderful allusions to Christ's character and work as expressed by each of these Old Testament prophets when speaking of "the Branch":

> Twice in Jeremiah do we get the Lord Jesus alluded to as the Branch, or Sprout (Jer. 23:5, 33:15); but there what is emphasized is righteousness. It is the character He displays rather than the Source from whence He springs. Again in Zechariah the expression occurs twice (Zech. 3:8, 6:12). There the emphasis lies on the fact that though He springs forth from Jehovah, He is to take the place of the

Servant, and enter into Manhood to serve. Reading the five occurrences in the fuller light of the New Testament, we see how full these early predictions were as to our blessed Lord. The one in our chapter [v. 2] is the first and deepest of them all.[22]

"The Branch of the Lord" is the deepest of the "Branch" expressions because it proclaims Christ's essential divine glory, His sovereign rule over the earth, and over His people, and that He alone is the source of life and blessing.

Washed and Restored

The reference to *"the daughters of Zion"* (3:16, 17, 4:4) is unique to Isaiah, except for one reference in the Song of Solomon (Song 3:11). The prophet uses the title to refer to the embodiment of the degenerate spirit that infested the Jewish people, an ill that had been passed down from previous generations (i.e., Zion their mother – "her"). Spiritually speaking, the Jews were suffering from chronic deep-seated rebellion and coldness of heart towards God. God's solution would be painful, but afterwards, surviving Jews will realize that God's purifying fire (His chastening) had cleansed away their filth and made them a holy people (vv. 3-4). Ultimately, in the Kingdom Age, Israel will be the glory of God in Zion, and will never again be referred to as *the daughters of Jerusalem* in the negative sense.

After their exodus from Egypt, the Jewish nation experienced God's abiding presence; a divine cloud overshadowed them by day and a pillar of fire shone upon them at night. This was a foretaste of what Israel will enjoy in the Kingdom Age (vv. 5-6). The Jewish nation will again bask in God's glory and enjoy His unbroken fellowship, blessing, and protection. God will never again need to withdraw from His covenant people, because they will always honor and obey Him.

Not only will the entire Jewish nation see God's glory then, they will also properly reflect it to all nations. This will fulfill the Lord's original intention for them. Sadly, the centuries of their waywardness have tarnished God's name among the nations. Paul indicts his own countrymen on this matter: *"the name of God is blasphemed among the Gentiles because of you"* (Rom. 2:24). But Isaiah tells us this will not be the case in the Millennial Kingdom of Christ: *"I bring My righteousness near, it shall not be far off; My salvation shall not linger. And I will place salvation in Zion, for Israel My glory"* (46:13). Israel

Sorrow and Comfort

will be to God's glory and all nations will not only esteem them most blessed, but will also come to worship Israel's God – Jehovah.

Ezekiel tells us that after the nations witness God's jealousy for and faithfulness to the Jewish people, *"then they* [the nations] *shall know that I am the Lord their God"* (Ezek. 28:26). Zechariah prophesied that, *"In those days ten men from every language of the nations shall grasp the sleeve of a Jewish man, saying, 'Let us go with you, for we have heard that God is with you'"* (Zech. 8:23). In a coming day all the nations of the earth will honor and worship the Jewish Messiah, the Lord Jesus Christ!

Meditation

> The Lord, that sits above the skies, derides their rage below;
> He speaks with vengeance in His eyes, and strikes their spirits through.
> "I call Him My eternal Son, and raise Him from the dead;
> I make My holy hill His throne, and wide His kingdom spread.
>
> "Ask Me, My Son, and then enjoy the utmost heathen lands:
> Thy rod of iron shall destroy the rebel that withstands."
> Be wise, ye rulers of the earth, obey the anointed Lord,
> Adore the King of heavenly birth, and tremble at His Word.
>
> — Isaac Watts

The Fruitless Vineyard
Isaiah 5

Centuries earlier, Asaph spoke of Israel as a vine brought out of Egypt that had once flourished under God's care, but, because of the nation's unfaithfulness, had been repeatedly trampled on by invaders (Ps. 80). Hosea, Jeremiah, and Ezekiel use similar imagery in their prophecies (Hos. 10:1; Jer. 8:13, 12:10-13; Ezek. 15). In this chapter Isaiah also likens the Jewish nation to a worthless vineyard (v. 1) and then exclaims six woes over the fruitless nation. As previously mentioned, a "woe" is an abrupt expression of distress often associated with God's displeasure and imminent judgment. Today, we might convey this thought by slowly shaking our heads saying, "Oh Israel." This chapter contains more woes than any other in the Bible; clearly Isaiah is deeply moved on God's behalf as he laments in a song the spiritual condition of his countrymen.

The Vineyard Parable

Isaiah begins the lyrics of this vine allegory by tenderly speaking of the Lord as *"my Beloved"*: God labored to plant a vineyard on a specific hill with the richest soil (v. 1). In most vineyards there are many grape vines, but in God's vineyard, there was only one choice vine – the nation of Israel. Israel was planted by Him for His enjoyment. He placed a high tower in his vineyard to secure and guard the vine as it flourished and spread (v. 2). This structure was likely constructed from the stones removed to ready the soil. Given this ideal environment, a winepress was erected beside the vine with the expectation of an abundant harvest.

However, the vine bore wild grapes (picturing Israel's rebellion and idolatry); it did not yield good fruit (i.e., faithfulness and obedience) as expected (v. 4). God challenged the inhabitants of Judah to consider the analogy and to offer a suggestion as to what more He could have done for His vine to cause it to bear bountiful, delicious fruit (v. 3). The question implies that God did everything possible to make Israel fruitful, meaning that she was responsible for failing to please God.

Isaiah acknowledges that the only solution for an unfruitful vine was to remove its hedge of protection (often vineyards were surrounded by a barrier of thorn bushes), to tear the vine down from its trellis, chop it up, and burn it (vv. 5-6). Furthermore, God promised to limit rainfall in His dismantled vineyard, meaning that only briers and thorns would prosper in its fertile soil.

The Explanation

Isaiah makes it clear that the Lord was including Judah, the southern kingdom, as part of His overall analogy when speaking of "Israel" (v. 7). The nation divided four centuries after God had planted His people in Canaan to be His choice vineyard. God was now posed to act against His vine because justice had been replaced with oppression and bloodshed, and righteousness with cries of distress.

Although Isaiah's song concludes in verse 7, the remainder of the chapter is a fitting sequel – a six fold indictment against Israel (i.e., a further explanation of Israel's sour fruit). Each indictment is introduced by a "woe" expression. The first two woes pertain to materialistic abuse, and are followed by a "therefore" interruption to explain why God's punishment is fitting for the offense named. Another "therefore" occurs after the sixth woe to accomplish the same objective; this follows four woes which address Judah's moral and spiritual failures.

In summary, darkness, death, and judgment would reign over Judah because of their entrenched evil. Not until the next chapter will we see a ray of comfort for Israel – God will mercifully send them Isaiah to rebuke them and to inspire hope in what God will still do. But for the present, the sour fruit Israel was bearing must be divinely repudiated.

Woe to Materialism (vv. 8-10)

Because God had given His people the land of Canaan as an inheritance, they were not to get rich at the expense of others. For this reason, the Law prohibited the permanent sale of houses in unwalled villages and also the sale of agricultural land. A debt incurred or legal restitution might prompt a Jew to temporarily sell their inherited property to resolve the financial need. However, no matter what transactions had occurred previously, property was to revert to its original owner every fifty years (in the year of Jubilee; Lev. 25:10).

Regrettably, there is no evidence in Scripture that the Jewish nation ever obeyed this command. As a result, many Jews had lost their God-given inheritance and had become impoverished, while others profited from their hardship. This omission had not gone unnoticed by the Lord, who promised to make vacant the mansions of the rich and cause their agricultural enterprises to fail.

To illustrate this point, Isaiah says, *"For ten acres of vineyard shall yield one bath, and a homer of seed shall yield one ephah"* (v. 10). Albert Barnes explains the ancient references to areas and volumes and Isaiah's intended meaning:

> **Ten acres** - An "acre," among the Hebrews, was what could be plowed by one yoke of oxen in a day. It did not differ materially from our acre.
>
> **Shall yield one bath** - One bath of wine. The "bath" was a Jewish measure for liquids, containing about seven gallons and a half. To say that "ten acres" should produce no more wine than this, was the same as to say that it would produce almost nothing.
>
> **And the seed of an homer** - An "homer" was a Hebrew measure for grain, containing about eight bushels.
>
> **An ephah** - The "ephah" contained about three pecks. Of course, to say that a homer of seed should produce about three pecks, would be the same as saying that it would produce almost nothing.[23]

Materialism is an ideology that has plagued God's people through the ages. The Lord Jesus warned His disciples not to be influenced by *"the leaven of Herod"* (Mark 8:15). Herod, a Jew, was in league with the Roman Empire, and was, therefore, a friend of the world (Jas. 4:4). For Herod and those like him, love for God and His Word had been supplanted by the love for materialism, fame, and political ambition. Little in one's life has value to God after a man or a woman has become mesmerized by earthly things which must ultimately be lost and burnt up!

> He is no fool who gives what he cannot keep to gain what he cannot lose.
>
> — Jim Elliot

Woe to Drunkards (vv. 11-12)

Apparently, drunkenness was prevalent in Isaiah's day as he mentions this social vice twice in this chapter (vv. 11, 22). When the cognitive abilities of intoxicated people are impaired, they usually do things which the Lord disapproves of; hence, the Law prohibited drunkenness (Lev. 10:9; Num. 6:3; Prov. 20:1). For this reason, at mealtimes, and at feasts and celebrations the Jews commonly drank diluted wine to avoid intoxication. Sobriety, however, was not practiced in Isaiah's day, as many were partying from the break of day until night and allowing the wine, not prudence, to control their actions. These drunkards pursued their own pleasures. They did *"not regard the work of the Lord, nor consider the operation of His hands"* (v. 12). The latter phrase likely speaks of people; God specially created Adam with His hands for the purpose of bearing His image.

King Lemuel was counseled by his mother to avoid intoxication and the sexual temptation of wayward women (Prov. 31:1-2). Immorality and drunkenness walk together – both should be avoided. Those who represent God's authority should not become inebriated, as they are to reflect God's character in their office and in their judgments (1 Tim. 3:8). Hence, Lemuel concludes that a drunken governor will pervert justice, will forget what is noble, and disregard problems that need resolution. He will not rule in righteousness nor care for the poor and needy (Prov. 31:4-9). This social travesty is exactly what Isaiah is describing.

The Consequences of Judah's Sin – Part 1 (vv. 13-17)

Isaiah interrupts his indictment against Judah, to announce the consequences of their sinful lifestyle. Most would die or be exiled and no social class would be exempt from starvation and thirst (v. 13). The revelers and merrymaking drunkards, of whom Isaiah has just spoken, would be swallowed up by Sheol (i.e., they would die; v. 14). God's judgment would humble all His people and also honor His holy and righteous character (vv. 15-16). The possessions of the wealthy will be plundered, which will also benefit "the lambs" of the nation, meaning that the common people would be able to scavenge what the invaders did not pillage (v. 17).

Woe to Doubters (vv. 18-19)

The prophet's next rebuke is against those thoroughly entangled in sin by cords of vanity (v. 18) and who yet had the audacity to challenge God, *"Let Him make speed and hasten His work"* (v. 19). These doubters did not believe that God was in control or that He would move against them; these agnostics were basically challenging God to prove Himself to them. Isaiah promises that He would, but it would not be a pleasant demonstration of His authority.

The leaven to be avoided in the believer's life comes in diverse varieties. Not only did the Lord Jesus warn His disciples against worldliness (*"the leaven of Herod"* as discussed in the first woe), He also warned them concerning *"the leaven ... of the Sadducees"* (Matt. 16:6). The Sadducees were materialists who denied the existence of the supernatural, the spiritual nature of man, and the idea of a future resurrection.

In our present day, the ideologies of the Sadducees live on in intellectualism, humanism, higher criticism, post-modernism, and naturalism. These ideologies challenge God's sovereignty and, like the doubters in Isaiah's day, challenge God to prove Himself as the One in control. There is a coming day when God will do just that, but let us be thankful that in the interim *"the Lord is not slack concerning His promise, as some count slackness, but is longsuffering toward us, not willing that any should perish but that all should come to repentance"* (2 Pet. 3:9).

Woe to Those Calling Evil – Good (v. 20)

Isaiah applies a Hebrew parallelism to introduce his next woe: *"Woe to those who call evil good, and good evil; who put darkness for light, and light for darkness; who put bitter for sweet, and sweet for bitter!"* (v. 20). Solomon confirms God's revulsion for those calling evil – good: *"He who justifies the wicked, and he who condemns the just, both of them alike are an abomination to the Lord"* (Prov. 17:15). Proper order in the affairs of life, including our worship, is exceedingly important to God, *"for God is not the author of confusion but of peace"* (1 Cor. 14:33) and He desires that *"all things be done decently and in order"* (1 Cor. 14:40). Satan is the author of deception and confusion (John 8:44), but God sets in place standards of proper order to confound his attempts to pervert divine truth.

Sorrow and Comfort

Satan rarely presents outright lies; rather, he depends upon a series of blurred deceptions to gain his footing and to wreak havoc within the Church. I will illustrate this point: "Despite what you might have thought previously, black really means white." You say, "No, black is the opposite of white." But then I pick up a reliable dictionary, perhaps *The American Heritage Dictionary*,[24] and show you that the meaning of "black" is "dark," and then I confirm that one of the meanings of "dark" is "dim." Finding the entry for "dim" I prove to you that "dim" can denote "pale." And finally I look up the word "pale" and verify that one of the connotations of "pale" is "white." I have proven to you using a series of only four imprecise meanings (variations of the best meaning, if you will) that black is equal to white.

If the devil can deceive the believer into compromising even a small portion of the truth, be sure that he will return to accomplish the same objective again and again. He may wait a bit until we become comfortable in our complacency, but he will always come back! Dear believer, stand fast with the belt of truth securely fastened and resist Satan's attempts to lure you into compromise through his lying and deception (1 Pet. 5:8-9). Let us stand fast in the light of divine revelation and not be moved into the darkness by the enemy's trickery!

Woe to the Conceited (v. 21)

The fifth woe is concise: *"Woe unto them that are wise in their own eyes, and prudent in their own sight"* (v. 21)! Human pride is a frequent subject in the book of Proverbs. In Proverbs 6, Solomon reminds his son of seven things God hates: a proud look, a lying tongue, murder, devising wicked schemes, a swift inclination to do mischief, a false witness, and those who sow discord among God's people (Prov. 6:16-19). These abominations include one sin of attitude, one of thought, two of speech, two of action, and one of influence, showing that the full product of the first six sins results in the latter offense of discord and division.

As we will see in the next chapter, pride results when men do not extol the Lord and give Him proper place in their thinking. *"The fear of the Lord is to hate evil, pride and arrogance, and the evil way"* (Prov. 8:13). When God's people rely on and glory in His strength and wisdom, they realize there is nothing to be proud about, except the Lord. Unfortunately, pride is the evil fountainhead by which many needless and divisive currents flow among God's people, and the Lord hates it! The Jewish nation thought they could protect themselves from God's chastening hand. Israel was about to learn just how much God despised their proud, self-preserving attitudes.

Woe to Bribe-takers (vv. 22-23)

A specific condemnation is pronounced against those leaders who were more concerned for their own pleasure and social status than caring for the needy and upholding the rights of the innocent. David affirms that righteous leaders will keep their commitments even though it costs them to do so; they will not take advantage of the impoverished, nor will they accept bribes against the innocent (Ps. 15:5).

Jewish leaders, many of whom were drunkards, had impaired judgment; they were not exhibiting God's holy character in executing the authority they had received from Him. Isaiah promises that these rulers would be severely punished.

The Consequences of Judah's Sin – Part 2 (vv. 24-30)

The prophet had previously hinted at the consequences of the before-mentioned sins in verses 13-17. Now in verses 24-30, he more elaborately describes God's indignation towards those offending Him. Using an allegorical description, these verses describe how those under Isaiah's indictment would burn like stubble, like dry grass in a prairie fire. Though they appeared to be a blooming plant, their roots would be dried up and they would be blown away like dust (v. 24). Isaiah then describes their doom in plain language: *"Their carcasses were as refuse in the midst of the streets"* (v. 25). These rebels had aroused the Lord's anger to the extent that He was now poised to raise His hand and pass judgment on them. The ramifications of doing so would be stunning, even causing the mountains to quake before Him.

God's raised hand would signal the nations (Egypt, Assyria, and later Babylon) to quickly assemble against Jerusalem for war. God promised an innumerable host of well-armed invaders would respond to His command and decimate Judah (vv. 26-28).

The chapter concludes with a double analogy of helplessness: When the invaders arrive in Judah, the Jewish people will be as helpless as a lion's prey and as a storm-battered sailor stranded at sea with no land in sight (vv. 29-30). Isaiah was warning Judah that a cloud of death and destruction would soon envelop them and there was nothing they could do about it. God is faithful to recompense wickedness!

Sorrow and Comfort

Notwithstanding, a key component of Isaiah's second message (2:1-4:6) is that human sin cannot frustrate God's ultimate purposes for Israel and that His mercy always finds a way to triumph over the desperate consequences of sin.

Meditation

>Woe to the men on earth who dwell,
>Nor dread the Almighty's frown,
>When God doth all His wrath reveal,
>And shower His judgments down!
>
>Who then shall live and face the throne,
>And face the Judge severe?
>When heaven and earth are fled and gone,
>O where shall man appear?
>
>— Charles Wesley

God's Throne and Altar
Isaiah 6

Isaiah writes: *"In the year that King Uzziah died, I saw the Lord sitting on a throne, high and lifted up, and the train of His robe filled the temple"* (v. 1). Whether Isaiah was physically at the temple to worship the Lord and saw this vision (i.e., received God's word while there), or if the Lord simply transported him in spirit into heaven to witness His throne is unknown. The former setting seems more applicable as God's holy robe filled the Most Holy Place in the temple, and the doorposts at the entrance were shaking from the shock and awe emanating from God's presence. Regardless of the vision's location, we do know when it occurred, what Isaiah saw, and the effect it had on him.

There are various time references throughout Isaiah which supply order to the book and help us correlate certain events (v. 1, 7:1, 14:28, 20:1, etc.). The timing of Isaiah's vision was not coincidental, but was directly linked to King Uzziah's death. Isaiah began his ministry while Uzziah was still alive (1:1), so why did Isaiah reckon his commission with Uzziah's death later that year? This is unusual, as no other Old Testament prophet dates any event by a death, but Isaiah does twice (v. 1, 14:28). The proper protocol would have been to say: "In the fifty-second year of Uzziah, I saw...". Uzziah was sixteen when he became king of Judah and he reigned for fifty-two years, but for the first twenty-four years he was coregent with his father, Amaziah.

The answer to the above question must relate to Isaiah's view of Israel at the time, which he felt was depicted in King Uzziah's situation – a proud king in seclusion because of leprosy with death looming over him. To better understand the ramifications of this association we need to first survey Uzziah's history as king, and then review the imagery and types presented in this chapter.

Sorrow and Comfort

King Uzziah

King Uzziah was better than many kings who ruled over the Southern Kingdom: *"King Uzziah did what was right in the sight of the Lord, according to all that his father, Amaziah, did"* (2 Chron. 26:4). Uzziah was divinely blessed for his determination to follow the Lord: *"as long as he sought the Lord, God made him prosper"* (2 Chron. 26:5). His leadership brought Judah economic prosperity, technological improvements, and vast military strength (2 Chron. 26:6-15). However, these accomplishments caused him to think more highly of himself than he did of his God. In arrogance he brought a censer into the temple to offer worship to Jehovah. This was an intrusion upon the priesthood which God had strictly forbidden (i.e., only priests could perform such tasks and then only per the Law). What happened next is astounding:

> *But when he was strong his heart was lifted up, to his destruction, for he transgressed against the Lord his God by entering the temple of the Lord to burn incense on the altar of incense. So Azariah the priest went in after him, and with him were eighty priests of the Lord – valiant men. And they withstood King Uzziah, and said to him, "It is not for you, Uzziah, to burn incense to the Lord, but for the priests, the sons of Aaron, who are consecrated to burn incense. Get out of the sanctuary, for you have trespassed! You shall have no honor from the Lord God."*

> *Then Uzziah became furious; and he had a censer in his hand to burn incense. And while he was angry with the priests, leprosy broke out on his forehead, before the priests in the house of the Lord, beside the incense altar. And Azariah the chief priest and all the priests looked at him, and there, on his forehead, he was leprous; so they thrust him out of that place. Indeed he also hurried to get out, because the Lord had struck him. King Uzziah was a leper until the day of his death. He dwelt in an isolated house, because he was a leper; for he was cut off from the house of the Lord* (2 Chron. 26:16-21).

When King Uzziah served the Lord obediently, he was blessed. Yet, when he went his own way, God humbled him. King Uzziah was struck with leprosy of his head, which symbolizes the sin of pride (Lev. 13:29). The Lord will not tolerate pride, especially in those ruling His people. There was no cure for leprosy in Old Testament days; it brought social isolation and a slow, agonizing death. Its damage to the nervous system often prevented individuals from being properly treated for injuries, as typically no pain was felt when the injury occurred.

Like Uzziah the leper, Israel's ongoing sin had made them numb to the pangs of their conscience, and they were further injuring their souls through idolatry. Pain is generally a good thing because it alerts us to what needs attention, but Israel was ignoring the warnings given by God's prophets. Hence, the nation, like Uzziah, was isolated, suffering, and heading towards death. This is likely the reason Isaiah ties his prophetic calling to Uzziah's death and not to his life – there is no life apart from God.

It seems likely, therefore, that the very temple that unholy Uzziah sought to enter is the same one Isaiah now sees full of God's glory. The proud and dying king is clearly contrasted with the majesty and holiness of God. The empty throne of Israel is juxtaposed with the never unoccupied throne of God; He always rules over Israel despite the failures of her kings. Hence, the focus of this chapter is not the Law, which demanded the death of the transgressor (Uzziah), but God's just means of imparting mercy to the repentant (Isaiah) and preparing him for ministry.

Thrones and Altars

The pairing of a throne and an altar in this chapter is representative of timeless truth depicted throughout Scripture. To better understand God's tie between His throne and His altar, let us consider two other examples before examining Isaiah's vision in this passage.

First, Adonijah, who had aspired to be king, feared his brother Solomon after their father David had put Solomon on the throne. Adonijah fled to the Bronze Altar in the temple. As he embraced the horns of the altar, Solomon granted him mercy; however, Solomon's mercy was contingent upon Adonijah's continued well-doing. Solomon's warning was not heeded, and Adonijah was judged (I Kgs. 1:48–52). In this story, we first read of the throne (a symbol of authority); after this authority was understood, the altar was sought to obtain mercy.

Second, in Exodus 21 and 24 Mount Sinai is God's majestic throne, His glorious habitation before His people, though not intimately among them. Gazing upon God's throne-mountain, the Israelites witnessed His awesome nature and received His righteous Law (Ex. 21). Their immediate response to God's holiness was to fear and to stand afar off

Sorrow and Comfort

– this is the proper response of sinful man to God's throne. The chapter then closes with God's provision for His people to worship Him – an altar upon which to present burnt offerings and peace offerings (Ex. 21:24). The altar did not allow the people to come intimately near Jehovah, but it did allow them to worship Him from a safe distance and the nation's leaders to have fellowship with God on the lower part of the mountain (Ex. 24:9-11). The pattern observed in the above passages is also apparent in Isaiah's vision in this chapter and will be further discussed below.

The Trinity

More than any other Old Testament writer, Isaiah provides frequent allusions to the Trinity, as we have in this chapter. In some of his references, there are clearly three separate voices speaking as God, which affirm the unique personages and roles of each member of the Trinity. F. B. Hole explains to us the representation of the Trinity in this chapter:

> It is instructive to note New Testament references to this scene. In John 12:41, the blind rejection of Jesus is the theme, and we discover that Isaiah "saw His glory, and spoke of Him." Then in Acts 28:25, Paul refers to our chapter and says, "Well spoke the Holy Ghost . . ." So here is one of those allusions to the Trinity, which are embedded in the Old Testament. In verse 3 we have "Holy," repeated, not twice nor four times but **three;** and Jehovah of hosts is before us. In verse 5, "the King, the Lord of hosts," whom we find to be the Lord Jesus. In verse 8, "the voice of the Lord," which is claimed as the voice of the Holy Ghost. God is One and yet Three: Three and yet One. Hence, "Whom shall **I** send, and who will go for **US**?"[25]

The Angel of the Lord

Having contemplated the expression of the Trinity, let us consider the role of God's Son in this chapter. Isaiah refers to the One sitting on the high throne as *"the Lord"* (v. 1) and the Seraphim identify Him as *"Holy, holy, holy, the Lord of Hosts"* (v. 3). Later, Isaiah will refer to *"The Angel of the Lord"* (37:36), but he does not refer to the high and lofty One, whose judicial robe filled the temple, by that title here. Why? In Isaiah's vision the Lord's majesty is connected with His heavenly seat of all power and authority, rather than His role of being God's Messenger to the earth. In the Old Testament, when the One shown enthroned here visits humanity (usually taking human form, but sometimes in an unusual depiction), He is referred to as "The Angel (i.e., *Malak* or "Messenger") of the Lord." This title is unique and should not be confused with the phrase "an angel of the Lord," which may refer to the manifestation of one of many holy angels.

Contextual observation confirms that appearances of "the Angel of the Lord" were *theophanies*. A theophany is a pre-incarnate visit of the second person of the Godhead to the earth as God's messenger. The Lord Jesus stated that no one had ever personally seen God the Father (John 6:46). The Lord also said that anyone who had seen Him had seen the Father (John 14:9). This means that God the Father did not appear to anyone in Old Testament times, but rather the only One who could perfectly represent Him did so by concealing the fullness of His essence and appearing in a way that man could perceive and appreciate His glory without being consumed. For this reason, some refer to these supernatural Old Testament appearances as *Christophanies*, or literally, "Christ appearances."

The role of the Son in the Trinity is to do the Father's will (Isa. 48:16; John 5:23, 30, 36-37), and part of that task involves communicating the Father's will to humanity (John 3:16, 5:18, 8:28). When the Son does this in the Old Testament, He is referred to as "the Messenger (Angel) of the Lord" and hence He identifies Himself as God (Gen. 31:11-13; Ex. 3:2-6) and receives worship (Judg. 6:18-20). This is why Jacob referred to the Lord as his "Redeeming Angel" (Gen. 48:16). Similarly, in the New Testament, the Son of God is called the Word which always existed (John 1:1; 1 Jn. 1:1); the Son became a man to bring the ultimate message of God to humanity. The Lord Jesus was a living message sojourning on the earth; He was both the message and the messenger of God.

There are references in the New Testament to these Old Testament divine appearances. For example, John refers to Isaiah's vision of God while explaining that Christ was fulfilling Isaiah's prophecies:

Therefore they could not believe, because Isaiah said again: "He has blinded their eyes and hardened their hearts, lest they should see with their eyes, lest they should understand with their hearts and turn, so that I should heal them." These things Isaiah said when he saw His glory and spoke of Him (John 12:39-41).

Sorrow and Comfort

John confirms that the Lord Jesus fulfilled the prophecies of Isaiah, and that the prominent One that Isaiah saw ("the Lord") in his glorious vision was the same One John loved and served – the Lord Jesus Christ. These temporary visitations of the Son of God to earth are not needed now to make individuals aware of God's will for their lives or to execute justice on wickedness as in the Old Testament. God's Word is complete (Jude 3) and reveals His will for all believers (Eph. 5:17; 1 Thess. 3:4; 1 Pet. 2:15). The matter of justice will be handled when the Lord Jesus returns to the earth on a future day (John 5:22; Jude 15).

Currently, there is a Man in the glory who waits to appear again on earth and to establish His kingdom. The Lord Jesus cannot abandon His humanity now or in the future to assume different discrete forms as He did in Old Testament days. Though human, His divine character and essence are unchanged; thus, He continues to possess all the power, wisdom, and insight to accomplish whatever the Father desires Him to do! Consequently, the eternal Word, the Son of God, no longer appears as "the Angel of the Lord," but rather is the incarnate Word of God for all of eternity.

Seraphim

Isaiah saw seraphim (or "burning ones") heralding praise above God's heavenly throne. They are not specifically referred to elsewhere in Scripture, although these beings are similar to the four living creatures John describes in Revelation 4. In every aspect, what is described to us about the seraphim in Isaiah 6, the cherubim in Ezekiel 1, and the four living creatures in Revelation 1 reflect the glory of Christ. What is not described to us is an intrinsic glory that God wants covered in His presence; the wings of these spiritual beings accomplish this. It is not that what is covered is not beautiful; rather, it is not what the Holy Spirit wants us to be occupied with. Isaiah provides no description of the seraphim's wings, except as to their number, which provides essential information to their ministry. (They fly above the throne of God with two wings, and they conceal their own intrinsic glory with four wings.) Their wings are mentioned to highlight their use in God-ordained ministry, not to emphasize their aerodynamic abilities. The specific language ensures all glory is of and to God.

Understanding the symbolic significance of each of the revealed portions of these spiritual beings is integral to appreciating the fuller glory of God; else why would the Holy Spirit have intentionally provided the extra revelation? The importance of the symbolic ministry of the four living creatures, the seraphim, and the cherubim before the throne of God has been acknowledged by many theologians.

> Matthew Henry: [Why do the Seraphim cover themselves in God's presence?] "This bespeaks their great humility and reverence in their attendance upon God, for He is greatly feared." "... in the presence of God, they cover ... because, being conscious of an infinite distance from the divine perfections, they are ashamed to show their faces."[26]

> Albert Barnes: [Why do the Seraphim cover their faces?] "This is designed, doubtless, to denote the reverence and awe inspired by the immediate presence of God." "The seraphim stood covered, or as if concealing themselves as much as possible, in token of their nothingness and unworthiness in the presence of the Holy One."[27]

> William MacDonald: "The creatures symbolize those attributes of God which are seen in creation: His majesty, power, swiftness, and wisdom." Of the Seraphim he writes, "with four wings for reverence and two for service. These celebrate the holiness of God."[28]

The willingness in these powerfully created beings to cover their own intrinsic glories to ensure that only God's glory is seen and appreciated in heaven serves as a personal salute to the glory and authority of God. Unfortunately, there is a similar symbol of God's authority that often receives little acknowledgement among Christians today. Paul instructs that when believers are in God's presence for the spiritual exercise of prayer or prophecy (teaching), there should be a visible salute to His authority. This salute, or sign of authority, is the covered head of the woman and the uncovered head of the man: *"For this cause ought the woman to have* [a sign of authority] *on her head"* (1 Cor. 11:10). The veil is a symbol of submission to God's authority; by wearing it, the woman shows visible agreement with divine order (1 Cor. 11:3).

The man is God's representative (God's glory) and is to remain uncovered; however, the woman, representing man's glory, is to be covered (1 Cor. 11:4-7). Long hair is a fitting covering for the woman, but this covering is also a glory in itself (1 Cor. 11:15), which must be covered so as not to compete with God's glory. When the brothers remain uncovered and the sisters covered during church meetings, all competing glories are thus concealed and only God's glory is seen. In this way, only God's glory, as represented by uncovered men, is seen by God and the angels overlooking the assembly – a visible salute to Christ's headship and God's order is thus affirmed for all to see. This pictures the scene in heaven as seraphim and cherubim cover their own glories with their wings in the presence of God, so God's glory is preeminent (v. 2; Ezek. 1:11).

The angels are at present learning about submission to divine order from observing the Church's submission to it (1 Cor. 11:10; Eph. 3:10). In a spectacular way, God is using the Church to testify to all creation of His manifold wisdom (Eph. 3:10). What God commands is clearly right, but some things are right only because they are commanded. So in such matters it would be good for us to follow the example of the Seraphim, who covered their eyes, but did not cover their ears – they did not judge anything by its appearance, but by God's Word alone.

The Holiness of God

Through encountering the Lord at the burning bush at Sinai, Moses was made aware of God's awesome holiness and his own futility (Ex. 3:1-12). This realization then enabled Moses to properly serve the Lord. Isaiah has a similar experience with God in this chapter. Besides a rumbling, smoked-filled temple to announce God's presence (v. 4), Isaiah saw seraphim flying overhead, crying out to each other, *"Holy, holy, holy is the Lord of hosts; the whole earth is full of His glory!"* (v. 3). Centuries later, John was caught up in the Spirit to a similar heavenly scene (Rev. 4:8) where he witnessed the glory of Christ (Rev. 1:12-18).

After seeing the majestic glory of God upon His throne, Isaiah's response was: *"Woe is me, for I am undone! Because I am a man of unclean lips, and I dwell in the midst of a people of unclean lips; for my eyes have seen the King, the Lord of hosts"* (v. 5). At that moment, Isaiah was not mindful of what he had or had not done, nor of what he should have done, but of his spiritual position before Almighty God. When man stands before the throne of God, there is no excuse, nowhere to shift blame; outside of Christ, we all stand condemned as sinners. This is what God wants us to realize!

As soon as Isaiah acknowledged his condition before God, God's response was immediate and effectual. A seraph hovering about the throne of God swooped down and snatched a hot coal from the altar and pressed it to Isaiah's lips saying, *"Your iniquity is taken away, and your sin purged"* (vv. 6-7). The coal would have been taken from the Bronze Altar and not the Golden Altar of Incense. Sins were atoned for on the Bronze Altar through blood sacrifices which foreshadow the once-for-all propitiation and redemption Christ would provide at Calvary. Additionally, no veils are mentioned, meaning there was free access to the altar mentioned. That would not be the case for the Golden Altar in the Holy Place of the temple.

The altar here demonstrates God's ability to purify sinners who understand who He is and who willingly humbly themselves to accept what only He can do – cleanse sins. The Hebrew verbs translated "touched" and "is taken away" in verse 7 are co-ordinate perfects, stressing that as soon as one happened the other action also happened.[29] Through confession and the altar, Isaiah received instant grace, and a holy, blameless standing before God. This wonderful spiritual connection between God's throne and His altar (i.e., to provide mercy to repentant sinners) is noticed throughout Scripture.

> Lord, Thy glory fills the heaven;
> Earth is with its fullness stored;
> Unto Thee be glory given,
> Holy, holy, holy Lord!
>
> Thus Thy glorious Name confessing,
> We adopt the angels' cry,
> "Holy, holy, holy" blessing
> Thee, the Lord of Hosts Most High!
>
> — Richard Mant

After Isaiah's sins were purged, the Lord inquires openly (He did not speak to Isaiah directly): *"Whom shall I send, and who will go for Us"* (v. 8)? This inquiry prompted Isaiah to immediately reply *"Here am I, send me."* It is important to observe that God did not give the call for service, nor did Isaiah respond to it, until his sin had been cleansed. Having realized his doomed position before a holy God and then experiencing God's mercy and cleansing, Isaiah became a clean vessel, fit for service. Notice Isaiah did not suggest to the Lord what kinds of ministries he would enjoy doing. Nor did he even ask the Lord what He would have him do. Isaiah was completely available and willing to do whatever God told him to do. This is evidence of true salvation –

consecrated and faithful service no matter the cost to the servant personally.

Peter understood that if a believer lives for Christ, he or she will suffer for it. But such suffering would be a sweet savor in the nostrils of God because it would remind Him of the way His Son suffered for doing His will.

> *When you do good and suffer, if you take it patiently, this is commendable before God. For to this you were called, because Christ also suffered for us, leaving us an example, that you should follow His steps: "Who committed no sin, nor was deceit found in His mouth"* (1 Pet. 2:20-22).

> *For it is better, if it is the will of God, to suffer for doing good than for doing evil. For Christ also suffered once for sins, the just for the unjust, that He might bring us to God, being put to death in the flesh but made alive by the Spirit* (1 Pet. 3:17-18).

Yet, there is another benefit of suffering with endurance in the will of God. Paul told both the saints at Philippi and Thessalonica that suffering patiently for the cause of Christ was a token of (a proof of) their salvation (Phil. 1:28; 2 Thess. 1:5). Naturally speaking, it is not possible to suffer patiently for doing what is right; however, it is possible for a Christian who draws on supernatural power from on high. Thus, suffering patiently in the will of God becomes a powerful witness to the lost; in fact, this was the testimony that brought one thief, crucified with the Lord, to repentance.

Preparation for Service

After Moses, Isaiah, and John became aware of God's unapproachable nature and then experienced His mercy, they all became available for lifelong service. The understanding of who God is and who we are before Him leads us to salvation. The outcome of experiencing God's grace is a passionate desire to serve the Lord in meekness and holiness. This is what the young prophet Isaiah learned from his encounter with God, and it is what we must learn also.

Isaiah was called to declare God's word to his countrymen who would ultimately be judicially blinded and hardened for rejecting his message and would suffer much for doing so (vv. 9-10). The goal of Isaiah's ministry was not to condemn Judah, but to graciously warn them of coming judgment if they did not repent (though he knew ahead of time that they would not turn back to the Lord).

And He said, "Go, and tell this people: 'Keep on hearing, but do not understand; keep on seeing, but do not perceive.' Make the heart of this people dull, and their ears heavy, and shut their eyes; lest they see with their eyes, and hear with their ears, and understand with their heart, and return and be healed" (vv. 9-10).

W. E. Vine describes the type of people that Isaiah was called to preach to:

The people had so persistently perverted their ways that they had gone beyond the possibility of conversion and healing. A man may so harden himself in evil as to render his condition irremediable, and this by God's retributive judgment upon him.[30]

Understanding the unpopular nature of his message and that he had not been promised any positive result for preaching it, Isaiah asked, *"Lord, how long?"* This clarification was not an attempt to evade his divine calling, but to determine the duration of God's judgments on his stubborn countrymen (v. 11). The Lord then answered Isaiah's question – until the cities of Judah are laid waste and uninhabited, and the land is utterly desolate.

Lest this news be too overwhelming for His new seer, the Lord did say that He would spare a remnant (a tenth) from destruction, but then added, that His people must suffer much tribulation to be cleansed of their idolatry (v. 12). This remnant, the *"holy seed,"* would be like a living stump of a great tree after the rest of the tree has been cut down. This meant that God would reestablish the Jewish nation in the land of Israel through the preserved remnant.

To devote one's entire life to such an arduous ministry without any observable benefit would be difficult unless that person was sold out for God. Isaiah was, and although he did not personally suffer in his prophetic ministry as Jeremiah did, he and his family endured many hardships. Isaiah did not witness a positive outcome of his preaching and writing ministry during his lifetime, but the impact of his faithfulness to God is still benefiting God's people today.

Sorrow and Comfort

Meditation

One great hindrance to holiness in the ministry of the word is that we are prone to preach and write without pressing into the things we say and making them real to our own souls. Over the years words begin to come easy, and we find we can speak of mysteries without standing in awe; we can speak of purity without feeling pure; we can speak of zeal without spiritual passion; we can speak of God's holiness without trembling; we can speak of sin without sorrow; we can speak of heaven without eagerness. And the result is a terrible hardening of the spiritual life.

— John Owen

Isaiah Visits Ahaz
Isaiah 7

In the previous chapter we saw the majesty of God revealed and how He righteously dealt with Isaiah's sin to prepare him for service. If the Lord could deal so prudently with the prophet's sin, could He not also erase Israel's debt? In this sense, Isaiah represented the entire nation, which meant that all was not lost. This realization would instill hope in the minds of the faithful remnant – a holy seed would eventually prosper in the land after their chastening was over.

Isaiah apparently chose to situate this narrative pertaining to Ahaz after his own calling to contrast two official realities. First, the weak and vulnerable throne of Ahaz is shown to be far inferior to the invincible and unthreatened throne of God. Second, the proud and ungodly Ahaz did not respond to his kingly office with the same humility and submission that Isaiah had shown in executing his prophetic office.

The Syrian-Israeli Alliance

Ahaz was the second king after Uzziah. The prophet completely skipped over Jotham's reign likely because he followed the Lord throughout his royal tenure. Isaiah surveys the political landscape at that time: Ahaz reigned over Judah; Pekah was the king of Israel, and Rezin, the king of Aram or Syria, northeast of Israel. Pekah and Rezin were gathering their armies to launch a second invasion into Judah (v. 1; 2 Chron. 28:5-8). Although Israel's alliance with Syria had been established for several years, and though their previous attempt to take Jerusalem had failed, the fresh amassing of troops along Judah's border was disheartening (v. 2).

The use of *"the house of David"* (v. 2) and *"O house of David"* (v. 13) is significant, as Isaiah uses the phrase only three times (vv. 2, 13, 22:22), and Zechariah is the only other prophet to invoke the reference. The foreign alliance was seeking to end the House of David, so its meaning is personified in its current king, Ahaz; thus, *"your father's house"* in verse 17. This was a time of crisis: Would David's dynasty end? How would Ahaz respond to preserve it? The Lord responded to this situation by sending Isaiah and his son Shear-Jashub to the end of the aqueduct from the upper pool to the Fuller's Field to meet with King Ahaz (v. 3). This is where the people would spread out their freshly-washed clothes to bleach and dry in the sun.

Isaiah's message to the king was concise: Do not fear Rezin and Pekah. They are merely two smoking firebrands and their efforts will fail; they will not replace you with the son of Tabeel (a puppet-king); rather you will remain on the throne of Judah (vv. 4-7). Indeed, Rezin and Pekah were like the faint smoke of nearly consumed firewood, as both men would die two years later in 732 B.C. Isaiah's lack of esteem for Pekah is obvious in that he refers to him only by name once. Four times Isaiah refers to the king of Israel as merely as "the son of Remaliah." Thus the conspiracy to destroy Judah, which seemed so overwhelming to Ahaz because of his dull conscience towards the things of God, brought this divine revelation: The menacing kings were doomed and the confederacy between Israel and Syria would come to nothing.

Then Isaiah prophesied that within sixty-five years Ephraim, speaking of the Northern Kingdom, would be broken (or shattered), meaning they would lose their autonomy, distinction, and would be scattered (vv. 8-9). Isaiah was obviously a married man with at least one child, Shear-Jashub. The Lord asked that the son accompany his father on this errand because the meaning of his name harmonized with Isaiah's message to Ahaz concerning the fall of the Northern Kingdom. Shear-Jashub's name means "a remnant will return." Standing by his father, "Jehovah is Salvation" conveyed a prophetic affirmation that God would gather His people back to their homeland after their chastening and dispersion was over.

The names of those opposing Judah also conveyed an important message in keeping with their character. Rezin's name means "self-willed," and Pekah, "to open the senses," by implication to be observant. When we judge matters of life by our senses and with a self-willed disposition, we will assuredly be opposing God's means of mercy! Rezin and Pekah would learn this truth only moments before their death.

Devotions in Isaiah

Since Assyria conquered Israel in 722 B.C., only twelve years after Isaiah's prophesy to Ahaz, why did he impose the sixty-five-year decree? John A. Martin offers this explanation:

> When Assyria conquered Israel in 722, many Israelites were deported to other lands by Assyria and foreigners were brought into Samaria (2 Kgs. 17:24). However, in 669 many more foreigners were transferred to Samaria by Ashurbanipal (Ezra 4:10), king of Assyria (669-626 B.C.). This "shattered" Israel, making it impossible for her to unite as a nation ("a people").[31]

In summary, Israel was conquered in 722 B.C., but it was the vast settling of foreigners in Samaria by Assyria in 669 B.C. that vanquished the already struggling Jewish culture. At that juncture, Israel lost its identity altogether and was shattered as a society.

Isaiah then challenged Ahaz to believe that what God had said would come true: *"If you will not believe, surely you shall not be established"* (v. 9). The horrific trial that Ahaz was facing was a faith-building opportunity to move closer to God, which is what God desired him to do. The Jews, by nature, have always been a people that must see to believe. Paul acknowledged this tendency in his day with the statement, *"For Jews request a sign, and Greeks seek after wisdom"* (1 Cor. 1:22). God was willing to work a miracle to help Ahaz more easily trust in His word declared by Isaiah. However, the Lord also knows that faith based on sight will be shallow and will be liable to falter when tested. God-pleasing faith takes God at His Word, apart from sensual or intellectual validation. This type of faith rises above natural experiences to connect with supernatural power. Overall, Ahaz failed to properly represent God to the people; this was his opportunity to be spiritually revived by exercising faith in God's Word and by experiencing the wonder of God.

God wanted Ahaz to believe that both of Isaiah's date-specific prophecies would be fulfilled; the Israel-Syrian alliance in Ahaz's day would soon fail, followed by a total collapse of the Northern Kingdom within sixty-five years. Obviously, Ahaz would not be alive to see the latter fulfilled, so Isaiah offers Ahaz an opportunity to see a supernatural sign of his choosing to affirm that Isaiah was speaking for the Lord. This would hopefully bolster Ahaz's resolve to exercise faith in all God had spoken through Isaiah (vv. 10-11).

Sorrow and Comfort

Amazingly, Ahaz declines Isaiah's offer for God to work a spectacular sign, *"I will not ask, nor will I test the Lord"* (v. 12)! J. N. Darby writes: "Ahaz, feeling the proximity of God, shrinks, under the form of piety, from the offered sign, and God takes up the matter in grace as to Messiah, but in the revelation of judgment."[32] The king's mock piety demonstrates that he was unwilling to abandon his trust in Assyria for protection. Matthew Henry suggests that Ahaz's response indicates the reality of his dissatisfaction with God: "Secret disaffection with God is often disguised with the color of respect to him; and those who are resolved that they will not trust God, yet pretend they will not tempt him."[33] Ahaz had drifted so far from the Lord that he just did not care what God had to say or would do. To grow as cold in spirit as to not want the Lord to interfere with one's plans is to be in a nosedive towards the hard ground of apostasy. Indeed, Ahaz did much evil; rather than seeking Jehovah's help, he sought Baal's favor by offering his own children as burnt sacrifices (2 Chron. 28:2-3).

While it is wrong to request a sign from God in order to trust in Him (Matt. 12:38-39; John 6:30), it is also a mistake to reject Him when He offers to demonstrate His glory. Gideon asked for a sign from the Lord, not because he disbelieved or doubted God's word, but to be doubly sure that he was in God's will. Ahaz's response demonstrates a deficient trust in the Lord and that he was counting on a different solution to Judah's threatening situation. He probably thought that with the help of a foreign alliance Jerusalem's fortifications would hold. Whatever the reason, Ahaz's false piety demonstrates that he is willing to face this ominous military threat without God's involvement.

One cannot escape trusting in something to interpret life. The atheist trusts science to explain life. Those who reject God's revelation of truth will fall for anything; they will not be established. Twentieth-century British mathematician and philosopher-atheist Bertrand Russell once wrote, "What is wanted is not the will to believe, but the will to find out, which is the exact opposite." [34] But scientific truth is only a statistical interpretation of ultimate truth. Man's systems of reasoning and empirically determined parameters of our existence are imperfect, meaning it requires faith to trust in scientific findings. Unfortunately, Russell learned this reality too late. Just before his death he said, "Philosophy has proven a washout for me." Russell proved the reliability of David's assessment, *"The fool hath said in his heart, there is no God"* (Ps. 14:1). Life without God as the center of existence is meaningless. Without God, man has no ontological foundation to reckon anything true. Without exercising faith in what God reveals as true, we cannot do anything to please Him. *"For without faith it is impossible to please God"* (Heb. 11:6).

Ahaz had no desire for God to draw near, so God answers his snub with "Immanuel" – God would indeed come to Israel. Although Ahaz did not want a sign, God would supply one anyway. Isaiah responds to Ahaz by unfolding future events:

> *Hear now, O house of David! Is it a small thing for you to weary men, but will you weary my God also? Therefore the Lord Himself will give you a sign: Behold, the virgin shall conceive and bear a Son, and shall call His name Immanuel. Curds and honey He shall eat, that He may know to refuse the evil and choose the good. For before the Child shall know to refuse the evil and choose the good, the land that you dread will be forsaken by both her kings* (vv. 13-16).

God's response to Ahaz's irreverent reply demonstrates the longsuffering nature of God. Isaiah's prophecy, given to the house of David (not just to Ahaz), has three components: First, a virgin would conceive and give birth to a son (v. 14). Second, this son would arrive during a time of national calamity. Milk (needed for curds) and honey are in abundance during distressing times because the death of new calves leave cows with excess milk and untilled fields naturally produce wildflowers from which bees make honey (v. 15).[35] There are a variety of interpretations of the "curds and honey" reference, but this understanding fits best given the political situation threatening Judah at that time (and also later when Christ would be born). Third, before the son would be old enough to know right and wrong, suggesting a young age of perhaps two, the Syrian-Israeli alliance would be broken (v. 16).

The Hebrew word *almah* is translated "virgin" in verse 14. *Almah* occurs seven times in the Old Testament and is rendered "virgin," "damsel," or "maiden" to speak of an unmarried woman of a marriageable age (i.e., who is sexually mature; Deut. 22:19). For example, it is the word used to describe the virgin Rebekah, Isaac's future wife in Genesis 24:43. It also unmistakably refers to virgins in Exodus 2:8 and Song 6:8. Some argue that the Hebrew word *bethulah* is more commonly rendered "virgin" in the Old Testament and that Isaiah would have used that word here instead of *almah* if he meant a virgin. While the first part of this argument is true, *bethulah* is also

Sorrow and Comfort

used to speak of a young married woman as in Joel 1:8, whereas *almah* is never used to refer to a married woman. So, given the context of the passage and how these two Hebrew words are used elsewhere in Scripture, *almah* is the better choice – otherwise the sign could relate to a married woman (not a virgin) conceiving, which is a natural event and not a supernatural miracle.

The definite article "the" before "virgin" is significant and implies that one specific virgin is in view. There is only one other salvation prophecy in Scripture to which this can refer, God crushing Satan's head through *"the seed of a woman"* (Gen. 3:15). All other humans would be born of a woman through the seed of a man, but not the Messiah. He would be born of a virgin (not the result of normal human conception).

Isaiah's prophecy has been interpreted in various ways, but it is obvious that there must also be a direct fulfillment of it that Ahaz could witness as a sign which pertained to Judah's present threatening situation. The likely meaning is that before a virgin woman conceived (meaning she was just married and could not have been pregnant beforehand), before she carried the baby for nine months, before she gave birth to a son, and before that son was old enough to make moral decisions, the Syrian-Israeli alliance would fail. The Hebrew text indicates that the "son," Immanuel, in verse 14 cannot be *"the youth"* (v. 16), meaning Isaiah's son was too old to fulfill the prophecy. This distinction eliminates confusion as to the timing of Isaiah's prophecy – the alliance threatening Judah would be abolished within, say, three years.

Indeed, that is exactly what happened. In 732 B.C. Assyrian king Tiglath-Pileser III invaded and destroyed Damascus and put Rezin to death. Ahaz could then know that God's word spoken through Isaiah was true and know for certain that God was with the nation. This would illustrate the meaning of the child's name, *Immanuel*, which means "God is with us." However, as we soon shall see, this did not mean that Judah would not be punished for her wickedness.

As with many prophecies in the Old Testament, there is often a near-term meaning and a remote meaning. So while Ahaz may have understood the more immediate meaning of the prophecy as it related to dissolving the threatening alliance, Matthew proclaimed that Isaiah's prophecy was fulfilled over seven hundred years later when Mary conceived Christ of the Holy Spirit (Matt. 1:21-23).

This is why Isaiah's prophecy is addressed to *the house of Judah* and not just to Ahaz; it further foretold the conception and birth of the Jewish Messiah of David's seed. Matthew affirms that Mary was a virgin when she conceived the Lord Jesus and that she still was a virgin when she gave birth to Him (Matt. 1:18, 25). This meant that not only was God's presence with Israel (as shown in Ahaz's day), but that God incarnate would be among His people in the future. When Isaiah says that Judah and Israel would be scattered among the nations and would need to be regathered by the Messiah, a distant future meaning of this prophecy is ensured (8:11-12, 11:12). Only then would the ultimate fulfillment of the Lord's names *Immanuel* – "God is with us" and *Jesus* – "Jehovah's Salvation" be realized.

The Assyrian-Judah Alliance

Although the Lord promised to deliver Judah from the Syrian-Israeli alliance, Isaiah told Ahaz that an even greater military threat was looming over Judah – Assyria (v. 17). Albert Barnes summarizes the horrific events which prompted Ahaz to seek Assyrian assistance, rather than the Lord's:

> Though the siege which Rezin and Pekah had undertaken was not at this time successful, yet they returned the year after with stronger forces, and with counsels better concerted, and again besieged the city. This was in consequence of the continued and increasing wickedness of Ahaz (2 Chron. 28:1-5). In this expedition, a great multitude were taken captives, and carried to Damascus (2 Chron. 28:5). Pekah at this time also killed 120,000 of the Jews in one day (2 Chron. 28:6); and Zichri, a valiant man of Ephraim, killed Maaseiah the son of Ahaz. At this time, also, Pekah took no less than 200,000 of the kingdom of Judah, proposing to take them to Samaria, but was prevented by the influence of the prophet Oded (2 Chron. 28:8-15). In this calamity, Ahaz stripped the temple of its treasures and ornaments, and sent them to Tiglath-pileser, king of Assyria, to induce him to come and defend him from the united arms of Syria and Ephraim. The consequence was, as might have been foreseen, that the king of Assyria took occasion, from this, to bring increasing calamities upon the kingdom of Ahaz. He first, indeed, killed Rezin, and took Damascus (2 Kgs. 16:7). Having subdued the kingdoms of Damascus and Ephraim, Tiglath-pileser became a more formidable enemy to Ahaz than both of them.[36]

Sorrow and Comfort

In the coming days, the Assyrians would inflict on Judah the worst attacks that they had experienced in three centuries. Tiglath-Pileser levied heavy tribute on Judah during Ahaz's reign, and later Sennacherib invaded northern Judah and would have slaughtered Hezekiah and his entire army if God had not miraculously intervened (chps. 36-37). Later, we will see that Hezekiah initially sought help against the Assyrian invasion from the declining Egyptian Empire, but God did not permit that to happen.

Returning to the present situation, Isaiah told Ahaz that God was in full control of Judah's future. He could whistle for bothersome flies from Egypt or summon buzzing bees of Assyria as He determined (vv. 18-19). These metaphors colorfully describe the multitudes of soldiers that would eventually cover the entire land, like swarms of flies and hives of bees. The meaning of Isaiah's message is clear: Do not rely on your own reasoning or on anyone else's strength to resolve this crisis – put your trust in the Lord. To trust in Assyria would be like grabbing a tiger by the tail!

In a coming day Assyria would divest and humiliate Judah. Isaiah says that Assyria would be a razor that would shave Judah's hair (v. 20). In the Jewish culture, a shaved head was a sign of grieving or misery (15:2; Jer. 47:5; Ezek. 7:18). The Assyrian calamity would distress the entire nation as signified by the abundance of milk (for curds) and honey (vv. 21-22; see earlier explanation for v. 15). Unattended vineyards and untilled farmland would soon be overtaken by grass, wildflowers, briars, and thorn bushes and thus be fit for only grazing livestock (vv. 23-25).

Ahaz was afraid of the Syrian-Israeli alliance, but through the Assyrians, God was going to inflict a much harsher blow to chasten His people. The Northern Kingdom would be conquered and shattered, and the Southern Kingdom would be greatly distressed. In the next chapter Isaiah will speak more of how the Southern Kingdom would be delivered. Thankfully, this chapter foretells the One who will ultimately deliver the Jewish nation from their sin, their rebellion, and all their distresses – His name is Immanuel.

Meditation

> The great God of Heaven is come down to earth,
> His mother a virgin, and sinless His birth;

Devotions in Isaiah

The Father eternal His Father alone:
He sleeps in the manger; He reigns on the throne.

Lo! here is Emmanuel, here is the Child,
The Son that was promised to Mary so mild;
Whose power and dominion shall ever increase,
The Prince that shall rule o'er a kingdom of peace.

— Henry R. Bramley

Fear the Lord, Not the Assyrians
Isaiah 8

This chapter is a sequel to the previous one in that deliverance from the Syrian-Israeli alliance was assured; however, the coming Assyrian invasion would eventually affect all of Israel. Where the previous chapter focused on Ahaz's disbelief and the cruelty of the future Assyrian conquest, this chapter highlights positive aspects of the ordeal, namely, that God would deliver His people from oppression. In the next chapter, this deliverance will introduce the nation's ultimate Deliverer.

A Second Sign

Isaiah begins by issuing a second prophecy relating to the dissolving of the Syrian-Israeli alliance foretold in chapter 7. But in this prophecy, the son would be born to Isaiah and his wife (v. 3). His name was to be called Maher-Shalal-Hash-Baz (hopefully this wee lad had a nickname); his name means "speed the spoil; hasten the booty," and it pointed to Assyria's invasion of Israel and Syria (v. 1). This prophecy was to be handwritten in common letters on a large scroll or tablet. Two witnesses, Uriah the priest and Zechariah the son of Jeberechiah, were to authenticate the timing of what was written (v. 2). (This would be similar to a notary public countersigning documents today.) Uriah is likely the same man mentioned in 2 Kings 16:10. He was the accomplice of Ahaz in corrupting the people, but apparently his testimony would carry weight with Ahaz, so he was summoned.

The large scroll (really a huge placard) was then to be publicly posted for all to read. The Message: Before Isaiah's son would be old enough to cry *"'My father' and 'My mother,' the riches of Damascus and the spoil of Samaria will be taken away before the king of Assyria"* (v. 4). The testimony of the two prominent witnesses ensured that scoffers could not later accuse Isaiah of penning the message after the fact. The extra effort of safeguarding God's Word serves as a good reminder for us to be able not just to present Scripture accurately, but also to defend its authenticity when it is attacked by critics.

It is observed that Isaiah's wife is referred to as a prophetess (v. 3), either because she was married to a prophet and could testify of his messages, or because God spoke directly through her. Isaiah's wife is one of seven women in the Bible who are referred to as prophetesses, two of whom did not speak for God (Noadiah, Neh. 6:14; Jezebel, Rev. 2:20). Generally speaking, when the Jewish nation was thriving under prudent male leadership, God did not use women to speak publicly for Him. However, at times in which this was not true, God did use women to convey important information or messages. God publicly acknowledged the poor condition of the nation by doing so.

For example, at a time when Israel was steeped in spiritual darkness and void of godly leadership, Deborah gave wise counsel from her home to all who sought wisdom from the Lord (Judg. 4:4). Elderly Anna also identified the Lord Jesus Christ as the future redeemer of Jerusalem (Luke 2:36-38). Again, at a time when Israel's leadership was destitute of spiritual vigor, God chose common people, like Zachariah and Simeon (and Anna) who were consecrated to the Lord to announce His son's birth and mission. In the apostolic period of the Church Age, some women were also given the gift of prophecy; Philip had four virgin daughters who prophesied (Acts 21:8). While the nature of this gift (private counsel, teaching women only, public evangelism, etc.) is not stated, these applications would certainly comply with stated church order in Scripture (1 Cor. 14:34; 1 Tim. 2:11-12).

Returning to the text, we conclude for several reasons that this prophecy is not the same as the one recorded in the previous chapter: First, the sons referred to have different names (Immanuel in 7:13, Maher-Shalal-Hash-Baz in v. 1). Second, Isaiah's wife was not a virgin (7:3). Third, this child would be younger than the one in chapter 7 when the Syrian-Israeli alliance collapsed (i.e., old enough to verbalize "daddy" and "mommy" vs. contemplating moral decisions). This meant that Ahaz would have two birth-related signs of the same prophecy to consider: the birth of the son in chapter 7 a year or more before Isaiah's son in chapter 8.

Warning of Invasion

Starting in verse 5, Isaiah brings another word from the Lord. Judgment was pronounced on *"these people"* (v. 6). The expression

Sorrow and Comfort

seems to refer to the Jewish nation as a whole, but with a stronger focus on the Northern Kingdom. Just as Isaiah had prophesied, the initial attack by Assyria in 732 B.C. (two to three years after Isaiah's prophecy) caused the Syrian-Israeli alliance to fail. Ten years later, after a three-year siege (started by Shalmaneser V), Samaria fell and was plundered by Assyria's king Sargon II in 722 B.C. (or the ninth year of Hoshea; 2 Kgs. 17:3-6). An Assyrian cuneiform states that 27,290 captives were taken from Samaria at this time.[37] Isaiah will later refer to Sargon by name to acknowledge that his prophecy had been fulfilled (20:1).

The Northern Kingdom rejoiced with Syrian Rezin instead of identifying with their countrymen in Jerusalem. Water gently flowed from the spring of Gihon east of the Water Gate into a small reservoir (Shiloah or Siloam) within the walls on the southeast side of Jerusalem. Since Israel had refused the soft-flowing water in Jerusalem (Immanuel's land), God promised to punish them by an Assyrian flashflood spilling over from the banks of the Euphrates ("the river" which flows through Assyria) and engulfing the entire land (v. 7). Additionally, the chastening floodwaters would spread over *"Immanuel's Land"* (v. 8). This is the first of seven references in Isaiah to the Jewish nation residing on God's land. Moses told the Israelites that God owned Canaan, but would permit them to be stewards of His land. If they were faithful in the land, then they would remain, but if not, He would remove them, which He later did (Lev. 25:23). J. A. Motyer notes the significance of the twofold reality of Immanuel mentioned in verses 8, 10:

> The two *Immanuel* references link this section with the last [7:14]. In 8:8 *Immanuel* shares the suffering of His land and in 8:9-10, though the nations worldwide prepare for battle, their plan will be frustrated because "God is with us." *Immanuel* is a truth as well as a name – the truth of the Lord's presence with His people and the security which it brings.[38]

The coming devastation in the north of Immanuel's land would be catastrophic, but the Assyrian flood would rise only to the necks of those in Judah, meaning they would not be drowned or be swept away like the Northern Kingdom would be. The reason is that God would spare Judah by spreading His wings over them. Just as Israel would know that Immanuel was responsible for dissolving the military threat

Devotions in Isaiah

against them (chp. 7), God would be known to be among His people in the Southern Kingdom through sparing them from the full brunt of the Assyrian war machine. Isaiah was confirming that God would be with Judah through the upcoming trial and that they need not heed the political propaganda or war cries coming out of Assyria. They would not be successful in their attempted conquest of Judah (vv. 9-10).

Many Jews doubted God's promises of protection for Israel (chp. 7) and of Judah (chp. 8); therefore God exhorts Isaiah not to be like them (vv. 11-12). *"For the Lord spoke thus to me with a strong hand, and instructed me that I should not walk in the way of this people, saying"* (v. 11). A parent might admonish a young child while shaking a finger back and forth to emphasize the message, but when God shakes his hand while speaking, He is not only confirming the message, but enforcing it by His power. This realization brought peace to Isaiah's heart, although everyone else was in a frenzy.

God would be a sanctuary for the faithful during the Assyrian invasion; therefore, His people were to fear only Him, not the heathen nations (v. 13). Isaiah eloquently presents God's promise:

> *He will be as a sanctuary, but a stone of stumbling and a rock of offense to both the houses of Israel, as a trap and a snare to the inhabitants of Jerusalem. And many among them shall stumble; they shall fall and be broken, be snared and taken* (vv. 14-15).

The Jews were God's chosen people, from among all people, and the temple in Jerusalem is where God chose to reside among His people when they were in communion with Him. We often think of a sanctuary as a place of asylum. But no building in Jerusalem would be a safe place to hide from the Assyrians, not even the temple. The idea here is that God would be among only those faithful Jews aspiring to be holy as He is holy. Those who stumbled over His word and would not seek Him as a holy sanctuary would not be preserved, but would fall into the Assyrian snare and be taken away (v. 15). In short, those who would believe and obey the Lord would also know His presence and deliverance; those who did not would experience His chastening.

It is difficult to pass over the language of verses 14 and 15 without thinking of what David wrote earlier concerning another future opportunity the Jewish nation would be given for deliverance. But sadly, they rejected both God's message of salvation and His Messenger – the Lord Jesus Christ their Messiah.

Sorrow and Comfort

> *The stone which the builders rejected has become the chief cornerstone. This was the Lord's doing; it is marvelous in our eyes. This is the day the Lord has made; we will rejoice and be glad in it* (Ps. 118:22-24).

Psalm 118:22 is quoted several times in the New Testament, where it is evident the reference to the rejected cornerstone relates to Israel's refusal of Jesus Christ as their Messiah. The psalmist says, *"this is the day which the Lord has made"* (Ps. 118:24). The Lord Jesus Himself acknowledged that this verse spoke of Him (Matt. 21:42; Luke 20:17), as did the apostles (Eph. 2:20; 1 Pet. 2:6-7). After being rejected by the Jewish nation, the Lord suffered and died at Calvary. Then He was resurrected to the highest station in heaven, and in a future day He will return to the earth to establish His throne as Israel's King – the day that the psalmist was rejoicing in. The Hebrew word *yowm*, normally translated as "day," appears frequently in the Old Testament; however, in the Hebrew expression that correlates to the English phrase, "on that day" or "this is the day" is it used only about twenty times. This expression first appears in Leviticus 16:30 in reference to the Day of Atonement. We find it again in Psalm 118:24 where it refers to a specific day that God had marked on His calendar since before the foundations of the world were laid – the day propitiation was offered by His own Son for all humanity's sins (Heb. 2:9; 1 Jn. 2:2). It was the day redeeming blood flowed from Immanuel's veins to ensure the redemption of all those who exercise faith in God's message of salvation.

Israel considered Christ the Rock of Offense and at His first advent rejected Him as their Cornerstone at His first advent. Thankfully, He became the Foundation Stone of the Church (1 Cor. 3:11). Hence, believers in the Church Age can rejoice with the psalmist in *the day the Lord has made.*

Two Responses

Isaiah then confirms his resolve to inscribe God's Word on the hearts of both faithful disciples and his own children. He also resolves to wait patiently on the Lord; their hope was in Him alone (vv. 16-17). These faithful believers in coming days would be a strong testimony of God's sovereign rule in Israel; in that aspect they would be a sign and wonder to the dissident: *"Here am I and the children whom the Lord has given me! We are for signs and wonders in Israel"* (v. 18). William

Kelly identifies these faithful Jewish disciples as those present in Jerusalem at Pentecost when the Church was formed (Acts 2):

> Now it is certain that those "disciples," who had trusted in the Christ, while the mass of the Jews rejected Him, as they do still, became at Pentecost the nucleus of Christianity, and were "added together daily" by the Lord, and formed "their own company" (Acts 4:23), distinctly called "the church" (Acts 5:11) thereafter. But this heavenly transformation is quite omitted here, and left as a secret to be made known in the New Testament. The prophet looks onward to the accomplishment of their hopes as Israel for the earth under the Messiah in the latter day. In neither the Old Testament is Israel transferred to the church, nor in the New Testament the church incorporating Israel by-and-by. But the church itself, as Christ's body, is in no way revealed here. It is left as a heavenly secret to be revealed to the holy apostles and prophets by the Spirit in the New Testament. And we pass over from the godly remnant at our Lord's first advent to the troublous and dark scene which precedes the day of His appearing at the end of this age. This, which is the evident and simple truth of the passage, cuts up by the root the allegorizing fancy that Judah or Israel means the church.[39]

This understanding reflects the prophetic meaning of verse 17, which is quoted in Hebrews 2:13 and rightly applied to Christ: *"I will put My trust in Him...Here am I and the children whom God has given Me."* But obviously there was a near-term prophecy and application associated with the passage also. Isaiah is voicing his commitment to faithfully shepherd his children and other sheep that had been entrusted into his care. This also was the resolve of the Lord Jesus Christ who is the Captain of salvation for all the sons of glory; these He promises to lead in singing praises to God (Heb. 2:10-11). None of God's spiritual children will be lost; thus their hope is solely in Him.

In the coming years, Isaiah also knew that the meaning of his name and that of his two sons would be fulfilled: Isaiah – "Jehovah is Salvation," Shear-Jashub – "a remnant will return from captivity," and Maher-Shalal-Hash-Baz – which implied that "the Syrian-Israeli alliance would be broken." God had provided for His people a prophetic portrait of ultimate things.

It is natural for man to want to know the future, but Isaiah rebukes his countrymen for consulting mediums and other pagan practices of divination (v. 19). In contrast to Isaiah's acceptance of God's promises

Sorrow and Comfort

by faith, other Jews were seeking wisdom from satanic sources. M. C. Unger summarizes what will happen to those who will not heed Isaiah's warning: "Those who relied on occult religion would become utterly despondent and blasphemous in the approaching time of distress and hunger."[40] This is a timeless truth with pertinent ramifications for the Church Age. W. E. Vine reminds us that today's infatuation with the occult and spiritism is nothing new:

> Before every great crisis in human affairs there has been an outburst of spiritism. So it was in Judah and Israel just before the captivity. So it was at the time of Christ's incarnation and atoning death. So it is today. God has provided all that is requisite for our guidance and spiritual needs in the Scriptures of truth (2 Tim. 3:16-17).[41]

The prophet warns: Rather than trying to contact the dead for counsel why not trust in the omniscient, immutable, eternal God who has already spoken all that is needed for His people to navigate safely and properly through life (v. 20)? Mediums, wizards, and the like will come under God's judgment because their mutterings oppose God's revealed Word and they lead many astray (v. 21). They and those who follow them will be driven into eternal darkness and will suffer anguish forever (v. 22; 1:31).

Meditation

> The remarkable thing about God is that when you fear God, you fear nothing else, whereas if you do not fear God, you fear everything else.
>
> — Oswald Chambers

> It is one thing to fear God as threatening, with a holy reverence, and another to be afraid of the evil threatened.
>
> — John Owen

The Coming Deliverer
Isaiah 9

The two previous chapters promised the birth of two sons as specific signs to the Jewish nation of God's deliverance from the Syrian-Israeli alliance. In this chapter, a third son, alluded to in chapter 7, is promised, but He will be Israel's Deliverer and Messiah. In Him, God will fulfill all that was promised to Abraham and to David; through Him, Israel will come into their full inheritance and blessing. In a few years the chastening of the Northern Kingdom would end, but Messiah's blessings to Israel would be forever.

Two Comings

Verse 1 identifies the region from which the promised Deliverer would come, the tribal lands of Zebulun and Naphtali. These regions were near the international highway known to invading nations as *"the way of the sea."* Christ's hometown of Nazareth was in Zebulun's territory, and Naphtali composed much of Galilee where the Lord spent most of His earthly sojourn, hence a great light was afforded to those residing in Zebulun and Naphtali (v. 2; Matt. 2:2). Since Matthew quotes verses 1-2 and directly applies them to the ministry of the Lord Jesus in Galilee, we can be assured that this is Isaiah's meaning (Matt. 4:13-17).

God the Father, by sending His own Son into the world, would provide sufficient light to deliver His people depicted in the last chapter as groping about in the darkness of sin, ignorance, and confusion (v. 2). Just as people rejoice over a bountiful harvest or the spoils of war, God's people will be elated by their deliverance by Messiah (v. 3). He will break the yoke of bondage and will bring to an end the years of oppression that the Jewish nation has suffered.

Isaiah provides two examples of God's past faithfulness to reemphasize this point (v. 4). First, the Lord crushed Egypt to deliver His people out of bondage and to deliver them from that land. Second, God's appointed deliverer, Gideon, led three hundred men victoriously

Sorrow and Comfort

against a massive Midianite army (Judg. 6-8). Likewise, there will be no lasting opposition against Israel under Messiah's rule; in fact, all implements of war will be burned (v. 5). As is often presented in this book, we see the two advents of the Lord Jesus: first to bring light to Galilee (vv. 1-2) and then later to bring joy and deliverance to the Jewish nation (vv. 3-5).

A Child Is Born – A Son Is Given

Isaiah continues his delightful prophetic message – God's Messiah is coming to Israel:

> *For unto us a Child is born, unto us a Son is given; and the government will be upon His shoulder. And His name will be called Wonderful, Counselor, Mighty God, Everlasting Father, Prince of Peace. Of the increase of His government and peace there will be no end, upon the throne of David and over His kingdom, to order it and establish it with judgment and justice from that time forward, even forever. The zeal of the Lord of hosts will perform this* (vv. 6-7).

The *"For unto us"* supplies the basic premise on which the prophecy rests: the Child born and the Son given would be for Israel. The two initial expressions confirm both the humanity and the deity of the coming Savior, says H. A. Ironside:

> The "child…born" refers to His humanity. As we have already seen, He was to come into the world as the virgin's Son. As such He was true Man – spirit, soul, and body. The "son…given" refers to the Savior's deity. He was born of Mary, but without a human father. The eternal Son of the Father, Christ came from the glory that He had with the Father throughout all the past eternity. The Son was given in grace for our redemption.[42]

Additionally, the double reference to the first advent of the Lord Jesus is of great importance. The Holy Spirit carefully chose the specific phrases and their order. The Lord was not "a child given," nor "a son born" – He was the unique child born, because He was the unique Son given. John tells us that the spirit of Antichrist is evident when one denies that God's Son *came* from heaven to the earth to be born of a virgin:

> *By this you know the Spirit of God: Every spirit that confesses that*

Jesus Christ has come in the flesh is of God, and every spirit that does not confess that Jesus Christ has come in the flesh is not of God. And this is the spirit of the Antichrist, which you have heard was coming, and is now already in the world (1 Jn. 4:2-3).

The coming Son would be called *Wonderful-Counselor* or literally "Wonder-Counselor." This title speaks of His supernatural character and attributes which are evident while ruling on the throne of David and teaching the nations God's Word. *Wonderful* here is a noun, not an adjective; the noun form is derived from a Hebrew verb *pala* meaning "to separate or to distinguish to mark greatness." The Lord Jesus is truly *Wonderful* because His power, knowledge, and wisdom are beyond human comprehension.

Solomon requested and received wisdom from God to rule His people. The result of this divine provision was that *"Solomon's wisdom excelled the wisdom of all the men of the East and all the wisdom of Egypt. ... He was wiser than all men"* (1 Kgs. 4:30-31). But Solomon was not the wisest man to ever live on the earth. During the Lord's earthly pilgrimage, He acknowledged that Isaiah's foretold Counselor had arrived, for *"indeed a greater than Solomon is here"* (Matt. 12:42).

The Son given is *Mighty God.* This title speaks of Messiah's divine essence. The supreme Ruler of all creation is able to work incredible feats of righteousness and goodness. The Lord Jesus quoted Psalm 82:6 to combat the Pharisees' charge that He had blasphemed because He claimed to be *"the Son of God"* (John 10:34). The Lord reasoned that, if God called those who were His representatives *"the sons of God,"* how could they accuse Him of blasphemy? While it is true that the Lord Jesus was representing God's authority on the earth at that time, He is the only One to be worshipped as "the Son of God" for all time (John 1:34, 9:35-38; Heb. 1:6-8).

Although the Son given to Israel would be born of a virgin, He would also be considered *the Everlasting Father,* or perhaps better rendered *"the Father of eternity."* While the Father and Son enjoy perfect oneness, each is a distinct person. The only human who could truly say, *"I and My Father are one"* is the Lord Jesus (John 10:30). When anyone looked at Him, he or she saw the glory of the Father (John 14:7-11). This oneness causes many commentators to view the "Father of Eternity" title as an expression of the Son's unique connection with God the Father and that the Son represents Him in all things. While this is true, it is the author's opinion that Isaiah is not

Sorrow and Comfort

referring to God the Father directly, as that would cause a contextual difficulty with the other titles in the same verse, but rather he is speaking of the Messiah Himself. This is in keeping with the usual custom in Hebrew and in Arabic, where he who possesses a thing is called "the father" of it.[43]

Since all the promises of God throughout all ages have their fulfillment in Christ, He is "the Father of Eternity" or "the Originator of All Ages to Come." Without Christ, the eternal Son of God, there would be absolutely nothing to look forward to. Death would be merely the doorway leading to eternal doom.

The eternal sonship of Christ does not hinge on the phrase, "the Father of Eternity" in Isaiah 9:6; there are many other Scriptures which affirm that fact. For example, John 16:28 teaches that Christ came forth from the Father, while John 17:5 and 24 indicate that there was a Father/Son relationship in the Godhead even before the creation of the world. Hebrews 1:2 also states that the Son created all things. God gave His Son (John 3:16), implying that Christ was God's Son before He was given – He did not give one that would become His Son, but One who was already His Son. Isaiah 48:16-17, Psalm 40:6-8, and Hebrews 10:6-9 also confirm this same understanding. Many other passages speak of the Father "sending" His Son; these all imply that Christ existed as God's Son prior to His mission (John 20:21; Gal. 4:4; 1 Jn. 4:10, 14). Proverbs 30:4 and Psalm 2:7-12 indicate that the Father had a Son prior to the Lord's incarnation. In Proverbs 30:4, Solomon implies that the Son has the same characteristics as God has; God who is the Creator has a Son of the same nature. Clearly, the Son existed eternally in the bosom of the Father (1 John 1:18) and He alone enjoyed the fellowship of that relationship prior to His incarnation.

He is also *the Prince of Peace*. The Lord will ensure peace and justice are maintained throughout the earth forever, for *the government will be upon His shoulder*. To rule the world requires but one of Christ's shoulders (a symbol of strength in Scripture), but to properly secure His sheep the Lord carries them on both His shoulders (Luke 15:1). These are those who were once lost, but through repentance were found and brought to safety by Christ. The Good Shepherd knows how to protect and keep His sheep for all eternity.

Some Orthodox Jews and modern Rationalists have tried to dismantle the prophecy by manipulating the Hebrew text and ascribing its full ramifications and fulfillment to Hezekiah. However, Hezekiah clearly did not bring peace without end to Israel nor did he sit on the throne of David forever. Other Hebrew interpreters view the passage as messianic in nature but yet unfulfilled (i.e., the *Talmud* and *Midrash* do acknowledge that these names refer to the future Messiah). Old Testament prophets spoke of, but did not understand that there would be a lengthy gap between the Lord's first and second advents to fulfill all God's promises. Before the Savior could ascend the steps of His throne, He first had to be nailed to a cross and to shed His blood to redeem those who then could rest under His care.

Anger Not Quenched

Verse 8 transitions from the glorious promise of the Jewish Messiah and what He will accomplish for Israel in the future to the sorry state of the nation in Isaiah's day. Perhaps the prophet arranged his book this way to contrast the righteous and just leadership of the Messiah with the degenerate leadership in Israel at that time. The measure of a shepherd is evident in the disposition of the sheep that are in his care towards God. The Messiah has the highest zeal for God; hence those in His care will wholeheartedly seek the interests of the Lord. This was not so in Isaiah's day. Israel's shepherds were worldly and scorned the things of God, including His Word. God was about to get their attention.

This section (9:8 10:4) is addressed to Jacob and recommences forecasting God's judgment on the Northern Kingdom of Israel (v. 8). This dirge actually began in chapter 5, but was interrupted by Isaiah's commissioning and by the divine signs of coming deliverance. This warning is organized into four stanzas, each ending with the refrain: *"For all this His anger is not turned away, but His hand is stretched out still"* (vv. 12, 17, 21, 10:4). Although the coming Assyrian judgment was mainly against Ephraim, the Northern Kingdom, Judah would learn from the Assyrian scourge that God must recompense rebellion harshly.

In the near-term, God would summon the Syrians from the east and the Philistines from the west to oppress Israel (vv. 11-13). This was not a full judgment for Israel's sin, nor would the Northern Kingdom turn from sin. Rather, Israel would brag that their setbacks were temporary and they would reestablish themselves by rebuilding what was destroyed or taken away (vv. 9-10). Isaiah's words are staggering: *"For all this His anger is not turned away, but His hand is stretched out*

Sorrow and Comfort

still" (v. 12). God loves His people too much to give up on them. Israel's stubborn pride called for more drastic measures – a crushing blow by Assyria (v. 14).

The writer of Hebrews tells us that God's chastening of His children is proof of His love for them (Heb. 12:6). God loves us too much to leave us the way we are. Though the Jews had repeatedly failed God, He had not deserted them. Paul reminds Timothy of this wonderful truth: *"If we are faithless, He remains faithful; He cannot deny Himself"* (2 Tim. 2:13). We have the Lord's promise to bring us safely through to the conclusion of our salvation – glorification with Christ:

> *Being confident of this very thing, that He who has begun a good work in you will complete it until the day of Jesus Christ* (Phil. 1:6).

> *For our citizenship is in heaven, from which we also eagerly wait for the Savior, the Lord Jesus Christ, who will transform our lowly body that it may be conformed to His glorious body, according to the working by which He is able even to subdue all things to Himself* (Phil. 3:20-21).

The Lord is faithful and has been shown faithful to His Word throughout Scripture and throughout history. Dear believer, the Lord will get you home with Christ-likeness one way or another, but the route you take to get there is largely up to you.

Israel's stiffed-necked disposition would require *"the Lord to cut off the head and tail from Israel"* (v. 14). This is a *merism*, a figure of speech which identifies the extreme ends in order to include everything in between. For example, Jeremiah used a merism of "north and south" to address all the Jews in between either end (Jer. 2:10). Today, we might say, "We looked high and low," to indicate that we searched everywhere for something. The meaning of Isaiah's merism is explained in verses 15-16. The humanly admired elder represented the *head* and the lying prophets represented the *tail*, meaning Israel's leadership was debased across the spectrum. This implied that everyone they guided (the young men, the fatherless, the widows, etc.) were corrupt too – therefore all would be judged by God.

When man rejects God's rule, the worst in man becomes apparent (Rom. 1:19-23). So, not only would God and foreign nations inflict hardship on Israel, the Jewish people would also turn on each other (v.

18). The prophet said that *"the people shall be the fuel for the fire"* (v. 19). In the way that an inferno can devour an entire forest, Israel would be consumed by its own wicked deeds. Those in the Northern Kingdom would oppress and take advantage of each other, and this tribal strife would further weaken their ability to withstand a foreign invasion (v. 20).

When there is no fear of God, it is only a matter of time before our self-focused and selfish fallen nature completely ruins us. Appropriately, Isaiah ends his message by repeating the refrain for the third time: *"For all this His anger is not turned away, but His hand is stretched out still"* (v. 21). Even to this day, God's hand is "stretched out still" against spiritually blind Israel, but the time is nearing when the Good Shepherd shall appear and gather His sheep upon His shoulders forever.

Meditation

One great power of sin is that it blinds men so that they do not recognize its true character.

— Andrew Murray

I am convinced that the first step towards attaining a higher standard of holiness is to realize more fully the amazing sinfulness of sin.

— R. C. Ryle

A Contrast of Kingdoms
Isaiah 10

Before contrasting the fall of the Assyrian Empire (chp. 10) with the greatness of the Kingdom Age (chp. 11), Isaiah pauses to utter a woe against Israel's corrupt leaders and those who follow them. In the last chapter, these civil and religious leaders were found responsible for the pitiful spiritual condition of the Jewish people.

Isaiah identifies six behaviors for which these leaders were guilty (vv. 1-4): First, they approved unjust laws. Second, they issued oppressive decrees. Third, they robbed the needy of justice. Fourth, they were stripping the people of their civil rights. Fifth, they were taking advantage of widows. Sixth, they were stealing from orphans. Jewish rulers were to represent God's character in executing their offices. They should have known better than to take advantage of those who counted on them to uphold their rights and to render justice.

For violating God's Law which protected the poor, widows, and orphans, the nation would experience *"desolation which shall come from afar"* (v. 3). When the Assyrians did come, there would be no one to save those who had led the people astray; *"they will fall down among the slain"* (v. 4). Just as they did not assist the poor and destitute, no one would rescue them. Even after Assyria's invasion of Israel, God's anger would not be fully vindicated for her wickedness; His hand would remain outstretched over the land until her full chastening was complete.

God's use of a more wicked nation (Assyria) than Israel to punish His people reminds us that God often uses man's wrathful behavior to accomplish His purposes. The psalmist puts the matter this way, *"Surely the wrath of man shall praise You"* (Ps. 76:10). In God's timing, Assyria would be severely punished, but not until God was finished using that pagan nation to accomplish His purposes.

Assyria to Be Judged

Having declared the woe, Isaiah launches into a lengthy comparison of the Assyrian Kingdom with the Millennial Kingdom of Christ (10:5-12:6). Although God would use the Assyrians as a rod to chasten His people (vv. 5-6), He was infuriated by Assyria's haughty demeanor towards Israel (vv. 7-11). In God's holy indignation against His sinful people, Assyria would be permitted to plunder Israel's cities and mercilessly trample down the Jews in the streets (v. 6). But Assyria was wrong to assume that Israel was just like other nations it would conquer, for that would mean Israel's God was like the defeated gods of other nations (v. 7).

Assyria was high on herself and her past achievements. Because the gods protecting the cities of Calno, Carchemish, Hamath, Arpad, Damascus and Samaria had failed to stop the Assyrian expansion, Assyria believed that Jerusalem would be an easy target because Israel's God was inferior to the gods of the other cities already taken (vv. 8-11). But verse 12 tells us that when God's purposes for Israel had been accomplished through Assyria, then He would teach Sennacherib just how different Jehovah was than the false gods he had conquered: *"When the Lord has performed all His work on Mount Zion and on Jerusalem, that He will say, 'I will punish the fruit of the arrogant heart of the king of Assyria'"* (v. 12). The proud Assyrian king would learn the hard way that Jerusalem was off limits, because Jehovah had decreed it so.

God loathed the Assyrian king's haughty looks of self-achievement; he had thought that all had prospered by his own power and wisdom (vv. 13-14). Sennacherib used the pronoun "I" six times and "my" three times in a two verse tirade. Caught in his own ego, he ruthlessly oppressed nations. He likened his escapades to rifling a nest, driving the mother bird away, and gathering up her abandoned eggs. Isaiah rhetorically inquires of the king: *"Shall the ax boast itself against him who chops with it? Or shall the saw exalt itself against him who saws with it"* (v. 15)? The obvious answer is no; the ax and the saw are just tools used in the woodsman's hand. They have no mind of their own, no ability in themselves. The Assyrian king was a tool, a rod of discipline, in Jehovah's hand – nothing more.

Assyria was an evil nation, and when they had fulfilled God's purpose, He promised to destroy them by leanness (i.e., pestilence) and by fire (vv. 16-17). The Assyrian soldiers would be consumed like trees

Sorrow and Comfort

in a windblown forest fire; so many would die by fire that even a small child could count the survivors (vv. 18-19). God was true to His word, for when Sennacherib threatened King Hezekiah and Jerusalem in 701 B.C., God sent the Angel of the Lord who slew 185,000 Assyrian soldiers in one night. There were no survivors (none merely wounded; 2 Kgs. 19:35); however, some low-ranking soldiers and Sennacherib were left alive to tell the story of what had happened (31:8; 2 Chron. 32:21).

We will later learn that after Sennacherib found his army massacred, he returned to Assyria and while worshipping in the temple of Nisroch (his god), two of his sons murdered him (2 Kgs. 19:36-37). How blinding is pride to the reality of things. Insanity and pride often walk together. Even after witnessing the God of the Jews wipe out his entire army in one night, Sennacherib still clung to his pagan god.

Now, the meaning of verse 18 becomes clearer: *"And it will consume the glory of his forest and of his fruitful field, both soul and body; and they will be as when a sick man wastes away."* The soul and body speak of the totality of man (all that he is). The man here represents Assyria, who was once full of vigor and strength, but is now diseased, pining away, and will finally sink into the grave. The highwater mark of the Assyrian Empire had passed!

The Assyrian Kingdom lasted another 92 years after this event, but finally succumbed to the Babylonians in 609 B.C. As Habakkuk, Jeremiah, and Ezekiel tell us, wicked Babylon would be God's new rod of discipline against His wayward people in Judah and against the Assyrians to punish them for their arrogance. These prophets also tell us that when Babylon had served her purpose, she too would be punished for afflicting God's people beyond what was permissible, and also for their vanity.

Isaiah indicates that after the devastation caused by Assyria, some Jews would choose to return to northern Israel from exile (vv. 20-23). This likely did not happen until years later when Cyrus the Persian overthrew the Babylonian Empire in 538 B.C. and issued an emancipation decree permitting all Jews to return to their homeland.

Given the above information, those in Jerusalem should not fear the Assyrian army, for after they had served God's purposes in chastening the Northern Kingdom, they would be removed from the region and, eventually, the entire empire would fall (vv. 24-26). Isaiah again refers to the historical motifs introduced in the previous chapter to reinforce this providential outcome (9:4-5). Just as God had used the Red Sea to vanquish Pharaoh's army, and had enabled Gideon to slaughter the armies of Midian at the rock of Oreb, He would miraculously deliver His people once again.

God was going to pour out a flood of judgment on the Assyrians to remove the burden from the shoulder of His people and the yoke from their neck (v. 27). *Burden* in this verse symbolizes "rendering service," whether willful or not, and the yoke pictures being "under orders" – being controlled by another. Judah therefore should not be afraid of the Assyrians; their time of oppressive control would be brief.

To show that this prediction concerning Assyria was sure, Isaiah even informs his audience of the route the invaders will take through Israel to attack Jerusalem (vv. 28-32). They would come from the north through Aiath or Ai (about twelve to fifteen miles north of Jerusalem) and then through Nob (about two miles north of the city). Isaiah is moved again to remind his audience (the remnant in Judah) that they do not need to fear the Assyrians; God would not permit them to take Jerusalem. Rather He will topple the Assyrian soldiers like a lumberjack clear-cuts a thick forest (vv. 33-34). God is sovereign over His people and He rules the nations also!

R. P. Smith contrasts the temporary aspects of the Assyrian kingdom spoken of in this chapter with the eternal kingdom to come, whose glorious capital shall be Jerusalem, as foretold in the next chapter:

> The prophet at once marks the difference between the two kingdoms. The one has a definite place in the Divine economy; the other is used but for a temporary object. For the moment, therefore, it may triumph; but it has no mission of its own, no settled final purpose in the world, and therefore no special providence hems it around. But Jerusalem, however unworthy, was the actual center of the world's history; and in spite of her feebleness in spite of her comparative insignificance she must outlive the far mightier kingdoms of Nineveh and Babylon, of Persia and Macedon and Antioch; for on her existence depended the accomplishment of God's unchanging counsels.[44]

After serving God's purposes, Assyria would fall, but though Jerusalem would suffer much oppression through the centuries, she will be the capital city of Christ's future kingdom.

Sorrow and Comfort

Meditation

Guidance, like all God's acts of blessing under the covenant of grace, is a sovereign act. Not merely does God will to guide us in the sense of showing us his way, that we may tread it; he wills also to guide us in the more fundamental sense of ensuring that, whatever happens, whatever mistakes we may make, we shall come safely home. Slippings and strayings there will be, no doubt, but the everlasting arms are beneath us; we shall be caught, rescued, restored. This is God's promise; this is how good he is."

— J. I Packer (*Knowing God*)

"Thy Kingdom Come"
Isaiah 11

Through the destruction of Jerusalem and the temple in 70 A.D., God put an end to the Levitical system that the Jews had transformed into their own works-based religion (Gal. 1:13-14). No more would God tolerate ceremonial lip service devoid of spiritual value. Through the New Covenant sealed by Christ's own blood, God would forgive the sins of Israel and Judah, pour out His Spirit upon them, and restore them to Himself.

While during the Church Age some Jews have certainly come to faith in Christ, the nation as a whole will not turn to Him until His second advent at the end of the Tribulation Period. At that moment, *"the time of the Gentiles"* will conclude (Rom. 11:25) and Christ will establish His Kingdom on earth; this is the focus of Isaiah's prophecies in this chapter. With this overview in mind, we will consider God's wonderful plan for Israel's future spiritual renewal and restoration to Jehovah. God's promises to Israel are still valid, for as Paul affirms, *"God has not cast away His people whom He foreknew"* (Rom. 11:2).

The Righteous Branch of David

The dual title of the Messiah in verse 1 is remarkable in that the coming King is both a "stem" ("shoot") and the "Root of Jesse." *"There shall come forth a Rod from the stem of Jesse, and a Branch shall grow out of his roots"* (v. 1). J. A. Motyer explains the striking features of the dual titles relating to Christ in this verse:

> The reference to Jesse indicates that the *shoot* is not just another king in David's line but rather another David. In the books of Kings, successive kings were assessed by comparison with "their father David" (e.g. 2 Kgs. 18:3) but no king is called "David" or "son of Jesse." Among the kings, David alone was "the son of Jesse" (e.g., 1 Sam. 20:27-33; 1 Kgs. 12:16), and the unexpected reference to Jesse here has tremendous force: when Jesse produces a shoot it must be

David. But to call the expected king *the Root of Jesse* is altogether another matter, for this means that Jesse sprang from him; he is the root support and origin of the Messianic family in which he would be born. ... In the same way, here, the Messiah is the root cause of his own family tree pending the day when, within that family, he will shoot forth.[45]

The house of David was in spiritual decline, but suddenly out of this decaying branch a fresh shoot of promise springs out. Hence, the Messiah, the *Rod* or *Branch* of David, will spring up from the *stem of Jesse*, but He will also be the *root cause* of this new life (vv. 1-2).

The prophet Samuel anointed David, a man after God's own heart, as the king of Israel; he was the eighth son of Jesse (1 Sam. 17:12). In David's autumn years the Lord promised him, through the prophet Nathan, that a new and everlasting dynasty would be established and one of David's descendants would sit on his throne forever:

When your days are fulfilled and you rest with your fathers, I will set up your seed after you, who will come from your body, and I will establish his kingdom. He shall build a house for My name, and I will establish the throne of his kingdom forever. I will be his Father, and he shall be My son. If he commits iniquity, I will chasten him with the rod of men and with the blows of the sons of men. But My mercy shall not depart from him, as I took it from Saul, whom I removed from before you. And your house and your kingdom shall be established forever before you. Your throne shall be established forever (2 Sam. 7:12-16).

Besides the prophecy in verse 1 stating that the Messiah must be in the royal line of David, we also know that He could not be a descendant of evil King Jeconiah, on whom Jeremiah pronounced a curse (Jer. 22:30). Jeremiah's prophecy then magnifies the incarnation of the Lord Jesus Christ as Messiah. Joseph, the husband of Mary (the mother of the Lord Jesus), was a descendant of Shealtiel who was the son of Jehoiachin or Jeconiah (Matt. 1:12; 1 Chron. 3:17). Therefore, no son of Joseph could sit upon David's throne. Mary, however, was also a descendant of David through Nathan (Luke 3:24-38). Thus, the son of Mary could fulfill both prophecies if she conceived supernaturally through the power of the Holy Spirit and not by Joseph her husband.

Devotions in Isaiah

Besides this confirmation, Isaiah's prophetic depiction of the coming Messiah's character in verses 3-5 aligns well with what Jeremiah foretells concerning Him:

> *Behold, the days are coming, says the Lord, that I will perform that good thing which I have promised to the house of Israel and to the house of Judah: In those days and at that time I will cause to grow up to David a Branch of righteousness; He shall execute judgment and righteousness in the earth. In those days Judah will be saved, and Jerusalem will dwell safely* (Jer. 33:14-16).

In summary, a David-like Jewish Messiah would originate His own birth as a descendant of David in such a remarkable way that He would avoid the curse of Jeconiah. Therefore, He would not be corrupted by the fallen nature inherited from Adam, but would be the rightful heir to the throne of David forever.

Before leaving verse 1, we note that the Hebrew word for "branch" is *netzer*, which in the Greek is translated "Nazareth." Matthew writes: *"And he came and dwelt in a city called Nazareth, that it might be fulfilled which was spoken by the prophets, 'He shall be called a Nazarene'"* (Matt. 2:23). As the town of Nazareth is not mentioned in the Old Testament, Matthew may be referring to Isaiah's statement.

The Holy Spirit

The Messiah will be a descendant of David who in His first advent will be endowed with the Spirit of the Lord (v. 2). The One ruling over the Apocalypse will have the full plenitude of the Holy Spirit's divine power, which Isaiah describes in seven distinct ways to express His perfection: The Spirit of Jehovah, the Spirit of wisdom, the Spirit of understanding, the Spirit of counsel, the Spirit of might, the Spirit of knowledge, and the Spirit of the fear of Jehovah. John, describing God's throne room in heaven, refers to the Holy Spirit in a similar way: *"Seven lamps of fire were burning before the throne, which are the seven Spirits of God"* (Rev. 4:5). At His second advent, the Son will accomplish the will of the Father in the full wisdom, counsel, power, etc. of the Holy Spirit. On this point, F. B. Hole writes:

> The Lord Jesus is the "Rod [or, Shoot] out of the stem of Jesse," and the "Branch," and the chapter presents Him in the power and glory of His second coming. That the Spirit of the Lord, in sevenfold fullness,

rested upon Him at His first coming is very true, and when we read of our Lord that, "God giveth not the Spirit by measure" (John 3:34), there may be a reference to what is stated here, as also there is in "the seven Spirits," mentioned in Revelation 1:4, 3:1, 4:5, 5:6; and in this last reference they are "sent forth into all the earth," as will be the case when the Shoot of Jesse comes forth endowed with this sevenfold fullness.[46]

The cults teach that the Holy Spirit is neither divine nor a person. The Jehovah's Witnesses believe that the Holy Spirit is an invisible force that produces visible results, while Mormons teach that the Holy Spirit is an influence of God completely distinct from God the Father and His son Jesus (whom they identify as one of the Father's many spiritual children). However, Scripture teaches that the Holy Spirit is much more than a mere influence or force which God uses to accomplish His will, for the Spirit has a will of His own (1 Cor. 12:11). These groups also deny the deity of Christ and, accordingly, the triune nature of God.

The deity of the Holy Spirit is expressed in various ways in Scripture, but one of the most obvious is through His direct association with the other Persons of the Godhead. The Holy Spirit is directly associated with the other members of the Trinity some sixteen times in the New Testament. For example, He is called "the Spirit of God" (1 Cor. 6:11), and "the Spirit of Jesus" (Acts 16:7). Clearly, the Spirit of God has full association with the other members of the Godhead (Matt. 28:19; 2 Cor. 13:14). While forgiven sinners can obtain a position of holiness in Christ through justification, individual believers are never called "Holy" by name. However, "Holy" is a personal name for God, speaking of His uniqueness (Ps. 111:9; Isa. 57:15). There are approximately eighty references to "the Holy Spirit" or "Spirit Holy" in Scripture. God does not attribute His name to others, so it is evident that His Spirit is a person within the Godhead.

The Holy Spirit has divine attributes clearly consistent with each member of the Godhead:

- Omniscience: the Holy Spirit knows the things of God (1 Cor. 2:11-12).
- Omnipresence: we cannot flee from the Spirit's presence (Ps. 139:7).
- Eternal Existence: He is the "Eternal Spirit" (Heb. 9:14).

- Omnipotence: the Holy Spirit was involved in creation (Job 33:4; Ps. 104:30).
- Without error: the Holy Spirit is "the Spirit of Truth" (1 Jn. 5:6).
- Divine Wisdom: no one can counsel God's Spirit (40:13).
- Immutable: The Holy Spirit does not change (11:2).

The Holy Spirit is divine; in essence He has the same attributes and character qualities as the other members of the Godhead. As God, the Holy Spirit is a person who unmistakably disapproves of sin, is deeply grieved by it, and works to save sinners from its deadly influence. As Isaiah alludes to, the Holy Spirit works to convict sinners of their need for a Savior by impressing them with the truth and the fearful consequences of rejecting God's offer. The Lord Jesus said the Holy Spirit would be about the same type of work during the Church Age: *"He will convict the world of sin, and of righteousness, and of judgment"* (John 16:8).

Consequently, when the Messiah appears to judge, the entire world will know that He is full of wisdom, understanding, knowledge, power, and reverence for God (v. 3). He will judge the nations justly and will be a champion of the poor and meek (v. 4). He will govern the earth by the rod of His mouth and with the slightest breath will slay the wicked (v. 5). The Messiah will be characterized by the holy righteousness of God and complete faithfulness to uphold God's name in the earth (v. 6). After telling what the Branch of David would be like, Isaiah begins to describe the era of bliss that inhabitants of the earth will enjoy under His rule.

The Millennial Kingdom

Isaiah has already told us in chapters 2 and 4 how the Millennial Kingdom of Christ will be marked by strange phenomena throughout the earth. Additionally, Isaiah informed us that Jerusalem would be the religious center of the world (2:1-5). Indeed, the faithful from the Gentile nations will gather with the Jewish nation to honor Christ at Jerusalem (vv. 1-11, 60:14, 65:18-25; Rev. 21). Christ will reign from Jerusalem and all the nations will come there to praise, to worship, and to learn of Him. Isaiah also revealed to us that the Jews who live through the Tribulation will gaze upon Christ (the Branch of the Lord) and will appreciate His splendor, glory, fruitfulness, and beauty (4:2-4).

In this chapter, the prophet explains more about the changes that will occur in nature during Christ's kingdom. The wolf and the lamb

Sorrow and Comfort

shall dwell together, as will the kid of the goat with the leopard, and the calf with the lion (vv. 6-7). Toddlers will be able to play by the hole of the asp and at the adder's den without fear of a deadly attack (v. 8). The glory of the Lord will be displayed in the world as abundantly as *"the waters cover the sea"* (v. 9). As a result, not only the Jewish nation, but also the Gentiles will see the Root of Jesse, for His resting place shall be glorious (v. 10). As John tells us, the Lord Jesus in His second advent will be proven to be "the root and offspring of David" (Rev. 22:16). He is not merely a descendant of David who rules, but He is the Root causing it to happen!

Later in the book, the prophet reveals that death during the Millennial Kingdom will be a rare event and mainly the result of willful sin of those not yet in glorified bodies or not controlled by the Holy Spirit. (That would be those Gentiles who survived the Tribulation Period and their descendants.)

> *No more shall an infant from there live but a few days, nor an old man who has not fulfilled his days; for the child shall die one hundred years old, but the sinner being one hundred years old shall be accursed. ... They shall not hurt nor destroy in all My holy mountain* (65:20, 25).

What a wonderful event it will be when the curses that were put on the earth (resulting from man's sin) are lifted in the Kingdom Age (Rom. 8:21-22). A handful of seed casually scattered on a mountaintop will produce a great harvest (Ps. 72:16), longevity will be restored to humanity, weapons will be used as agricultural implements (Mic. 4:3), and a spirit of peace and tranquility will engulf the earth (v. 9). All this and more Christ shall do! Isaiah will later tell us that so great will be the glory of the Lord on the earth that there will be no need for the sun or moon to illuminate it (60:18-20). These circumstances, though wonderful, should not be confused with the *Eternal State* in which there is a new heaven and new earth where no evil will be present (Rev. 21:1). (See further explanation below.)

Establishing His Kingdom

Isaiah then explains how Christ will establish His kingdom (vv. 11-16). First, from all over the world He will gather to the land of Israel the remnant of the Jewish people who survived the Tribulation (vv. 11-12). Ezekiel says that the Lord will not leave one Jew outside of Israel

(Ezek. 39:28). Then Ezekiel states that the Lord will pour out the Holy Spirit upon His people (Ezek. 39:29). The prophet Joel foretold the same truth:

> *Then you shall know that I am in the midst of Israel: I am the Lord your God and there is no other. My people shall never be put to shame. And it shall come to pass afterward that I will pour out My Spirit on all flesh* (Joel 2:27-28).

Not only will all Jews have the Holy Spirit in the Kingdom Age, they also will be one nation again, not two kingdoms (v. 13). Ezekiel also prophesied that Judah (the southern kingdom) and Israel (the northern kingdom) would no longer be two nations when they come into their inheritance in Christ's Kingdom, but that they would be one (Ezek. 36:16-21). The prophet symbolized this truth by taking two sticks and making them one, the result of which he called "Israel" (Ezek. 36:28). This was the name God gave to Jacob, the father of the nation (Gen. 32:28). Jeremiah foretold the same event (Jer. 3:18), but only Ezekiel foretells that this united nation would be called "Israel."

Israel to Plunder the Surrounding Nations

At the commencement of the Millennial Kingdom, when all Jews worldwide return to Israel, there will be nothing blocking their way. God promises to dry up the Gulf of Suez to permit Jews to leave Egypt as well as the Euphrates River and its tributaries to permit His people from the east to return home (v. 15). In one sense, this regathering is reminiscent of God dividing the waters of the Red Sea to escort His people out of Egypt long ago. Now He will open the way for all His people in the world (including Assyria, which was the world power at the time of Isaiah's writing) to return to Him in Israel.

One of the first acts of this newly established nation of Israel will be to despoil the Philistines, the Moabites, the Ammonites and the Edomites; these were nations who had laid claims to Israel's land or had taken advantage of the Jews in Old Testament days (vv. 13-14). Daniel tells us that the Antichrist will not conquer the territories of Edom, Moab, and Ammon during the Tribulation Period because of more pressing challenges to his authority (Dan. 11:40-45). Perhaps this is God's way of preserving the best to reestablish His covenant people, who will lose everything during the Tribulation Period. In any case, divine judgment of these regions is to be executed by Israel under Messiah's rule.

The Millennial Kingdom and the Eternal State

While all this information concerning the Kingdom Age is wonderful, we should not confuse it with the Eternal State in which there is a new heaven and earth. There are several clear distinctions between the Kingdom Age and the Eternal State. For example, the seas and oceans we know today will still be present during the Kingdom Age (v. 9; Ezek. 47:18; Zech. 14:8), but there will not be any sea in the new earth (Rev. 21:1).

Peter identifies the Kingdom Age as the Day of the Lord (2 Pet. 3:10), and the Eternal State as the Day of God (2 Pet. 3:12). At the end of the Day of the Lord (i.e., at the end of Christ's Millennial Kingdom), the heavens and the earth shall pass away with a great noise and their elements shall melt with fervent heat and be burned up (2 Pet. 3:10). Isaiah states that *"all the host of heaven shall be dissolved, and the heavens shall be rolled up like a scroll"* (34:4). He later foretells that, after the Millennial Kingdom, God will create a new heaven and new earth (65:17).

Furthermore, a literal Kingdom Age must precede the Eternal State. The Kingdom Age cannot be some spiritual existence during the Church Age, as amillennialism teaches. Clearly, the Jewish nation is not in the land specified for them and the millennial tribal allotments have not yet been delegated (47:13-23). Likewise, geographic locations on earth today will exist in the Millennial Kingdom (Joel 3:18; Zech. 14:16-21), but obviously not in the new earth. In summary, the new heaven and earth will not be created until after the Kingdom Age is concluded, Satan's last rebellion on earth is quelled (Rev. 20:7-10), and the planet we live upon today is destroyed (Rev. 20:11).

"Thy Kingdom Come"

What a day of blessing it will be when the curses that were put upon the earth as a result of man's sin will be lifted. Seed casually scattered on a mountaintop will produce a great harvest. Weapons will be used as agricultural implements. The glory of God and a spirit of peace and tranquility will permeate the whole world. Christ's kingdom will fulfill Jacob's prophecy recorded in Genesis 49 concerning his son Judah. Jacob foretold that through Judah, kings would rule over Israel, and one day the scepter "would come to the one it belongs to" (the literal meaning of *"until Shiloh come"*), and it would never depart and *"to Him shall be the obedience of the people"* (Gen. 49:10). During the Kingdom Age everyone will seek the Lord. All this and more Christ shall do: *"Even so, come, Lord Jesus"* (Rev. 22:20)!

Meditation

> Crown Him! Crown Him! Crown the Saviour King of kings;
> In your hearts enthrone Him, Lord and Master own Him;
> Crown Him! Crown Him! While heaven exultant rings;
> Crown the blessed Saviour King of kings.
>
> Soon He is coming back again, a thousand years on earth to reign;
> We'll see Him by and by, we'll see Him by and by;
> All the redeemed with Him He'll bring,
> Who in their hearts have crowned Him King,
> And they shall live and reign with Him on high.
>
> — Leila N. Morris

The Remnant Rejoices
Isaiah 12

In the previous chapter, Isaiah revealed that at the commencement of the Millennial Kingdom the Lord would bring the Jews from all over the world back to their homeland. This chapter records their rejoicing once they are reestablished in Israel and under Messiah's rule. Their song has two stanzas, both beginning with *"In that day you will say"* (vv. 1, 4).

Isaiah has already explained that the phrase *"that day"* relates to their final deliverance from Gentile oppression and when God fulfills all His promises to them (i.e., this phrase links back to 11:10-11). Isaiah mentioned the exodus from Egypt at the conclusion of chapter 11 to better introduce Israel's future rejoicing after being delivered from the Antichrist and in their homeland again. Paradoxically, after experiencing God's great deliverance through the Red Sea, as recorded in Exodus 14, the Israelites commenced singing praises to God in the next chapter; this pattern will occur again in "that day."

Exodus 15 records both the first occurrence of singing in the Bible, as well as the lyrics of Scripture's first song. The Israelites had escaped death twice in recent days and euphoria swept through their ranks as they marched further into the wilderness under the shadow of Jehovah's cloud. Remarkably, the last mention of singing in the Bible is associated with this same song of redemption that the Israelites sang after God vanquished Pharaoh's army in the Red Sea.

In the book of Revelation, John describes the redeemed singing *the song of Moses, the servant of God, and the song of the Lamb* and again the words of the song are recorded (Rev. 15:2-4). This song will not be sung by those just escaping death to begin a journey with Jehovah through the wilderness, but rather by those who will have suffered death at the end of their journey to escape the Antichrist on earth. These saints will choose to die rather than to bow to the Antichrist and to take his identifying mark. The heavenly inheritance that the Israelites long ago sang about will now be theirs as well to enjoy forever.

Devotions in Isaiah

Throughout the Bible we read of only the redeemed singing to God. Apparently, singing praises to God is reserved for those individuals who have experienced God's salvation, that is, those who have been redeemed by the blood of His dear Son.

With this understanding we have a better appreciation of the song Isaiah prophetically voices to reflect Israel's enthusiasm for God. This song of "the Day" is in two parts: Israel's praise for what God has done in delivering them from death and sin's captive grip (vv. 2-3), and a call to each other to praise God in His dwelling place on earth – at Jerusalem (vv. 4-6):

Behold, God is my salvation, I will trust and not be afraid; "for YAH, the Lord, is my strength and song; He also has become my salvation." Therefore with joy you will draw water from the wells of salvation (vv. 2-3).

Praise the Lord, call upon His name; declare His deeds among the peoples, make mention that His name is exalted. Sing to the Lord, for He has done excellent things; this is known in all the earth. Cry out and shout, O inhabitant of Zion, for great is the Holy One of Israel in your midst (vv. 4-6)!

Throughout the Bible, the redeemed of God break into spontaneous exclamations and songs of praise to express their excitement at God's abiding presence which has been achieved through redemption. It is obvious that the redeemed ache to be with the Lord. Dear believer, do you long to be with your Redeemer? Thousands of years ago the Israelites sang and danced before the Lord and a billion years from now the redeemed of the Lord *"will have no less days to sing God's praise than when we'd first begun."* A mark of God's redeemed is their joyous singing.

While the unregenerate may experience a degree of happiness in life, God is, in fact, the only source of true joy. Those who have not turned to Him seek fulfillment at broken cisterns, but those who come to the wells of salvation find true joy (v. 3; Jer. 2:13). Indeed, the saved may well rejoice when thinking of what Christ accomplished at Calvary, as various songwriters have attested. An anonymous psalmist, yet on the preceding side of Calvary, called God *"my exceeding joy"* (Ps. 43:4), while David penned these words: *"You will show me the path of life; in Your presence is fullness of joy; at Your right hand are*

Sorrow and Comfort

pleasures forevermore" (Ps. 16:11). Fullness of joy is in God's presence. But is He not present with us now? Are you experiencing His fullness of joy?

Meditation

>Redeemed, how I love to proclaim it! Redeemed by the blood of the Lamb;
>Redeemed through His infinite mercy, His child and forever I am.
>I think of my blessed Redeemer, I think of Him all the day long;
>I sing, for I cannot be silent; His love is the theme of my song.
>
>— Fanny J. Crosby

Judgment Against Babylon
Isaiah 13:1-14:27

The Lord directs Isaiah to prophesy against the surrounding pagan nations who afflicted the Jews and contributed to their moral downfall (chps. 13-23). Correspondingly, Jeremiah and Ezekiel also warn the adjacent people groups to Israel of forthcoming judgment (Jer. 46-51; Ezek. 25-32). Although this chapter begins a major thematic shift in Isaiah's book, he still weaves suggestions of kingdom glory into the text to give Israel a continuing hope of future deliverance.

The framework of this next section involves ten oracles of judgment revealed in two series. In the first series, five judgments are levied against an identified people and God's punitive response relates to their history (13:1, 14:28, 15:1, 17:1, 19:1). In the second series, four of five recipients of judgments have enigmatic titles (21:1, 11, 13, 22:1) and one a plain title (23:1). Those being addressed by enigmatic titles can be identified by the context of the passage. As we will soon see, some received a double portion of judgments (i.e., they are listed in both series). J. A. Motyer notes the series order for this section of judgments against particular peoples and nations:

Series 1	Series 2
Babylon (13:1-14:27)	The Desert by the Sea (Babylon; 21:1-10)
Philistia (14:28-32)	Silence (Edom; 21:11-12)
Moab (15:1-16:14)	Evening (Arabia; 21:13-17)
Damascus (17:1-18:7)	The Valley of Vision (Jerusalem; 22:1-25)
Egypt (19:1-20:6)	Tyre (23:1-18)[47]

Notice that both series begin with judgments against Babylon, the first series detailing the fall of her political power, and the second the demise of her pagan religious system (which has caused God's people so much harm through the centuries; Rev. 17:2-6).

We understand from Isaiah's opening remarks that pronouncing waves of divine retribution on various people groups was burdensome

Sorrow and Comfort

for him (v. 1). This attitude marks a true servant of the Lord who is in tune with God's own heart. Speaking for the Lord, Ezekiel said that God has no pleasure in the death of the wicked (Ezek. 18:23). Because God is holy, He must judge those guilty of wickedness, that is, those who do not repent of their rebellion and take advantage of His mercy. However, God does not (nor should His people) enjoy seeing anyone suffer His wrath, knowing His mercy could have tempered the outcome.

Every person, saint or unregenerate, will stand before God and be evaluated. The believer will stand at the Judgment Seat of Christ, immediately after Christ's return for His Church (2 Cor. 5:10). Paul says, *"So then each of us shall give account of himself to God"* (Rom. 14:12). It is important to the Lord that His people in every dispensation understand that He derives no enjoyment in punishing the wayward, but rather yearns for all to repent and receive His blessing through exercising faith in His revealed will. For those in the Church Age that means trusting Christ as Savior and submitting to His lordship while waiting for His return. With the Church removed from the earth, God will pour out His vengeance on the living wicked and then for eternity in Hell after the Great White Throne Judgment (Rev. 20). This is called *"the Day of the Lord"* (v. 6; Jer. 46:10; Ezek. 30:3).

Isaiah begins this section by pronouncing judgment on Babylon, the future rod of chastening that God will use to punish both His people and other societies. Jeremiah ends his section of Gentile judgments with sentencing Babylon. This pictures the culmination of divine judgment upon the nations during the Tribulation Period when all that is related to Babylon, the originator of rebellion against God on earth (Gen. 10), will be once and for all destroyed (Rev. 18). Thus, the prophetic declarations of both Isaiah and Jeremiah swirl with both near-term and far-reaching statements.

God Mobilizes His Army

Jeremiah gives us two reasons that God promised to punish Babylon. First, God avowed, *"I will bring judgment on the carved images of Babylon"* (Jer. 51:47). God hates paganism; it robs Him of His rightful honor as Almighty God, Lord Supreme, and Creator of All. Second, He promised, *"I will repay Babylon and all the inhabitants of Chaldea for all the evil they have done in Zion in your sight"* (Jer. 51:24). The Jews are the apple of God's eye, His covenant people.

Zechariah proclaimed that any nation which persecutes the Jews will ultimately be judged by God: *"For thus says the Lord of hosts, 'He sent Me after glory, to the nations which plunder you; for he who touches you touches the apple of His eye'"* (Zech. 2:8). Babylon would be no exception.

Bringing the Jews back to Israel from Babylon would mean that another world empire would have to conquer the Babylonians. Prophets Isaiah and Daniel explain that indeed this was God's plan and He would use the Medes and the Persians to accomplish this feat (v. 17; Dan. 7:5, 8:3, 20).

Two Babylons Judged

Isaiah colorfully describes God amassing a vast number of soldiers from faraway places to strike Babylon which would then permit His mercy to be shown to Israel (vv. 2-5). Once assembled, *the Day of the Lord* will begin and God will judge Babylon with fierce anger and without mercy (vv. 6-9). Although Isaiah is metaphorically describing the calamities that Babylon is doomed to suffer by the armies of the Medes and the Persians, there is much in his prophecy that goes beyond the sixth century B.C. For instance, Isaiah says that in the Day of the Lord, God will judge sinners worldwide with such ferocity that the sun, moon, and stars will be darkened (would not be visible from the earth; vv. 10-11) and *"the earth will be moved out of her place"* (v. 13). Indeed, this is figurative language for the sixth century, but not for the Tribulation scene that John describes in the Apocalypse.

Babylon of the sixth century was a melting pot of various cultures and peoples. When the Persians did invade Babylon, panic and chaos would result: *"every man will turn to his own people, and everyone will flee to his own land"* (v. 14). Those not able to escape to their homelands would be pillaged and slaughtered, children dashed to pieces and women ravished (vv. 15-16).

Jeremiah's prophecies against Babylon also contain both a near-term and far-reaching conclusion (Jer. 50-51). He states that Babylon would be attacked and conquered by an army from the north and that the city would be laid waste (i.e. destroyed by fire – Jer. 50:32). Both Jeremiah and Isaiah state that after Babylon's destruction the city would be uninhabitable forever (vv. 17-22; Jer. 50:39). This does not describe how the Medes and Persians actually conquered Babylon – by diverting the Euphrates River and taking the drunken city without much

Sorrow and Comfort

opposition (Dan. 5). Additionally, history shows that Babylon was used as a Persian outpost for two centuries before being dismantled by one of Alexander the Great's successors, Seleucus, to obtain building resources for another city 30 miles away.[48]

We conclude that the events related to Babylon's capture in 539 B.C. and its eventual disassembling over two centuries later do not conform to the specific prophecies of Isaiah and Jeremiah. To date, for example, Babylon has never been destroyed by fire. Since the Lord says that it must be destroyed by fire, the rebuilding of a city known as "Babylon" is guaranteed (Rev. 18:10).

Another prophecy regarding Babylon in Jeremiah 51:26 further substantiates this point: *"They shall not take from you a stone for a corner nor a stone for a foundation, but you shall be desolate forever."* Reliable evidence shows that at least six cities contain building materials which originally belonged to ancient Babylon. Hillah, which is near ancient Babylon, was built almost entirely from its ruins about two hundred years after its fall to Cyrus.[49] According to the Bible, when Babylon is destroyed by fire, it will never be inhabited again, nor will debris from its ruins be profitable for reuse. Since this type of destruction has not yet occurred, the fulfillment of this prophecy is yet to come.

So, when will Isaiah and Jeremiah's prophecies concerning Babylon's final destruction be fulfilled? John addresses this question in the book of Revelation. He informs us that Babylon will be: destroyed suddenly (Rev. 18:8, 10, 17, 19), destroyed by fire (Rev. 18:8-9, 18), completely destroyed (Rev. 18:21), and will remain uninhabited forever (Rev. 18:22). Indeed, John reconfirms much of what Jeremiah and Isaiah predicted seven to eight hundred years earlier concerning Babylon's final destruction. Not only will the literal capital city of wickedness be destroyed by Christ, but all of its religious and economic influence throughout the world will be vanquished forever.

> The mighty God, that rules the skies,
> Shall Babel's rage restrain;
> In vain she forms her cruel schemes,
> And boasts her power in vain.
>
> That bitter cup which she has mixed,
> Once more herself shall drink;
> As falls the millstone in the deep,

Proud Babylon shall sink.

Rejoice, ye saints, the vengeance long
Is laid for her in store;
And Babylon, that scarlet whore,
Shall sink to rise no more.

— C. H. Needham

The Lord Jesus Christ will destroy wicked Babylon (the city and its evil influence) at His second coming. The anti-God spirit that started in Nimrod's time will culminate in the Tribulation Period with the political and religious system of the Antichrist. As previously mentioned, this rebel movement has been responsible for the deaths of millions of God's people: *"In her* [Babylon] *was found the blood of prophets and saints, and of all who were slain on the earth"* (Rev. 18:24). God will judge all those who have oppressed and persecuted His people down through the ages. In Jeremiah's day, the fall of Babylon signaled that the time of Jewish chastening had ended, that it was time for the Jews to return to Israel, and that they would enjoy God's protection and blessing there. The future and final fall of Babylon will indicate the same realities, only ever so much more so.

Meditation

Reflecting on the certainty of God's Word and the ultimate fall of Babylon (the anti-God system that opposes Christ and His followers in every way), William Kelly provides this lovely devotional thought:

> God thinks of Christ, who is more precious to Himself than all besides. It is in virtue of Christ that there can be a holy purpose of good brought to issue in such a world as this has been. For it is not possible that the creature itself could have any intrinsic value in the sight of God. That which merely flows out of the sovereign will and almighty hand of God can cease to be. He that made can destroy; but when you come to Christ, you have that which, we may reverently say, nothing can annul; yea all the efforts of man or Satan to oppose and dishonor Him have been only turned, in the mighty and gracious wisdom of God, into a display of all-surpassing glory.

Sorrow and Comfort

Hence we arrive at the great truth for our everyday walk, no less than for eternity and God Himself. We have to do with One now, whose love nothing can exhaust, whose ways too are all perfect; we have to do with Him day by day, to wait on Him, to expect from Him, to trust Him, and to be sure of His admirable care for us. Christ is worthy that our hearts should confide in Him, and He cannot be confided in without the blessing that ever flows out. Thus God proves Himself greater than all that can be against us. Apart from Christ there is nothing even that He Himself made but what, connected with man on earth, soon had a cloud over it. Nay, it is wider still: look where you may, above or below; look at any creature height or beauty apart from Christ, and what is the security?[50]

Judging Pride
Isaiah 14

In this chapter, Isaiah speaks of Israel's future rejoicing over the fall of Babylon and its haughty ruler, the historical fall of proud Lucifer from God's holy mount, and the forthcoming judgments on overconfident Assyria and Philistia.

Israel to Rejoice Over Babylon's Fall (vv. 1-11)

Isaiah begins by confirming God's compassion towards His people. The prophet is writing as if the events nearly two hundred years into the future have already happened. Previously, Isaiah foretold that God would not have compassion on Judah when He raised His disciplinary rod (i.e., the Babylonians in the sixth century; 9:17). However, the fall of Babylon signaled a new era for the Jewish nation; God would bring them home from exile and shower them with His tender mercies. Some believe that the tyrant spoken of was Sennacherib, the king of Assyria who also ruled over Babylon. While this is possible, the outcome of Sennacherib's fall did not resettle Israel in their homeland or initiate God's blessings on the nation (v. 1). These blessings did accompany the Jewish people after the fall of Babylon in the sixth century. The entire sixth-century scene is a prophetic blueprint of the final demise of Babylon and her tyrant at Christ's second advent.

The prophet Jeremiah suffered with his countrymen during Judah's chastening under Babylon, but he also experienced God's abundant grace during that long trial. As a result, he was able both to sympathize with his people and to inspire them to seek the same solace he had found during arduous circumstances – trusting in Jehovah alone.

Difficult trials often cause God's people to sink into spiritual despondency. Even Jeremiah, during a moment of despair, said, *"my strength and my hope have perished from the Lord"* (Lam. 3:18). But after calling on God to remember his past afflictions, Jeremiah also recalled God's past faithfulness enabling him to persevere through adversity (Lam. 3:19-20). Jeremiah had learned through experience that

Sorrow and Comfort

God's children should never feel hopeless, for they are always established in God's eternal love and His promises:

> *Through the Lord's mercies we are not consumed, because His compassions fail not. They are new every morning; great is Your faithfulness. "The Lord is my portion," says my soul, "therefore I hope in Him!" The Lord is good to those who wait for Him, to the soul who seeks Him. It is good that one should hope and wait quietly for the salvation of the Lord* (Lam. 3:22-26).

Yes, God had punished Judah for her idolatry and unfaithfulness, but He could not reject or discard His covenant people. He could not undermine His unconditional promises to them despite their poor behavior. This meant that the fall of Babylon was proof of God's abiding love to the Jews in Daniel's day and will be proof again when Babylon is finally destroyed forever. Then the Jewish nation will be fully restored to Jehovah and established in their land inheritance. This seems to be the fuller meaning of verses 1-2, which is addressed to Jacob (i.e., the entire nation of Israel), and not just to Judah. In the Millennial Kingdom, the Jews will *"rule over their oppressors"* – that has not happened yet (v. 2).

Verses 3-21 record the song of those Jews freed from the brutal tyranny of Babylon's ruler. The initial verses show the visible tyrant defeated when God brought down Babylon, but the latter verses refer to Lucifer, whose power and authority incited Babylon's rebellion against God and His people. Isaiah informs us that Lucifer was brought down long ago because of pride and rebellion against God.

God would put to an end the Babylonian king's fury, *"who struck the people in wrath"* and *"ruled the nations in anger"* (v. 6). His death will usher in a time of peace and rest, a joyful reality that people will sing about for generations (vv. 3-8). Isaiah foretells that Babylon's ruler will then join the spirits of other deceased leaders and kings in the grave (v. 9). In poetic satire, Isaiah says that in Sheol, these rulers would express their surprise that the great king had become weak and had joined the ranks of the dead (v. 10). While maggots and worms devour the corpse in the grave, the souls of the dead are constrained in *Sheol* (v. 11).

The Hebrew word translated "hell" in verse 9 is *sheol*, which is rendered "pit," "grave," or "hell" throughout the Old Testament (2 Sam. 22:6; Ps. 9:17, 18:5). It is the equivalent of the Greek word *hades*, used in the New Testament. In Luke 16, we learn that this spiritual domain secures disembodied spirits in one of two compartments: Abraham's Bosom where faithful souls await resurrection unto life through Christ, and a place of torment where the wicked continue to wait for their resurrection to stand before the Lord at the Great White Throne. Their eternal punishment in the Lake of Fire will follow.

Hades is a domain of sorrow; it is the place the wicked go after death. Luke 16, which is not a parable, highlights the fact that souls are completely conscious of their situation (i.e. these souls are not sleeping), and are in torment. Hence, the rich man suffering torment pleaded that Lazarus be permitted to return from the dead and warn his five brothers about the horror of Hades. During the Church Age the spirits of the redeemed will be with the Lord after death (Phil. 1:21-23; 2 Cor. 5:8). They do not go to where Abraham was, an abode called *Abraham's bosom*. This is where (i.e., a compartment associated with, but distinct from hades) faithful souls once joyfully waited for Calvary's completed work (Luke 16:22-23). In contrast, the souls of unbelievers continue to descend into Hades (the compartment of torment) where they wait to be reunited with a resurrected body, which at the Great White Throne Judgment will be condemned to the Lake of Fire (Luke 16:19-31; Rev. 20:11-15).

There is no opportunity for these souls to escape their eternal destination. The writer of Hebrews sums up the matter this way: *"It is appointed for men to die once, but after this the judgment"* (Heb. 9:27). Death seals one's eternal fate; there are no second opportunities to be saved from God's wrath. In Isaiah's prophecy, the tyrant of Babylon took his place down in Sheol alongside other doomed rebels. At this present moment, Babylon's ruler has endured the torment of Hades for 2,500 plus years. He continues to await final judgment with all other wicked, disembodied souls since the time that man became subject to death in Eden (Rev. 20).

Lucifer's Fall (vv. 12-17)

Isaiah prophetically peers beyond Babylon's visible leader to the one who will prompt his brutality – Lucifer. Ezekiel refers to Lucifier as the anointed cherub that was created in perfection, sheathed with precious stones, and was in the Garden of Eden (Ezek. 28:13). Apparently, Lucifer was created with a provision of timbrels and flutes to offer music before God, and perhaps even to lead the angels in

Sorrow and Comfort

worship. In the celestial realms, worship (accompanied by music) was being offered by spiritual beings to their Creator, even before man was created (Job. 38:7).

As the anointed covering cherub, Lucifer may have had a view of God's majesty and glory that no other created being was afforded – He was with God on His holy mountain and enjoyed a state of perfection (Ezek. 28:14-15). Charles Ryrie writes that this is "evidently a reference to Satan, because of Christ's similar description (Luke 10:18) and because of the inappropriateness of the expression of Isaiah 14:13-14 on the lips of any but Satan (1 Tim. 3:6)."[51] Satan then became obsessed with his own beauty and wanted to be worshipped as God. In mutiny, the "light bearer" (Lucifer) became the ruler of darkness, and immersed the world in deceit, corruption, and violence (vv. 16-17). In depicting Satan's pride, Isaiah first recalls Lucifer's five "I will" statements and then details the consequences of his rebellion against God:

> *How you are fallen from heaven, O Lucifer, son of the morning! How you are cut down to the ground, you who weakened the nations! For you have said in your heart: "I will ascend into heaven, I will exalt my throne above the stars of God; I will also sit on the mount of the congregation on the farthest sides of the north; I will ascend above the heights of the clouds, I will be like the Most High." Yet you shall be brought down to Sheol, to the lowest depths of the Pit* (vv. 12-15).

In summary, Lucifer was a spectacular creature that had been created to bring God glory; however, his prestigious position in creation and his unique vantage point of God's preeminence led him to be dissatisfied with God's creation order. Lucifer no longer desired to cover himself and protect the sanctity of God's glory; he wanted his glory to be visible above the stars of God and the heights of the clouds (v. 13). He would no longer conceal his personal glory in God's presence, but being "lifted up" in pride sought to be like "the Most High" (v. 14). God responded by casting him off the Holy Mount (Ezek. 28:16) and destining him to eternal judgment in the Lake of Fire (Matt. 25:41). Lucifer's rebellion in heaven also resulted in the fall of a third of all created angels (Rev. 12:3-4, 9).

These fallen angels have various biblical distinctions and evil agencies: demons, spirits of divination, foul spirits, unclean spirits, and familiar spirits. Like the holy angels, fallen angels have ranks of differing authority and power (Eph. 6:12). Apparently, the angel sent to Daniel was opposed by a fallen angel of greater authority – one that Satan had assigned to manage his agenda in the Persian Empire (Dan. 10). We mortals cannot really imagine the spiritual warfare behind world affairs, especially in the dealings of God's covenant people, whom the devil utterly hates.

Babylon to Be Swept Clean (vv. 18-23)

Having identified the rebel authority behind Babylon, Isaiah offers a colorful taunt to mock its fallen leader. The one who leveled cities and inflicted worldwide destruction would not even get a decent burial; he would be cut down by the sword and trampled underfoot (vv. 18-19). Initial survivors of God's judgment on Babylon, including descendants of Babylon's fallen ruler, would not assume power in Babylon again, for God promised *"to cut off from Babylon the name and remnant, and offspring and posterity"* (vv. 20-22). God promised to thoroughly sweep Babylon with *"the broom of destruction"* (v. 23). Afterwards, its muddy marshes would be a home fit for porcupines, but not for humans.

Assyria's Army to Be Destroyed in Israel (vv. 24-27)

Assyria was a pagan nation, and when they had fulfilled God's purposes in chastening the Northern Kingdom, God promised to destroy them on the mountains of Israel – on His turf, so to speak (v. 25). When Sennacherib threatened King Hezekiah and Jerusalem in 701 B.C., God fulfilled this prophecy by slaying 185,000 soldiers of the Assyrian army in one night (2 Kgs. 19:35). This illustrated to the Jewish nation that no one, nor any kingdom on earth, could thwart God's plans for Israel, nor save themselves from His judgment:

Surely, as I have thought, so it shall come to pass, and as I have purposed, so it shall stand (v. 24).

For the Lord of hosts has purposed, and who will annul it? His hand is stretched out, and who will turn it back? (v. 27).

When faith is anchored in the revealed will of God and His sovereignty, God's people can move forward with confidence and with the expectation of being honored by the Lord no matter the outcome of any trial. Israel had this wonderful assurance from the *"Lord of hosts."*

Philistia to Be Dissolved (vv. 28-32)

Although Isaiah had previously received this oracle from God in the year King Ahaz died (715 B.C.), he was not led to disclose it until now (v. 28). The revelation of Philistia's judgment with the fall of Babylon and Assyria was to further encourage God's people with His sovereign purposes for the Jewish nation.

The Philistines dwelt directly west of the Judean foothills and had been enemies of Israel since Joshua led the Israelites into Canaan (Judg. 3:1-4). During the era of the Judges, the Philistines had repeatedly attempted to expand their dominion by invading Jewish territory. The conflict raged back and forth for hundreds of years until King David subdued Philistia (2 Sam. 8). King Solomon continued to hold Philistia with a firm grip, but after the Jewish kingdom split during the reign of Solomon's son Rehoboam, the wrangling for superiority began again between these two people groups.

Jeremiah also informed the Philistines that the sword of the Lord was against them (Jer. 47:6). And the prophet Ezekiel explained one of the reasons that Philistia deserved to be punished: *"Because the Philistines dealt vengefully and took vengeance with a spiteful heart, to destroy because of the old hatred"* (v. 15). Prompted by deep hatred and by a vengeful spirit, the Philistines had opposed the Jews for centuries and had repeatedly tried to remove them from the land which Jehovah had given them.

Isaiah rebuked Philistia for rejoicing that the rod that had struck them was broken (v. 29). Who is the rod? Some think that it is referring to Ahaz who had attacked the Philistines previously (2 Chron. 26:6-7) and that Isaiah was promising that one of his descendants would attack them again like a viper and a fiery flying serpent (2 Kgs. 18:8). While this is possible, the context of this section better implies that the broken rod symbolizes the end of Assyrian brutality. (The Assyrian Empire conquered Philistia in 711 B.C.)

In either case, there was no reason for Philistia to feel secure, for God promised to strike them with famine and that invaders from the north would cover the land like smoke (vv. 30-31). As a nation, Philistia would be dissolved! Babylon invaded Philistia in 604 B.C., and destroyed many cities, such as Ashkelon. However, God's people in Zion need not fear the Babylonian invasion at the time of Philistia's fall, for Jerusalem would be a safe refuge then; her judgment would come years later (in 586 B.C.).

Devotions in Isaiah

There was much pain and suffering ahead for Isaiah's Jewish audience, but as each of the above prophecies unfolded in time, they would be encouraged to trust in God's sovereignty and faithfulness. He would work all their ills for a greater good, both for them and to honor Himself before the nations.

Meditation

Nothing paralyzes our lives like the attitude that things can never change. We need to remind ourselves that God can change things. Outlook determines outcome. If we see only the problems, we will be defeated; but if we see the possibilities in the problems, we can have victory.

— Warren Wiersbe

Judgment Against Moab
Isaiah 15:1-16:14

Jeremiah's prophecies against the Moabites are more extensive (Jer. 48:1-47) than Isaiah's 23 verses and Ezekiel's four verses (Ezek. 25:8-11). The Moabites were descendants of Lot (through his older daughter). Although more friendly to Israel than most other nations in the region, the Moabites did have a long history of conflict with the Jews reaching back to the days of Moses (i.e., the Moabites tried to impede the Israelites from entering Canaan; Num. 22-24). The Moabites greatly oppressed the Israelites under the reign of King Eglon early in the era of the judges (Judg. 3:12-30).

Ezekiel prophesied against the Moabites for one particular reason. Like the Edomites, Moab had concluded that Israel's destruction proved she was no different than any other nation: *"Look! The house of Judah is like all the nations"* (Ezek. 25:8). Their envy and hatred of the Jewish people caused them to deny the validity of God's promises to the Jews. Not only did the Moabites rejoice in Israel's devastation, but they had also mocked Jehovah, suggesting that His covenant with Israel was a hoax. Since they thought that Israel was no different than any other nation, and Israel's God no different than the gods of the Gentiles, Moab too would be invaded by Babylonian armies and decimated (Ezek. 25:9-10). Then, they would know that Jehovah is Lord (Ezek. 25:11).

Jeremiah said that Moab was exceedingly proud, arrogant, and high-minded (Jer. 48:29) and that Moab had magnified himself against the Lord (Jer. 48:26, 42). Although Moab had not previously experienced the cruel reality of invasion and exile, Moab's immorality and conceit demanded God's remedy (Jer. 48:11-13). A century earlier, Isaiah had proclaimed the same truth: *"We have heard of the pride of Moab – He is very proud"* (16:6). Isaiah, Jeremiah, and Ezekiel all agree as to why Moab deserved to be punished – they were a proud people.

Judgment Against Moab

Isaiah first describes Moab's present situation – the nation was already lamenting over the destruction of several of their key cities by the Assyrians (15:1). The survivors shaved off their beards and the hair on their heads (signs of deep mourning in ancient times) and were clothed in sackcloth (15:2-3). Soon the entire land would be filled with wailing and, though many would venture to their pagan high places and temples to beseech their gods for assistance, no help would come (16:12). The surviving soldiers of Moab's army also wept because they had failed to defend their cities against the Assyrian invaders (15:4).

Because the slaughter of Israel's neighbor to the east was then in progress, the prophet was deeply moved for Moab (15:5). It is one thing to pronounce judgment on a people long into the future; it is quite another to know that thousands, including women and children, were being brutally slashed to pieces while speaking. Regardless of his own heaviness in the matter, Isaiah declared his message: just as a "three-year-old heifer" is fitly suited for sacrifice (or possibly the yoke is meant), so was vigorous Moab prime for slaughter and servitude.

The Moabites were fleeing southward as the Assyrian army advanced from the north (15:6). Finding the waters of Nimrim in southern Moab dried up, they would continue southward to the *"Brook of the Willows"* (Arabim), likely at the southern tip of the Dead Sea (15:7). There was wailing in the cities of Eglaim and Beer Elim (identities are unknown, but likely near Moab's southern border; 15:8). The city of Dimon is a wordplay on Dibon of verse 2, as the Hebrew word for "blood" resembles *dimon*. Dimon had suffered a great slaughter and their water supply was polluted by the blood of the slain (15:9). Although they were already distressed, Isaiah foretold that more terror was coming to Moab. He likened their situation to being hunted by relentless lions that would chase them down and devour them (speaking of the Assyrian soldiers).

Some Moabites had fled into Edom to take refuge in strongholds as far south as *Sela* (or Petra, meaning "a rock" located some fifty miles within Edom's territory; 16:1). However, Isaiah suggests that the lambs (i.e., the refugees, probably including the princes of Moab) should have been sent like tribute to Jerusalem for safekeeping. This was because he had already prophesied that the Assyrians would not prevail against that Jewish capital (10:24-34). The instruction alludes to the time when Moab sent regular tribute to David in Jerusalem (2 Sam. 8:2), and at a

Sorrow and Comfort

later date sent a hundred thousand lambs annually to the king of Israel (2 Kgs. 3:4-5).

Isaiah then likens the fleeing Moabite women wandering at the fords of Arnon to frantic birds that have been thrown out from their nest (16:2). These women begged for help and protection but there would be none until the time their oppressor would be destroyed (16:3-4). Obviously, there was no one from Moab who could accomplish this, but Isaiah knew of One who could. Using the plight of the Moabite people as a backdrop, the prophet affirms God's promise that in a future day, One from the house of David will sit on His throne forever and judge all the earth with justice and righteousness (16:5). There will be no oppressors or aggressors during Christ's rule.

God Must Judge Pride

Isaiah said that Moab was very proud (16:6). From Genesis to Revelation, the Bible declares God's contempt for pride and His commitment to judge it. As the proverb says, *"Pride goes before destruction and a haughty spirit before a fall. Better to be of a humble spirit with the lowly, than to divide the spoil with the proud"* (Prov. 16:18-19). Both James and Peter proclaim that *"God resists the proud, but gives grace to the humble"* (Jas. 4:6; 1 Pet. 5:5). Solomon wrote, *"When pride comes, then comes shame; but with the humble is wisdom"* (Prov. 11:2). The psalmist declared, *"The sacrifices of God are a broken spirit, a broken and a contrite heart"* (Ps. 51:17). The opposite of pride is a broken spirit and a contrite heart.

To be broken before the Lord is to be a qualified recipient of His grace. Our failures should lead to personal brokenness, which should then cause us to cast ourselves upon the Lord in a way that we were hesitant to do beforehand. Our victories, won by His grace, only prompt us to praise His name! The outcome of testing, then, is that the believer knows and trusts the Lord with a greater patience and confidence than he or she had before. This is why the Lord longs for us to come to Him with all of life's burdens.

The Moabites did not do this. Instead of realizing their vulnerability before the Assyrians and retreating into Israel for safety and trusting Israel's God, they sought to save themselves by fleeing southward, and many were slaughtered. Because of their pride, God promised to limit agricultural productivity throughout Moab; this would likely be accomplished through drought (16:7-10). Without the benefit of their vineyards, orchards, and farmland to sustain them in a siege or while fleeing, the Moabites would become easy prey for the Assyrian army.

For a second time, Isaiah expresses his emotional burden for the suffering people of Moab (16:11). Just as the strings of a harp promptly respond when played, Isaiah's heart vibrated with abrupt groaning over Moab's calamity. Although Moab had already suffered greatly, Isaiah concluded his prophecy against that nation by foretelling that there would be much more devastation to come, and that Moab would completely fall within three years (16:12-14). The reference to *"the years of a hired man"* simply meant that just as a hired worker watches the clock to ensure that he does not work more than what he agreed to, Moab's ruin would conclude before the foretold time. This probably referred to the Assyrian conquest of Moab commencing in 735 B.C. and ending with Tiglath-Pileser's full invasion in 732 B.C. If that is the case, Isaiah would have written this prophecy in 735 B.C. and then predicted Assyria's final push to conquer Moab three years later. The fall of Moab would be proof to Israel that God will not tolerate pride.

Meditation

> None are more unjust in their judgments of others than those who have a high opinion of themselves.
>
> — Charles H. Spurgeon

Judgment Against Damascus
Isaiah 17

In this chapter, Isaiah pens a prophecy against Syria (the capital city being Damascus) and her ally, the Northern Kingdom of Israel (7:2). Both kingdoms would fall to Assyrian invaders.

Writing two centuries in advance, the prophet Amos, an older contemporary of Isaiah and Hosea, described the overwhelming destruction of Damascus and why it would occur. Amos stated that the Babylonians would silence the soldiers of Damascus, and her fortifications would be burned (Amos 1:4). The prophet asserted that Damascus, the capital of Syria, had rebelled against God's covenant. As no specific covenant is mentioned, the transgression is likely against the universal covenant God instituted with Noah, which forbade murder, and installed civil authority to punish the guilty.

Damascus, the capital city of Syria, had often meddled in Jewish affairs (7:1; 1 Chron. 18:5) resulting in much harm to God's people. Amos acknowledges why God would punish Damascus, *"because they have threshed Gilead with implements of iron"* (Amos 1:3). Gilead was situated on the Eastern Plateau, the region given to the tribes of Reuben, Gad, and the half tribe of Manasseh for an inheritance. As Syria's king Hazael invaded *"all the land of Gilead"* (2 Kgs. 10:32-33), Amos has the entire region east of the Jordan in view. The Syrians not only conquered Gilead, but also massacred many Jews by running over them with threshing implements. Pulling threshing implements over people would both crush and cut to shreds their bodies. Such devaluation of human life and brutality was a war crime that would not go unpunished. The Lord promised that Syria would be invaded, their cities would be captured and burned, their rebel king killed, and many of their inhabitants would be enslaved and exiled to Kir (Amos 1:4-5).

Jeremiah tells us more than a century later that Damascus would be conquered again by the Babylonians (Jer. 49:23-27). Jeremiah also predicted that the mighty fortress of Ben-hadad (named after the dynasty that ruled Damascus during the 9th and 8th centuries B.C.) would be destroyed at that time.

The Assyrians would decimate the city of Damascus and make it uninhabitable; it would become a fitting home for wild beasts (vv. 1-2). The Assyrian conquest would take Ephraim and all of Syria (even as far south as Aroer, which is in Moab; v. 3). Syria was conquered in 732 B.C. and northern Israel fell in 722 B.C.

Isaiah has previously stated repeatedly that the Syrian-Israeli alliance to invade Judah and to also withstand the Assyrian conquest would be broken. "In that day" appears three times in this chapter (vv. 4, 7, 9) to commence three different sections detailing the aftermath of that failed alliance. Isaiah often uses this phrase "in that day" to first pronounce a judgment and then to acknowledge the blessing that it eventually achieves.

In the first "in that day" expression, the prophet predicts that many in Israel will be slaughtered, and that the remaining survivors will face widespread starvation because farmland (e.g., the fertile Valley of Rephaim running southwest from Jerusalem) and the olive groves will be nearly barren (vv. 4-6).

The second "in that day" phrase again relates solely to Israel (v. 7). After experiencing God's rod of affliction through the Assyrians, Israel *"will have regard for his Maker and his eyes will look to the Holy One of Israel"* (v. 7). The ten northern tribes will realize too late that the pagan gods they had honored by their many altars and idols (including the Asherah poles) had no power to save them (v. 8).

While Satan does mimic God's handiwork and does deceive mankind through supernatural signs, he cannot explicitly control future events or create life (Ex. 8:16-19), nor is he omniscient, knowing the end from the beginning. Only God can forecast and govern forthcoming events with precision and accuracy. Isaiah will later explain to his fellow countrymen that this was why much of God's message to them was prophetic in nature – He wanted them to know He was the one true God so they would reject the many false gods of their day. *"Even from the beginning I have declared it to you; before it came to pass I proclaimed it to you, lest you should say, 'My idol has done them, and my carved image and my molded image have commanded them'"* (48:5). Only the true Creator and Sustainer of all things could possibly know what will transpire in the future – Jehovah was proving to His people that He was the omnipotent, omniscient, immutable, and eternal

Sorrow and Comfort

God. This is why the majority of prophecy in the Bible relates to God's covenant people. Jehovah wanted the Jews to flee idolatry and to embrace Him, the one true God.

The third "in that day" statement pertains to Syria (v. 9). Damascus and other fortified Syrian cities would be destroyed and abandoned; thick underbrush would spring up in these ruins (v. 9). Because the Northern Kingdom must bear her share of Damascus' judgment because of their alliance verses 10 and 11 may apply to Israel directly, as F. B. Hole explains:

> In the days of Isaiah, Damascus had been allied with the ten tribes. Its "burden" fills the three verses that open Isaiah 17. The prophetic strain however quickly passes from Damascus to the children of Israel for disaster was to come on both, since both had united in alliance against Judah. The figure is used of harvest, whether of corn or of grapes, which would leave them poor and thin, yet a remnant would be left, like a gleaning of grapes or a few berries on an olive tree, and that remnant will turn their eyes to "the Holy One of Israel" (v. 7) and away from the idolatrous things that formerly held them.[52]

Israel had been unfaithful to and then forgotten the one true God (v. 10). Consequently, they would come to realize that despite how hard they worked to replant vineyards, it was not a time of peace (v. 11). Isaiah promised that what they had planted would become diseased and that the people would suffer much anguish. Yet, God sought to preserve for Himself a remnant in the land that would honor Him.

The remaining section of the chapter stands alone as a reminder that though Assyria had inflicted much death and destruction, soon enough they would be under God's judgment. The prophet therefore pronounces a "woe" on Assyria. Although the Hebrew word *howy* can be translated as "oh," as in verse 12, it is the same word Isaiah repeatedly employs to express "woe" when addressing someone or a people group (e.g., 10:1, 18:1).

Like a flashflood that soon passes, or like chaff that blows away from the threshing floor, the Assyrian Empire would soon be suddenly vanquished, in the same way that terrors in the night vanish in the morning (vv. 12-14). As mentioned previously, this is what happened to the Assyrian army, when it was slaughtered overnight by the Angel of the Lord (2 Kgs. 19). Sennacherib was threatening Judah, which was off limits to his conquest, and as a result he returned to Assyria in shame and was later murdered by two of his own sons.

Meditation

> We all believe in one true God,
> Who created earth and heaven,
> The Father, who to us in love
> Hath the right of children given.
>
> We all believe in Jesus Christ,
> His own Son, our Lord, possessing
> An equal Godhead, throne, and might,
> Source of every grace and blessing.
>
> We all confess the Holy Ghost,
> Who sweet grace and comfort gives
> And with the Father and the Son
> In eternal glory lives.
>
> — Martin Luther

Judgment Against Cush
Isaiah 18

Matthew Henry refers to this chapter as one of the most obscure in Scripture. The use of poetic metaphor in this passage has resulted in several different understandings as to whom the prophet is addressing.

The ancient nation of Cush (from the Hebrew *Kuwsh* in verse 1) occupied southern Egypt, Sudan, and northern Ethiopia. *Kuwsh* is often translated "Ethiopia" in Scripture, but strictly speaking Cush's boundaries went far beyond the modern borders of that country. Isaiah also identifies Cush as *"the land shadowed with buzzing wing,"* which may refer to the locust that plagued them (v. 1). The region addressed was divided by many rivers, which may refer to the Nile's tributaries (v. 2), but as J. N. Darby suggests, it is more likely that the rivers are boundaries describing an arid region between the Nile and the Euphrates: "The 'rivers of Cush' I take to be not only the Nile but the Euphrates, as if he should say, 'I am now speaking of a land or people beyond those in point of distance, which now are the extremities of and affect the Jewish land and people.'"[53]

Apparently, these tall, smoothed-skinned, fearsome-looking people sent envoys to Israel in swift-moving papyrus boats with the objective of securing an alliance with Israel against the Assyrians. Isaiah instructed the Cushites to return home, as no human alliance would defeat the Assyrians, but God would vanquish them at the proper time (v. 3). The determination of the Cushites for preservation represented the desire of all people groups throughout the region at that time; no one wanted to be brutalized by the Assyrians. Isaiah foretells that God would take down Assyria in such a dramatic way that all nations would know it was His doing, but for now His plans would linger on, like summer heat and the harvest dew (v. 4).

When would God act against Assyria? After that nation had accomplished God's objectives in chastening the Northern Kingdom and in punishing Israel's neighbors (which is the theme of this portion of Isaiah's book). When Assyria is like ripening grapes before harvest, then the Lord will cut down her branches (v. 5). The bodies of Assyrian soldiers will be shattered on the mountains of Israel and so numerous that birds would feed on them all summer long and wild beasts would still be cleaning up their bones in winter (v. 6).

Isaiah closes his prophecy against Cush on a positive note by stating that sometime after the fall of Assyria they will bring presents to the Lord of hosts at Mount Zion (speaking of Jerusalem; v. 7). Whether this occurred in or after Hezekiah's time is unknown. Certainly, the story of how Jehovah saved Jerusalem by slaughtering most of the Assyrian army in one night (without a single Jewish soldier unsheathing his sword) must have resonated throughout the region. No nation had been able to stand against the Assyrian threat, but the God of the Jews had suddenly wiped them out and sent the king reeling back to Assyria in disgrace.

As Isaiah has been intermingling rays of future Kingdom glory throughout the section of judgments on the nations, verse 7 is probably another glimpse of the Millennial Age. Then all nations, including Ethiopia, will come to Jerusalem to worship Jehovah.

Meditation

God of the nations, near and far,
Ruler of all mankind,
Bless Thou Thy people as they strive
The paths of peace to find.

O Father! from the curse of war
We pray Thee give release,
And speed, O speed the blessed day
Of justice, love and peace!

— John H. Holmes

Judgment Against Egypt
Isaiah 19-20

Jeremiah and Ezekiel both prophesied against Egypt within a couple of centuries after Isaiah did. Jeremiah gave two distinct messages against Egypt, both of which have already been fulfilled (Jer. 46): Pharaoh-Neco's failed attempt to invade Babylon (609 B.C.) and Nebuchadnezzar's invasion of Egypt (571-567 B.C.).

Egypt's Fall

. Ezekiel levied seven prophecies against Egypt. In his first oracle, Ezekiel explained that one of the reasons Egypt deserved divine retribution is that they had been an untrustworthy ally (Ezek. 29:8-9). Pharaoh had promised to assist Judah against the Babylonians, but failed to honor that commitment when Nebuchadnezzar attacked Jerusalem, though he did make a halfhearted attempt to do so. Not only had Egypt led His people astray in rebelling against Babylon, but God promised to smite Egypt with a sword and make it a desolate land because of their deceitful assurance of support.

These prophecies confirm the big picture of Egypt's decline and eventual collapse foretold by Isaiah in the next two chapters. Many nations in Isaiah's day thought that Egypt was the only nation strong enough to confront Assyria's quest. Isaiah refutes that notion, because Egypt was also under God's judgment. The prophet portrays God as gliding over Egypt on a swiftly moving storm cloud and dispensing His wrath like lightning bolts. This action would cause Egypt's idols to tremble before Jehovah (19:1) and would result in civil unrest (19:2) The Egyptians would soon realize that their idols were powerless to deliver them. Isaiah foretold that the Egyptians would also be given *"into the hand of a cruel master, and a fierce king will rule over them"* (19:3-4). The "fierce king" may refer to Psammetichus, who subdued eleven rival kings to rule over Egypt. This occurred in the twentieth year of the reign of Manasseh. Psammetichus reigned fifty-four years.[54]

Devotions in Isaiah

To prove that Egypt's judgment was originated by God, He would also smite the land with a severe drought. Egypt was largely desert with a narrow strip of fertile land bordering both sides of the Nile. The Hebrew word for Egypt is *Mitsrayim* (or *Mizraim*), which means "double straitness," and undoubtedly refers to the two straits of land on either side of the Nile. It was these irrigated strips of sand that gave Egypt her prominence. Because the Nile brought life to Egypt, the river was honored. The miracle of turning the Nile's water into blood in Moses's time proved that the God of heaven was superior to the god of the Nile. Now the prophet Isaiah pronounces another judgment on the Nile: God would dry up the river so as to make it stagnate and foul, resulting in a great loss of revenue and creating a life-threating situation for the nation (19:5-10). The fishing, papyrus, and flax industries would all be greatly impacted.

Egypt was known for her wisdom, but Isaiah says that even the esteemed officials from Zoan (in the Nile delta), the counselors of Pharaoh, and the wise rulers of Memphis (Noph) would have no counsel that could alleviate God's judgment against Egypt (19:11-14). No one in Egypt can thwart the counsel of God; no head or palm branch (speaking of leaders), nor tail or bulrush (speaking of the general populace; 19:15).

Egypt's Future Conversion

Then Isaiah confirms that the only people on earth who would be permitted to have control over what happened in Egypt would be Israel, once restored to Jehovah (19:16-25). The prophet applies the familiar "in that day" phraseology five times in this section to indicate that the outcome of past judgments will result in specific blessings in Christ's Millennial Kingdom. Much of the content of chapters 13-23 dealing with the judgment of the nations is now historical, but this passage undeniably relates to end-times events.

Though Israel had often sought Egypt's help during times of crisis (and did so until the sixth century B.C.), there was a time coming in which Egypt would be under the uplifted hand of the Lord of Hosts (i.e., under His judicial sway; 19:16). In the Kingdom Age, Egypt would come to know Israel's God as the true God and would tremble before Him in fear, like helpless, unprotected women (19:17).

Egypt (as represented by five key cities) will then come to Jerusalem to worship the Lord, meaning that they will have to learn

Sorrow and Comfort

Hebrew to some extent to offer sacrifices in Jehovah's name (19:18; Zech. 14:16-19). One of the five cities is probably Heliopolis (also called Aven; Ezek. 30:17), which was a religious center in the Nile delta for worshipping the sun. Hence, *"the city of Destruction"* probably should be rendered "the city of the Sun" as it is in the Vulgate and the Revised Standard Version of the Bible.

The point is that even the deep-seated pagan centers of Egypt will turn to the Lord to acknowledge His authority. While it is true that thousands of Jews fled to Egypt (taking Jeremiah with them) when Jerusalem was destroyed by the Babylonians, that scenario does not fit with what the previous verses describe concerning God's judgment of Egypt. However, it does align well with the prophetic events associated with the Kingdom Age.

As a national display of Egypt's loyalty to Jehovah, they will set up a monument with an altar on the border of their land (19:19-20). Though Josephus states that this prophecy was fulfilled in 1 B.C. when Onias, the high priest, fleeing from Jerusalem, obtained permission to erect an altar in Egypt, the fuller meaning of the prophecy is clearly millennial in nature. For only in the Kingdom Age will Egyptians gladly worship in Jerusalem with the appropriate offerings and sacrifices and make petitions and vows in Jehovah's name and in the Hebrew language. As a result, God will in turn honor their faithfulness by extending to them the same protection and blessing that He will bestow to Israel (19:21-22).

Charles Russell, the founder of the Watchtower organization (now known as the Jehovah's Witnesses), taught that the pillar mentioned in verse 19 referred to a great pyramid in Egypt. This speculation led to several date-specific prophecies concerning the second coming of Christ; all have proven to be bogus. The pillar is established at the onset of the Kingdom Age by Egyptians as a memorial to Jehovah; the pillar is not the tomb of some long-dead Egyptian Pharaoh. Just in case the reader might think Egypt was enjoying something that other nations would not under Messiah's kingdom, Isaiah mentions that Assyria will benefit in the same way (19:23-25).

Once bitter enemies, Egypt, Assyria, and Israel will all enjoy fellowship with each other because they will all be in jubilant communion with Israel's Messiah. A highway granting free access to Jerusalem will actually connect all three nations in Christ's kingdom. This lovely reality will be the fulfillment of God's promise to Abraham millennia earlier, *"I will bless those who bless you, and I will curse him who curses you; and in you all the families of the earth shall be blessed"* (Gen. 12:3). In Christ – all will be blessed!

Egypt's Soon Captivity

Isaiah inserts a parenthetical exhortation in chapter 20 to reiterate his main point of the two previous chapters – it is foolish for Judah to form an alliance with foreign nations that God has destined to be judged by Assyria. Isaiah says the capture of the Philistine city of Ashdod (a seaport city between Askelon and Ekron) by Assyrian King Sargon II in 711 B.C. proves his point – Judah should trust in the Lord and not in the failing might of its neighbors (20:1).

It was at this time that Isaiah informs us of an awkward aspect of his prophetic ministry. The Lord commanded Isaiah to be an object lesson to illustrate a message to his audience concerning Egypt and Cush: *"'Go, and remove the sackcloth from your body, and take your sandals off your feet.' And he did so, walking naked and barefoot"* (20:2). Such a public spectacle pictured how surviving captives of Cush (mainly Ethiopia) and Egypt would be treated after being defeated by Assyria.

Of considerable debate among commentators is what "naked" means in verse 2. Many have suggested that Isaiah removed only his outer prophetic garment (the sackcloth), but had a loin cloth or some inner covering and was not totally naked. Albert Barnes is one such commentator to hold this view:

> That is, [he was] walking "without this special prophetic garment. It does not mean that he was in a state of entire nudity, for all that he was directed to do was to lay this garment - this emblem of his office - aside. The word "naked," moreover, is used in the Scriptures, not to denote an absolute destitution of clothing, but that the "outer" garment was laid aside.[55]

This understanding would agree with David's conduct when he put off his royal apparel (outer garments) to dance "naked" before the ark that was being carried into Jerusalem. The nation saw David not in his kingly attire, but in a linen ephod (2 Sam. 6:14). This was extremely rare. So unusual was David's behavior that his estranged wife Michal accused him of shamefully uncovering himself in front of Israel's maidens (2 Sam. 6:20). David's behavior was prompted by joy in the

Sorrow and Comfort

Lord, while Isaiah's lack of attire was in obedience to the Lord's command. The world does not know God or His purposes, so what He commands His people to do will often appear strange to them. Matthew Henry notes a good application of Isaiah's example for believers today:

> The world will often deem believers foolish, when singular in obedience to God. But the Lord will support his servants under the most trying effects of their obedience; and what they are called upon to suffer for his sake, commonly is light, compared with what numbers groan under from year to year from sin. Those who make any creature their expectation and glory, and so put it in the place of God, will, sooner or later, be ashamed of it. But disappointment in creature-confidences, instead of driving us to despair, should drive us to God, and our expectation shall not be in vain. The same lesson is in force now; and where shall we look for aid in the hour of necessity, but to the Lord our Righteousness?[56]

Given the number of Scriptures prohibiting public nakedness and promoting modesty (Ex. 20:26, 28:42; Ezek. 16:8; Hab. 2:15), it is most likely that Isaiah put aside only his prophet's attire (the sackcloth) to expose an undergarment of some sort. With this said, however, the next verse confirms what the prophet's actions were to represent, the shameful treatment of Egyptian and Ethiopian captives by the victorious Assyrians – which included being stripped naked.

> *Just as My servant Isaiah has walked naked and barefoot three years for a sign and a wonder against Egypt and Ethiopia, so shall the king of Assyria lead away the Egyptians as prisoners and the Ethiopians as captives, young and old, naked and barefoot, with their buttocks uncovered, to the shame of Egypt* (20:3-4).

These poor captives would be butt-naked and publicly shamed by the Assyrians. The next difficulty of this sign is how long did Isaiah walk around in Jerusalem in his undergarments. Many commentators think that the three-year period relates to Egypt and Ethiopia's humiliation, not Isaiah's. Barnes suggests the following meaning of the Hebrew text:

> The entire sense of the phrase can be expressed by translating it: "My servant Isaiah hath walked naked and barefoot, 'a three years' sign and wonder' that is, a sign and indication that 'a three years'

calamity' would come upon Egypt and Ethiopia. Whether this means that the calamity would 'commence' in three years from that time, or that it should 'continue' three years, perhaps we cannot determine.[57]

This seems to be a reasonable understanding of the message as the event would occur soon, and a three-year illustration was not necessary to convey the prophet's message. The entire drama was to prove to Judah the utter futility of trusting in those the Lord had promised to judge – it was best to put their confidence in God alone and to trust His word as declared by His prophets (20:5-6).

If your Christian ministry ever seems too arduous to endure, remember how the prophets of old drank from their own ministries. In order to better communicate God's pain when His people engage in worldliness and idolatry, Hosea was permitted to feel the pain of a lascivious wife (Hos. 1). According to Isaiah's prophecy, Daniel and his friends were likely made eunuchs (Isa. 20:18, 39:7). God told Ezekiel that the death of his beloved wife would be an object lesson to motivate exiled Jewish captives (Ezek. 24:18). Jeremiah was thrown in a deep, muddy pit and left to die (Jer. 37:11-38:13). And as we just saw in this chapter, Isaiah was commanded to publicly strip off his prophet's attire to demonstrate how Assyria would shame their captives. These servants of the Lord suffered daily hardships, threats against their lives, and the loss of loved ones to remain faithful to their God-ordained calling. They were God's servants doing God's will and were thus invincible until God's mission for their lives was complete. May we learn from their example – lest we ever think that the Lord asks more from us than what He deserves (Luke 17:10).

Meditation

> I have a secret thought from some things I have observed, that God may perhaps design you for some singular service in the world. ... We should always look upon ourselves as God's servants, placed in God's world, to do his work; and accordingly labor faithfully for him; not with a design to grow rich and great, but to glorify God, and do all the good we possibly can.
>
> — David Brainerd

Judgment Against the Desert and Edom
Isaiah 21

Isaiah speaks three oracles of judgment against Babylon, Edom, and Arabia in this chapter. The actual timing and the events of the first prophecy have been debated.

A Prophecy Against "the Wilderness by the Sea" (vv. 1-10)

The region of focus, *"the wilderness by the sea,"* likely speaks of a portion of Babylon adjacent to the Persian Gulf. Because Elam and Media are mentioned in verse 2 and Babylon in verse 9, many Bible commentators apply this prophecy to the fall of the Babylonian Empire in 539 B.C., when conquered by the Medes and Persians. In this view "the wilderness by the sea" is understood to be figurative: Babylon is spiritually dry because God does not dwell there, and being near to a sea speaks of her influence over many nations (e.g., Rev. 17:15). However, there is good historical evidence to suggest that this prophecy actually relates to events toward the conclusion of the eighth century B.C.

Ancient Elam (later Media – the Medes), located north and east of Babylon (in modern Iran) experienced a long autonomy from before the time of Abraham until overtaken by Cyrus and the Persian Empire at about 539 B.C. The Medes increased their control of much of Babylon's territories from 600 to 553 B.C. However, the Persians surged north and east from 553 B.C. through 550 B.C. to take control of Media's portion of Babylon's kingdom. Then the Persians (now in control of Media's army) continued extending their territory east and south until the city of Babylon was conquered in 539 B.C.

Although this was accomplished by the joint confederacy of Medes and Persians, the Medes were subject to the Persians under Cyrus' rule. The Jews would rejoice at the fall of Babylon in 539 B.C. because their exiled captives would be able to return home. Both Isaiah and Daniel

Devotions in Isaiah

foretell the identity of Babylon's conquerors, the Medes and Persians (Isa. 13:17, 44:28; Dan. 8:20) and Jeremiah gave the timing of their victory (Jer. 25:11-12).

Indeed, these are all wonderful fulfillments of Bible prophecy. But these events are not likely what Isaiah was addressing; in fact, he was keenly distressed and grieved by the meaning of this prophecy (vv. 2-4). So if this prophecy is not speaking of the later fall of the Babylonian Empire, what is it addressing?

Thus far, nearly all of Isaiah's prophecies of judgment in chapters 13-20 have related to the invasion of Assyria in the eighth century. Even before this prophetic section, Isaiah foretold how Assyria's advance would crumble the Syrian-Israeli alliance. Therefore, as John A. Martin explains, it seems probable that Isaiah's prophecy (vv. 1-10) relates to another situation occurring during the Assyrian offensive in the latter days of the eighth century:

> In 722 B.C. a Chaldean prince from the Persian Gulf region, named Marduk-apal-iddina (called Merodach-Baladan in 39:1), revolted against Assyria, captured Babylon, and was crowned king of Babylon. Elam, a nation northeast of Babylon, supported his revolt. Not till 710 B.C. was Sargon able to evict Marduk-apal-iddina from Babylon. After the death of Sargon in 705 Marduk-apal-iddina along with Elamite troops revolted against Sennacherib. In 702 Sennacherib finally defeated him (and Elam) and devastated his home area around the Persian Gulf. Undoubtedly Isaiah was prophesying about this situation. Hezekiah, king of Judah, and other members of his royal court felt that Marduk-apal-iddina would be able to break the strength of the Assyrian Empire. But Isaiah was warning them that this would not happen.[58]

This historical explanation seems to better fit the tenor of Isaiah's prophecy. Proceeding with that assumption, the invader approaching the region of Babylon-by-the-sea like a desert storm would be Marduk-apal-iddina (v. 1). The battle cry heard in verse 2 was that of the invaders from Elam and Media rallying to liberate Babylon-by-the-sea from Assyria's control. It pained Isaiah greatly to utter this frightening and perplexing prophecy; he likened the effort to that of a woman in childbirth (vv. 3-4).

Verse 5 better explains the prophet's anxiety: *"Prepare the table, set a watchman in the tower, eat and drink. Arise, you princes, anoint*

Sorrow and Comfort

the shield!" The Jews were hopeful that Marduk-apal-iddina's rebellion against Assyria would prosper and would ultimately liberate Judah from its control. So no doubt when some of the rebel's men came to Jerusalem (chp. 39), there was merrymaking; however, the Lord had already revealed to Isaiah that Assyria's devastating blow would be accomplished by Him and in the mountains of Israel. Rather than feasting about what would never happen, Marduk-apal-iddina's soldiers should have been preparing for battle by oiling their shields (shields of animal skin had to be oiled often to keep them from cracking; v. 5).

God told Isaiah to post a watchman (as if he were located in Babylon-by-the-sea) to look eastward for a messenger bearing news of the conflict between Assyria's and Marduk-apal-iddina's soldiers (vv. 6-7). Day after day there was no news, until finally a message was delivered: Though the cavalry of the Medes and the Elamites had advanced gallantly in pairs, the Assyrians had roared upon them like a lion with a terrible slaughter. Babylon had fallen and her gods lay shattered on the ground (vv. 8-9). How would Judah respond to this news? Isaiah says that as a grain is crushed on the threshing floor, so Judah will be devastated after learning of Marduk-apal-iddina's defeat (v. 10). It was now obvious that no earthly power could hinder Assyria's advance.

A Prophecy for Edom (vv. 11-12)

The Edomites were the descendants of Jacob's twin brother Esau, who settled in the region south of Moab and just east of the Dead Sea. The sibling conflict that began after Esau sold Jacob his birthright for a bowl of bean soup continued among their descendants. Edom became a heathen nation that loathed the Jews, their fraternal brothers (Ezek. 35; Obad. 15-16). Like Ammon and Moab, Edom had a long history of hostility toward the Jewish nation (e.g., 1 Sam. 14:47; 1 Kgs. 9:26-28; 2 Kgs. 8:20-21), which commenced when the Israelites were journeying to Canaan. At that time, the Edomites refused to allow the Israelites to pass through their borders, which added many more miles to their route (Num. 20:14-21).

Isaiah only briefly addresses Edom, but later, Jeremiah and Ezekiel will have much more to say against Edom (v. 11). Isaiah simply posts a watchman to observe Edom who was already paying tribute to Assyria (Tiglath-Pilesar in 734 B.C. and Sargon II in 711 B.C.). The watchman did not observe anything changing in Edom's situation and remained silent until someone in Edom called out to him: *"What of the night."* The Jewish watchman replied, *"The morning comes, and also the night. If you will inquire, inquire; return! Come back"* (v. 12)! This meant that nothing was going to change anytime soon concerning Assyria's oppression of Edom; though morning was coming, another night would soon follow. However, there was still time to seek and find out what the Lord had said, and then turn away from sin and rebellion to Him (v. 12).

Jumping ahead to the sixth century, Ezekiel tells us why God was angry with the Edomites; they had assumed Israel was a nation no different than any other. This conclusion challenged the importance of God's Word and His special relationship with the Jewish people (Ezek. 25:8). Furthermore, Edom's sin was great because they had actually assisted Nebuchadnezzar in defeating Judah (Ezek. 25:12). Edom had sided with Babylon in the defeat of Egypt in 605 B.C., but in 593 B.C. they agreed to be part of an alliance, which included Judah and other nations, to rebel against Nebuchadnezzar (Jer. 27:1-7). However, when Babylon came against Jerusalem in 588 B.C., double-crossing Edom switched sides again and assisted Babylon in brutally conquering the Jewish nation (Jer. 49:7-22).

Jeremiah posed a logical statement for the Edomites to consider: If the Lord was determined to cause the surrounding nations, who had no fraternal ties with the Jews, to drink from His cup of wrath, how much more judgment did the Edomites deserve for oppressing and betraying their own distant kin (Jer. 49:12)? Jeremiah specifically explains why God's wrath would be poured out on them: *"'Your fierceness has deceived you, the pride of your heart, O you who dwell in the clefts of the rock, who hold the height of the hill! Though you make your nest as high as the eagle, I will bring you down from there,' says the Lord"* (Jer. 49:16). Edom's pride had summoned God's judgment; they were high on themselves, but God would bring them low.

Ezekiel said that Edom's actions were motivated by hate and revenge (Ezek. 25:12). Consequently, God said He was furious and was going to stretch out His hand to execute His revenge on Edom. Unlike Egypt, Moab, and Ammon, the prophets did not promise Edom a future inheritance or restoration to their land. In fact, history records that in the years following the Babylonian invasion, the Nabateans drove the Edomites westward from their land into southern Judah. The descendants of the Edomites became known as the Idumeans.

Sorrow and Comfort

According to Josephus, the Idumeans became subject to John Hyrcanus I, a Maccabean, in 125 B.C. and were forced to accept Judaism; at that juncture, the Edomites ceased to be a distinct people.[59] Today, there are still remnants of the Moabites and Ammonites living in their respective regions; this cannot be said of the Edomites.

Why were the Edomites destined to lose their distinctiveness as a people? The answer originates in Exodus 17 and is then confirmed elsewhere in Scripture: the Edomites represent something which continues to oppose God and must therefore be eliminated. After crossing the Red Sea, the Israelites were brought into the wilderness by Moses. There they suffered an unprovoked attack by the Amalekites (Edomites). Amalek was the grandson of profane Esau, *"who for one morsel of food sold his birthright"* (Heb. 12:16). Consequently, both Esau and Amalek are used in Scripture to picture the lusting flesh which continues to war against God's people.

So why will the Edomites not have an inheritance in the Kingdom Age; why do they have no future identity as a people? This is a fair judgment for the nation's sins and it is symbolically fitting because the Edomites picture the flesh, which is in opposition to God (Gal. 5:17). God desires believers to *"make no provision for the flesh to fulfill its lusting"* (Rom. 13:14). This mindset is vital to victorious Christian living: *"For if you live according to the flesh you will die; but if by the Spirit you put to death the deeds of the body, you will live"* (Rom. 8:13). The stench of carnal flesh is what the Lord wants to remove from us; it will have no place in His kingdom, and neither will the Edomites.

A Prophecy for Arabia (vv. 13-17)

Tema was a renowned oasis in northwestern Arabia (Job 6:19) and the Dedanites resided in southern Arabia (vv. 13-14). Kedar was a nomadic tribe or league of tribes in the Arabian Desert. Kedar's warriors would be defeated and the survivors would flee for their lives (v. 15). Isaiah prophesied that the Assyrian invasion would affect all of Arabia within one year (vv. 16-17). Other tribal people, *"companies of Dedanites,"* would take refuge in forests to avoid capture. History confirms Isaiah's prophecies; Sargon II defeated a number of Arabian tribes and deported many of them to Samaria in 715 B.C.

Each of the above prophecies has been fulfilled. God's dealing with Edom is sobering and demonstrates just how much He hates our carnal

Devotions in Isaiah

nature and our stubborn pride. These hinder us from pursuing God and obtaining His best for us.

Meditation

> God may allow His servant to succeed when He has disciplined him to a point where he does not need to succeed to be happy. The man who is elated by success and is cast down by failure is still a carnal man. At best his fruit will have a worm in it.
>
> — A. W. Tozer

Judgment Against Jerusalem
Isaiah 22

The Assyrian takeover of the region had been largely successful. Although Isaiah does not date this prophecy, the mention of Shebna (vv. 15-19) and Eliakim (vv. 20-25), the Jewish negotiators at the time of Sennacherib's siege of Jerusalem, confirms the timeframe (36:3-37-2; 2 Kgs. 18:18-37). Additionally, the defensive improvements of Jerusalem described in this prophecy were accomplished in the days of Hezekiah in response to the Assyrian advance. The likely date of this oracle then would be just prior to Sennacherib's army surrounding Jerusalem in 701 B.C. (chps. 36-37).

The Valley of Vision – A Day of Trouble

Jerusalem, including the City of David, lies on the western slope of the Kidron Valley which passes between Mt. Zion to the west and Mt. Olivet to the east. As Isaiah was in Jerusalem when this vision was received, he introduces this oracle as *"the burden against the Valley of Vision"* (v. 1). The prophet explains that the inhabitants of Jerusalem were not responding properly to the Assyrian threat. God wanted His people to cry out to Him for deliverance; instead the Jews were attempting to better fortify the city (vv. 8-11). Others engaged in merrymaking because they believed their doom was inevitable no matter what they did (v. 2).

Isaiah desires his countrymen to see the futility of trusting in themselves against such a mighty foe. They must turn to the only One who could protect them – Jehovah. Instead of climbing on their flat rooftops to catch a glimpse of the Assyrian encampments (v. 1), they should be humbly beseeching the Lord for deliverance.

Sennacherib had already captured dozens of towns throughout northern Judah. Although initially some leaders were able to escape, many were later captured by the Assyrians (v. 3). Knowing that many of his countrymen had died or were being enslaved and oppressed grieved Isaiah (v. 4). Those within the walls of Jerusalem knew that *"a day of trouble ... by the Lord God of hosts"* had beset them (v. 5). Yet, they did not seek the One responsible for their trouble.

Throughout Israel's history God repeatedly chastened His wayward people to awaken them to their deplorable spiritual condition and cause them to repent and return to the Lord through obedience. God Himself has always been the greatest threat to the prosperity of the Jews; because He loves them, He cannot permit them to be ignorant of His Law or in rebellion against it. This is a good reminder for us in the Church Age: without ongoing spiritual revival, all our great accomplishments can easily be negated by lethargic attitudes that will eventually result in moral decline.

Isaiah notes that soldiers from Elam (east of Assyria; see discussion in 21:1-10) and Kir (possibly already conquered by Assyria) had joined ranks with the Assyrian troops (vv. 6-7). This was an unlikely mix of soldiers and suggests that some were either being forced into military service or were mercenaries. Isaiah probably mentioned this point and also the number of the enemy's chariots to heighten Jerusalem's awareness of how hopeless their situation was, that is, without the Lord (v. 7). Yet, the Jews withdrew their weapons and armor from storage (i.e., from Solomon's *House of the Forest*; v. 8; 1 Kgs. 7:2, 10:17-21).

The prophet then identifies how the Jews were bolstering Jerusalem's defenses to improve their chances of enduring a long siege (vv. 9-11). Hezekiah demolished houses to obtain stones for repairing the broken portions of the wall around the City of David (2 Chron. 32:5). He also collected water in the Lower Pool, while stopping up springs in the surrounding area (2 Chron. 32:4). Originally, the Lower Pool (likely located in the southwest of the city) was not protected by a wall, so Hezekiah enclosed the reservoir to protect the water supply from the Assyrians and to reserve it for the city (v. 11).

In Nehemiah's day, the Fountain Gate was located on the east wall just north of the Dung Gate. There was a man-made pool at this location called the king's pool (Neh. 2:14). This reservoir inside the eastern wall is likely the Pool of Siloam which Hezekiah connected by an underground water tunnel to the Spring of Gihon located outside the city and northeast of the pool (2 Chron. 32:30). Hezekiah had teams of engineers on each end of the tunnel digging through solid rock towards each other. The tunnel is about 1750 feet (533 m) long and maintains a steady 0.6 percent grade the entire length of the channel (i.e., a 10.5-foot drop on a one-third mile span). The tunnel was a great engineering feat, but the inhabitants of Jerusalem needed to realize that no technological achievement, no state-of-the-art weapon, or impenetrable armor could save Jerusalem; only the Lord could rescue them.

Instead of trying to withstand the Assyrians, which God had sent to test and to chasten them, the Jews should have realized their helplessness and sought the Lord. Isaiah says they should have pulled out their hair and worn sackcloth, both signs of mourning (v. 12). Apparently, many Jews did not consider Jehovah powerful enough to rescue them, so instead they became fatalistic: *"Let us eat and drink, for tomorrow we die"* (v. 13)! And that is what they did. Instead of humbling themselves and requesting deliverance, they chose drunken carousing and feasting – believing the end was near.

Paul quotes verse 13 in 1 Corinthians 15:32 to show the futility of life on earth, if Christ did not rise from the grave. Without His resurrection, believers would just be forgiven dead people who would never experience the vibrancy of His abundant life. In Him is the essence of light and life (John 1:3-4). If we are not baptized into a living Christ, there is no eternal life, and nothing in the future to hope for. If that were the case, then believers in the Church Age might well follow the example of the hopeless Jews in Isaiah's day. But, the Lord Jesus did experience Resurrection and every true Christian is spiritually connected to Him forever – that gives us hope for the future and is a defense against living for the present.

Judah's worldly course of action was so offensive to the Lord that he declared a fatal outcome for them: *"Surely for this iniquity there will be no atonement for you, even to your death"* (v. 14). These are chilling words from the One who controls all things. Although God would deliver Judah from Assyria in the near-term because of Hezekiah's humble, faithful leadership, the judicial demands of the Mosaic Covenant would eventually fall on Judah (Deut. 27:15-26).

Shebna and Eliakim

We are in a quandary as to why this next decree, which is of a personal nature, was inserted between sections pertaining to Jerusalem and Tyre. Shebna was a high-ranking Jewish officer (Hezekiah's treasurer) and was involved with negotiations with Sennacherib while Jerusalem was under siege (v. 15). Apparently, Shebna wanted to make a name for himself and had an elaborate sepulcher fashioned so that the people would remember him long after his death (v. 16). Shebna likely fostered the same attitudes that Isaiah was confronting in this chapter; Shebna may have even confronted Isaiah. The prophet informed Shebna what the consequences of his pride would be: you will be demoted, be carried away to *"a large country,"* and there you will die. So much for your fancy gravesite!

Isaiah even names Shebna's successor, Eliakim, who was a godly man, and also a high ranking administrator involved with Assyrian negotiations (vv. 20-21). Eliakim's name means "God will establish." The Lord knew that he would be a faithful leader of *"the House of David"* who would render wise and righteous decisions (v. 22). His godly leadership of the people is spoken of as a well-driven *"peg in a secure place"* (v. 23). He was God's man and God would honor him and so would both the common folk and the elite (v. 24). However, Isaiah closes this oracle by again reiterating his proclamation in verse 14; eventually even this peg would be removed and Judah would come under judgment (v. 25).

In this chapter, we are made aware of God's own heartache in being coldly rejected by His people. To willfully discount the Lord's position in one's life or His ability to control one's life is an offense with severe ramifications. Seeing how the Babylonians were permitted to decimate Jerusalem a few years later, one shudders to think of what God's wrath will be like against those who reject His gift of eternal life secured through the judgment and death of His own Son.

Meditation

> God's thoughts, his will, his love, his judgments are all man's home. To think his thoughts, to choose his will, to love his loves, to judge his judgments, and thus to know that he is in us, is to be at home.
>
> — George MacDonald

> What think we of Christ? Is He altogether glorious in our eyes, and precious to our hearts? May Christ be our joy, our confidence, our all. May we daily be made more like to Him, and more devoted to His service.
>
> — Matthew Henry

Judgment Against Tyre
Isaiah 23

Isaiah's prophecies against Tyre center on seventy years of trade disruption and economic oppression under the Assyrian Empire. Jeremiah prophesied briefly against the Phoenician cities of Tyre and Sidon when he listed all the surrounding regions that would be conquered during the Babylonian invasion (Jer. 25:15-26). Ezekiel, on the other hand, devotes three chapters to condemning Tyre, the capital city of Phoenicia (Ezek. 26-28).

Why was God going to judge Tyre? Jeremiah reveals two reasons: First, Tyre delighted in hearing of Jerusalem's destruction. Second, her proud deceit in causing King Zedekiah to ignore the prophecies of Jeremiah and to rebel against Babylonian rule (Jer. 52:2-3). As a result of choosing this plan, Nebuchadnezzar brought his armies westward and focused their attack first on Jerusalem and Judah. Thus, Tyre's influence on Zedekiah delayed Babylon's attack on Tyre for years. Tyre had no concern for the loss of life in Jerusalem, but rather how they could profit commercially from the situation. Jerusalem was a hub for inland trade routes, while Tyre was the chief seaport for merchant ships in the region. Tyre's actions angered the Lord!

God's judgment on Tyre would depress not only Tyre's economy, but also that of all those nations in the region who depended on Phoenican trade. For example, Cyprus, an island 150 miles northeast of Tyre, depended upon grain from Egypt (Shihor) shipped through Tyre (v. 3). Egypt and other countries would wail over the loss of trade with Tyre (vv. 4-5). When ship captains heard of the Assyrian attacks on Tyre, they would decide to stay anchored at Cyprus rather than risk sailing into Phoenician harbors and being destroyed or plundered (v. 2). This realization would cause the ships of Tarshish to wail over their losses (v. 1).

The identity of Tarshish is unknown. Scripture does speak of the ships and merchants of Tarshish to confirm its booming sea trade, especially in metals (Ezek. 27:4-6, 12). It may have been located in the western part of the Mediterranean Sea, such as southwestern Spain (the Iberian Peninsula is rich in metal deposits), or as some suggest, may even refer to the Isles of Britain lying north of Spain. History does record that the Phoenicians sailed to Cassiterides (the Tin Islands) in fifth century B.C. to obtain tin, as did the Greeks later. On the identification of Tarshish, H. A. Ironside writes:

> Tarshish is generally identified with the lands of the far west of Europe, including perhaps a part of Spain but very definitely Great Britain. It was from Tarshish of old that the Phoenicians obtained tin, and the word Britannia means "the land of tin."[60]

Indeed, Britain may be Tarshish of old; Cornwall in the British Isles has large deposits of tin and Tarshish in Ezekiel's day was a main supplier of tin (Ezek. 27:12). The amalgamation of tin and copper produces bronze, thus both metals were highly sought after during this era. Regardless of the identity of Tarshish, the people of that country would mourn over their financial losses connected with their inability to use Phoenician seaports (vv. 6-9).

Isaiah said that all the other ports throughout the entire Mediterranean Sea and beyond (e.g., Egypt, Tarshish, Cyprus, etc.) would mourn because of the fall of Phoenicia (vv. 10-12). Though Sidon and Tyre were fortified, they would fall into the hands of the Assyrians just like Babylon by the Persian Sea did (v. 13, 21:1-10). As a result, all the glamor and prestige associated with their wealth and all their rejoicing in their prosperity would cease in Phoenicia (v. 12). Isaiah concludes the oracle by instructing the ships of Tarshish to wail over Tyre and Sidon's judgment and their lost trade with Phoenicia (v. 14).

The Fall of Tyre

Isaiah, Jeremiah, and Ezekiel all prophesied against Tyre. Isaiah speaks mainly of Tyre's loss of commercial enterprise during a seventy-year period until the Assyrians lost their hold on the region (from about 700 to 630 B.C.; vv. 15-17). After seventy years, Tyre would return to her elite commercial role in the region. The prophet likens the city to a prostitute who was long-forgotten, but later returned to her sexual perversions; she would sing songs to lure past lovers back into her web of economic seduction.

Sorrow and Comfort

How the profits from Tyre's business dealings were to be set aside for the Lord and to benefit those who fear Him with food and clothing is unknown (v. 18). It is conceivable that under Cyrus' decree of 538 B.C., which commanded the Jews to rebuild the temple in Jerusalem, some of the supplies needed for its construction, to sustain the workforce, and to maintain Jewish sacrifices came from Tyre.

Jeremiah stated that Phoenicia would be punished for assisting the Philistines in their assault against the Jews (Jer. 47:4). In 585 B.C., a year after Jerusalem fell, Nebuchadnezzar confronted Tyre (Ezek. 26:7-14). After thirteen years of siege, the mainland portion of Tyre fell and was abandoned. Most of her inhabitants sought shelter in the island fortress, whose walls went straight down into the sea and were 150 feet high on the landward side. Tyre's island defenses held because the Babylonians could not prevent the city from being resupplied from the sea.

Ezekiel then prophesied that after Tyre was punished by Nebuchadnezzar, other nations would later arrive to destroy it (Ezek. 26:12). One of these nations would be Greece over two centuries later. Tyre rebelled against Alexander the Great who destroyed the mainland portion of the city and then built a causeway (a land bridge 200 feet wide and a half mile long) to attack the island fortress. The building materials were scavenged from the conquered mainland portion of the city. This fulfilled the first statement of Ezekiel's prophecy: *"break down your walls and destroy your pleasant houses; they will lay your stones, your timber, and your soil in the midst of the water"* (Ezek. 26:12).

Alexander was able to hammer at the walls of the city with floating rams until eventually a breech on a southern wall was achieved. His forces then entered and captured the city in 332 B.C. (after a seven-month siege). Nearly ten thousand of Tyre's citizens perished in the onslaught (including 2,000 crucified on the beach); another 30,000 were sold into slavery.[61] Alexander then destroyed much of the city – the once famed commercial metropolis was no more. Although the island has been inhabited through the centuries, the ancient island fortress of Tyre was never fully rebuilt, just as Ezekiel predicted (Ezek. 26:14). Historical information indicates that God's Word through all three prophets against Tyre has been fulfilled. Most of these prophecies were fulfilled by the Babylonian invasion during the sixth century B.C.

With that said, H. A. Ironside notes that the typological fulfillment of Tyre's destruction is still future:

> Tyre speaks of the world as a great commercial system where men seek to enrich themselves and their families through material pursuits. They revel in every kind of extravagance and forget about God. Such materialism pervades society today as nations reach out for commercial gain and people live on a scale of luxury unknown in previous centuries. But the time is soon coming when all the things on which men have set their hearts will be destroyed and the present world system will pass away. We may see a prediction of that day in the prophecy relating to the doom of Tyre.[62]

Isaiah has now foretold the doom of the wicked nations surrounding Israel. He hoped that this series of prophetic judgments would cause his countrymen to not seek protection from condemned Gentiles against Assyrian invaders, but to the Lord. The reality of the matter is that all of Israel's neighbors were going to experience God's wrath. Unfortunately, the Jewish nation continued to doubt God's faithfulness and His ability to protect them from harm. The prophecies offered adequate light for those to see who wanted to believe, yet enough dark obscurity for those to remain blind who would not trust God. This is God's way throughout the ages.

Meditation

> Faith certainly tells us what the senses do not, but not the contrary of what they see; it is above, not against them.
>
> — Blaise Pascal

> Faith is to believe what we do not see, and the reward of this faith is to see what we believe.
>
> — Augustine

The Apocalypse to Come
Isaiah 24

Having concluded the lengthy section that pronounced judgments on surrounding nations (chps. 13-23), Isaiah provides a four-chapter preview of things to come. Most of the prophecies in the previous section were fulfilled by the Assyrian invasion. Isaiah's previous ten "burdens" against various people groups were merely individual tributaries that now combine into an eschatological flashflood that sweeps over the entire planet.

This section is often referred to as *Isaiah's apocalypse*. The prophet uses the distressing Assyrian invasion as a backdrop to foretell a time of even greater worldwide chaos – the Tribulation Period. J. A. Motyer observes the following order for this four-chapter section:

> In chapters 24-27 there are no overt headings, and apart from references to Jerusalem (24:23, 25:6), Judah (26:1), Moab (25:10) and the cluster of Assyria, Egypt and Jerusalem (27:13), there are no plain pointers to history. The whole is impressionistic, rhapsodic and full of song (24:16, 25:1-5, 26:1-6, 27:2) and eschatological cantata on the theme of worldwide overthrow and rectification.[63]

Unfortunately, these prophecies have spawned many erroneous interpretations that have led to some wild assessments of future events. For example, the teachings of Ellen G. White, nearly two centuries ago, resulted in the origination of two major cults (Seventh-Day Adventism and Armstrongism/The Worldwide Church of God). She denied that Christ would establish His Millennial Kingdom on earth, but claimed instead that the earth would become the bottomless pit in which Satan would be bound and where he could do evil until his destruction a thousand years later in the Lake of Fire.

Undeniably, a single portion of Scripture can be twisted to form any kind of eschatological fantasy. But God's truth is declared in the whole, and the unity of all Old and New Testament prophecies guard against such abuses. What Isaiah teaches in this passage is consistent with what God has revealed to us throughout Scripture concerning "End Times" events.

Apocalypse Overview

At present, the Lord sits on His Father's throne (Rev. 3:21). At the end of the Tribulation Period, the Church will return with Christ to earth and He will defeat the Antichrist and his armies who have gathered to battle Israel (Zech. 14; Rev. 19). Shortly after this battle, Christ will separate those who are able to enter His kingdom from those who cannot; this is called the Judgment of Nations (Matt. 13:47-50; 25:31-47; Rev. 19:21). Then, the Lord Jesus will establish His righteous kingdom on the earth. Satan and demonic forces will be constrained within the bottomless pit during this one thousand-year period (Rev. 20:1-3) and the world will be governed by Christ from Jerusalem (Isa. 60:12-14, 66:10-14; Zech. 14:9). The curses that were placed on the earth in Adam's day will be lifted and the earth will be fully fruitful again (Ps. 72:16; Isa. 11:1-10; Rom. 8:18-22). Peace, prosperity, righteousness, justice, holiness, and the glory of God will be known throughout the planet.

Shifting from God's near-term judgment of the region by the Assyrians, Isaiah now focuses on a future worldwide judgment and the blessed aftermath under Messiah's authority. This change in prophetic emphasis is evident as the *"earth"* is mentioned fifteen times in this chapter. The only chapter in the Bible with more occurrences is Genesis 1, which speaks of the earth's creation.

The Scope and Reason

During the Tribulation Period the entire planet's ecosystem will be decimated through divine judgments and much death will result: *"Behold, the Lord makes the earth empty and makes it waste, distorts its surface and scatters abroad its inhabitants"* (v. 1). Isaiah says that during this time every level of society will be affected and no one's wealth will be able to save them from suffering (vv. 2-3). The entire planet and its inhabitants will languish together, not even the most important individuals will escape the desolation (v. 4). Thankfully, in the next chapter we see that Christ will completely renew the earth during the Kingdom Age and will remove the curses that God put in place as a result of human rebellion (Gen. 3:17-24; 66:17-22).

Sorrow and Comfort

God's judgment on the earth will be like a consuming fire in which only a few will escape (v. 6). Why will God levy such austere judgments on the earth during the Tribulation Period? Isaiah explains the reason: humanity has defiled the world with sin – man has *"broken the everlasting covenant"* with God (v. 5). God created the earth in perfection and put man in authority over it, but humanity has utterly ruined what God has made. God's conditional covenant with Adam in Eden put him under stewardship (Gen. 2:16-17): Obedience ensured life with God in paradise, but disobedience would result in hardship and death (including spiritual separation from God).

Man was created for God's pleasure and to glorify His name (Rev. 4:11). When man rejects the truth that God has revealed to go his own way – he has rebelled against the foundational purpose for which he was created. This is why Paul pronounces judgment on those who forsook the Creator to worship His creation:

> *For since the creation of the world His invisible attributes are clearly seen, being understood by the things that are made, even His eternal power and Godhead, so that they are without excuse, because, although they knew God, they did not glorify Him as God, nor were thankful, but became futile in their thoughts, and their foolish hearts were darkened. Professing to be wise, they became fools, and changed the glory of the incorruptible God into an image made like corruptible man -- and birds and four-footed animals and creeping things. Therefore God also gave them up to uncleanness, in the lusts of their hearts, to dishonor their bodies among themselves, who exchanged the truth of God for the lie, and worshiped and served the creature rather than the Creator, who is blessed forever* (Rom. 1:20-25).

Likewise, our first parents chose to rebel against revealed truth in Eden and sin intruded into humanity. As a result, sin, death, and suffering have passed down to each generation since that horrible day (Rom. 5:12). Man continues to defile God and dishonor the divine stewardship that he was originally placed under (Heb. 2:7-8).

Confusion and Desolation

During this tumultuous future period, earth's vineyards will all be dried up; there will be neither wine nor music for merry-making parties (vv. 7-9). Rather, the entire city (speaking of the civilized urban world) will be in utter confusion and broken down (v. 10). It is possible that *"the city of confusion"* may be one of several dozen titles for Jerusalem in Isaiah, but the context of this passage has a global bearing (i.e., it is not just speaking about Jerusalem being confounded). It seems more likely that Isaiah is reaching back to events in Genesis 11 to confirm his point – God is judging the entire world, which is symbolized by Babylon (Rev. 18:2).

After the flood, mankind rebelled against the Lord by remaining in one location (Babel) and sought to reach heaven (to be like God) by constructing a tall city/tower (10:10, 11:1-8). The Lord's response was one that caused complete hysteria and affected every person on the planet: *"Therefore its name is called Babel, because there the Lord confused the language of all the earth; and from there the Lord scattered them abroad over the face of all the earth"* (Gen. 11:9). A play on words in the Hebrew language occurs in this verse. The word *babal* is alluded to, which means "confusion." What the Babylonians had previously called "the gate to God" the Hebrews referred to as "confusion." Paganism finds its roots in Nimrod at Babel. Our English word *Babylon* is simply the word *Babel* with a Greek ending. The judgment of "the city of confusion" then speaks of God's wrath being poured out on Babylon and all the inhabitants of the earth which are under her sway (Rev. 17:1-6, 15).

All then will be gloomy and desolate; food will be scarce, like after the olive trees and grape vines have been thoroughly harvested (vv. 11-13). Matthew Henry reminds us that the desolation of earth's dainties and luxuries only serve to prove where true happiness is found – in the Lord:

> All whose treasures and happiness are laid up on earth, will soon be brought to want and misery. It is good to apply to ourselves what the Scripture says of the vanity and vexation of spirit which attend all things here below. Sin has turned the earth upside down; the earth is become quite different to man, from what it was when God first made it to be his habitation. ... The world we live in is a world of disappointment, a vale of tears; the children of men in it are but of few days, and full of trouble. See the power of God's curse, how it makes all empty, and lays waste all ranks and conditions. Sin brings these calamities upon the earth; it is polluted by the sins of men, therefore it is made desolate by God's judgments. Carnal joy will soon be at end, and the end of it is heaviness. God has many ways to

embitter wine and strong drink to those who love them; distemper of body, anguish of mind, and the ruin of the estate, will make strong drink bitter, and the delights of sense tasteless. Let men learn to mourn for sin, and rejoice in God; then no man, no event, can take their joy from them.[64]

A Remnant Preserved From Wrath

The first thirteen verses are filled with the gloom of earthly judgments, but the dawning of light begins in verse 14, when, in the darkest hour of the Tribulation Period, the remnant begin to sing of God's majesty (vv. 14-15). It seems likely that this is the Jewish remnant, but perhaps it includes Gentiles who have heeded the kingdom gospel message also.

In the previous chapters, it was evident that those deserving judgment, including God's covenant people, did not view the Assyrians, God's chastening rod, with acceptance. Rather, they complained about their invader's cruelty and thus mocked God's righteous chastening and retribution for their offenses against Him. However, the survivors of the Tribulation Period will acknowledge that all that God has done was deserved and just – no complaining or whining about God's vindication, but rather songs of *"Glory to the Righteous"* (v. 16).

In contrast to this future day of joyful praise, Isaiah groans in his spirit over the treachery and unfaithfulness of his countrymen to God in his day. Prophetically speaking, Isaiah understood Israel's future bliss with God, but also the terrible consequences of their rebellion to be exacted during the Tribulation Period. The prophet is prompted to mourn aloud: *"I am ruined, ruined! Woe to me"* (v. 16)!

God would not be mocked by His people; hence, all their treachery would be recompensed. The guilty would not be able to escape His vindication; rather, they would be like animals caught in a deep pit or a snare (vv. 17-18). God's retribution on the earth would be like a thunderous cloudburst sweeping defilers away or a great earthquake that would create enormous caverns to swallow up the wicked (v. 19). This earthquake would be so great that Isaiah likens the earth to a swaying drunkard; even flexible huts shall fall flat to the ground (v. 20). John reiterates the literal meaning of this prophecy toward the conclusion of the Tribulation Period: *"And there were noises and thunderings and lightnings; and there was a great earthquake, such a mighty and great earthquake as had not occurred since men were on the earth"* (Rev. 16:18).

Neither spiritual wickedness in high places (fallen angels), nor the political and military might of kings below will be able to circumvent the righteous judgments of God on the earth (v. 21). Wicked people will all be judged at the Second Advent of Christ and will be cast into the realm of torment (Hades) until their final judgment at the Great White Throne a thousand years later (vv. 21-22; Rev. 20). After this event, the Lord will create a new heaven and earth and He will reign from the New Jerusalem which is 1500 miles in width, height, and depth. This city does not need the sun or the moon to illuminate it, for the glory of God will permeate all the city as well as the new earth (Rev. 21:23). Isaiah seems to be referring to the same illuminating dynamic of God's glory commencing in the Millennial Kingdom and continuing throughout eternity:

> *Then the moon will be disgraced and the sun ashamed; for the Lord of hosts will reign on Mount Zion and in Jerusalem and before His elders, gloriously* (v. 23).

Notice the Lord reigns in glory "**before** His elders" or "ancients" (KJV) and not **over** them. This reminds us of the panoramic scene of God's heavenly throne room recorded in Revelation 5, before the Tribulation Period commences in the next chapter. A multitude of elders representing the redeemed are gathered around God's throne to witness His glory and to worship His Lamb – the Lord Jesus Christ. In the same way, the Jewish remnant will be witnesses of the Lamb's glory, when He reigns *before* them in Jerusalem.

Meditation

    I'll see the new Jerusalem when Christ to earth does come.
    I'll see Him then, will hear His voice, all Christians will rejoice.
    Of sun and moon there is no sign, God's light o'er all will shine.
    And then, when He has come with might, it never will be night.

    A stream of water, crystal clear, from His throne will appear.
    An end to struggle and all strife, that water brings new life.
    The tree of life brings forth its fruits, on ever growing shoots.
    With praise and music in the air, no thirst or hunger there.

Sorrow and Comfort

And all who served Him, with Him reign, now free from sin and stain.
How fathomless, dear Lord, the love, come to us from above.
That caught in bondage, fraught with strife, You bring eternal life!
One day, on Your eternal shore, we'll praise You evermore.

— Adrian V. Miller

We Have Waited for Him
Isaiah 25

The expression *"we have waited for Him"* occurs twice in verse 9, and is not found anywhere else in Scripture, though a similar phrase *"we have waited for You"* occurs in 33:2. A faithful Jewish remnant, now enjoying the blessings of the Kingdom Age, will offer this poetic tribute to their prodigious God. The restored Jewish nation now realizes that Jehovah brought to pass all that He promised, even after centuries of chastening turmoil; they are in full appreciation of God's pledge, *"I will not forget you"* (49:15).

Rejoice in the Lord

This psalm of praise commences by extoling God's good name, speaking of His holy character, acknowledging His wondrous works, and declaring that His word is forever faithful and true (v. 1). The particular focus is on God's judgment on the great city of foreigners and terrible nations (i.e., the entire Gentile world; vv. 2-3). Not only would Israel be delivered from Gentile oppression forever, but God's judicial role during the Tribulation Period will cause many Gentiles to turn to Him for salvation.

Today, Israel is not in her full inheritance; she is still under Gentile oppression, and the inhabitants of the world have not embraced Jehovah, Israel's God. Clearly, to date, God's covenant with Abraham has not been fulfilled (Gen. 12:1-3, 15:18-21; Josh. 21:43). However, through Christ, the Abrahamic covenant will be completely honored. Listen to the prophetic words of Zacharias, the father of John:

> Blessed is the Lord God of Israel, for He has visited and redeemed His people, and has raised up a horn of salvation for us in the house of His servant David, as He spoke by the mouth of His holy prophets, who have been since the world began, that we should be saved from our enemies and from the hand of all who hate us, to perform the mercy promised to our fathers and **to remember His holy covenant, the oath**

Sorrow and Comfort

***which He swore to our father Abraham**: To grant us that we, being delivered from the hand of our enemies, might serve Him without fear, in holiness and righteousness before Him all the days of our life* (Luke 1:68-75).

Matthew tells us in the opening verse of his gospel account that Christ is "Son of David," then "the Son of Abraham." Normally, when these two chief patriarchs of the Jewish history are mentioned, Abraham is referred to first, for he walked upon the earth more than a thousand years before David was born. The order arranged by Matthew, however, introduces us to the "authority" theme of his Gospel; he addresses the official glory of the Lord Jesus as rightful heir to the throne of David. The "son of David" refers specifically to the office of king. The Lord Jesus is the King of the Jews, but more than that, He is the King of kings and the Lord of lords (1 Tim. 6:15). He simply has not yet advanced to the earth to establish His throne; presently He resides upon His Father's throne in heaven (Rev. 3:21).

The reference to the "son of Abraham" is much wider in scope than the reference to the "son of David." Through the son of Abraham *"shall all families of the earth be blessed"* (Gen. 12:3). Paul speaks of Abraham as the spiritual father of all spiritual seed, and of the eternal blessings which God promised to Abraham that are likewise offered to all those (including Gentiles) who, like Abraham, would simply believe God's word (Rom. 4:13-16). The blessed reality that Isaiah is describing in this chapter proves that all God's promises to Abraham have been completely fulfilled. How did this come about? The answer is, because the Son of David and the Son of Abraham is ruling the world! Under His rule the helpless, poor, needy, and oppressed will be delivered and satisfied, but rebels and devisers of cruelty will be overcome by a cloud of judgment (vv. 4-5).

Blessings of the Kingdom

In the previous verses, the remnant praised God for His protection and for the elimination of their enemies. In verses 6-12, Isaiah identifies several divine achievements in the Kingdom Age that Israel will also rejoice in and be thankful for:

First, the prophet mentions that in God's mountain (speaking of His kingdom; Micah 4:1) there will be plenty to eat, and the food that He provides will be of the best quality (v. 6). All are invited to the Lord's banquet table and there will be no one who honors Him who will not be satisfied. Initially, only the righteous who survived the Tribulation Period will enter Christ's Millennial Kingdom, but their descendants (who still have a fallen nature) have the capacity to rebel against Christ, and indeed many do at the end of the Kingdom Age (Rev. 20). However, during Christ's reign He will rule the nations with a rod of iron and any rebellion will be quickly judged (60:12; Zech. 14:16-19); those who cherish Him will be fully satisfied with all good things.

Second, Isaiah says that God *"will swallow up death forever and the Lord God will wipe away tears from all faces"* (v. 8). In verse 7, the prophet refers to a shroud, or sheet, placed over a corpse to symbolize the separation and pain that the death of the deceased causes family members and friends. It is obvious that rebels will experience death during the Millennial Kingdom, but with the Genesis 3 curses lifted from the earth, longevity will be restored. It will be unusual for a child to die under a hundred years of age (65:20). Faithful individuals may live through the entire Kingdom Age. Then at the end of the Kingdom Age, just before God creates a completely new heaven and earth (Rev. 21:1-3) – death and sorrow will be done away with forever (Rev. 20:14, 20:4). How is this possible? Because sin, which caused such death and damage will never be known again. E. J. Young summarizes how God accomplishes this feat.

> Outwardly, evil culminates in death; subjectively, it leads to tears. For a parent to wipe away a child's tears is not difficult; but for God to wipe away the tears from His people's eyes, there must first be removed the evil which had caused those tears; and to remove evil, there must be a conquering of him who had the power of death. No longer, however, will the faces of His own be covered with tears, for God has removed the cause of those tears. The New Testament makes clear how He has done this. He has done it in the person of His Son, who offered Himself a sacrifice to put away sin. Behind the beauty and glory of the blessings herein depicted there stands the cross of Calvary.[65]

Dear believer, through His Son's finished work, God is going to powerfully remove all suffering related to sin, including the last teardrop of grief and regret to trickle down your face. What will it be like to be face to face with the One radiating the fullness of joy, and for Him to gently touch our cheek to remove the last reminder of former things?

Sorrow and Comfort

Paul quotes verse 8 (see 1 Cor. 15:57) to teach of the glorification of the Church which occurs when Christ descends to the clouds and "snatches up" His Church from the earth (1 Thess. 4:13-18). At that moment mortality shall put on immortality and what was corruptible, speaking of the believer's body, will become incorruptible forever (1 Cor. 15:53-54). Believers will receive a Christ-like body (Phil. 3:21) which cannot sin, age, or degrade in any way. At that moment the believer's salvation will be complete: the spirit and soul were saved at conversion through regeneration, but the body will not be saved from the presence of sin until glorification is experienced. Then believers will have bodies fit for heaven and will be with the Lord evermore (2 Cor. 5:1). What a joyful experience it will be to never have another putrid thought, never to say another stupid or hurtful thing, but rather to be filled with elation and praise for the Savior!

Third, the believing remnant of Israel will also be full of jubilant praise after experiencing all the goodness God lavished upon them in the Kingdom Age:

Behold, this is our God; we have waited for Him, and He will save us. This is the Lord; we have waited for Him; we will be glad and rejoice in His salvation (v. 9).

The rejoicing of future Israel in God's full salvation no doubt was a rebuke against Israel's waywardness in Isaiah's day. The implication is that God's people should always rejoice in Him, regardless of our temporal difficulties, and especially when such hardships result from our own foolishness. Paul exhorts the Christians at Thessalonica to *"rejoice evermore"* (1 Thess. 5:16). This is the shortest verse in the Greek New Testament, but one of the most important. Joy removes the burden. God's family should be a happy family, meaning we all must contribute to the atmosphere of joy. There is no room for a "doom and gloom" attitude. *"Yet, if any man suffer as a Christian, let him not be ashamed, but let him glorify God on this behalf"* (1 Pet. 4:16). As a believer chooses to rejoice in the Lord while in the midst of a dire situation, God often glorifies Himself by working a miraculous solution to end the trial.

It may be that our rejoicing does not specifically or immediately bring relief or conclusion to our difficulty, but God has promised to work a greater good and to glorify Himself through every situation (Rom. 8:28). Writing to the Corinthians, Paul relates some of the incredible difficulties he faced in his ministry, but then concludes by declaring, *"As sorrowful, yet always rejoicing"* (2 Cor. 6:10). The Lord had miraculously delivered him from many life-threatening circumstances (2 Cor. 11:23-28). He also informed the Corinthians that he had maintained a glad state, though his laboring among them had cost him greatly (2 Cor. 12:15, 13:9). Paul had a choice to complain or to rejoice in his laboring which in time brought the Corinthians to maturity.

Against much opposition Nehemiah led the Jews to rebuild the wall around Jerusalem in just fifty-two days. Afterwards he declared, *"...neither be ye sorry;* **for the joy of the Lord is your strength**" (Neh. 8:10). The Psalmist writes: *"Delight yourself also in the Lord; and He shall give you the desires of your heart"* (Ps. 37:4). Rejoicing in the Lord demonstrates a trusting faith in God's sovereign control over every matter of life. This is what Isaiah wanted his countrymen to understand – they should be rejoicing now; God should not have to wait for their joyful praise until He delivered them.

Fourth, Israel will rejoice in God's visitation on Moab. The Moabites were a proud people and so Isaiah uses them to typify all the rebellious, haughty people in the world; God will spread His hands out like a swimmer does to remove all that is in his way in order to pass through the water, so shall God by force vanquish all who oppose Him (vv. 10-12). The self wise and self-exalting rebels of the world will be brought low and will not be permitted to walk upon His mountain (i.e., to enter His kingdom centered in Zion). On the other hand, the refined nation of Israel and all those Gentiles willing to honor Israel's God will enjoy rich prosperity and blessing under Christ's rule.

Meditation

> To the quiet mind all things are possible. What is the quiet mind? A quiet mind is one that nothing weighs on, nothing worries, which, free from ties and from all self-seeking, is wholly merged into the will of God and dead to its own.
>
> — Meister Eckhart

The Redeemed Praise God
Isaiah 26

The previous chapter contained a psalm of praise reflecting Israel's joy in God's faithfulness to bring about all His covenant promises to Abraham. This includes deliverance from Gentile oppression forever and rich blessings within a land inheritance set aside for them.

In this chapter we have another song; Isaiah pictures himself alongside his restored countrymen in the holy land singing praises to God, and their Messiah, during the Kingdom Age. J. M. Riddle suggests the following outline for this chapter: "The praise of God's people (vv. 1-6); the path of God's people (vv. 7-11); the prosperity of God's people (vv. 12-15); the pain of God's people (vv. 16-19); the preservation of God's people (vv. 20-21)."[66]

The specific language that Isaiah applies in this song is much more than a poetic expression of himself standing with restored Israel in spirit; rather, Isaiah believed that he would be resurrected with other faithful saints to do so bodily (vv. 8, 18-21).

Some portions of Scripture seem to indicate that Old Testament saints will be raised up in glorified bodies when the Church is raptured to be with Christ prior to the Tribulation Period (e.g., 1 Thess. 4:13-18; Heb. 11:40). Other passages, however, such as verse 19 and Daniel 12:1-2, suggest that the resurrection of these saints will occur at the end of the Tribulation Period, when the martyred tribulation saints are glorified (Rev. 20:4). Regardless of when Isaiah and other Old Testament saints will be raised, all the redeemed will be with Christ in His kingdom and will be singing praises to Him.

Because the Messiah will dwell in Jerusalem with His covenant people, that city is said to be *"a strong city"* with salvation as its wall and ramparts (v. 1). Only the righteous, those who walk in truth, can enter its open gates (v. 2). Though all the nations of the world will come to Jerusalem to worship God during the millennial reign of Christ, Ezekiel indicates that the Jews will have a privileged position in the temple that Gentiles will not have (i.e., Gentiles will be limited to a "common" area outside the temple; Ezek. 42:20).

Furthermore, the priests (sons of Zadok) will have a priestly ministry that permits them to come closer to the Lord than ordinary Jewish worshippers. So, although God will commune among His covenant people, they will still be limited in how they can approach the Lord. There will be no such limitations for the Church, who will ever be with the Lord (2 Cor. 5:8). There will also be no restrictions for Old Testament saints or for tribulation saints who also have experienced *the first resurrection* and are, like the Church, in glorified bodies (Isa. 26:18-21; Heb. 11:40; Rev. 20:4).

During the Kingdom Age the righteous will enjoy a peaceful state of mind, because they will completely trust forever in their God of eternal strength (v. 4). Accordingly, Isaiah is suggesting to Judah that it is possible, despite their present hardships, to enjoy such a tranquil disposition now (before their national restoration with God): *"You will keep him in perfect peace, whose mind is stayed on You, because he trusts in You"* (v. 3). As in Israel then, and in the Church today, there is a danger that the redeemed may value the importance of corporate prayer, worship, and fellowship to the point that they forget to be watchful for their own souls. William Kelly reminds us that "strength depends upon what passes between our own souls and God, who in His gracious and vigilant care watches over His saints individually."[67] Therefore, believers should not forget or devalue the blessings of their corporate identity, but neither should they neglect their individual walk with the Lord. Each saint must personally appreciate and rest in Him to do what is appropriate and right each day.

In reference to verse 3, what does it mean to set one's mind on something? The prophet Samuel told Saul, who had been looking for his lost donkeys for three days, *"...set not thy mind on them; for they are found ..."* (1 Sam. 9:20). Clearly, it is possible to focus or set the mind on a particular thing by an act of the will. Isaiah informs us that this is ultimately how we maintain peace in our minds. Nearness to God is the greatest defense against depression and the best means of promoting a stable mind. In a coming day the Jews will seek peace with the Antichrist and will pay dearly for that mistake. True peace is found in God alone.

In the Millennial Kingdom, Israel's ultimate rest will be realized: all their foes will be defeated, they will be esteemed by their enemies,

Sorrow and Comfort

and will dwell in the presence of the Lord in complete peace (Zech. 8:20-23). Meanwhile, Christians are to eagerly long for all that Christ accomplished at Calvary to come to fruition in God's timing. The Lord Jesus Himself waits with blissful anticipation to be with His glorious bride and to establish His eternal kingdom (Isa. 53:11; Eph. 1:22-23). Until summoned home by the call of the archangel and the trump of God, may each believer count on the faithfulness of God to enter into His rest. This serenity of mind and soul is enjoyed only through ongoing dependence and ceaseless vigilance, for the adversary remains active.

The challenge, then, in any fearful disaster or sorrowful event, is to maintain an unruffled mind by determining to rest in Christ in heavenly places (Eph. 2:6). That is where all our spiritual resources are presently found (Eph. 1:3). All beneficial spiritual exercise then begins with resting in Christ. We are not to resort to carnal weapons to resolve our difficulties, nor to become depressed because our expectations are not met. We understand that whatever situation we face, He also faces and He is in full control. With our final rest still before us, let us take full advantage of the divine rest available for us today in Christ.

A woman said to evangelist D. L. Moody, "I have found a promise that helps me when I am afraid. It is Psalm 56:3 – 'What time I am afraid, I will trust in Thee.'" Mr. Moody replied, "I have a better promise than that! Isaiah 12:2 – 'I will trust and not be afraid.'"[68] Certainly, both promises are true and each has its own application, but the latter speaks of a settled mind without the distraction of fear. This settled mind immediately and completely trusts our helper, the Lord Jesus Christ, in unsettling times. Hudson Taylor once wrote from the China Sea concerning the Isaiah 12:2 promise, "Soon we shall be in the midst of the battle, but the Lord our God in the midst of us is mighty, so we 'will trust, and not be afraid' (Isa. 12:2)."[69] There is but one hiding place for the threatened, one solace for the brokenhearted, and one salve for the wounded soul – the Lord Jesus Christ. Believer, stay near to Him!

When Christ rules over the nations, all that were lofty in pride and affluence will be brought low, and those they took advantage of or ignored, such as the impoverished, will be well cared for by the Lord (vv. 5-6). Throughout Scripture, God consistently declares His concern for the poor, the widows, and the orphans. In the Kingdom Age, those deprived of life's good things will rejoice in God's justice over those who thought too highly of themselves to share what they had received from the Lord.

The Just and the Wicked

Isaiah then proclaims that the Most Upright One weighs out and blesses those who choose to walk on the path of righteousness with Him (v. 7). This does not mean that righteous people do not suffer trials, but rather that God will walk with them to smooth out the hardship as much as possible until it is overcome. Paul affirms a similar truth in the New Testament:

> *No temptation has overtaken you except such as is common to man; but God is faithful, who will not allow you to be tempted beyond what you are able, but with the temptation will also make the way of escape, that you may be able to bear it* (1 Cor. 10:13).

The Greek word for temptation in this verse is *peirasmos*, which means "a proving of" or, by implication "a test to prove fidelity." God promises not to test us above what we are able to endure without providing the necessary grace to sustain us in that particular trial. God's ways are perfect, so our ability to rest in God's faithfulness during adverse situations is the true measure of our fidelity (v. 8). The prophet clearly connects our faith in God with our loyalty to Him. We will not serve a God we do not know, and we will not seek to know a God we cannot trust. Those who truly know God and know that He is completely faithful will want others to learn of Him also. Hence, Isaiah captures the essence of loyalty to God – the exaltation of His name: *"The desire of our soul is to Your name"* (v. 8).

Sadly, for centuries Israel's unholy conduct caused Gentiles to blaspheme God's name (Rom. 2:23-24). It should be the deepest desire of all believers to uphold the name of God in all we do and say. This means our attitudes, motives, speech, and behavior must not cause the name of the Lord God to be blasphemed. The Lord affirmed that Paul was *"a chosen vessel unto Me, **to bear My name**"* (Acts 9:15). Paul faithfully declared the name of Jesus Christ before Gentiles, kings, and the children of Israel. The Church is commanded to go forth *"and teach all nations, baptizing them **in the name of the Father, and of the Son, and of the Holy Ghost [Spirit]**, teaching them to observe all things whatsoever I have commanded you..."* (Matt. 28:19-20). When you evaluate the options for living life, only two choices become evident:

Sorrow and Comfort

live to bear up the name of the Lord Jesus Christ, or live in such a way that causes others to blaspheme His name.

Isaiah says that merely living in the land of uprightness (i.e., the location in which God revealed His righteousness – Judah) is not enough to be deemed righteous (v. 10). Being a Jew meant nothing unless you obeyed the Law that God gave to the nation. Sadly, many have (including many Jews) refused God's grace as offered by accepting His righteous way. The Lord Jesus said, *"I am the way, the truth, and the life. No one comes to the Father except through Me"* (John 14:6). Ultimately, all those who go their own way will learn of God's righteous way through His Son when they are judged by Him (v. 11).

In contrast, the redeemed walk according to God's word and yearn intensely to be with God: *"With my soul I have desired You in the night, yes, by my spirit within me I will seek You early; for when Your judgments are in the earth, the inhabitants of the world will learn righteousness"* (v. 9). No doubt verses 10-11 were an indictment by Isaiah against Judah's lethargic attitudes towards the things of God then. But the prophet's rebuke is good for us to consider also – are we yearning for God and for what pleases Him, or are we snubbing His righteousness? Longing for God's righteousness now or learning of God's righteousness too late clearly determines whether we receive God's lovingkindness or judicial wrath.

Verse 9 closely parallels the warning in verse 21: *"For behold, the Lord comes out of His place to punish the inhabitants of the earth for their iniquity; the earth will also disclose her blood, and will no more cover her slain."* This relates to the Tribulation Period and to the Judgment of Nations at its conclusion (i.e., at the second advent of Christ). The Lord will preserve a remnant of His covenant people safely *through* this time of worldwide judgment.

In contrast to Israel (which still must be refined and must receive Christ to become righteous in the Tribulation Period), we have the examples of Noah and Lot. Both "righteous" men were saved out of catastrophic judgment and thus did not perish with the wicked: *"The Lord knows how to deliver the godly out of temptations and to reserve the unjust under punishment for the day of judgment"* (2 Pet. 2:9).

This is exactly what the Lord promises the Church at Philadelphia: *"Because you have kept My command to persevere, I also will keep you from the hour of trial which shall come upon the whole world, to test those who dwell on the earth"* (Rev. 3:10). John acknowledges that the Church will be brought home prior to the Tribulation Period. The Greek preposition *ek* is rightly translated "keep...from" in this verse; if the Lord were to preserve the Church *through* the Tribulation (as with the Jewish remnant), the Greek preposition *dia* would be required. Although the Church will be taken to heaven before the Tribulation Period, there is no promise of God to preserve Gentiles who turn to Christ after that event. In fact, many of those new believers will be slaughtered during the Tribulation Period (Rev. 7:9-14, 13:5).

Two Dominions

Paul tells us in Romans 11 that God has always maintained a faithful Jewish remnant down through the centuries of Gentile oppression. (From Pentecost to the rapture of the Church just prior to the Tribulation Period, these would be a part of the Church.) Rather than complaining about their long hardship, the faithful remnant coming through the Tribulation Period will voice their approval (as a restored nation) of what God accomplished in them through their ordeal (vv. 12-13). The attitude of the remnant is commendable, and being under His dominion, they will enjoy God's presence and peace.

When we willingly permit God to have His way with us, we are always better off than we were before – not only do we become more like God in character, but we also draw closer to Him. The remnant in the Kingdom Age will recognize that all who sought to dominate them have perished and that the dominion of the "prince of this world" (John 12:31, 14:30, 16:11) and "the god of this age" (2 Cor. 4:4) has ended. In Christ's kingdom the nation will be spiritually revitalized and richly blessed (even having larger borders), and most importantly, God's name will be exalted through them (vv. 14-15).

Of course, God's chastening hand put the Jewish nation in distress for a long time before spiritual rejuvenation was achieved. At times their sorrows were so heavy that *"they could only whisper a prayer"* (v. 16; NASB). Isaiah likens the nation to a woman in the travail of childbirth: her labor must continue once it has begun (v. 17). But Israel's suffering was so drawn out that it seemed that she could give birth only to wind, meaning she could not deliver herself from her ongoing sorrows (v. 18). H. A. Ironside explains why Israel's high expectations of deliverance have yet to be achieved.

Sorrow and Comfort

From time to time during Israel's dispersion and suffering under Gentile domination there have been what seemed like birth pangs, but all expectations have ended in disappointment. Christ has not yet been born as far as their comprehension is concerned. But in that day they will be able to understand the full meaning of the prophecy in Isaiah 9:6: *"Unto us a child is born, unto us a son is given."* Then in their own consciousness they will recognize in Jesus the man-child who is to rule the nations with a rod of iron.[70]

After the travail of childbirth, a mother is comforted by the outcome of her hardship – her newborn child. However, for Israel this spiritual outcome of birth has never been realized; her inhabitants remain unbelieving and thus continue to perish in the world without Christ. Although it must have pained Isaiah to admit that point, he did have confidence that God would renew the Jewish nation at the commencement of the Kingdom Age through the giving of the Holy Spirit (Ezek. 36:26-27; Joel 2:28-29).

Like Isaiah, the prophet Jeremiah also equates the travail of the Jewish nation to a woman giving birth, but he focuses on the idea that pain precedes deliverance (Jer. 30:6-7). Jeremiah exhorted his countrymen to encourage themselves during this period of intense suffering called *"the time of Jacob's trouble"* because that meant the fulfillment of the remainder of his prophecy was imminent. Most of the unfulfilled Bible prophecies pertaining to the Jewish nation of Israel focus on this timeframe.

Isaiah's point here is that the solution to Israel's sorrows was not in self-deliverance (pictured in her endless childbearing travail), but in experiencing supernatural rejuvenation, including resurrection, which the prophet likens to the morning dew which comes from above to refresh the grass below (v. 19; Hosea 14:5). Israel's restoration will be preceded by the darkest time in their history, the Tribulation Period.

The Jews should remain faithful to God during this time, and they should hide until the world's wickedness has been fully revealed and divinely judged (vv. 20-21). God will protect this faithful remnant both in foreign lands (Ezek. 39:28-29), and also in a specific location near Israel which is off-limits to the Antichrist (Rev. 12:13-17). Israel is and will be God's special treasure hidden in the world until He digs it up and recovers it (Matt. 13:44).

Several other prophets address this same timeframe to provide us with a concise picture of what will happen to Israel: Zechariah informs us that two-thirds of the Jewish people will die during the Tribulation Period because of the Antichrist's hatred of them (Zech. 13:8-9). The remaining third will be protected from harm (1:18; Rev. 12:5-6, 13-17), will experience spiritual rebirth (Joel 2:28-29; Ezek. 36:23-28), and will be restored to their Messiah, the Lord Jesus Christ (Rom. 9:27). In fact, 144,000 Jews (12,000 from each of the twelve tribes) will be specifically sealed and protected by God to preach the kingdom gospel message throughout the entire world during the Tribulation (Matt. 24:14; Rev. 7:4-8, 14:1-5).

Resurrection

There are a variety of explanations for verse 19: *"Your dead shall live; together with my dead body they shall arise. Awake and sing, you who dwell in dust; for your dew is like the dew of herbs, and the earth shall cast out the dead."* Some commentators think Isaiah is figuratively speaking of Jewish captives being released from Babylon (they were dead so to speak while there) and returning to their homeland. Others say that verse 19 is speaking of Israel's future national and spiritual revitalization as prophetically pictured in Ezekiel's valley of dry bones (Ezek. 37). Paul also speaks of this event as a resurrection of sorts (Rom. 11:15). Some believe Isaiah is speaking about bodily resurrection to life (in contrast with the wicked that would not experience such a resurrection; v. 14). In this view Isaiah himself looked forward to resurrection and observing Israel's future and final national revival.

The main focus of debate is whether verse 19 is speaking literally of physical resurrection or metaphorically of Israel's national resurrection (e.g., Ezek. 37:12-14). It is observed that the translators added the words "together with" without a corresponding Hebrew text. Furthermore, W. E. Vine suggests that "my dead body" is used in a collective sense, and should be rendered as Darby does: *"Thy dead shall live, my dead bodies shall arise"* (JND). This understanding seems to follow Ezekiel's metaphoric depiction of Israel being brought back to life, after being politically and spiritually deceased, so to speak.

Whether verse 19 is speaking of literal or national resurrection is not a critical point, as the *first resurrection* pertaining to Jewish saints and Israel's spiritual rebirth both occur at Christ's second advent at the end of the Tribulation Period (Joel 2:27-32; Dan. 12:2). However, it is also possible that these Old Testament saints (e.g., Isaiah) may

Sorrow and Comfort

experience resurrection when the Church is glorified (Heb. 11:40), just prior to the Tribulation Period and will return with the Lord from heaven seven years later to witness Israel's deliverance and spiritual restoration (Rev. 19). In either case, Isaiah would be an eyewitness of God's completed work in the Jewish nation.

Like Isaiah, Job believed that he would eventually experience resurrection also: *"All the days of my hard service I will wait, till my change comes"* (Job 14:14). He also knew that in a future day he would be able to enjoy fellowship with his Redeemer in a body not riddled with boils:

> *For I know that my Redeemer lives, and He shall stand at last on the earth; and after my skin is destroyed, this I know, that in my flesh I shall see God, Whom I shall see for myself, and my eyes shall behold, and not another. How my heart yearns within me!* (Job 19:25-27).

Not having divine revelation on the topic of heaven, Old Testament saints, like Job, hoped to enjoy God's presence on the earth after escaping the cold confines of Sheol through resurrection (Job 19:26; Dan. 12:2). Old Testament saints understood that death was unavoidable and that beyond the grave their souls would be sequestered in a spiritual abode called Sheol. The Lord spoke of this place during His earthly sojourn: redeemed souls were consciously residing in Abraham's bosom, while the wicked were suffering in Hades (Luke 16:19-31). The realm of Abraham's bosom was emptied after Christ's resurrection (Matt. 27:52; 2 Cor. 5:8).

Though not afraid of death itself, David was not too enthusiastic about the finality of death or his future stay in Sheol: *"The sorrows of Sheol surrounded me; the snares of death confronted me"* (2 Sam. 22:6; Ps. 18:5). Yet, he rejoiced and hoped in his future resurrection from Sheol in a new body:

> *Therefore my heart is glad, and my glory rejoices; my flesh also will rest in hope. For You will not leave my soul in Sheol, nor will You allow Your Holy One to see corruption* (Ps. 16:9-10; also Ps. 86:13).

David is still waiting for his new resurrected body. His earlier body did see corruption in the grave, but the body of Jesus Christ, of whom David spoke prophetically, did not; He was raised up from the grave after three days. This event not only fulfilled David's words, but also indicates his hope for a future resurrection. This is why Old Testament saints do not speak about dying and going to heaven – that is a mystery, not revealed until the New Testament, as a result of Christ's finished work at Calvary (2 Cor. 5:8; Phil. 1:23). There is a day coming when the redeemed dead shall receive glorified bodies and shall stand with the restored nation of Israel to sing songs of praise to their Redeemer – the Lord Jesus Christ. May God guard our hearts and minds with His perfect peace until we are with Him forever.

Meditation

> Peace, perfect peace, in this dark world of sin?
> The blood of Jesus whispers peace within.
> Peace, perfect peace, with sorrows surging round?
> On Jesus' bosom naught but calm is found.
> Peace, perfect peace, death shadowing us and ours?
> Jesus has vanquished death and all its powers.
> It is enough: earth's struggles soon shall cease,
> And Jesus call us to Heaven's perfect peace.
>
> — Edward H. Bickersteth, Jr.

"In That Day"
Isaiah 27

The phrase "in that day" occurs four times in this chapter to highlight various attributes of Israel's future salvation in the Kingdom Age. It is used in verse 1 to connect the worldwide judgment in the previous verse (26:21) with its culmination. This chapter is a capstone over all the preceding judgments that pertained: to Israel (chps. 1-12), to the nations (chps. 13-23), and to the entire world (chps. 24-27).

The Enemy Vanquished

Using figurative language, Isaiah describes God taking a sword and slaying the twisted serpent of the sea – the Leviathan. If it were not for the end-time context of the passage, this word picture would be challenging to interpret. One possibility is that Isaiah is speaking of God wiping out three ancient empires that once occupied and oppressed Israel to symbolically indicate that He will remove any who oppose Israel in the Kingdom Age. F. C. Jennings cites Delitzsch to explain the metaphors accompanying this view:

> Let us grant that Delitzsch is correct, and that the "swift-flowing serpent" ("piercing serpent," AV) is Assyria, represented by the swift Tigris; and that "the crooked serpent" is Babylon, represented by the winding Euphrates; and that the "dragon in the sea" is Egypt, represented by the Nile, termed a "sea," as any expanse of water was.[71]

There is good agreement among commentators as to what God is accomplishing in this allegory, but wide speculation as to what various symbols depict. John A. Martin offers an explanation based on popular Semitic legend:

> With a sword the Lord will cut up a great serpent called Leviathan. This gliding, coiling serpent is the many-headed sea dragon

mentioned in Psalm 74:13-14. In Ugaritic literature (of Ugarit, a city-state in North Syria) reference is made to a similar seven-headed creature. Isaiah, though not believing this ancient Semitic myth, simply referred to Leviathan to convey his point (cf. Job 3:8). Leviathan, the twisting monster of the sea, was viewed in Ugaritic literature as an enemy of order in Creation. But the Lord can stop this chaotic state and establish order on the earth and in people's hearts. When God's judgment comes in that day, when He slays the wicked at the end of the Tribulation, it will be like His slaying the chaotic dragon Leviathan.[72]

Regardless of what the specific components of this allegory represent, Isaiah is poetically affirming that God will restore proper order in the earth which has been under Satan's devastating control. This parable is followed by a second "in that day" reference which announces the song of the vineyard (vv. 2-6).

The Song of the Vineyard

The previous song of the vineyard (5:1-7) spoke of Israel's unfaithfulness to God and the necessity of her destruction in Isaiah's day – the nation bore sour grapes unfit to refresh God's heart. In contrast, this song highlights God's protection and care of His new vineyard which causes it to bear delicious fruit for Him (vv. 2-3).

If any nation chose to plant briers and thorns in the vineyard (depicting rebellion against His care for Israel), then God, as a good Husbandman, would be obliged to rectify the situation (v. 4). God would rather bestow His peace and blessing on the repentant than His wrath on the wayward, but He will protect His vineyard at all cost (v. 5). At the end of the Tribulation Period, not just the Jewish nation will be restored to God, but many Gentiles will humbly turn to Jehovah for salvation also. Isaiah promises, *"Those who come He shall cause to take root in Jacob; Israel shall blossom and bud, and fill the face of the world with fruit"* (v. 6).

While the context of this vineyard prophecy highlights Israel's spiritual rebirth and fruitfulness in the Kingdom Age, Ezekiel tells us that this event will be accompanied by her literal agricultural prosperity also. Under Christ's rule, Israel will no longer be plagued with drought and famine, but the land will be abundantly fruitful (Ezek. 36:29-30). Likewise, the Jews and their livestock will multiply radically (Ezek. 36:10-11). Most importantly, their return to the land of Israel will be permanent (Ezek. 36:12), for God will not permit the nations to oppress His people ever again (Ezek. 36:15).

Scripture foretells Israel becoming an agricultural icon in the world, which to some degree has already occurred in recent years. Isaiah not only speaks of this agricultural achievement, but also associates the timing of this complete revitalization to when Jehovah gathers His people out of the nations to worship Him in Jerusalem (v. 13). Though the Jewish nation has not fully returned to Israel (Ezek. 39:28), nor do they yet worship their Messiah (they have not taken root yet, v. 6), the process of gathering them back "one by one" has apparently already begun (v. 12). A century ago less than one percent of all Jews in the world lived in the holy land, but today forty-four percent of all Jews worldwide reside in Israel.[73]

Isaiah later writes again of Israel's future agricultural prosperity: *"The wilderness and the wasteland shall be glad for them, and the desert shall rejoice and blossom as the rose"* (35:1). After 2,500 plus years of having no homeland, the Jewish people became a political reality again within their ancient homeland in May 1948. A marked increase in agricultural productivity commenced at that time. From 1950 to 1984, the amount of irrigated land in Israel increased from fifteen to fifty-four percent and agricultural production has expanded sixteenfold (more than three times the rate of the population growth).

Seventy-five years ago, Israel was full of malarial swamps and deserts. Today, farms in Israel are bearing three and four bountiful crops a year and the replanted forests are thriving. After centuries of being mostly unproductive, Israel has become an agricultural marvel. However, Isaiah and Ezekiel tell us that what God will accomplish in the Millennial Kingdom will go beyond the present laws of nature – Israel will be the breadbasket of the world (35:1-7; Ezek. 47:1-12; Amos 9:13-14).

Desolation and Dispersion First

Israel becoming a spiritually fruitful vineyard in the Kingdom Age is a fitting testimony to what God can accomplish despite human failure. However, this future fruitful outcome will not be possible without severe divine chastening beforehand (v. 7). Isaiah's point here is that God has promised to deal differently with His covenant people's failures than with the failure of the nations. The prophet Amos explains why God treats the Jews differently than other people groups: *"You only have I known of all the families of the earth; therefore I will punish you for all your iniquities"* (Amos 3:2). God relates to the Jewish nation through a covenant of love (Ezek. 16:1-10). He promises not to deal with her as an enemy to be eradicated, but rather will teach her the error of her ways through warfare and exile (v. 8; Deut. 28:64-68).

Hence, the strong east wind in verse 8 likely refers to the Babylonian conquest in the next century which would sweep across Judah from the northeast and result in the exile of many Jews. The main purpose of this invasion was to destroy Israel's altar stones and Asherah poles that had been set up to honor false gods (v. 9). Paganism originated in Babylon and God was going to return Israel's idols to that place. Later He would retrieve Israel from exile, a now purified people back to the Promised Land.

The prophet Ezekiel says that these returning Jews (those who have been purged of their idols) foretell a similar future event when the entire nation would receive the Holy Spirit and never again rebel against the Lord. This will occur in the Millennial Kingdom. Israel's difficulties in Isaiah and Ezekiel's day resulted from a heart problem – their love for Jehovah had grown cold and they were no longer in awe of Him. God promised to fix that problem so His people could always enjoy His presence and communion. So while the returning Jews from Babylon had a change of heart concerning their idols and other detestable things, this transformation was only partial. God's ultimate solution of spiritual regeneration would occur later and nationally through the New Covenant (Ezek. 11:18-19). Only then will His covenant people have the wherewithal to walk in His statues and commandments forever (Ezek. 11:20). Those not experiencing this transformation will be judged for their rebellious ways (Ezek. 11:21).

Consequently, the Babylonian invasion would have severe ramifications. Israel's fortified city (i.e., Jerusalem) would be destroyed and the entire region devastated (v. 10). Because of His jealous anger, God would not be moved to show compassion to His covenant people when the Babylonians came. The resulting calamity would be so vast that cattle would be forced to graze among Jerusalem's ruins and strip the trees of their bark to survive and women would then gather the bare branches for firewood (v. 11).

Final Deliverance

The Spirit of God now moves past the Babylonian captivity and all the centuries of Jewish heartache to speak of Israel's final deliverance. At the end of the Tribulation Period (i.e., in that day), *"the Lord will thresh, from the channel of the River to the Brook of Egypt; and you will be gathered one by one, O you children of Israel"* (v. 12). Before God resettles His dispersed people in the region of Israel, He first must prepare the land for them through the judgment of Jewish oppressors. (This will occur at the Judgment of Nations at the conclusion of the Tribulation Period.) God will completely cleanse from all defilement the land set aside for Israel's possession. Then the Jewish nation will receive what was promised to Abraham long ago (Gen. 15:18), the region between the Euphrates in the east (Assyria) to the Wadi El-Arish in the southwest (Egypt).

In that day, God will blow a trumpet to summon His dispersed people hiding in Egypt, Assyria, and throughout the world to return to Palestine; they will worship and commune with Him in Jerusalem (v. 13). Revelation chapters 8-11 record seven distinct trumpet blasts that signal various judgments on the earth during the Tribulation Period. As stated in Revelation 12, God will preserve a remnant of the Jewish nation during this time, and then, at the last trumpet blast of the Tribulation Period, *every* Jew will be gathered back to the land of Israel (Ezek. 39:28-29). This refined remnant will then receive the Holy Spirit and God will finally have His fruitful vineyard on the same holy hill He set apart for it long ago (Jerusalem).

At this time the words of the prophet Zechariah will be fulfilled:

> *Thus says the Lord of hosts: "I am zealous for Jerusalem and for Zion with great zeal. I am exceedingly angry with the nations at ease; for I was a little angry, and they helped -- but with evil intent." ... "I am returning to Jerusalem with mercy; My house shall be built in it ... My cities shall again spread out through prosperity; the Lord will again comfort Zion, and will again choose Jerusalem"* (Zech. 1:14-17).

So much for Replacement Theology – the Lord is going to return to Jerusalem with mercy and comfort. He will reestablish His covenant people of old in the land He set aside for them and He will remain with them and they will worship Him in His temple! This is Israel's hope, not the Church's. Dark times will precede the curtain call of the Church

Age (2 Thess. 2:3), yet believers have the hope of their *Bright and Morning Star* (Rev. 22:16). He shall come for His beloved bride just moments before the dawning of the Day of the Lord, and then the *Sun of Righteousness* (Mal. 4:2) shall rise in His full fury and flood the earth with His glory!

Meditation:

> In hope we lift our wishful, longing eyes,
> Waiting to see the Morning Star arise;
> How bright, how gladsome will His advent be,
> Before the Sun shines forth in majesty!
>
> How will our eyes to see His face delight,
> Whose love has cheered us through the darksome night!
> How will our ears drink in His well-known voice,
> Whose faintest whispers make our soul rejoice!
>
> — James G. Deck

Refusing to Believe
Isaiah 28

In the previous section (chps. 13-27), Isaiah pronounced a series of "woes" on the nations to declare God's disdain for the proud and for those who had oppressed Israel. Many of these judgments have already occurred, but all will have their complete fulfillment in the Kingdom Age. In chapters 28-33, Isaiah switches back to the tumultuous political situation of his day; the key question being – would the Jews trust in Jehovah or the Egyptians to thwart the Assyrian invasion?

The prophet launches into a new series of five messages, which contain six woes levied on various groups within Israel who were rejecting his prophetic messages and warnings (28:1; 29:1; 29:15; 30:1; 31:1; 33:1). He rebukes Israel's leaders for thinking that either their wealth (chp. 28), their vain religiosity (chp. 29), or their foreign alliances (chps. 29-30) would save them from the Assyrian invasion. Only Israel's God could deliver Israel from Gentile oppression and, ultimately, that would be through His chosen Deliverer, the Messiah, at the conclusion of the Tribulation Period (chps. 31-32).

It becomes evident that with this series of oracles, Isaiah has established a routine to further encourage Israel to trust in the Lord. The prophet concluded his first series of messages to Israel (chps. 1-12) by referring to their regathering to worship God in Jerusalem (12:6). Likewise, the prophet's second series of messages to the nations finished with the same promise (27:13). Clearly by design, this third series of messages to the wayward in Israel ends with the same decree (35:10). Though Israel's chastening would be long and burdensome, the prophet consistently reminds his countrymen that it will not last forever. Eventually, and at the appropriate time, God will fulfill all His promises to the Jewish patriarchs; their descendants will be blessed in the Promised Land and they will worship Jehovah in Jerusalem unhindered by anyone.

Isaiah's first woe is directed at two groups of people: the Northern Kingdom (Ephraim; vv. 1-13) and then the Southern Kingdom (Judah; vv. 14-29).

The Northern Kingdom

Twice the prophet addresses the capital city of the Northern Kingdom, Samaria, which was *"at the head of the verdant valleys"* (v. 1) and *"the crown of pride, to the drunkards of Ephraim"* (v. 3). This region of Israel was known for its fertile valleys and beautiful, flowering countryside, but God was about to severely judge the land by the Assyrians and change its esthetic landscape (vv. 1-3).

The Assyrian invasion would be like a powerful hailstorm that would pulverize Ephraim's beauty. Indeed her flowering wreath of pride, Samaria, *"will be trampled underfoot"* (v. 3). Samaria's fall is likened to *"the first fruit before the summer, which an observer sees; he eats it up while it is still in his hand"* (v. 4). In the same way that the early fig (ripening in June) would be spotted, plucked, and eaten with greediness and haste, so shall Samaria be seized and destroyed by its enemies. Although the Lord extended a measure of grace to withstand the Assyrian siege for three years (v. 6; perhaps as an opportunity for repentance), the Northern Kingdom would not be protected against the Assyrians and all Ephraim's boasting would be a fading glory.

Isaiah then imposes the *"in that day"* terminology from the last chapter to contrast with the previous verses: In the Kingdom Age, Israel will consider the Lord Almighty as their *beautiful diadem*; He is much more glorious than a withering wreath of beautiful foliage, for His splendor never diminishes (vv. 5-6). The remnant will not be ensnared by vanity; rather than glorying in their feeble achievements, they will extol God's greatness.

Isaiah's exhortation to avoid the pride of seeking empty glory is still pertinent today. Paul likewise exhorted the church at Philippi, which was thriving and doctrinally sound, not to be lifted up in "vain glory":

> *Fulfill my joy by being likeminded, having the same love, being of one accord, of one mind. Let nothing be done through selfish ambition or conceit, but in lowliness of mind let each esteem others better than himself. Let each of you look out not only for his own interests, but also for the interests of others* (Phil. 2:2-4).

Sorrow and Comfort

How is it possible for believers from different cultural and social backgrounds, with unique problems and difficulties, to have one mind? The answer is revealed in the next verse, which exhorts, *"Let this mind be in you, which was also in Christ Jesus"* (Phil. 2:5). When all believers have the lowly mind of Christ, we will be of one mind. It is a mindset that is not puffed up in vain glory, but is focused on the needs of others. Christ was the Servant of servants before He was the King of kings (Phil. 2:6-10). Let this mind be in you.

Returning to the narrative, Isaiah explains why the Northern Kingdom is in such a pathetic spiritual condition – their leaders (including the prophets and priests) were intoxicated much of the time. Instead of properly caring for the people, they sat at banqueting tables covered with vomit and while in their drunken stupor they claimed to receive further revelations from God (vv. 7-8). Obviously these men were false prophets and would reap God's vengeance for leading His people astray.

These so-called prophets were offended by Isaiah's message; after all, they were adults and Isaiah was rebuking them as foolish children (vv. 9-10). So they mocked Isaiah by speaking back to him the same child-like message he had given them: *"precept upon precept, precept upon precept, line upon line, line upon line, here a little, there a little"* (v. 10). This was toddler-talk, the most basic message of dos and don'ts that might be taught to a young child. To summarize, Isaiah's audience, Ephraim, did not want to hear his message, nor did they esteem him as a true prophet of God. Rather they jeered and derided him.

The Sign of the Unknown Tongue

Isaiah then warned Ephraim that if they did not want to hear God's simple message through him, the Lord would deliver it again through a foreign nation whose tongue they did not understand (speaking of the Assyrians; vv. 11-13). A little over a century after this, the men of Judah rejected Jeremiah's call to submit to the Babylonians (Jer. 27). He warned that if they did not do so, Jerusalem would be destroyed and the nation would be exiled to Babylon (Jer. 22:5-10; 25:8-11). This demonstrates that God was willing to temper His discipline if His people humbly accepted His chastening.

The Jews hated this message and, in time, plotted to kill God's messenger, Jeremiah (Jer. 26:7-24). The people would not listen; they accused Jeremiah and the other godly prophets of being full of wind

(Jer. 5:13). In response to this accusation, God declared that His words would instead be like a fire that would consume both the people and the land. The people would know that judgment was near when they heard a language that they did not recognize (Jer. 5:14-15). Eventually, Babylon destroyed Judah's best fortifications and battlements. Without the Lord's assistance to preserve them, the Jews had no hope of thwarting God's instrument of justice against them.

The sign of the unknown tongue is used throughout Scripture as a warning to the Jewish people of imminent judgment. Moses told the people that if they rebelled against the Lord, He would punish them through a nation whose language they would not understand (Deut. 28:49). This meant that God would use an army from a distant land instead of a neighboring nation. As we have just witnessed, Isaiah warned idolatrous Israel by imposing this sign just prior to the Assyrian invasion (vv. 11-12) and Jeremiah referenced it as a final warning to Judah of imminent judgment for the same deeply-rooted sin (Jer. 5:15). But the Jews ignored the warnings of Moses, Isaiah, and Jeremiah; the sign of the unknown tongue was issued and severe judgment ultimately came. Yet, this was not the last time God would use the sign of an unknown tongue to alert the Jews of impending judgment for their unfaithfulness.

According to Acts 2:9-11, at least ten specific languages were heard in Jerusalem at the Feast of Pentecost, just after Christ's ascension into heaven. This was the day the Church Age began (Acts 2:4; 1 Cor. 12:13). The Holy Spirit came to the believers as promised by the Lord Jesus, baptized them into the body of Christ, bestowed spiritual gifts on them, and enabled them to supernaturally serve the Lord. This event served two main purposes. First, it verified in the sight of the Jews that the apostles were continuing the ministry of Christ and were doing so by His power (Acts 2:22). Second, it served as a final warning to the nation of Israel to repent and turn to God through Christ (1 Cor. 14:23). As a nation, they had rejected and crucified their Messiah, but, as individuals, they now had the opportunity to be saved. Unavoidable judgment was coming upon the nation of Israel, and trusting Christ for salvation was the only way for them to obtain God's forgiveness.

In A.D. 70, that crushing judgment came. A vast Roman army of about 70,000 soldiers was led by the future Emperor Titus to besiege and conquer Jerusalem. The temple, that had been built by the Jewish captives who returned from Babylon towards the end of the sixth century B.C. and that had then been renovated by Herod the Great some five centuries later, was destroyed. There were to be no more offerings, or sacrifices, no Levitical priesthood, or stench of humanized religion in the nostrils of Jehovah. Even to this day, although the Jews are back in their land and are a self-governing nation, they have no temple or priesthood to reinstate what God put away. This is how the message in tongues is presented in Scripture – it was a message delivered in a foreign language to warn Israel of God's imminent judgment if they did not repent.

God told Isaiah that Ephraim would not heed His message; they would not choose to rest in Him and be refreshed. Therefore, Ephraim would *"fall backward, be injured and snared and captured"* (v. 13). The Lord would deliver this punitive message through the Assyrians, who spoke a language unknown to the Hebrews.

The Southern Kingdom

In verse 14, Isaiah turns his attention to the Southern Kingdom by addressing Judah's leaders who should have been guiding God's people in the godliness of His laws, but were not. Rather, these men had sealed a secret "covenant with death and Sheol" (probably referring to the false gods of Egypt) to save them from the Assyrians but God knew all about it:

> *We have made a covenant with death, and with Sheol we are in agreement. When the overflowing scourge passes through, it will not come to us, for we have made lies our refuge, and under falsehood we have hidden ourselves* (v. 15).

John A. Martin suggests that Isaiah was using imagery rich in the symbolism of Semitic mythology to indict Judah:

> In the Ugaritic pantheon, death was personified as the god of the underworld. The Jerusalem leaders were trusting in other gods to save them from the coming scourge, the Assyrian invasion. However, to trust in false gods was futile.[74]

By revealing their secret allegiance, Jehovah was demonstrating His superiority over the gods that Judah was covertly trusting in. However, Isaiah says that it is God alone who sets the cornerstone and foundation of salvation and all who trust in it (Him) will not be ashamed of doing so: *"Behold, I lay in Zion a stone for a foundation, a tried stone, a precious cornerstone, a sure foundation; whoever believes will not act hastily"* (v. 16). Notice that the cornerstone is tried, precious, and sure and therefore typifies Christ's faithfulness, proven impeccability, and fruitful ministry.

The Lord Jesus Christ is often likened to a stone in Scripture to portray either His character, His work, or how others respond to Him. For example, He was the Rock struck by God's rod in the wilderness so Moses could supply life-sustaining water for the thirsty Israelites (Ex. 17:1-6; compare with John 4:6-14, 7:37-39). He was the Rock of Offense, the rejected Cornerstone over which the nation of Israel stumbled at His first advent to earth (1 Pet. 2:6-8). He is the Rock of Strength (Deut. 32:4) and the Foundation Stone of the Church (1 Cor. 3:11). For those who will not trust in Him, He will be the Smiting Stone (Dan. 2:44-45) and a Grinding Stone (Matt. 21:44-45). Isaiah's message to Judah is simple: Those who trust in God's cornerstone alone for salvation will experience God's eternal peace and joy – these will be gladly broken upon their divine Stone!

As God's salvation can be received only through faith in revealed truth, He had a twofold solution for Judah's secret doings: First, their lie would be swept away (v. 17) and their covenant with death annulled (v. 18). Second, He would chasten them day after day with a scourge (the Assyrians) until they realized the utter futility of seeking the protection of false gods (v. 19). Isaiah likened the inadequacy of resting in false gods to lying in a bed shorter than one's stature and trying to wrap up with a narrow blanket to stay warm. As Albert Barnes explains, it just does not work (v. 20)!

> This is evidently a proverbial saying, and means that they would find all their places of defense insufficient to secure them. They seek repose and security – as a man lies down to rest at night. But they find neither. His bed furnishes no rest; his scanty covering furnishes no security from the chills of the night. So it would be with those who sought protection in idols, in the promises of false prophets, and in the aid which might be obtained from Egypt. So it is with sinners. Their vain refuges shall not shield them. The bed on which they seek rest shall give them no repose; the covering with which they seek to clothe themselves shall not defend them from the wrath of God.[75]

Sorrow and Comfort

The point is: it is best to rest in the Lord and not in a human haven (a short bed) with inadequate benefit (covering)!

Although Judah would not be fully conquered by Assyria, the invasion would sweep over Mount Perazim (which was connected with the Valley of Rephaim to the west of Jerusalem) and the Valley of Gibeon northwest of Jerusalem. This invasion would be enabled by the Lord in the same way He had previously empowered the Israelites to vanquish the Canaanites in the Valley of Gibeon (Josh. 10:10-14) and David to overcome the Philistines in the Valley of Rephaim (2 Sam. 5:20-21). This foretold outcome should be sufficient to convince Isaiah's skeptical audience that his message was from the Lord God (vv. 21-22). In 701 B.C. the Assyrians did invade and conquer these regions of Judah.

In verse 21, Isaiah calls our attention to the fact that God's anger and subsequent wrath are not part of His primary work. God's anger leading to acts of judgment is a necessary aspect of God's sovereignty, but His usual and normal work arises from His gracious, loving nature.

> *For the Lord will rise up as at Mount Perazim, He will be angry as in the Valley of Gibeon – that He may do His work, His awesome work, and bring to pass His act, His **unusual act** (v. 21).*

> *The Lord will rise up as he did at Mount Perazim, He will rouse himself as in the Valley of Gibeon – to do His work, **His strange work**, and perform His task, **His alien task** (v. 21 NIV).*

God's anger prompts His secondary (unusual) work. It is not that righteous wrath is less noble than divine love, for each necessitates the other, but God would rather shower His people with blessings than be angry with them. Amen!

Isaiah concludes his first woe message in this series with a farming analogy so as to instill hope and provide comfort to the afflicted, faithful remnant. God is the Master Farmer: He knows when and how long to plow (i.e., trials have a discrete duration to accomplish the best result). He also rightly discerns when to plant (to ensure good germination and proper growing time), how to plant (sowing in rows or scattering), and what to plant (to obtain His desired harvest; vv. 23-26). This means that God skillfully chooses the type of discipline and other factors of correction to lead us heavenward and to accomplish His purposes in the best way possible.

Furthermore, the Lord knows the most productive means of obtaining what He wants from us and removing what is undesirable. Correspondingly, the way the Farmer harvests wheat, separates the chaff from it and stores it in His barn is much different than the process used for obtaining and preserving delicate spices (vv. 27-28). The Lord knows how to best work with His people to get out of them what He desires!

The Southern Kingdom therefore should not trust in false gods, but in *"the Lord of hosts, who is wonderful in counsel and excellent in guidance"* (v. 29). We should also trust in His sovereign care.

Meditation

In contemplation of the vast treasury of Old Testament prophecies, it is quite obvious that Israel does have the hope of glory. We agree with the prophet Isaiah's assessment of the Kingdom Age: *"In that day the Lord of hosts will be for a crown of glory and a diadem of beauty to the remnant of His people"* (v. 5). Israel's only hope is centered in the second coming of their Messiah, the Lord Jesus Christ, whom they previously rejected!

O Israel, hope in the Lord; for with the Lord there is mercy, and with Him is abundant redemption. And He shall redeem Israel from all his iniquities (Ps. 130:7-8).

Choosing to Be Blind
Isaiah 29

Isaiah continues his rebuke against Judah from the previous chapter in his second and third of six "woe" decrees in this section. The prophet again states that the Assyrian invasion will cause havoc in Judah and will threaten Jerusalem, but would be averted by the Lord. No such promise was given to the Northern Kingdom. *Ariel* is another name for Jerusalem, which Isaiah has not used previously.

Siege and Rescue

To Jerusalem, the prophet says, *"Add year to year; let feasts come around"* (v. 1). Isaiah's sarcasm was to show the irony of doing thoughtless religious activities year after year. Ariel was David's home and the location where the Jews held their feasts and offered sacrifices. Apparently nostalgia, and not devotion, prompted the Jews to continue these observances as mere formalities.

Ariel means "altar hearth" or "lion of God," which by implication means *heroic* or *strong*. In Ezekiel 43:16, Ariel is associated with the altar. Jerusalem was Judah's stronghold and place of worship, which Isaiah says would suffer distress because of a long siege and because of being pounded with battering-rams (v. 2).

Although the Assyrians would surround Jerusalem, God was clearly inferring that He was the One directing their attack: *"I will encamp against you all around, I will lay siege against you with a mound, and I will raise siege-works against you"* (v. 3). Can man fight with God and win? No. But Isaiah says the purpose of this attack (i.e., by Sennacherib in 701 B.C.) was not to destroy Jerusalem, but to teach her humility (v. 4). Jerusalem prided herself in her own strength, but soon she would learn the value of a *"low"* position and of *"speaking out of the ground."*

Though the multitude of the *"terrible ones"* was like the *"dust of the earth,"* the Lord would vanquish them *"in an instant, suddenly"* with powerful awe-inspiring means (vv. 5-6). This prophecy refers to

Devotions in Isaiah

the sudden destruction of the Assyrian army in one night as recorded in Isaiah 37.

The Lord continues to speak in the first person in verses 7-8, but the focus of His wrath changes from a single nation, Assyria, to *"the multitude of all the nations who fight against Ariel"* (v. 7). There would be a coming day in which a large-scale invasion of many nations would threaten Jerusalem's existence, but the Lord would suddenly come and vanquish that enemy (v. 8).

The prophet elegantly poses "dream" imagery to express two ideas: First, to express the great yearning of Sennacherib to vanquish Jerusalem. He was like a hungry and thirsty man who dreams of food and drink, but awakens from sleep still unfulfilled. Second, Isaiah indicates that the Lord's deliverance will be so sudden, it will be like being abruptly awakened in the midst of a dream, and, before it is forgotten, the dreamer realizes that what was dreamt was not real. While the Assyrian invasion is in the foreground of verses 7-8, the reference to *"the multitude of all the nations"* attacking Jerusalem better describes a much later event – the second advent of Christ to deliver Jerusalem from the Antichrist and his armies.

Both Zechariah and John describe this horrific future scene for us: Jerusalem will have been conquered and half the city enslaved when Christ returns from heaven to protect His covenant people and to destroy the Antichrist (Zech. 14:2-3). He will land on the Mount of Olives and will split the mountain in half, such that a river of water will flow to the east and to the west out of the newly formed ravine (Zech. 14:4-8). The returning Messiah will be King over the whole earth (Zech. 14:9). He will cause the Jews' oppressors to fight each other and then cause their bodies to dissolve where they stand (Zech. 14:12-13). John provides the number of those soldiers gathered in the Jezreel Valley for the battle of Armageddon: 200,000,000 (Rev. 9:16). He then explains that the entire valley will become a giant winepress, for when Christ destroys this great army, their blood will freely flow out of its basin for 182 miles (Rev. 14:19-20). By the sword out of His mouth (His words) the Lord Jesus will dissolve in a moment of time all of Israel's enemies where they stand.

Judah's Spiritual Condition

Sadly, Judah was in such a poor spiritual condition that they could not comprehend Isaiah's message concerning God's sudden

Sorrow and Comfort

intervention to deliver them from Assyria. The Jewish prophets could neither read nor understand what Isaiah had written on a scroll because they, through disobedience, had chosen to ignore the truth and to remain blind (vv. 9-10). God responded by deepening that blindness, for without the help of the Holy Spirit man cannot understand the things of God (1 Cor. 2:9-14). As a result, Israel's prophets were illiterate in the things of God (vv. 11-12). So when Isaiah says, *"the book is delivered,"* he was implying that Israel's prophets were just as ignorant of the true meaning of God's revelation as a man was of the contents of a book he was unable to read. When it comes to knowing God's will, ignorance is not bliss; it is always damaging.

Spiritual blindness clouds human reasoning, perverts logic, and distorts our perception of reality. This is why, in spiritual matters, man must ignore sight-based faith and mutable feelings, and must simply trust God at His word; this is true faith and the only kind that pleases God (Heb. 11:6). God rewards true faith by opening our eyes to deeper spiritual truth; naturally speaking, we cannot understand the things of God without His help (1 Cor. 2:14). The Lord Jesus told His disciples, *"Know the truth, and the truth shall make you free"* (John 8:32). God has offered mankind a choice – to hide in the calamity of darkness and experience eternal death, or to abide in divine light and experience life in and with God. There can be no fellowship with God in darkness!

Judah was still holding on to the religious form that the Law demanded, but there was no sincerity in their prayers, offerings, feasts, etc. They were religious but not spiritual, and God rebukes them for their vain piety:

> *Inasmuch as these people draw near with their mouths and honor Me with their lips, but have removed their hearts far from Me, and their fear toward Me is taught by the commandment of men* (v. 13).

Dear believer, how close is your heart to God's? Are you merely performing futile religious routines because you know you should or because others do? Or are you motivated to experience the wonder of God's presence and the power of His essence? Do you yearn to know God more deeply through His Word and to have daily enjoyment in Him? God longs to demonstrate the wonder of Himself to those who will draw near to Him, but woe to those who snub God's *"marvelous work and a wonder"* and cause others to ignore Him also (v. 14). They will be judged and their vain wisdom will vanish. God was going to cause such a calamity that even the most experienced and wisest of the Jews would be baffled. Thus *"the wisdom of their wise men shall perish."* The Jews in Isaiah's day were ignoring their spiritual deadness and sinfulness; until they saw their problem as God did, they could not experience His deliverance, His fellowship, or His goodness.

> Those whimpering Stateside young people will wake up on the Day of Judgment condemned to worse fates than these demon-fearing Indians, because, having a Bible, they were bored with it – while these never heard of such a thing.
>
> — Jim Elliot

Man has no choice in being a part of God's plan, but as a moral and a conscious being, he has every choice in how he will answer God's call and how he will be used within God's unfolding design. Whether or not we yield to His call, God will be glorified through our choices; He will use us either as vessels of mercy prepared for glory, or as vessels of wrath fit for destruction (Rom. 9:14-23). God prepares yielded vessels for glory and rebellious vessels prepare themselves to receive His wrath.

For instance, God did not force Pharaoh to worship Egyptian gods, but He did intervene to harden Pharaoh's heart on certain occasions in order to accomplish the release of His people from Egypt. The fact that Pharaoh hardened his own heart afterwards (some ten times) demonstrates he still had free choice in the matter. God would have been perfectly just to destroy a pagan like Pharaoh, but instead He designed ten specific plagues to prove to Pharaoh that He was superior to a number of specific Egyptian gods. Pharaoh rejected this revelation and hardened his own heart against the Lord – he proved himself to be a vessel of wrath fit for destruction. God brought glory to His name by honoring Pharaoh's decision, which God already foreknew. This example shows how human responsibility and sovereign design work cooperatively to ensure that God will receive all the glory in every situation. Isaiah puts the matter this way to introduce his third woe in this series of messages:

> *Woe to those who seek deep to hide their counsel far from the Lord, and their works are in the dark; they say, "Who sees us?" and, "Who knows us?" Surely you have things turned around! Shall the potter be*

Sorrow and Comfort

esteemed as the clay; for shall the thing made say of him who made it, "He did not make me"? Or shall the thing formed say of him who formed it, "He has no understanding" (vv. 15-16)?

A vessel is used to hold or to transport something – it is what a vessel does and not what it is that is important. Consequently, Scripture refers to individuals as vessels and states that God will use both the yielded and the rebellious vessels to work His eternal purposes and to uphold His glory. The prophet was warning those who attempt to conceal their "true" intentions under a credible religious veneer, who look good outwardly. To exchange mere formality for true spirituality was *"turning things around"* (we would say "upside down"). Hence, *"Woe to those who seek deep to hide their counsel far from the Lord, and their works are in the dark,"* as God sees beyond showmanship into a person's heart. He knows who are truly yielded vessels fit for glory and who are not – God cannot be conned!

On this point, Paul implores Timothy to flee youthful lusts so he will be a vessel of honor fit for God's intended use (2 Tim. 2:21). God fashions perfectly, but we can corrupt what He creates for Himself. For Isaiah's audience to say that God does not see their plans, and does not control their doings would be as absurd as a clay jar accusing the Potter who fashioned it of being ignorant. In fact, it was not God who was uninformed, but the people who chose to be oblivious of His ways.

In the Christian experience it is only through submitting to God's ongoing work of sanctification that one is able to know God's purpose for his or her life. Without the work of sanctification, service to God is impossible. A servant is not defined by fanciful words or good intentions. His or her character is the message. A Christian who lacks Christ-likeness will fail miserably in representing Christ to the lost. May the divine Potter have His way with each of us and may each vessel He fashions glisten with sovereign grace for all to see!

Judah's Future Transformation

Isaiah concludes his third woe message by stating that in the Kingdom Age, *"in a little while"* from God's perspective, Israel would be such a vessel of honor (vv. 17-24). In that day, there will be no spiritual blindness and no poverty, but rather there will be understanding of the truth and fruitfulness. All the inhabitants of the earth will rejoice in the Lord – *"the Holy One of Israel"* (vv. 17-19).

Devotions in Isaiah

There will be good reason to rejoice, because the Lord will cut off the beast (the Antichrist) and will judge all those who followed him in persecuting Israel: *"For the terrible one is brought to nothing, the scornful one is consumed, and all who watch for iniquity are cut off"* (v. 20; Rev. 19:11-21). No scoffer, swindler, liar, or distorter of justice will be permitted in Christ's kingdom. The poor in spirit shall be exalted, and those who oppressed them will be judged (vv. 20-21).

At that time, the attitude of the Jewish nation (Jacob) will be changed forever. No longer will they need to be ashamed of their waywardness or be humbled by foreign invaders because of disobedience. Instead, they will honor and rejoice in the Lord and His Word (vv. 22-24). Never again will *"Jacob's face now grow pale"* with fear and disappointments!

While in earnest prayer, Daniel acknowledged the sins of the Jewish nation, which had resulted in their *"shame of face"* (Dan. 9:8). God had a much higher calling for the Jewish people; they were to stand forth as *"a light to the Gentiles, that You should be My salvation to the ends of the earth"* (49:6). Israel was to be a great witness to the entire world of God's faithfulness, mercy, and longsuffering. However, in their rebellious condition, the Jews did not represent God by being a holy people – the outcome of which was shame. In the Millennial Kingdom, the Jewish nation will heed instruction and will be all that God desired them to be from the beginning – a beacon of light to reflect His Glory to all nations.

Meditation

> Darkness is my point of view, my right to myself; light is God's point of view.
>
> — Oswald Chambers

Rebellious Children
Isaiah 30

The fourth (chp. 30) and fifth (chp. 31) woes in this series of messages are directed toward Judah, who was seeking an alliance with Egypt to thwart the Assyrian threat – this was against God's will (v. 2). The irony of the situation was that the Egyptian Empire was in decline and would be a weak ally anyway. Why would Judah's leadership be more willing to trust a declining nation that had repeatedly oppressed them rather than their God who had consistently loved them and knew what was best for them? The fact that Egypt was in such a weakened state made Judah's decision even more insulting to the Lord.

Rebellion Against God

"The Holy One of Israel" occurs three times in this chapter, as in Isaiah 41. No other chapter in the Bible has more references to this title of God. In contrast to God's holiness, His "rebellious children" were not holy. They did not seek counsel from Him, nor did they permit the Holy Spirit to guide their plans (v. 1). A delegation from Judah traveled to two Egyptian cities (Zoan and Hanes) seeking to establish an alliance (v. 4). This pursuit of an alliance was in direct rebellion against God's revealed word, and as a result, the Jews were *adding sin to sin* (v. 1)! Albert Barnes notes an important application drawn from this situation: "Sins do not usually stand alone. When one is committed, it is often necessary to commit others in order to carry out and complete the plan which was contemplated."[76] Judah's leaders were not following the Lord and were causing others to stray from Him too.

Without God directing us in life, we go our own way and, unavoidably, make a mess of things. Isaiah promised that Judah's decision to seek help from Egypt, who could not assist them, would lead to their shame and humiliation (vv. 3, 5). H. A. Ironside admonishes Christians to learn from Israel's mistake:

May we not see in Judah's attitude a lesson for ourselves today? How apt we are in times of stress to depend on some human expedient instead of relying on the living God! It is always an evidence of declension when Christians look to the world for help rather than turning to the Lord Himself, who may be chastening them because of unjudged sin. He always stands ready to meet His people in grace (1 John 1:9). ... But we are prone to forget this and to try to find a way out of our difficulties by human means instead of reliance on the omnipotent God.[77]

As Abraham learned long ago, when God's people venture into Egypt (a symbol of *humanism*) to resolve life's difficulties, it always costs more than what was hoped to be gained.

Isaiah says that in journeying to Egypt, the Jewish envoy and their donkeys laden with riches would risk being attacked by dangerous wild beasts of the Negev (e.g., lions and vipers) and, of course, by bandits (v. 6). All this effort to secure Egyptian support would be of no benefit to Judah in thwarting the Assyrian invasion: *"For the Egyptians shall help in vain and to no purpose. Therefore I have called her Rahab-Hem-Shebeth"* (v. 7). John A. Martin explains the meaning of the expressions "Rahab-Hem-Shebeth":

In Ugaritic literature Rahab was the name of a female sea monster associated with Leviathan. Perhaps the hippopotamus, an animal that often sits in the water of the Nile doing nothing, represents that mythical water beast. Understandably Rahab came to be a poetic synonym for Egypt (and also for a demon behind Egypt) when God overpowered the Egyptian soldiers in the sea at the Exodus. So Egypt, Isaiah wrote, was good for nothing; she could not assist Judah in any way.[78]

Whether the hippopotamus is the Leviathan that God speaks to Job about is doubtful (Job 41), but the symbolism of this Ugaritic legend fits the context of the verse – Egypt would be like the do-nothing mythical water beast.

Because the Jews were acting like rebellious children who would not heed His warnings, God told Isaiah to preserve the message by writing it down on a tablet and a scroll (vv. 8-10). The scroll would later rebuke God's people as He continued to chasten them to achieve their repentance and restoration. But for now, not only were they ignoring God's warning, they did not even want Him ruling over them:

Sorrow and Comfort

"Get out of the way, turn aside from the path, cause the Holy One of Israel to cease from before us" (v. 11). Judah was acting like a toddler throwing a temper tantrum to get his or her own way. God had a solution that would get their attention – a painful one. F. B. Hole explains why God is especially offended when His people seek from Egypt what they can receive only from Him.

> This reliance upon Egypt was especially offensive to God, since from that very people He had delivered them by His judgments at the start of their national history. It is equally offensive to God if the Christian, who has been delivered from the world-system and its coming judgment, goes back to it, relying on its power or its wisdom, instead of finding his resource in God as emergencies arise. Egypt had its **pleasures** and its **treasures,** from which Moses turned, and they typify the things which are **not** for the believer.[79]

Even though they were rejecting Isaiah's message, he continued to warn his countrymen that oppressing God's Word and those who declare it would not go unpunished (v. 12). They would not only suffer the deceit of Egypt (i.e., Egypt would take Judah's payment but would not render assistance), but also God's displeasure. His judgment on His people would be like a bulging stone wall whose foundation had eroded: it would suddenly crack and collapse on them (v. 13). Besides being abrupt and unexpected, God's retribution would be thorough, like the smashing of a clay pot into such small pieces that it was good for nothing (not even the removal of hot coals from a fire; v. 14). This is not what God wanted for His people; He desired to bestow on them deliverance and strength in response to sincere repentance and faith, but Judah did not want God, or His help (v. 15).

The principle of restoration within verse 15 is still valid today. When we stumble off the path of righteousness let us remember: *"In returning and rest you shall be saved; in quietness and confidence shall be your strength."* Without the Lord we can do nothing (John 15:5); therefore it is foolish to wander away from Him – that path leads us nowhere but into fruitless misery. Communion is restored through "returning and resting." Consequently, all beneficial spiritual exercise begins with resting in Christ, who is in heavenly places (Eph. 2:6).

Unfortunately, Judah would not return to their God through repentance, neither would they rest in Him to obtain His power. The Southern Kingdom would soon learn the sorrow of relying on military might (symbolized by the warhorses) instead of on divine resources (v. 16). They thought they would speedily flee to Egypt and to safety, but the Lord said if you do not trust Me, you shall instead swiftly retreat from the enemy (Assyria). Not even a thousand Jews would be able to withstand one attacker (v. 17).

In the aftermath of God's chastening, they would be left destitute and alone. They would become a flimsy banner dangling from a scrawny pole on a hilltop to warn other nations what happens when you trust in military might to avert God's will (v. 17). And for two-plus millennia this ensign has characterized the dispersed Jewish people; they have been powerless and without influence, and thus they are still a warning beacon to the nations. Today, Israel has regained some measure of influence; they again have military clout. There can be little doubt that this is all part of the final earthly scene of God's design before the curtain falls on their centuries of suffering.

Mercy for Israel

Despite His people's infidelity, God was in a covenant relationship with them and therefore He longed to show them His goodness and compassion (v. 18). Justice for offenses would occur, but ultimately those in Jerusalem who trusted the Lord would experience His communion and enjoy His manifold blessings (v. 19). *"For the Lord is a God of justice; blessed are all those who wait for Him."* Much hardship will occur for the Jewish people prior to this time, as depicted by their survival diet: *"the bread of adversity and the water of affliction"* (v. 20). But this lean diet would lead them into better things, such as listening to and obeying God's prophets (i.e., they would no longer be gathered and pushed into a corner), and also counting their idols as filth which must be discarded (vv. 21-22).

Once restored to God in the Millennial Kingdom, Israel will be blessed with an abundance of rain, good pasturelands for livestock, and with bountiful harvests (vv. 23-24). Israel will be delivered from all Gentile oppression *"in the day of the great slaughter,"* which likely speaks of the Battle of Armageddon (v. 25; Rev. 16:14-16, 19:17-19). The earth will have polluted drinking water (Rev. 8:10, 16:4) and will be covered with a cloud of dust and debris that blocks sunlight during much of the Tribulation Period. However, God will heal the earth, and the sun and moon will shine with a brighter intensity than they had previously and He will bind up the wounds of His covenant people and heal them (v. 26).

Wrath for Assyria

Having hopefully stirred up Israel's longings for their future deliverance and restoration, Isaiah transitions to promising God's swift deliverance in their present situation – the Assyrians had besieged Jerusalem (v. 31). Judah was not to fear them; God would abruptly beat them down with His rod. His righteous indignation was full, His anger burned hot, and His arm was fully flexed to show His mighty power against them (vv. 27, 30).

Verse 27 is a figure of speech called an anthropomorphism, which assigns to God the physical characteristics of man in order to better convey the meaning:

> *Behold, the name of the Lord comes from afar, burning with His anger and His burden is heavy; His lips are full of indignation, and His tongue like a devouring fire.*

Anthropomorphisms are used throughout Scripture as a means of emphasizing God's emotions in a way that we can better empathize with (e.g. Ex. 33:11, 20; 2 Chron. 6:40; Job 34:21; Jas. 5:4).

The prophet then paints a word picture to illustrate the meaning of his message: Just as a farmer sifts his grain to remove unwanted debris, God would shake Assyria and her allies in His sieve to remove them from the land of Israel; Jerusalem would then rejoice greatly (vv. 28-29, 32). J. A. Motyer sees Isaiah using the historical Assyrian threat as a sort of epic trailer to the Lord's fiery action against "nations" and "peoples" in verses 27-33:

> This balance is now reversed. Assyria is veiled behind the description destroyer and traitor, and the climax is a fire of judgment upon the peoples. There is, however, the same sense of an "eleventh-hour" divine rescue, with the people of God just managing to live one day at a time, despair taking hold within a wasted world (vv. 7-9) and the dramatic threefold divine *Now* of verse 10.[80]

The invading Assyrians would be gathered up like firewood for a huge bonfire. Perhaps this was an indictment against those Jews who had sacrificed their children to Molech. Isaiah compares the immensity of God's fire to that which the pagans would kindle at Topheth, above the Hinnom Valley south of Jerusalem: *"For Tophet was established of old, yes, for the king it is prepared"* (v. 33). The difference was that God's own breath would ignite and make this inferno so intensely hot that the blaze would consume the Assyrian army and its wicked king (v. 33). Isaiah is not saying that God will punish the Assyrians for King Hezekiah's sake, but rather that the wicked king of Assyria will be consumed by the fires of divine judgment.

The fire of God at Topheth *"established of old"* pictures the fires of hell which await Satan's false king – the Antichrist, whom Christ will cast into the Lake of Fire (Rev. 19:20). While teaching about Hell, the Lord Jesus referenced the Hinnom Valley and Gehenna, the location where perpetual fires burned the carcasses of criminals and beasts, and Jerusalem's garbage (Mark 9:44-49). The Jews understood the symbolism. Prophetically then, verse 33 speaks to the doom of both the Assyrian king and the eternal judgment of the Antichrist in the Lake of Fire.

God's Anger

In the passage before us, God's anger is described in its full development: *"the indignation of His anger and the flame of a devouring fire"* (v. 30). Thankfully, Scripture teaches us that this is not God's normal disposition, nor does His anger rise quickly to vent indignation. He is not an angry God, even though His righteous character is angered by the behavior of the wicked every day (Ps. 7:11). Believers would do well to learn the characteristics of God's anger, and to pray for grace to conform the working of their own anger to His.

God is slow to anger:

> *The Lord is gracious, and full of compassion;* ***slow to anger****, and of great mercy* (Ps. 145:8).

Inherently, God is slow to anger, so we should be also. The fact that God's anger is not quickly kindled does not mean He is negligent. His slowness to anger ensures a deliberate response at the appropriate time. By His own character, God demonstrates that anger is to be a secondary, not a primary, emotion. If anger were a primary emotion, it would rule our lives with a heavy hand. Anger is not to be a quick-triggered emotion that abruptly enters and exits our daily routine. *He that is slow to anger is better than the mighty; and he that rules his spirit than he that takes a city* (Prov. 16:32). God desires for us to have a long-suffering attitude, which allows anger to deliver a measured response at the most advantageous time.

God is provoked to anger:

> *When you beget children and grandchildren and have grown old in the land, and act corruptly and make a carved image in the form of anything, and do evil in the sight of the Lord your God* ***to provoke Him to anger*** *(Deut. 4:25).*

The Lord is not a furious God, but He is "provoked" to anger. Either an appalling event or a series of distressing circumstances should occur before anger heightens the body into action. The Lord Jesus said, *"That whosoever is angry with his brother without a cause shall be in danger of the judgment"* (Matt. 5:22). One of the first questions we should ask ourselves when first feeling angry is, "Do I have a righteous cause to be angry?" If the situation does not demand anger-induced behavior, we have been wrongly provoked to anger. If not extinguished, anger is too powerful an emotion to control – it will lead us into sin: *"Be ye angry, and sin not: let not the sun go down upon your wrath: Neither give place to the devil"* (Eph. 4:26-27, KJV).

God's anger is kindled:

> *And when the people complained, it displeased the Lord: and the Lord heard it;* ***and His anger was kindled****; and the fire of the Lord burnt among them, and consumed them that were in the uttermost parts of the camp* (Num. 11:1; KJV).

The Hebrew word translated as "kindled" in the above verses is *charah* (khaw-raw'), which means "to grow warm." It is normally applied in a figurative sense, "to blaze up." The word describes the igniting of combustible materials and the nursing of the initial spark into the desired conflagration. Not only is God slow to be angry, but once provoked to anger, His anger fully develops before action is rendered, as shown in this chapter. God's anger requires sufficient kindling before flaming vengeance is released. God shows us that righteous provocation and a period of anger development are necessary before proper action is discharged.

Living a Christ-centered and disciplined life will reduce the number of occasions on which we feel inappropriately and unnecessarily angry. While in close fellowship with the Lord, the power of the Holy Spirit will effectively control and mold our anger to accomplish the righteousness of God – *"for the wrath of man does not produce the righteousness of God"* (Jas. 1:20). However, God's wrath does uphold His righteousness: *"For the wrath of God is revealed from heaven against all ungodliness and unrighteousness of men, who suppress the truth in unrighteousness"* (Rom. 1:18). In this chapter, Isaiah promises Israel what Paul also confirms to the Church: *"the wrath of God is coming upon the sons of disobedience"* (Col. 3:6). Accordingly, may we not be numbered with or imitate "the rebellious children" who break God's heart (v. 1).

Meditation

> I have been learning all along my pilgrim journey that the more my heart is taken up with Christ, the more do I enjoy practical deliverance from sin's power, and the more do I realize what it is to have the love of God shed abroad in that heart by the Holy Spirit given to me, as the earnest of the glory to come.
>
> — H. A. Ironside

The Folly of Not Trusting the Lord
Isaiah 31

The subject of Judah trusting in Egyptian military might to avert the Assyrian conquest continues into this chapter.

Why Trust Egypt?

To emphasize the foolishness of trusting in Egypt instead of in the Lord, the prophet adds an additional woe to his message to Judah (v. 1). The Lord, who is wiser and stronger than the Egyptian army despite all their horses and chariots, would certainly judge Judah's offense (v. 2). The Jews were not thinking straight, for *"the Egyptians are men, and not God and their horses are flesh and not spirit"* (v. 3). If Judah continued pursuing this foolish course of action, their all-powerful God promised to stretch out His mighty hand over the situation and both the supposed helpers (the Egyptians) and those they helped (the Jews) would fall down and perish together (v. 3).

Just as a fierce lion attacks a flock of sheep without fear of its shepherds, God was not afraid of the Assyrians – they were no match for Him (v. 4). If His people chose to trust in Him, rather than the Egyptians, then He promised to be like flocks of birds flying overhead (i.e., an impenetrable shield over Jerusalem; v. 5). Seeing that God's deliverance of Jerusalem would be sure, Isaiah then implores his countrymen to turn back to the Lord (v. 6). Eventually, God would purge them of their idolatry (30:22), so would it not be wise to abandon their idols now? Isaiah's logic is sound: having hope in God's glorious kingdom to come should affect the behavior of God's people now.

This same exhortation is repeated in the New Testament for believers in the Church Age. As a result of spiritual regeneration, Christ is presently with all believers on earth; in the future, His Church will be with Him in heaven. His forever abiding presence with us is certain, though our intimacy with Him each day depends on our desire for it. With His exaltation looming, Christians are to live each day in the anticipation of Christ's coming (2 Tim. 4:6-8). There is a reward for those who do, and their lives will be more joyful and fruitful in light of that imminent expectation.

In a twinkling of an eye, what was corruptible will become incorruptible, and what was mortal will become immortal (1 Cor. 15:51-52), and we will be caught up into the air to be ever with the Lord (1 Thess. 4:13-18). At this event, often referred to as the Rapture of the Church, sin and pain will cease to exist within all believers in Christ. The believer's glorified body will be able to worship and to please God without any hindrance from the flesh or any ills of its previously fallen state.

Paul had one hope (Eph. 4:4), one earnest expectation, the *blessed hope*: *"Looking for the blessed hope and glorious appearing of our great God and Savior Jesus Christ"* (Titus 2:13). While this may include aspects of Christ's future kingdom, the believer's faith and hope finish their course at Christ's coming for the Church (the rapture), yet love, as previously mentioned, continues forever (1 Cor. 13:8, 13). The Church is not to be waiting for the Antichrist to appear (his coming is a sign to the nation of Israel; Dan. 9:27), but for Christ Himself to translate them from the earth into heaven. The Church is not waiting for the inhabitants of earth to be slaughtered during the Tribulation Period, but rather longs to be removed from this wicked world to be with Christ. As John puts it, this is a purifying hope:

> *Beloved, now we are children of God; and it has not yet been revealed what we shall be, but we know that when He is revealed, we shall be like Him, for we shall see Him as He is. And everyone who has this hope in Him purifies himself, just as He is pure* (1 Jn. 3:2-3).

This was the message that Isaiah wanted his fellow Jews to heed – those who truly have the hope of glory purify themselves now. The Lord is pure and saints having the blessed hope will want to be found living purely when He suddenly returns from heaven.

Assyria Shall Fall

Isaiah concludes his fourth woe oracle by again confirming that Assyria would *"fall by a sword not of man"* (v. 8). God would soundly defeat the Assyrian army; their soldiers will fall or be captured and Judah's battle standard shall strike terror into the minds of the Assyrians (v. 9). God's incredible victory will completely remove the Assyrian threat. This meant that fire on the Bronze Altar in Jerusalem's

Sorrow and Comfort

temple would continue to burn (i.e., worship at the temple would not be interrupted).

Isaiah foretold that some younger men in Sennacherib's army would survive and would become forced laborers. This was desirable, as these survivors would provide a testimony of what happened to other nations. The massacre would demonstrate that God was quite capable of protecting Jerusalem in the future; for example, no invader in the Kingdom Age will be permitted to interfere with sacrifices on the Bronze Altar in Jerusalem.

As we learn in chapters 36-37, all came about as God had promised. Unfortunately, Judah did not purify herself of her idols, and God's glory later departed from Jerusalem in the days of Ezekiel (just before the temple was destroyed by Babylon). May we remember the main points of Isaiah's message: First, it is foolish to entrust our difficulties to men, rather than to the Lord. Second, those who truly have the hope of glory live purely now!

The writer of Hebrews acknowledges this strong connection between the believer's faith and hope – that both have their culmination in Christ's coming for the Church. *"For yet a little while, and He who is coming will come and will not tarry. Now the just shall live by faith"* (Heb. 10:37-38). Although Scripture repeatedly emphasizes hope in the Christian experience, many believers today unfortunately do not know what their hope is. Some dread the future and live in fear of it. This was not the disposition of the apostles, who lived out their lives exuberantly for Christ because they expectantly and joyfully anticipated being with Him. Regrettably, much of the Church maintains a dismal outlook of the future rather than contemplating their blessed hope and joyfully resting in God's promises. As Isaiah has told us, a lack of compassion for the poor and needy and no remorse for perishing souls are symptoms of misplaced hope. Fear creates bondage, but hope liberates the redeemed soul to serve with joy (Heb. 2:15).

Meditation

Look, ye saints! The sight is glorious: see the Man of Sorrows now;
From the fight returned victorious, every knee to Him shall bow:
Crown Him, crown Him, crown Him, crown Him, crown Him, crown Him.
Crowns become the Victor's brow, crowns become the Victor's brow.

— Thomas Kelly

Until the Spirit Is Poured Out
Isaiah 32

This chapter is a refreshing oasis in a wilderness of woes. Isaiah carries the idea forward of God's protection of Judah (then to ensure temple sacrifices would continue) to God's ultimate securing of Jerusalem in the Kingdom Age.

The King Is Coming

One of the amazing aspects of Isaiah's book is how various series of messages are organized to repeat key conclusions through developed patterns. As J. M. Riddle explains, we have another such pattern in the transition between chapters 31 and 32, when compared with the transition between chapters 10 and 11.

> Chapter 10 describes the advance of the Assyrian on Jerusalem, and concludes, "Behold, the Lord, the Lord of hosts, shall lop the bough with terror: and the high ones of stature shall be hewn down, and the haughty shall be humbled. And he shall cut down the thickets of the forest with iron, and Lebanon shall fall by a mighty one" (vv. 33-34). Chapter 11 commences, "And there shall come forth a rod out of the stem of Jesse, and a Branch shall grow out of his roots ... And righteousness shall be the girdle of his loins, and faithfulness the girdle of his reins" (vv. 1, 5). Similarly, chapter 31 concludes, "Then shall the Assyrian fall with the sword ... And he shall pass over to his stronghold for fear" (vv. 8-9). Chapter 32 commences, "Behold, a king shall reign in righteousness, and princes shall rule in judgment" (v. 1). Whilst, undoubtedly, the historical Assyrian is first in view in chapters 10 and 31, the past Assyrian anticipates the Assyrian of the future who will invade the land, and suffer defeat at the hand of Israel's Messiah. The Lord Jesus will then "reign in righteousness" (v. 1).[81]

Christ will reign in righteousness and those entering His kingdom will be those who pursue justice and purity. This will include Gentiles who did not side with the Antichrist and who lived through the Tribulation Period, the restored nation of Israel, and glorified saints (Old Testament believers, the Church, and previously martyred Tribulation saints). Some within the Jewish nation – *"princes will rule with justice"* (v. 1), glorified Tribulation saints (Rev. 20:4), and of course the Church (2 Tim. 2:12; Rev. 5:10) will rule and reign with Christ during the Kingdom Age.

Think of a world which has no political agendas, no warring factions, no unethical dealings and is void of rebels and wickedness. Such a utopia will exist in Christ's kingdom; furthermore, citizens of His kingdom will be protective of each other. While some commentators think the "man" in verse 2 is Christ, the idea of believers under His rule better fits the context of verses 2-8. Subjects of the King will be like a shelter in a windstorm to each other, and they will seek to refresh each other, like a rock casting its shadow or a cool drink of water for those suffering in desert heat (vv. 1-2). This attitude is just one of the evidences that the Spirit of God has free recourse to bless humanity during the Millennial Kingdom.

Isaiah says that in the Kingdom Age the inhabitants of the earth will see, hear, and discern spiritual things properly (vv. 3-4). They will know and choose to obey God's laws. Isaiah strikes a strong contrast between how Israel will behave in the future with their poor conduct towards the Lord now. In God's kingdom, those who resort to deceitful ways take advantage of the poor or engage in foolish endeavors to get ahead will not be respected; ungodliness of any sort will not be tolerated (vv. 5-7). Rather, subjects of Christ will seek to care for those in need, and will pursue righteousness; God promises that such a person has His favor and will continue to stand (i.e., live with His blessing; v. 8).

Assyria Is Coming

Turning again to the time of his ministry, the prophet sternly addresses the women of Judah for a second time (vv. 9-14). They should not think that God's judgment would never come; rather it would begin in a little over a year (vv. 9-10). F. C. Jennings explains why Isaiah refers to the feminine gender in admonishing the nation: "The women are here addressed because of the peculiar sensitiveness of the feminine temperament, quick to catch the first sight of coming danger and to take alarm. But these see no cause for anything but confidence and pleasure."[82]

Apparently, the Jewish women were just going on with the affairs of life with no care as to what God was saying to the nation through Isaiah. Rather than being complacent, they should humble themselves by wearing sackcloth (v. 11). Darby translates verse 12: *"They shall smite on the breasts* [in lamentation] *for the pleasant fields, for the fruitful vineyards."* The beating of one's breasts expressed the epitome of maternal agony. Soon, Assyria would ravage the land and steal their harvest and mothers would not be able to feed their starving children, or nurse their babies.

Although Isaiah is speaking of the coming Assyrian invasion, the entire scene is a prophetic allusion to the greatest crisis to engulf the Jewish people – the Tribulation Period. The Lord Jesus, speaking of this time, echoes the maternal sentiment that Isaiah mentions:

Therefore when you see the "abomination of desolation," spoken of by Daniel the prophet, standing in the holy place (whoever reads, let him understand), then let those who are in Judea flee to the mountains. Let him who is on the housetop not go down to take anything out of his house. And let him who is in the field not go back to get his clothes. ***But woe to those who are pregnant and to those who are nursing babies in those days*** (Matt. 24:15-19).

Until Christ's second coming, Israel will be marked by sorrow and spiritual complacency (Dan. 9:26), but nothing, including the Assyrian invasion, can compare to the holocaust the Jews will experience during *the time of Jacob's Trouble*.

Many Jewish cities would be destroyed by Assyria and abandoned. Herds would be confiscated, and fields and vineyards left unattended for a time, thus producing unfruitful briers and thorns (vv. 13-14). Although Jerusalem did not fall during the Assyrian invasion, Sennacherib's Prism, discovered in the ruins of Nineveh in 1830, claims that the king conquered forty-six Judean cities.[83] The divine chastening, that began with the Assyria conquest in 701 B.C. to awaken the Jews to their abhorrent spiritual condition, would continue until Jerusalem was destroyed by the Babylonians in 586 B.C. Between these two days, there would be two brief glimmers of hope for Judah: Hezekiah and then Josiah. But as shown by history, the doings of a righteous king cannot effect revival for an entire despondent nation.

The Kingdom Is Coming

This dismal time for the Jewish nation is then contrasted with a future time in which the entire nation would experience spiritual revival and would bask in God's goodness. Joel, Isaiah, and Ezekiel all prophesy of a future day when God will create in His covenant people a new heart by pouring out His Spirit upon them:

Until the Spirit is poured upon us from on high (v. 15).

Then you shall know that I am in the midst of Israel: I am the Lord your God and there is no other. My people shall never be put to shame. And it shall come to pass afterward that I will pour out My Spirit on all flesh; your sons and your daughters shall prophesy, your old men shall dream dreams, your young men shall see visions (Joel 2:27-28).

A new heart also will I give you, and a new Spirit will I put within you (Ezek. 36:26).

The Holy Spirit will ensure that the Jewish nation will never again depart from Jehovah for false gods; instead, they will continue in His Law and be His people (Ezek. 36:26-27). Having received God's Spirit, the refined and restored nation of Israel will not bring dishonor on Jehovah's name ever again. Accordingly, the nations will never have a reason to blaspheme God's name because of hypocritical Jewish conduct (Rom. 2:23-24). Speaking of this event, Jeremiah says that God's Law will be deep inside His people and that all the Jews from the oldest to the youngest will intimately know Jehovah and identify Him as *"The Lord of Hosts"* (Jer. 31:33-35).

After receiving the Holy Spirit, Israel will be able to look back on their history with honest integrity and lament their past sinful ways (Ezek. 36:31-32). So deep will be Israel's remorse that she loathes herself – why would God so abundantly bless an adulterous wife? At that moment, they will realize how undeserving they are of God's forgiveness and that they were not preserved because of their own merits, but because God sought to sanctify His great name among the nations. Therefore, He will purify Israel of her impurities, return her to the land promised her, and richly prosper her in that land (Ezek. 36:33-38).

These events commence the Kingdom Age; then a wilderness will be as a fruitful field and a fruitful field will be like a dense forest (v. 15). Justice and righteousness will fill the earth, the nations will be at peace with each other, and Israel's full confidence will be in the Lord forever (vv. 16-17). After centuries of divine chastening by Gentile oppression, Israel will forever be at rest because they will have a peaceful habitation with their God (v. 18). After over two millennia of constant distress, Jerusalem, which means "founded in peace," will finally experience the reality of her name.

Thankfully, believers in the Church Age do not have to wait until the Kingdom Age to enjoy having peace with God and the peace of God. The former occurs through yielding to the gospel of Jesus Christ, the latter when we align our thinking with God's mind and yield to His will. This is why Paul instructed the believers at Philippi to *"be anxious for nothing, but in everything by prayer and supplication, with thanksgiving, let your requests be made known to God; and the peace of God, which surpasses all understanding, will guard your hearts and minds through Christ Jesus"* (Phil. 4:6-7). Being in happy communion with God ensures that we can enjoy His peace of mind also.

Meditation

> Like a river glorious is God's perfect peace,
> Over all victorious, in its bright increase;
> Perfect, yet it floweth fuller every day,
> Perfect, yet it groweth deeper all the way.
> Stayed upon Jehovah, hearts are fully blest
> Finding, as He promised, perfect peace and rest.
>
> — Frances R Havergal

The Plunderer to Be Plundered
Isaiah 33

The sixth and final *woe* in this series of five messages that began in chapter 28 is pronounced against the enemies of God's covenant people. If you are counting, this is the twenty-first of twenty-three "woes" in Isaiah's book. After a relatively long season of woe-lessness, the final two will be pronounced in chapter 45.

This chapter is equally divided, with Isaiah first describing God's judgment on the unrighteous (vv. 1-12) and then concluding with God's wonderful blessings for the redeemed during the Kingdom Age (vv. 13-24).

The Plunder

The metaphor in verse 1 causes some difficulty in identifying who Isaiah is talking about. The overall subject matter of the previous chapters (chps. 28-32) would suggest that the unnamed "plunderer" ("the spoiler"; KJV) would be the Assyrians. *"You who deal treacherously"* may refer to those Jews who sought Egyptian assistance instead of God's protection. If "the treacherous" refers to the individual in verse 8 who broke his covenant, then the reference would be to Sennacherib, who agreed to received gold and silver from Hezekiah to halt the Assyrian invasion of Judah, but later declined to do so after receiving the tribute (2 Kgs. 18:13-17). Regardless of who the treacherous are, God's sovereign plans for Israel cannot be frustrated by the violence of Assyria or by the unfaithfulness of anyone, including His people. Hence, the plunderer was destined to be plundered and the traitor(s) would be betrayed.

Verse 2 introduces us to the righteous remnant (including Isaiah) who are waiting and praying for the Lord's deliverance: *"O Lord, be gracious to us; we have waited for You."* These faithful saints put their full confidence in the Lord; they knew that He would deliver them from their oppressors scattering their armies and plundering their goods (v. 3). The latter point is affirmed by two metaphors: *"Your plunder shall be gathered like the gathering of the caterpillar, as the running to and fro of locusts, he shall run upon them"* (v. 4). Albert Barnes explains the allegorical meaning of this verse:

> The meaning here is, undoubtedly, that the plunder of the Assyrian army would be collected by the Jews, as the locust gathered its food. The sense is that as locusts spread themselves out over a land, as they go to and fro without rule and without molestation, gathering whatever is in their way, and consuming everything, so the Jews in great numbers, and without regular military array, would run to and fro collecting the spoils of the Assyrian army. In a country where such devastation was made by the caterpillar and locust as in Palestine, this was a very striking figure.[84]

Isaiah responds to their declaration of faith by affirming that God (in the Kingdom Age) would be exalted in Zion and would rule from there with justice and righteousness (v. 5). It is interesting that Ezekiel spoke of invading marauders from the North, Gog and Magog, that would attempt to despoil Israel in the midst of the Tribulation Period, but the Lord would intervene to defeat them and then Israel would plunder their dead (Ezek. 38-39). Again, we have a near-term prophecy with a far-reaching meaning, but the point is the same: God, in His manifold wisdom and power, has promised His people complete deliverance and the spoil of the enemy, but they must continue to fear Him and trust Him.

This is the thought Isaiah conveys in verse 6, *"Wisdom and knowledge will be the stability of your times, and the strength of salvation; the fear of the Lord is His treasure."* J. A. Motyer says the literal meaning of this is "the fear of the Lord is the key to this treasure." He then clarifies the gender components of the Hebrew text to identify whose treasure is being referred to – it is "the Lord's ... He has treasure in store for His people."[85] God has reserved a great reward for those who faithfully fear and venerate Him.

The lack of reverential awe and fear of the Lord is a growing problem among Christians today. The writer of Hebrews addressed the same issue in his day by reminding his audience that the God who violently shook Mount Sinai in Moses's day is the same God who rules over the Church today: *"Wherefore we receiving a kingdom which cannot be moved, let us have grace, whereby we may serve God acceptably with reverence and godly fear: for our God is a consuming*

Sorrow and Comfort

fire" (Heb. 12:28-29). When God's people cease to revere the Lord, they inevitably will exalt themselves and legitimize their sin. Isaiah wanted his people to maintain an elevated view of God and low estimation of themselves and so to receive His good favor.

A century later, the prophet Jeremiah told Judah that they had forsaken the Lord and did not fear Him any longer (Jer. 2:19). The fear of the Lord involves a proper understanding of who God is and a proper reverence for Him. This was sorely lacking among the Jews, and was a matter that would be remedied by devastating judgments at the hands of the Babylonians – God would soon have His people's respect again.

The Traitor

Having discussed the demise of the plunderer (Assyria), Isaiah then speaks about the fate of those *"who deal treacherously"* (vv. 7-12). As mentioned above, perhaps the traitor refers to those Jews who had sought security through an Egyptian alliance instead of trusting in the Lord. If that is the case, the Assyrian invasion would cause even the mighty of Judah to be fearful and weep (v. 7). However, it seems more likely that the traitor is Sennacherib, and the "valiant ones" crying outside (perhaps near the wall of Jerusalem) are his leaders (e.g., Rabshakeh).

This would mean that the distraught *ambassadors of peace* (v. 7) may refer to the delegation Hezekiah sent to Sennacherib who was also attacking Lachish at the time (2 Kgs. 18:13-17). Hezekiah offered to pay tribute to Assyria to obtain peace. Sennacherib assessed Judah three hundred talents of silver and thirty talents of gold. So Hezekiah gave the Assyrian king all the silver in the temple and in the king's treasury and then stripped the gold from the doors and pillars in the temple to buy off Sennacherib. The wicked king received the tribute but then brought his army against Jerusalem anyway. Isaiah said that the Jewish envoy would weep over their mission that failed to avert the invasion of Judah.

Not only would it be unsafe to travel in Judah, the Assyrians were going to decimate the entire region (v. 8). The forests of Lebanon in the north would wither, the fertile coastal Plain of Sharon to the west would become like the arid region of Arabah to the south, and the meadows and farmlands of Bashan on the Eastern Plateau and the thick forests of Mount Carmel would be laid waste (v. 9).

Jehovah to Intervene

Why was God permitting the Assyrian army to so violently ravage Israel? To demonstrate to His people that all their efforts to bring peace to their homeland through the Egyptians or by any other means would come to nothing. These Jewish doubters were like a mother giving birth to nothing but chaff and straw, which were easily burnt up (vv. 11-12). The Lord knew that He must put His people in a place of utter desperation before they would turn to Him for help and that was exactly what He was doing.

God would be exalted by the outcome and His people would learn to depend on Him alone (v. 10). Hence, Isaiah's exhortation: *"Hear, you who are afar off, what I have done; and you who are near, acknowledge My might"* (v. 13). While it is possible that this is merely a general call of people everywhere to consider God's righteous and powerful ways, it seems more likely that this is a twofold invitation for Israel. God's marvelous doings through the Assyrians would strengthen the faith of the remnant who were near to God and hopefully would awaken and revive the vast majority who were not. The Jews had God's Law, but they really did not know and trust the Giver of it. God's people will not trust, nor live for, a God they do not know!

Who Shall Dwell With God?

Having described the ultimate demise of the plunderer and the traitor, Isaiah concludes his message by describing the person that God delights in, the one who will experience His salvation (vv. 14-16) and also the blessings they will receive (vv. 17-24). Having witnessed God's fury and powerful judgments, the fearful sinner asks, *"Who among us shall dwell with the devouring fire? Who among us shall dwell with everlasting burnings?"* (v. 14). (This is speaking of God's consuming holiness and awesome unapproachable presence; Heb. 12:29.) Isaiah answers this question:

> *He who walks righteously and speaks uprightly, he who despises the gain of oppressions, who gestures with his hands, refusing bribes, who stops his ears from hearing of bloodshed, and shuts his eyes from seeing evil* (v. 15).

Isaiah had already told his countrymen in his first message that the only solution to their pitiful spiritual condition was wholesale repentance, which is evidenced by ongoing godly conduct (1:16-17). Sinners who wanted to have communion with the One who dwells high above the earth could do so through repentance. This meant that true confessors would cease from evil, seek justice, and do what was good and proper, like assisting those in need (v. 16). Those who return to God in faith would be protected and not lack when God judged the nation; furthermore they *"will see the King in His beauty; they will see the land that is very far off"* (v. 17). Not only would the faithful be preserved from the Assyrians, but they would be a part of Messiah's kingdom, *"still far off"* in the future. The promise would imply that resurrection from the dead was a certainty, as both Isaiah and Daniel affirm (26:26; Dan. 12:2). It is possible (given the threatening situation of that day) that Isaiah was referring to preservation of righteous King Hezekiah, but as a prelude to a "very far off" presentation of the coming Messiah.

The Zion to Come

In the Kingdom Age, the faithful will reflect on former days of hardship and be elated that no rebel or foreign invader can be found in the land (e.g., no Assyrians who spoke an unknown tongue; vv. 18-19). In that day Jerusalem will be completely secure, at peace, and God's tabernacle will be in place there:

> *Look upon Zion, the city of our appointed feasts; your eyes will see Jerusalem, a quiet home, a tabernacle that will not be taken down; not one of its stakes will ever be removed, nor will any of its cords be broken* (v. 20).

This is the Zion to come and no war-galleys filled with invading troops will ever threaten her again (v. 21). Who will ensure that Israel's security and peace will continue during the Kingdom Age? The restored Jewish nation answers this question: *"For the Lord is our Judge, the Lord is our Lawgiver, the Lord is our King; He will save us"* (v. 22). The One who is their Judge and Lawgiver, is also their King and Savior – this is a strong affirmation of the deity of the Lord Jesus Christ. Quoting Isaiah, Matthew asserts, *"And she will bring forth a Son, and you shall call His name Jesus, for He will save His people from their sins"* (Matt. 1:21). Later, the Lord speaking through Isaiah declares, *"I, even I, am the Lord, and besides Me there is no Savior"* (43:11).

Commentators disagree as to whom the shipping analogy in verse 23 refers and also its prophetic timing. Some believe it refers to the despoiling of Assyrian soldiers slaughtered by the Angel of the Lord. Given this understanding, those who plundered Israel (the Assyrians) are likened to a colossal shipwreck on Israel's Mediterranean shore which provides so much spoil that there will be plenty for even a lame person arriving sometime later to have a generous share.

But this explanation hardly fits the context of the verses on either side of verse 23, which have unarguably a Millennial Kingdom connotation: *"the Lord is our King; He will save us"* (v. 22) and *"the inhabitant will not say, 'I am sick'; the people who dwell in it will be forgiven their iniquity"* (v. 24). If the shipping parable does pertain to the second advent of Christ, then the crippled ship with its rigging loose, mast rickety, and sails unhoisted represents Zion. Though battered through the centuries, she still limps along and receives the spoil from the Battle of Armageddon which is won by another – the Lord Jesus.[86] Christ will provide and care for all those in His kingdom; no one will say *"I am sick,"* for disease will be a thing of the past and all will rejoice to be forgiven for past iniquities (v. 24).

It is with this contemplation that Isaiah concludes this series of messages which began back in chapter 28. He has sought to inspire his countrymen to look to the Lord rather than to Egypt to overcome the Assyrian threat. Lasting preservation, prosperity, and peace are sovereign works of God in response to genuine faith; these blessings cannot be achieved through carnal methods (e.g., foreign alliances). For the Jews to put their trust in Egypt instead of in the Lord, who loved them, would be a poor decision with painful consequences! To enjoy God's goodness, His people must first be broken and yielded to His will. Thankfully, as we will see shortly, King Hezekiah heeded Isaiah's warning and experienced God's amazing and complete deliverance.

Meditation

> We need to remember that we cannot train ourselves to be Christians; … we cannot bend ourselves to the will of God: we have to be broken to the will of God.
>
> — Oswald Chambers

Sorrow and Comfort

To accept the will of God never leads to the miserable feeling that it is useless to strive anymore. God does not ask for the dull, weak, sleepy acquiescence of indolence. He asks for something vivid and strong. He asks us to cooperate with Him, actively willing what He wills, our only aim His glory.

— Amy Carmichael

The Day of Vengeance
Isaiah 34

Chapters 34 and 35 provide a capstone to the judgment and deliverance themes developed by Isaiah up to this juncture. First, God's promises to deliver and bless the faithful and to judge the wicked necessitate purging the nation of immorality and idolatry. Second, He will judge the tool used to punish Israel (the Assyrians). Third, He will restore and bless the faithful remnant. Intermingled with prophecies pertaining to Isaiah's day is the wider perspective which foretells Christ's coming to accomplish the same feats by establishing His kingdom. He will judge the world during the Tribulation Period, deliver His covenant people from the Antichrist, and fulfill all His promises to Abraham.

Isaiah has already explained how God is able to accomplish all this. God will give His own Son to be Messiah (9:6). He will be born of a virgin and will be called *"God with us"* (7:14), and the Holy Spirit will be upon Him (11:2). During His first advent, God's Servant-Messiah would *"be a stone of stumbling and a rock of offense to both the houses of Israel"* (8:14). Israel will condemn Him to death and He will suffer at Calvary for human sin. Yet, after His death the Messiah will judge the wicked and rule the world in righteousness and power (11:1-5). The curses of the earth will be removed and the entire planet will be full of the knowledge of God (11:6-9). During this time even the Gentiles will seek the Jewish Messiah and worship Him (11:10). Although this revelation was divinely given to Isaiah, the understanding that the Messiah must come to the earth on two different occasions to accomplish it all was not plainly explained to him. Thankfully, we have New Testament revelation which enables us to interpret Old Testament Scripture and to understand the fuller picture of Christ's second coming.

The wonderful time of worldwide blessing in chapter 35 is preceded by the Day of the Lord in this chapter. God must judge wickedness throughout the earth. Isaiah begins by extending an

Sorrow and Comfort

invitation to all nations to consider the Lord (v. 1). This is followed by an announcement of judgment on the nations who follow the Antichrist (vv. 2-4), all of which is typified by God's judgment of Edom (vv. 5-17).

Christ's Second Coming (vv. 2-4)

There will be many types of judgments levied on the earth during the Tribulation Period. (Revelation identifies twenty-one specific judgments.) In verse 2, Isaiah characterizes the vast destruction inflicted by God's wrath on the nations at that time:

> *For the indignation of the Lord is against all nations, and His fury against all their armies; He has utterly destroyed them, He has given them over to the slaughter* (v. 2).

There are three significant judgments that will occur during the Tribulation Period which effectively wipe out all the Gentile armies (followers of the beast) who are bent on destroying Israel. First, there will be the Battle of Gog and Magog to enter Israel near the mid-portion of the Tribulation Period (Ezek. 38-39). Second, there will be the Battle of Armageddon when the Antichrist and Gentile armies invade Jerusalem at the end of the Tribulation (Zech. 14:1-13; Rev. 14:14-20, 19:17-20). Third, the Judgment of Nations will occur directly after the Battle of Armageddon to ensure that all those who sided with the Antichrist will be promptly killed (Matt. 13:47-50, 25:31-46; Rev. 19:21). Rightly named, the Tribulation Period is called "the Day of the Lord" throughout the Old Testament – it is when God's righteous indignation is released against nations (v. 2). Isaiah refers to God's indignation more times than any other writer in Scripture. Stuart Briscoe accurately describes what indignation is:

> The wrath of God is as pure as the holiness of God. When God is angry, He is perfectly angry. When He is displeased, there is every reason He should be. We tend to think of anger as sin; but sometimes it is sinful not to be angry. It is unthinkable that God would not be purely and perfectly angry with sin.[87]

For centuries, Almighty God has been holding back His righteous fury against the nations until Christ completes His Church, so that God can then complete His plans for refining and restoring the nation of

Israel. This will occur in the Day of the Lord. Isaiah describes this event again with an eloquent metaphor:

> *Also their slain shall be thrown out; their stench shall rise from their corpses, and the mountains shall be melted with their blood. All the host of heaven shall be dissolved, and the heavens shall be rolled up like a scroll; all their host shall fall down as the leaf falls from the vine, and as fruit falling from a fig tree* (vv. 3-4).

Is the prophet forecasting the destruction of celestial bodies, or is he figuratively speaking of the judgment of fallen angels, or perhaps of the nations gathered against His people? Again commentators disagree as to how far the implication of this text reaches. We do know that fallen angels will be confined to the earth midway through the Tribulation Period (Rev. 12:7-9), then to the bottomless pit at the end of the Tribulation Period (Rev. 20:1-2), and ultimately into the Lake of Fire (Matt. 25:41; Rev. 20:10). The second of these events does coincide with the second coming of Christ, so perhaps sealing all demonic powers in the bottomless pit does explain some of the upheaval within the heavens.

Another possibility is that verse 4 is describing the Judgment of the Nations, which will determine who enters Christ's kingdom (Matt. 25:31-46; Rev. 19:21). Holding this view, Albert Barnes explains that the language of the text figuratively describes the worldwide fall of all political powers at Christ's second coming:

And all the host of heaven - The heavenly bodies often represent kings and princes (24:21).

Shall be dissolved - The sense is that the princes and nobles who had opposed God and his people would be destroyed, as if the sparkling stars, like gems, should melt in the heavens, and flow down to the earth.

And the heavens shall be rolled together as a scroll - The sense is that there would be great destruction among those high in office and in power – a destruction that would be well represented by the rolling up of the firmament, and the destruction of the visible heavens and their host, and by leaving the world to ruin and to night.

> **And all their host shall fall down** - That is, their stars; either by being, as it were, melted, or by the fact that the expanse in which they are apparently located would be rolled up and removed, and there being no fixtures for them, they would fall. The same image occurs in Revelation 6:13.[88]

While all the above is certainly true, there are wider implications of dealing with human rebellion and its effect on creation than just the toppling of secular governments or putting fallen angels into jail. A figurative interpretation of verse 4 does not fully match the literal language of verses 9, 10, 13, nor does it agree with other passages that depict stellar and terrestrial chaos at Christ's coming. The Lord Jesus, speaking to His disciples, described what the earth would be like at His return:

> *Immediately after the tribulation of those days the sun will be darkened, and the moon will not give its light; the stars will fall from heaven, and the powers of the heavens will be shaken. Then the sign of the Son of Man will appear in heaven, and then all the tribes of the earth will mourn, and they will see the Son of Man coming on the clouds of heaven with power and great glory* (Matt. 24:29-30).

Despite the stellar pandemonium, this passage affirms that the earth is not literally destroyed at Christ's coming. John and Peter both foretell that destruction of the heavens and earth will not occur until after Christ's Millennial Kingdom (2 Pet. 3:9; Rev. 21:1). Given these facts, reason suggests that God's indignation is so powerful against human wickedness and the earthly domains that oppose His people that creation itself convulses when Christ returns to remedy the situation. Human sin in Eden caused curses to be levied on the earth, and it has groaned with pangs to be delivered ever since:

> *For the earnest expectation of the creation eagerly waits for the revealing of the sons of God. For the creation was subjected to futility, not willingly, but because of Him who subjected it in hope; because the creation itself also will be delivered from the bondage of corruption into the glorious liberty of the children of God. For we know that the whole creation groans and labors with birth pangs together until now* (Rom. 8:19-22).

Devotions in Isaiah

So powerful will be God's wrath against the nations that mountains will be eroded by the blood pouring out of millions of bodies instantly eradicated by divine vengeance (v. 3; Zech. 14:12; Rev. 14:20). Celestial bodies and the earth itself will shudder with shock and awe (v. 4).

The Judgment of Edom (vv. 5-17)

As discussed previously, God had several reasons to be angry with Edom (21:11-12). Here Isaiah uses Edom to picture God's overall wrath against the nations described in the previous verses. It is likely that Edom was singled out to represent the nations because of their past treachery which resulted in a great slaughter of the Jews. Edom had sided with Babylon in the defeat of Egypt in 605 B.C., but in 593 B.C. they agreed to be part of an alliance, which included Judah and other nations, to rebel against Nebuchadnezzar (Jer. 27:1-7). However, when Babylon came against Jerusalem in 588 B.C., double-crossing Edom switched sides again and assisted Babylon in brutally conquering the Jewish nation (Jer. 49:7-22). It is this same kind of deceitful brutality which will be poured out by the nations on the Jewish nation during the Tribulation Period. According to Zechariah, two-thirds of the Jews worldwide will be exterminated during this time (Zech. 13:8-9).

Isaiah pictures God fiercely slaughtering Edom with His sword in order to offer a great sacrifice to Himself in Bozrah in southeast Israel (vv. 5-7). God is no respecter of persons; His sword will fall on both the common people (i.e., those who offer lambs, goats, and rams) and also on the nobles (who sacrifice the more expensive oxen and bulls).

"For My sword shall be bathed in heaven" (v. 5) is another metaphor which has perplexed translators. The sword is associated with judgment throughout Scripture and often with the idea of capital punishment. But what does *"bathed in heaven"* mean? The Hebrew word *ravah*, rendered "bathed" in verse 5, is also translated "make drunk," (take the) "fill," (abundantly) "satisfy," and "soak." Given how *ravah* is used elsewhere in Scripture and the context of verse 6, *"the sword is filled with blood,"* Albert Barnes explains the imagery of the "bathed" sword:

> The idea here is, not that the sword of the Lord was made drunk with blood in heaven, but that it was intoxicated, or made furious with wrath; it was excited as an intoxicated man is who is under ungovernable passions; it was in heaven that the wrath commenced,

and the sword of divine justice rushed forth as if intoxicated, to destroy all before it.[89]

What will motivate God to shed the blood of millions of people with such passion and fervency? Isaiah answers this question: *"For it is the day of the Lord's vengeance, the year of recompense for the cause of Zion"* (v. 8). All brutality by Gentile nations against God's covenant people through all the ages will be recompensed at one time. The "time of the Gentiles," as Scripture refers to it, will come to an end and the Jewish people will never be persecuted again.

The result of God's vengeance will leave the land of Edom in a blaze of burning sulfur and pitch; it will be desolate and uninhabitable for generations (vv. 9-10). No person will be able to live in Edom's destroyed cities, but birds and beasts of prey will populate their ruins (v. 11). There will be no surviving nobility, or perhaps, if some leaders do live, they will govern Edom's survivors; this will ensure lingering confusion and disorder throughout the land (v. 12). Edom's broken-down walled cities will be overgrown with thorn bushes and brambles and will be inhabited by a multitude of wild and dangerous creatures, which will thrive there (vv. 13-15). Why will these cities be full of snakes, jackals, hyenas, hawks, etc.? God's Spirit will direct these creatures to inhabit and propagate within Edom's ruins for generations as a powerful testimony of His wrath against the nations (vv. 16-17).

Isaiah's graphic description of Edom's utter devastation is a preview of what the entire world will be like by the conclusion of the Tribulation Period, as described earlier in the chapter. The nations will experience God's escalating fury for seven years with the quick sequence of the seven bowl judgments of Revelation being the grand finale. John informs us that the apocalypse of Jesus Christ will decimate the entire planet (Rev. 7-19). This staggering scene of death and destruction sets a dark, dreary backdrop for the wondrous blessings of the Kingdom Age which will immediately follow the darkest time in human history. Of the latter portion of the Tribulation Period, the Lord Jesus said:

> *For then there will be great tribulation, such as has not been since the beginning of the world until this time, no, nor ever shall be. And unless those days were shortened, no flesh would be saved; but for the elect's sake those days will be shortened* (Matt. 24:21-22).

Thankfully, the book of Isaiah does not conclude with the bleak predictions of chapter 34. Indeed, there is good news ahead (chp. 35) – Christ is coming back to make all things new again!

Meditation

> Break forth in hymns of gladness,
> O wasted Jerusalem;
> Let songs instead of sadness,
> Thy jubilee proclaim;
> The Lord, in strength victorious,
> Upon thy foes has trod;
> Behold, O earth, the glorious
> Salvation of our God.
>
> — Benjamin Gough

The Day of Blessing
Isaiah 35

The previous chapter foretold God's righteous indignation being unleashed against the nations for their wickedness and their ill-treatment of the Jewish nation. In this chapter, Isaiah foretells God's rich blessings to the refined Jewish nation and to surviving Gentiles who did not follow the Antichrist. The chapter is full of joy and gladness. It commences with jubilant rejoicing in God's goodness and concludes with the ransomed of the Lord returning to Zion to do the same. The main point of Isaiah's message is expressed in verses 3-4:

Strengthen the weak hands, and make firm the feeble knees. Say to those who are fearful-hearted, "Be strong, do not fear! Behold, your God will come with vengeance, with the recompense of God; He will come and save you."

Isaiah was encouraging the remnant to remain strong in the Lord, for He was coming to save them. God's vengeance against the nations would coincide with His deliverance and healing of Israel.

In the Kingdom Age the judicial, worldwide devastation described in the last chapter and the divine curses on the earth for original sin (Gen. 3) will be reversed (see Isa. 11 discussion). To this end, Scripture foretells Israel becoming an agricultural icon in the world during the Millennial Kingdom (vv. 1-2), which to some degree has already occurred in recent years. Isaiah speaks not only of this agricultural achievement, but also associates the timing of this realization with when Jehovah gathers His people out of the nations to worship Him in Jerusalem (27:13). Though the Jewish nation has not fully returned to Israel, nor do they yet worship their Messiah, the process of gathering them back "one by one" has apparently already begun (see 27:12 comments). This gathering process will conclude at Christ's second advent (Ezek. 39:28-29). Isaiah writes:

Those who come He shall cause to take root in Jacob; Israel shall blossom and bud, and fill the face of the world with fruit (27:6).

The wilderness and the wasteland shall be glad for them, and the desert shall rejoice and blossom as the rose (v. 1).

During the Kingdom Age, Ezekiel says fruit-laden trees will line the banks of a river which proceeds from Messiah's temple in Jerusalem. This river will cleanse the whole earth. This characterizes the Holy Spirit's influence among the nations during this time:

Along the bank of the river, on this side and that, will grow all kinds of trees used for food; their leaves will not wither, and their fruit will not fail. They will bear fruit every month, because their water flows from the sanctuary. Their fruit will be for food, and their leaves for medicine (Ezek. 47:12).

Imagine fruit that never drops to the ground and spoils, but is always available to refresh the one desiring to eat it. Even the leaves of these trees are always accessible to heal any ailment. The blind shall see, the deaf shall hear, the lame shall walk, and the dumb shall speak – genetic disorders causing disabling conditions will be a thing of the past (vv. 5-6). The entire earth will be well-watered and its fertile ecosystem will have been cleansed of pollution, toxins, and radiation (v. 7).

There will be nothing in the Kingdom Age to stop individuals from receiving God's blessings, other than their own exercise of faith and holiness. Isaiah informs us that there will be easy access to the Millennial Temple in Jerusalem during the Kingdom Age, despite the river of water coming out of it, which Ezekiel says splits in two flowages which terminate in the Mediterranean Sea and the Dead Sea:

A highway shall be there, and a road, and it shall be called the Highway of Holiness. ... But the redeemed shall walk there, and the ransomed of the Lord shall return, and come to Zion with singing, with everlasting joy on their heads. They shall obtain joy and gladness, and sorrow and sighing shall flee away (vv. 8-10).

Isaiah does not provide any more information about the Highway of Holiness in his book. J. A. Motyer notes: "Through this attractive, nourishing landscape runs a highway. Where it goes we are not yet

Sorrow and Comfort

told, only who may go on it." He also notes that the Hebrew word rendered "highway" is not found elsewhere, but has a similar meaning as $m^e silla$ – "a road built on a raised causeway and therefore visible and unmistakable."[90] Through comparing the books of Ezekiel, Zechariah, and Revelation, we can surmise a possible route of this highway.

In the book of Revelation, John foretells that five separate earthquakes will occur during the Tribulation Period, and that the last one is the mother of all earthquakes – mountains about the earth fall and islands vanish (Rev. 16:18, 20). This means that the world's geography will be quite different after the Tribulation Period. Zechariah records that Jerusalem is actually elevated at this time, while the highlands to the south become a flat plain. He also states that when Christ returns to the earth, He cleaves the Mount of Olives in two (i.e., what is remaining of it) and creates a valley running east and west (Zech. 14:4-8). Two rivers will then originate from the mount; one will flow westward to the Mediterranean Sea and the other eastward to the Dead Sea. The Mount of Olives is located just east of Jerusalem and was prophesied at Christ's ascension to be the location of His return (Acts 1:9-12). He will return to the mount in the same visible and bodily manner (Zech. 14:4; Rev. 1:7).

These events all happen just prior to the Kingdom Age and before the temple complex described by Ezekiel exists. The source of all life is Jesus Christ (John 1:1-4). When He lands on the Mount of Olives, refreshing rivers of life appear; when He is on His throne in the temple, living water will also flow freely. Perhaps then, this road called *"the Highway of Holiness"* will allow the redeemed (those walking in holiness) to travel northward from Jerusalem and to pass over the river in order to enter the temple complex (v. 8). This road permits safe passage for all righteous pilgrims traveling on it; no wild beasts will ever threaten or impede them from coming to the temple and worshipping the Lord (v. 9). The prophet Ezekiel describes in great detail the layout of the millennial temple and the types of sacrifices and offerings that will occur there, as led by Israel's prince and priesthood on behalf of the nation (Ezek. 40-44).

Although verse 10 speaks of all the redeemed, these words will be especially encouraging for the Jewish people who have been estranged from the Lord and have suffered much through the centuries: *"And the ransomed of the Lord shall return, and come to Zion with singing, with everlasting joy on their heads. They shall obtain joy and gladness, and sorrow and sighing shall flee away."* Because the Jewish nation will be indwelt by the Holy Spirit during the Kingdom Age, they will understand what God has accomplished in them, that He has kept His promises to them, and they will rejoice in their great God. Then Israel will be excited to worship their Messiah, the Lord Jesus Christ!

Dear believer, we have Scripture to understand what God has accomplished for us and we already have the Holy Spirit, so let us be excited to worship the Lord Jesus now! Our times of corporate worship should be joyful, fresh, and exhilarating. Is not our God worthy of such excitement?

Meditation

> We need to discover all over again that worship is natural to the Christian, as it was to the godly Israelites who wrote the psalms, and that the habit of celebrating the greatness and graciousness of God yields an endless flow of thankfulness, joy, and zeal.
>
> — J. I. Packer

A Blasphemous Rant
Isaiah 36

The key message that Isaiah has repeatedly delivered to Judah is, Do not put your confidence in foreign alliances; rather, trust in the Lord and He will mightily remove the Assyrian threat. Chapters 36 and 37 contain the historical record of how God kept His promise and astoundingly wiped out the invading army. This outcome was realized largely due to the faithfulness of godly King Hezekiah, who put the entire situation into the Lord's hands. This was exactly what the Lord wanted His people to learn through this trial. God is always strong, but He desires to demonstrate His manifold wisdom and power when His people put their complete confidence in Him.

Assyria, the dominant world power at that time, thought her military was invincible. Assyria's king, Sennacherib, chided Israel's God as being no different than other puny gods already defeated in their territorial conquest. Both facts are plainly stated within this historical narrative so that future readers would understand just how much God detests pride and how powerfully He acts against it.

The events of chapters 36 and 37 occurred in 701 B.C., the fourteenth year of Hezekiah's reign (v. 1). The Assyrians surrounded Jerusalem a few months after Hezekiah's healing (chp. 38) and shortly after the Babylonian delegation had left the city (chp. 39). Sennacherib had successfully invaded and conquered many cities in northern Judah. He directed one of his commanders, Rabshakeh, to remove his army from Lachish (a large, conquered city southwest of Jerusalem) and to surround King Hezekiah at Jerusalem (v. 2). Sennacherib's assault on Lachish is recorded in the Annals of the Assyrian king and was depicted on the walls of Sennacherib's palace in Nineveh.[91] Also, an inscription on Sennacherib's Prism extols his military accomplishments in Judea:

> As to Hezekiah the Jew he did not submit to my yoke. I lay siege to forty-six of his strong cities walled forts and to the countless small

villages in their vicinity. I drove out of them 200,150 people. Himself I made a prisoner in Jerusalem, his Royal residence, like a bird in a cage.[92]

Although the Assyrian army at Jerusalem's gates was indeed a sobering moment for Judah, Isaiah must have been ecstatic to witness the fulfillment of the prophecy he had uttered thirty years earlier (8:5-10).

It Would Be Wise to Surrender

Rabshakeh is not likely a proper name, but rather a title denoting high rank – a general, so to speak (similar to the title of Abimelech in Gen. 20:3). For this reason, many commentators refer to him as "the Rabshakeh." Hezekiah sent three distinguished representatives, Eliakim, Shebna, and Joah, to speak with and hopefully negotiate with Rabshakeh.

This meeting occurred by the aqueduct from the upper pool, on the highway to the Fuller's Field (v. 3). Isaiah and his son had conversed with King Ahaz at this location about thirty years earlier when Jerusalem was threatened by a Syrian-Israeli alliance (7:3). Ahaz did not believe that God would deliver Judah from their attack, but Isaiah told him that within three years the alliance would fail and it did. Now, the same prophet was delivering a similar message to Hezekiah. Would he follow in Ahaz's disbelief or would he put his confidence in the Lord? The historical significance of the meeting location certainly heightened the tension over the outcome of this question.

Rabshakeh immediately began to mock the Jews and their God by asking the three Jewish representatives as to whom they were depending on to defeat Assyria's unbeaten army. He suggested that Egypt was like a splintered reed and had no strength to help them (vv. 4-6). Ironically, on this point Isaiah was in full agreement with Rabshakeh.

The profane Assyrian commander, speaking in Hebrew and in the hearing of Jewish soldiers on the wall, provided three reasons why the Jews should surrender Jerusalem to the Assyrians.

First, he challenged the Jews not to say to him that *"we trust in the Lord our God"* (v. 7). He wrongly assumed that Hezekiah had angered God by removing all the high places and altars throughout Judah and limiting Jehovah worship to only one altar in Jerusalem. Obviously, the pagan commander did not understand that Hezekiah's reforms pleased the Lord because the king was ensuring that Jewish religious practices were in accordance with God's Law. Hezekiah had purged paganism and reestablished the Levitical priesthood as the only officiants who could offer sacrifices on the Bronze Altar.

Second, Rabshakeh insulted Judah's army as being minute and feeble. He offered to give Hezekiah 2,000 horses, if he could find enough cavalrymen to ride them. The gesture implied that Judah was unable to muster up any kind of a legitimate fight (v. 8). Then, in taunting rhetoric, the commander suggested that even if Judah had 2,000 skilled riders, all of them could not overcome even one low-ranking Assyrian officer in battle (v. 9).

Third, the Assyrian commander insisted that the Hebrew God, Jehovah, had commanded him to *"go up against this land, and destroy it"* (v. 8). This implied that God was infuriated with the Jews over the loss of the high places and wanted the Assyrians to punish His people. Obviously, none of this was true, but the Assyrian commander was a master of terrorizing those he wished to conquer. And what better way to demoralize Judah's army than to plant the thought that God was angry with His people and had turned His back on them.

The Hebrew delegation understood the seriousness of the tactic and requested that Rabshakeh speak to them in Aramaic and not in Hebrew during their negotiations (v. 11). The pompous Assyrian denied their request. He said that he had been sent to communicate his message to the general populous, not just Hezekiah's negotiators, who would likely filter out the nonsensical content of his message (v. 12). He conjectured that it was important for common soldiers to hear his message, because they would be forced to eat and drink their own waste in order to survive a long siege. So, Rabshakeh spoke with even a louder voice so even more Jews would hear his warning (v. 13):

> *Do not let Hezekiah deceive you, for he will not be able to deliver you; nor let Hezekiah make you trust in the Lord, saying, "The Lord will surely deliver us; this city will not be given into the hand of the king of Assyria"* (vv. 14-15).

Logically speaking, if Jehovah had sent Rabshakeh to punish Judah as he claimed, would not the message from heaven have been to repent and return to Jehovah who loves you, rather than "do not trust in Jehovah"? The weakness of the enemy's position was now revealed.

They did not fear the army of Judah, but rather feared that the Jews would put their full confidence in their God.

Such actions of faith by God's people today result in fresh proclamations of the devil's defeat at Calvary. Satan knows that if he can move the believer from the truth of the triumphant ground of Calvary, he can gain a victory. Watchman Nee summarizes this point in his book *Sit, Walk, Stand*:

> Christ's warfare was offensive; He gained the victory over the devil at the Cross. Our warfare is mostly defensive – we war against Satan only to maintain and consolidate the victory which Christ has already gained – we hold what Christ has gained against all challenges. If we fight with the concept of gaining a victory, then we lose the battle at the onset. The Christian walk and warfare draw their strength from sitting before God and resting in Him. Satan's objective is to move us from the perfect ground of triumph, thus our armor (Eph. 6) is essentially defensive.

Satan knows that he can overcome God's people only when they compromise the truth by doubting God's ability and promises. This is why James exhorts believers to *"submit to God. Resist the devil and he will flee from you. Draw near to God and He will draw near to you"* (Jas. 4:7-8). The prophet Ezekiel informs us that before his fall, Lucifer (now referred to as Satan or "the accuser") was a beautiful anointed cherub (Ezek. 28:11-16). He was likely the most powerful created being that God made and, thus, is a cunning and dangerous enemy that only God controls. Consequently, believers are not commanded to confront Satan, but rather to resist him by submitting to God in faith.

Believers are to be knowledgeable of the devil's tactics so that he does not gain an advantage over them through ignorance. Paul reminded the Christians at Corinth of this fact, saying, *"we are not ignorant of his devices"* (2 Cor. 2:11). Because Satan uses the same strategies repeatedly to oppose the things of God, believers are able to become more aware of his confrontational tactics by studying Scripture. The lesson for us in Isaiah 36 is that God's people must not compromise the truth no matter what the enemy says – it is best, if possible, not to even listen to what he says.

In the hearing of the Jewish soldiers on the wall, Rabshakeh continued his tirade by promising that if the Jews surrendered, they would receive homes, farms, and vineyards in another land and could

Sorrow and Comfort

get on with their lives in peace (vv. 16-17). Rabshakeh was too shrewd to try to hide Assyria's deportation policy of conquered people; hence, he exaggerates the so-called "opportunity" to make it appear as attractive as possible. Though this may have been an appealing option as compared to a long siege, it is doubtful that such terms would be honored after their surrender. Even if partially granted, the Jews would still be slaves and under heavy tribute in Assyria.

Rabshakeh concluded his blasphemous rant by again instructing the Jews not to listen to Hezekiah, nor to have confidence in their Jehovah:

Beware lest Hezekiah persuade you, saying, "The Lord will deliver us." Has any one of the gods of the nations delivered its land from the hand of the king of Assyria? Where are the gods of Hamath and Arpad? Where are the gods of Sepharvaim? Indeed, have they delivered Samaria from my hand? Who among all the gods of these lands have delivered their countries from my hand, that the Lord should deliver Jerusalem from my hand?" (vv. 18-20).

Reason begs the question, Why would Rabshakeh supposedly obey Jehovah's command to punish the Jewish people if he thought so little of Jehovah, even comparing Him to the gods of Hamath and Arpad in Aram? Furthermore, the Assyrian commander reminded the Jews, that no god had protected anyone in Samaria from being conquered by the Assyrians twenty-one years earlier. Why should they trust in their God now when He did not protect the Northern Kingdom from defeat and exile? Of course, all that had happened to Israel had been prophesied by Isaiah years before as part of God's chastisement for their stubborn idolatry (7:8). Judah had been spared a subsequent attack by Assyria largely because of Hezekiah's reforms and his purging of organized idolatry. The situation was much different in Judah than Israel, because Hezekiah was yielding to God's Law and, as we will see in the next chapter, he also had God's favor.

The Jewish Response

Although the Jewish delegation and soldiers were no doubt disturbed and perhaps even terrified after hearing Rabshakeh's taunts, they obeyed the king's command and answered him nothing (v. 21). Eliakim, Shebna, and Joah returned to Hezekiah with their clothes torn and reported all the Assyrian commander had said to them (v. 22). The tearing of one's clothes is an ancient Jewish tradition associated with mourning, grief, and loss. Jacob, for example, tore his clothes, put on sackcloth, and mourned many days when he thought his son Joseph had been killed by a wild animal (Gen. 37:34). The men in the envoy were publicly displaying their revulsion over Rabshakeh's blasphemy and threats. We will learn of Hezekiah's incredible response of faith to this situation in the next chapter.

Meditation

In his hatred of Christ, the devil will seek to rob us of the truth, or, failing to do this, he will seek to bring dishonor upon the Name of Christ and discredit the truth by bringing about moral breakdown amongst those who hold the truth. The more truth we have, the greater the dishonor to Christ if we break down by the allowance of the flesh. We must therefore be prepared to face conflict, and the more truth we have, the greater will be the conflict.

— Hamilton Smith

God Is Greater Than Assyria
Isaiah 37

The Humble King Is Assured

After King Hezekiah heard the envoy's report, he also tore his clothes, put on sackcloth, and then went to the temple (v. 1). As previously noted, tearing one's clothes was a dramatic gesture to express outrage or deep grief in response to some event. Wearing sackcloth was an ongoing expression of brokenness until the distressing situation had passed. Any Jew seeing Hezekiah without his royal attire and earnestly praying in the temple would have been deeply moved. Rabshakeh had blasphemed God and threatened to decimate Judah. Hezekiah knew the situation was desperate and that there was only one remedy – the hand of God.

The king sent Eliakim, Shebna, and the elders of the priests, also covered in sackcloth, to Isaiah with the king's request that he pray with them about this urgent matter (v. 2). This was significant, as some, like King Ahaz, did not view Isaiah's messages as being divine in origin. However, godly Hezekiah immediately seeks Isaiah's prayers and counsel. Hezekiah likens Jerusalem's situation to a woman who has been in the deep pangs of childbearing for an extended time and has no strength remaining to deliver her baby – meaning that Jerusalem could not deliver herself from this ominous circumstance (v. 3). The king was hoping that God took note of Rabshakeh's profane words and that He will move to vindicate Himself (vv. 4-5).

Speaking for the Lord, Isaiah assures Hezekiah that God heard every blasphemous word, and that Hezekiah was not to be fearful:

> *Do not be afraid of the words which you have heard, with which the servants of the king of Assyria have blasphemed Me. Surely I will send a spirit upon him, and he shall hear a rumor and return to his own land; and I will cause him to fall by the sword in his own land* (vv. 6-7).

Devotions in Isaiah

Rabshakeh had surrounded Jerusalem with a sizeable army, and the Assyrian king, Sennacherib, had moved his remaining soldiers from Lachish to Libnah, a city about five miles north of Jerusalem (v. 8). At about the same time that Rabshakeh sent a report to Sennacherib on the progress at Jerusalem, the king received another intelligence report that Tirhakah king of Ethiopia was moving north to war with him (v. 9).

Sennacherib withdrew from the region in order to properly array his troops for combat, but before doing so, he sent a parting message to Hezekiah: *"Do not let your God in whom you trust deceive you, saying, 'Jerusalem shall not be given into the hand of the king of Assyria'"* (v. 10). He then boasted that no god of any land that he had conquered had been able to deliver anyone from his hand. Sennacherib then supplied a list of key cities throughout the region which had succumbed to Assyria's conquest: Gozan, Haran, Rezeph, Eden, Tel Assar, Hena, and Ivah. (Some of these cities had fallen over one hundred years earlier; vv. 11-13.)

The Praying King Is Heard

After Hezekiah received Sennacherib's message, he again trekked to the temple and laid the letter before the Lord in prayer (vv. 14-15):

O Lord of hosts, God of Israel, the one who dwells between the cherubim, You are God, You alone, of all the kingdoms of the earth. You have made heaven and earth. Incline Your ear, O Lord, and hear; open Your eyes, O Lord, and see; and hear all the words of Sennacherib, which he has sent to reproach the living God. Truly, Lord, the kings of Assyria have laid waste all the nations and their lands, and have cast their gods into the fire; for they were not gods, but the work of men's hands – wood and stone. Therefore they destroyed them. Now therefore, O Lord our God, save us from his hand, that all the kingdoms of the earth may know that You are the Lord, You alone (vv. 16-20).

This is a remarkable prayer of faith, a model prayer in many respects. First, notice that Hezekiah did not rush into God's presence as a frantic, fearful king, but as a trusting worshipper. He commences his prayer with praise and worship. This is how the Lord Jesus taught His disciples to initiate their prayers (Luke 11:2). Hezekiah acknowledges that he is praying to the only true God, the One who dwells in heaven, who created all things, and controls the kingdoms of the world (v. 16).

Sorrow and Comfort

To enter God's presence with accolades of praise, expressions of thanksgiving, and heartfelt worship demonstrates to God that we know Him and trust Him. If we believe that God truly controls all things according to His sovereign plan, then we must also believe that time is not a limiting factor for Him to accomplish His best.

Second, Hezekiah asks God to take action against the Assyrians because of Sennacherib's blasphemous words (v. 17). Notice that Hezekiah did not repeat to God what Sennacherib actually said. The king of Judah understood that an all-knowing, all-seeing, and all-wise God did not need more information. Rather, God is honored when His people are in awe of Him and trust Him. The Lord's people should not waste time supplying God with facts about situations He is already completely aware of – He understands much more than we do anyway. Rather, we should be telling the Lord what we know about Him, giving thanks for what He has done, and expressing our confidence in His attributes and character to achieve the best outcome, even though we do not know what that might be. True faith wants what God wants.

Third, Hezekiah acknowledges the truth of Sennacherib's claim that no people groups (with all their pagan gods) have been able to resist Assyrian aggression (vv. 18-19). This is not to provide God with information, but to acknowledge the incredible prospect that God has to glorify His name. The stage is set, so to speak, and Jehovah has a wonderful opportunity to prove to all Gentile nations that the God of the Jews is indeed Lord of all (v. 20).

Hezekiah's actions reflect Peter's and James' exhortations to fellow believers in the Church Age when tested by trials:

> *Yes, all of you be submissive to one another, and be clothed with humility, for "God resists the proud, but gives grace to the humble." Therefore humble yourselves under the mighty hand of God, that He may exalt you in due time, casting all your care upon Him, for He cares for you. Be sober, be vigilant; because your adversary the devil walks about like a roaring lion, seeking whom he may devour. Resist him, steadfast in the faith, knowing that the same sufferings are experienced by your brotherhood in the world* (1 Pet. 5:5-9).

> *God resists the proud, but gives grace to the humble. Therefore submit to God. Resist the devil and he will flee from you. Draw near to God and He will draw near to you. Cleanse your hands, you sinners; and purify your hearts, you double-minded* (Jas. 4:6-8).

The king was literally "clothed with humility" and he humbled himself before the Lord. He effectually "cast his care on the Lord," that is, he laid Sennacherib's letter before the Lord – a gesture meaning "Lord you handle this." Walking in faith and truth, Hezekiah fully expected God to honor His name, just as David had three centuries earlier during a threatening situation:

> *Revive me, O Lord, for Your name's sake! For Your righteousness' sake bring my soul out of trouble. In Your mercy cut off my enemies, and destroy all those who afflict my soul; for I am Your servant* (Ps. 143:11-12).

And as we will see shortly, "in due time" God likewise delivered Hezekiah, as He did David. Accordingly, both Old and New Testaments present the same pattern for victorious living as poetically expressed in this hymn:

> When we walk with the Lord in the light of His Word,
> What a glory He sheds on our way!
> While we do His good will, He abides with us still,
> And with all who will trust and obey.
>
> Not a shadow can rise, not a cloud in the skies,
> But His smile quickly drives it away,
> Not a doubt or a fear, not a sigh or a tear,
> Can abide while we trust and obey.
>
> — John H. Sammis

The Waiting King Is Answered

The Lord God of Israel replied to the king's prayer of faith through Isaiah: *"Because you have prayed to Me against Sennacherib king of Assyria, this is the word which the Lord has spoken concerning him"* (v. 21). The Lord specifically states that He would do three things.

First, Assyrians would be turned back in such a powerful way that the virgin daughter of Zion (speaking of Jerusalem in poetic parallelism) would mock the Assyrians (v. 22). Jerusalem would revel over the ineffectual attempts of Sennacherib to take it, like a taunting young maiden. This mocking would rebuff Assyria's blasphemy of Israel's God and their triumphal endeavors (vv. 23-25).

Sorrow and Comfort

The felling of trees (the toppling of nations) and the drying up of brooks for defense (draining moats around cities) metaphorically represented Sennacherib's boasted achievements. But Isaiah likens the nations that Assyria conquered to grass on a flat housetop. These countries were easily overcome because Israel's God had weakened those opposing Assyria, whom He was using to punish them (vv. 26-27). But because of Sennacherib's rage against God, God promised to put a hook in his nose and a bridle in his mouth and to lead him like a captive slave back to Assyria (vv. 28-29).

The second thing God promised was to maintain a remnant in Judah and to return agricultural productivity back to normal after two years (vv. 30-32). This sign would dissuade anyone from thinking that the Assyrian withdrawal had happened by chance. The Jews would glean what God caused to spring up naturally in their fields, but in the third year they would be able to sow and reap again. Isaiah then compares this agricultural promise to what God would accomplish spiritually in His people: *"And the remnant who have escaped of the house of Judah shall again take root downward, and bear fruit upward"* (v. 31).

This scenario provides a lovely application: believers must root down to bear up fruit to God. Many Christians, often those who are infants in the Lord, are zealous to serve the Lord, but do not want to expend the time to "root downward" first. When Christians try to do something for the Lord without a good scriptural foundation, an understanding of their spiritual calling and gifts, and exercising dependence on the Lord, the result is usually harmful to the name of Christ. Young believers desiring to branch out before they are sufficiently rooted in the Lord to sustain the work of ministry will tend to topple over. Thus the wisdom of Isaiah's statement – believers must "take root downward" before they can "bear fruit upward."

To summarize this second decree, some cities had been conquered and vineyards, orchards, etc. had been destroyed by the Assyrians, but all this devastation would be remedied soon. It would take only a couple of years for there to be the rooting down and the bearing up of fruit again. God promised to do this because of His great zeal for Judah.

The third promise of the Lord centered in the protection of Jerusalem and the ultimate destruction of the Assyrian army:

> *"He shall not come into this city, nor shoot an arrow there, nor come before it with shield, nor build a siege mound against it. By the way that he came, by the same shall he return; and he shall not come into*

this city," says the Lord. "For I will defend this city, to save it for My own sake and for My servant David's sake" (vv. 33-35).

God was long-suffering with Judah because of His unconditional covenant with David. God promised David that one of his descendants would sit on his throne forever, which meant the seed royal had to be preserved. Hence, God informs Hezekiah that Sennacherib will not step foot in Jerusalem. He would not even have time to build a siege ramp because God would turn him back to Assyria via the same route he arrived. Isaiah had already stated that Sennacherib would die by the sword in his own land (v. 7).

The Trusting King Is Delivered

The chapter concludes with the fulfillment of much of what Isaiah had previously prophesied concerning the fall of the Assyrians (e.g., 30:27-33, 31:8-9, 33:18-19). Because this is one of the most spectacular defeats in all Scripture of an army threatening Israel, the single verse account seems almost anticlimactic: *"Then the angel of the Lord went out, and killed in the camp of the Assyrians one hundred and eighty-five thousand; and when people arose early in the morning, there were the corpses – all dead"* (v. 36). This is the only time in his book that Isaiah refers to *the Angel of the Lord*; the only other prophet to employee this title is Zechariah.

Chapter 6 has a fuller discussion of who the Angel (or Messenger) of the Lord is. It suffices here to acknowledge Him as a theophany of the second person of the Godhead. Later He, the Word, became flesh to become both the Message and the Messenger of God to humanity.

The slaughter by the Angel of the Lord occurred at night. How it was accomplished has been the source of much speculation. It was not likely pestilence, for the Jews would have been apprehensive about despoiling the dead Assyrian soldiers. Some have suggested that the army was struck by a colossal hailstorm. But that would have damaged the goods and livestock that the Lord was providing for His people through the victory, and also does not explain how Sennacherib survived. We learn from 2 Chronicles 32:21 that the entire Assyrian army was not destroyed, but the Angel *"cut down every mighty man of valor, leader, and captain in the camp of the king of Assyria."* The selective nature of this judgment further substantiates its divine origin (i.e. the Lord disabled the Assyrian army by eliminating all of its leadership and skilled soldiers). Perhaps the best explanation is that the Lord, who is the essence of all life, simply snuffed out the lives of 185,000 specific men in a single moment of time.

We do know that the next morning the Jews awoke to find 185,000 corpses and that Sennacherib had returned to Assyria with only a remnant of his army. The reason the king was permitted to survive was so that Hezekiah could see that God was in control of every detail of Judah's deliverance. Isaiah had foretold that Sennacherib would return to Assyrian and die there by the sword.

The last two verses of the chapter confirm that is what happened. Over the next twenty years, Sennacherib engaged in several military exploits, but he never returned to Israel. While the king was worshipping in the house of Nisroch his god in Nineveh, his sons Adrammelech and Sharezer struck him down with the sword (vv. 37-38). They escaped into the land of Ararat, and Esarhaddon, one of the sons of Sennacherib, ruled in his place.

God permitted Sennacherib several years to reflect on what he had witnessed, that is, much of his army being selectively wiped out without the presence of a visible enemy. Instead of believing that he had actually offended the one true God and lost, he turned to his own gods who did not protect him, nor provide him answers for the calamity. There is an insanity to pride, the ultimate expression being that somehow a man or an angel can overcome their Creator and rule in His place. This was Lucifer's sin which caused his ruin and it is the same mindset that his children, the sons of disobedience, continue propagating today through a variety of world religions (such as New Age, Mormonism, and Hinduism). Rejecting God, or desiring to be on His throne, never ends well, but humbling ourselves before Him always will.

Meditation

> The Assyrian came down like the wolf on the fold,
> His cohorts were gleaming in purple and gold;
> The sheen of their spears was like stars on the sea,
> When the blue wave rolls nightly on deep Galilee.
>
> Like the leaves of the forest when Summer is green,
> That host with their banners at sunset were seen:

Devotions in Isaiah

Like the leaves of the forest when Autumn hath blown,
That host on the morrow lay withered and strown.

For the Angel of Death spread his wings on the blast,
And breathed in the face of the foe as he passed;
And the eyes of the sleepers waxed deadly and chill,
And their hearts but once heaved, and forever grew still!

And there lay the steed with his nostril all wide,
But through it there rolled not the breath of his pride;
And the foam of his gasping lay white on the turf,
And cold as the spray of the rock-beating surf.

And there lay the rider distorted and pale,
With the dew on his brow, and the rust on his mail:
And the tents were all silent, the banners alone,
The lances unlifted, the trumpet unblown.

And the widows of Ashur are loud in their wail,
And the idols are broke in the temple of Baal;
And the might of the Gentile, unsmote by the sword,
Hath melted like snow in the glance of the Lord.

— George Gordon

Hezekiah's Extra Years
Isaiah 38

Hezekiah's Illness and Warning

Thirty-nine-year-old Hezekiah was sick and near death when Isaiah visited him and said, *"Thus says the Lord: 'Set your house in order, for you shall die and not live'"* (v. 1). The prophet had spoken in the name of the Lord, therefore what Isaiah said was sure to come to pass, correct? Isaiah spoke only what God told him to and though the statement conveyed urgency, it did not affirm imminent death.

Though Hezekiah could probably ensure that the affairs of state were in good order, he apparently did not have a son to set on the throne in his place. Manasseh was born about three years after the events in this chapter; he assumed Hezekiah's throne at the age of twelve (2 Chron. 33:1). As long as Judah had a throne, the Davidic dynasty must not be broken, meaning, Hezekiah needed to have a natural son. Most kings took many wives to ensure they would have plenty of sons and heirs. However, the king had either neglected this matter in his early years (perhaps thinking he had plenty of time to marry and have children), or perhaps he was married, but only daughters had been born to him. The king had been quite occupied with spiritual reform in Judah and with fortifying Jerusalem.

Hezekiah's Prayer

After Isaiah delivered his message and departed, Hezekiah turned and faced the wall, tearfully uttering this brief prayer: *"Remember now, O Lord, I pray, how I have walked before You in truth and with a loyal heart, and have done what is good in Your sight"* (v. 3). Why would the king remind God of His integrity and good deeds? In the Old Testament illness and disease were often associated directly with divine punishment for sin. This appears to be Hezekiah's thinking in appealing to the Lord, for later he will connect his deliverance from death with the forgiveness of his sins (v. 17).

Notice that Hezekiah did not bother to tell God what he wanted; he knew that God was already aware of the desires of his heart. Rather, he reminded the Lord that he had walked in truth and had faithfully led His people to honor Him. He was not a wayward king deserving the death penalty. Few of us could ever pray such a prayer, but the fact that God respected Hezekiah's prayer tells us that it was a genuine statement – Hezekiah had been a loyal king of high morals and he had brought many reforms to Judah during his tenure.

Hezekiah's Answer

The parallel account recorded in 2 Kings 20 tells us that Isaiah had not yet departed from the palace before the Lord, responding to Hezekiah's prayer, instructed the prophet to return to the king with a second message (2 Kgs. 20:4):

> *"I have heard your prayer, I have seen your tears; surely I will add to your days fifteen years. I will deliver you and this city from the hand of the king of Assyria, and I will defend this city. And this is the sign to you from the Lord, that the Lord will do this thing which He has spoken: Behold, I will bring the shadow on the sundial, which has gone down with the sun on the sundial of Ahaz, ten degrees backward." So the sun returned ten degrees on the dial by which it had gone down* (vv. 5-8).

One thing that we learn from God's decree is that the events in chapters 38 and 39 slightly preceded the events in chapters 36 and 37. Since Hezekiah died in 686 B.C., the events of this chapter would have occurred early in 701 B.C., just prior to Rabshakeh's advance on Jerusalem recorded in chapter 36. Why did Isaiah arrange the narrative out of its natural chronology? Probably to place Hezekiah's folly in showing the Babylon delegation all of Judah's wealth (chp. 39) in such a way as to preface the prophecies pertaining to Babylon (chps. 40-48). In this nine-chapter section, God promised to chasten His idolatrous people by the Babylonians and then remove the Babylonians from power by the Medes so that the Jews could return to Israel to rebuild the temple the Babylonians had destroyed.

Isaiah told Hezekiah that God had heard his prayer and would heal him and add fifteen years to his life. Isaiah also promised Hezekiah that he would be healed quickly. *"On the third day you shall go up to the house of the Lord"* (2 Kgs. 20:5). Why the king asked for a sign from

Sorrow and Comfort

God proving that he would be healed is unknown (2 Kgs. 20:8), but God granted his request. Isaiah asked the king if God should cause *"the shadow go forward ten degrees or go backward ten degrees"* (2 Kgs. 20:9). John A. Martin explains the choices Isaiah was offering Hezekiah:

> Apparently a special stairway had been built as a time device, a kind of sundial. As the sun went down in the west, a shadow would move upward on the staircase so that people could ascertain the time of the day. Interestingly Ahaz had rejected a sign from the Lord (7:10-12) but now on a staircase named for him his son Hezekiah was given a sign.[93]

Since it is natural for a shadow to advance as the sun declines in the horizon, Hezekiah chose the latter option. Isaiah promptly petitions the Lord and *"He brought the shadow ten degrees backward, by which it had gone down on the sundial of Ahaz"* (2 Kgs. 20:11). How this miracle was achieved is unknown. It may have been a local phenomenon at the obelisk or one on a grander scale that actually affected the earth's rotation, the sun's disposition, or a redirection of light. What is evident is Isaiah's faith; he did not hesitate to ask God to do what seemed impossible, that is, something beyond what natural law can rationalize.

This all was good news for the king. However, we can only imagine what it was like for Hezekiah to live out his final years knowing exactly when he would die. What effect would that information have on a God-fearing individual? Knowing that you were invincible until God said your time on earth was over might either embolden zeal for the Lord or reckless thrill-seeking. The brevity of our sojourn on earth should cause all believers to evaluate life's priorities and pursue what is best in his or her remaining days.

The psalmists offer many aspiring prayers which should encourage us to value each day God has granted to us. For example:

> *O God, You have taught me from my youth; and to this day I declare Your wondrous works. Now also when I am old and grayheaded, O God, do not forsake me, until I declare Your strength to this generation, your power to everyone who is to come* (Ps. 71:17-18).

So teach us to number our days, that we may gain a heart of wisdom (Ps. 90:12).

Paul reminded the Ephesian Christians that the only reason we exist is for *"the praise of His glory"* (Eph. 1:12-14). We were created for God's good pleasure and to accomplish His purposes; nothing beyond that has any value for eternity (Eph. 2:10; Rev. 4:11).

Being healed of a fatal disease and observing a supernatural celestial event likely explains why Hezekiah was prompted to immediately humble himself and to put Sennacherib's threatening letter before the Lord in the temple. Unfortunately, we do not read of Hezekiah doing any other great feats for the Lord in his later years. In fact, the next chapter records that Hezekiah was lifted up in pride. He boasted of Judah's great resources to a visiting Babylonian delegation as if they were his.

Hezekiah's Praise

Verses 9-20 record Hezekiah's song of praise and thanksgiving after being healed. In the first stanza, the king speaks of his illness (vv. 9-15) and in the second stanza of his healing (vv. 16-20).

Hezekiah's illness seized hold of him during the prime of his life and was going to pull him through the gates of death (v. 9). He loathed the fact that he would be removed from the world of the living and would no longer be blessed by or able to worship the Lord (vv. 10-11). The king laments that his life would be cut off like a piece of cloth from the weaver's loom and that his body would soon be dismantled like the taking down of a temporary shepherd's tent (v. 12). Hezekiah hoped that he would get well, but as the days dragged on, he only got worse. He describes his emotional anguish over this as if God were a lion breaking all his bones (v. 13).

Lastly, he likened his painful groaning to the endless chattering of a crane or a swallow and his mourning to the doleful songs of a turtledove (v. 14). The turtledove is sometimes used in Scripture to represent mourning (59:11). Despite the prospect of nearing death, Hezekiah knew that God was in control of his life and had permitted this disease: *"O Lord, I am oppressed; undertake for me! ... He Himself has done it"* (v. 15). Realizing that God was in control of his illness, Hezekiah knew that he should choose to walk carefully and humbly before the Lord.

Sorrow and Comfort

In the second stanza, Hezekiah praises the Lord for restoring him to health and also for the experience; he discerned that he had benefitted from it (v. 16). The Lord loved Hezekiah too much to leave him the way he was, so he permitted a life-threatening disease to challenge and refine him. Likewise, He loves you and me too much to leave us the way we are. God specializes in managing crisis situations for our good and His glory.

While enduring a distressing situation, David wrote, *"I would hasten my escape from the windy storm and tempest"* (Ps. 55:8). If given a choice between enduring hardship with the Lord or having a life of ease, the flesh will also pick the latter. It is so easy to run from our difficulties, unless we understand that God has His way in the storms of life and that, if we flee prematurely, we are actually withdrawing from God's presence. J. N. Darby puts the matter this way: "Although God in His faithfulness be with us, we are not always with Him."[94]

After feeding five thousand men (plus women and children), the Lord sought solitude in order to pray to His Father. He sent His disciples by boat to the other side of the Sea of Galilee. Those twelve men, obedient to their Lord, launched out into a sea that soon met them with life-threatening force. They toiled all night in a raging storm but did not prevail against it. The disciples believed death crouched within each wave that broke upon their battered vessel. Yet, they were safer in that boat than any other place on earth. Why? Because they had been obedient to the Lord's command and were in the center of His will.

The very thing that the disciples feared – the raging sea – was what the Lord used to bring Himself closer to them; He walked upon the sea to meet them. God's presence enables us to overcome what is feared. The result will be a greater appreciation for His faithfulness and we will be more likely to confidently engage the next challenge in faith. This is why Hezekiah could say that he had benefitted from his near-death experience.

Every devoted Christian is destined for trouble, but not for despair: *"Yes, and all who desire to live godly in Christ Jesus will suffer persecution"* (2 Tim. 3:12). It is a promise of God that if you live to serve Christ, you will suffer for it. Dear believer, do not expect anything less and you will not be disappointed. Prepare your mind for the struggles ahead, and don't get bogged down in self-pity, grappling with despair when those forecasted storms of life arrive. If Christian in

John Bunyan's *Pilgrim's Progress* had girded his mind, he would have likely avoided the "slough of despond." Every Christian who righteously suffers for the cause of Christ will be rewarded: *"If we suffer, we shall also reign with Him"* (2 Tim. 2:12, KJV).

Through this bitter trial, Hezekiah saw more clearly God's love for him; he understood that the illness was not to punish him for sin, but to refine him (v. 17). Souls in Sheol, the realm of the dead, cannot praise God, so Hezekiah was thankful for the opportunity to do so in life. He promised to declare to others God's goodness and faithfulness to him (vv. 18-19). It is noteworthy that Hezekiah defines "the living" as those who enjoy doing what he was doing then, that is, praising and giving thanks to God. The redeemed in heaven agree; we exist only to refresh the heart of God and honor His name: *"Thou art worthy, O Lord, to receive glory and honor and power: for Thou hast created all things, and for Thy pleasure they are and were created* (Rev. 4:11; KJV). Because God had added fifteen years to Hezekiah's life, the king said he would happily use them to sing praises to God in His temple (v. 20).

Whether or not Hezekiah should have requested the Lord's intervention in his medical crisis is debated. From a logical perspective, we might conclude that it would have been better for the king to die from his illness. Hezekiah later fathered Manasseh, the most wicked king to sit on the throne of Judah. Hezekiah brought great religious reform to Judah, even removing the high places, but his son Manasseh plunged Judah into gross idolatry for decades before turning to the Lord near the end of his fifty-plus-year reign. Certainly much heartache for the remnant and for the Lord would have been avoided if Hezekiah had died instead of appealing to the Lord in this chapter.

Yet, all these things are within God's purposes: Manasseh's wicked ways would test the faithfulness of those loyal to Jehovah and set the stage for a great revival under Josiah, two years after Manasseh's death. Godly Josiah would cause the Word of God to be heard and honored again in Judah and he ushered in sweeping reforms. If there had been no Manasseh, there would have been no Josiah. In summary, God's ways are above our ways, and Hezekiah's foreknown failure had already been incorporated into God's sovereign plan for refining and restoring His covenant people to Himself. Through Hezekiah's faith, Assyria would be brought down as God said; through Hezekiah's failure, God announced the next phase of Judah's refinement – the Babylonians.

Hezekiah's Healing

The final two verses of the chapter describe the king's healing. Isaiah directs the king to apply a poultice of dried figs to his boils or ulcers (v. 21). This was a common medicinal treatment in those days for such inflammations, but it also offered a test of faith. Isaiah also told Hezekiah that he would be healed in three days (2 Kgs. 20:5). Because of Hezekiah's prayer, God was going to heal him through the poultice, but the king had to act in faith to apply it for three days and wait, which he did. But though Hezekiah was willing to proceed in faith, he also asked for a sign to confirm God's promise of his healing (v. 22).

Was this request a lapse of faith? It seems more likely that the opposite is true – a supernatural sign would infallibly confirm God's word in the matter. That is, a sign would prove that God had intervened in saving the king's life, and that the king had not been cured just by good medicine. So Hezekiah did not doubt God's word, but rather wanted to confirm it in such a way that no one else would doubt it either. This is a good example of faith-centered prayer, the Lord, and medicine all having their part in the healing process.

Meditation

> Lord, Thy Word abideth, and our footsteps guideth;
> Who its truth believeth light and joy receiveth.
> When the storms are o'er us, and dark clouds before us,
> Then its light directeth, and our way protecteth.
> O that we, discerning, its most holy learning,
> Lord, may love and fear Thee, evermore be near Thee!
>
> — Henry Baker

The Babylonians Are Coming
Isaiah 39

God's divine intervention in wiping out the Assyrian army in one night occurred a few months after Hezekiah's healing in the last chapter and likely just after the events in this chapter. Merodach-Baladan, the son of Baladan, king of Babylon, heard of Hezekiah's recovery and dispatched an envoy carrying letters and gifts to congratulate the king (v. 1). Merodach-Baladan was mentioned previously in chapter 21. Subsequent history suggests that the king of Babylon may have had an alternative motive in contacting Hezekiah besides just expressing goodwill. John A. Martin explains:

> Merodach-Baladan was Marduk-apal-iddina, the invader. Twice he had tried to break away from the Assyrian Empire, and once had succeeded in taking the city of Babylon. After his second reign (of nine months in 703-702 B.C.) he was deposed by Sennacherib and went to Elam. While there (and while still known as the king of Babylon) he actively tried to form an alliance with other nations to throw off the Assyrian yoke. Undoubtedly his friendly visit after Hezekiah's illness was intended to persuade the king of Judah to join the rebel alliance in the fight against Assyria.[95]

Hence, Hezekiah's showing the Babylonian envoy all *"the silver and gold, the spices and precious ointment, and all his armory – all that was found among his treasures"* was a foolish thing to do (v. 2). He was trying to impress his pagan visitors by acting as if all the riches of Judah belonged to him, but that was not the case – the wealth of Judah belonged to God.

Isaiah had already stated that Assyria was God's chastening rod on the entire region, so commiserating with those rebelling against God's expressed will (i.e., the Babylonians) was an indiscretion that God did not take lightly. A few months earlier, God had tested Hezekiah's faith through a fatal illness; now he would test the king's heart: *"Regarding the ambassadors of the princes of Babylon, whom they sent to him to*

Sorrow and Comfort

inquire about the wonder that was done in the land, God withdrew from him, in order to test him, that He might know all that was in his heart" (2 Chron. 32:31). In other words, the Lord wanted to show Hezekiah himself the terrible consequences of pride.

Solomon reminds us that God often sends trials our way to test the purity of our hearts and to expose what is dross: *"The refining pot is for silver and the furnace for gold, but the Lord tests the hearts"* (Prov. 17:3). It would be easy, after reading this story and with historical hindsight, to condemn Hezekiah's behavior, however, H. A. Ironside reminds us that God permits these types of tests in our lives to show us what is lurking in our hearts:

> Few of us could stand such a test. If we were left alone by God so that our hearts would be exposed and our inmost thoughts revealed, we without doubt would suffer moral and spiritual breakdown. Hezekiah failed the test because of self-confidence. He acted on his own judgment instead of turning to the Lord for guidance, and the inevitable result was harm instead of blessing.[96]

Hezekiah's response shows us that we can trust and serve the Lord, but still have pride hiding in our hearts. It is one thing to rest in the Lord and be delivered, but it is an entirely different disposition of mind not to rob glory from Him after being blessed. No wonder the Lord often keeps us immersed in trials; it keeps us humble and dependent on Him. Our self-dependence results in the loss of divine blessing and, as Hezekiah would soon learn, is usually harmful to others in our care.

This seems to be the reason that Paul had to struggle with an ongoing infirmity, though he had repeatedly petitioned the Lord to remove it. The Lord explained to Paul why He was not going to remove it: *"My grace is sufficient for you, for My strength is made perfect in weakness"* (2 Cor. 12:9). Once Paul understood why he must continue suffering with his infirmity he declared: *"Therefore most gladly I will rather boast in my infirmities, that the power of Christ may rest upon me. Therefore I take pleasure in infirmities, in reproaches, in needs, in persecutions, in distresses, for Christ's sake. For when I am weak, then I am strong"* (2 Cor. 12:10). The Lord delights to demonstrate His power through the weakness of His people, and it liberates our minds to realize that this is good for us and honors Him.

After hearing about the foreign delegation, Isaiah visited Hezekiah and asked him, *"What did these men say, and from where did they come to you?"* (v. 3). The prophet's questions were not to obtain information, but to assist the king in realizing the gravity of his error. Hezekiah told Isaiah from where they came, Babylon, but not what they had said. This withholding of information may indicate that the Babylonian delegation had indeed solicited Hezekiah's assistance against Assyria (vv. 4-5). After learning that the king had shown the Babylonians all the wealth of Judah, Isaiah issues a twofold prophecy:

> *"Behold, the days are coming when all that is in your house, and what your fathers have accumulated until this day, shall be carried to Babylon; nothing shall be left," says the Lord. "And they shall take away some of your sons who will descend from you, whom you will beget; and they shall be eunuchs in the palace of the king of Babylon"* (vv. 6-7).

First, Isaiah said that all Hezekiah had shown the Babylonians would be carried back to Babylon. This seemed unlikely at the time, as Assyria was the dominant world power and the rebel Babylonians were on the run. Second, the prophet told the king that some of his descendants would be made eunuchs and would serve in the royal court of Babylon. These prophecies were fulfilled during three separate Babylonian invasions in which Judah was despoiled and captives were taken back to Babylon:

First Invasion: Not long after Josiah's death, Pharaoh Neco replaced Jehoahaz with his brother Jehoiakim. In 605 B.C. the Babylonians came to Jerusalem to confront the Egyptian puppet, Jehoiakim. To save the city, the king pledged allegiance to Babylon, and Nebuchadnezzar took silver and gold from the temple and many captives back to Babylon. The prophet Daniel, and other young men including those of the king, were among these early exiles and many were made eunuchs (Dan. 1).

Second Invasion: King Jehoiakim again switched sides in 601 B.C. to ally with Egypt. Nebuchadnezzar returned to put down his rebellion in 597 B.C. Jehoiakim died during the siege and his son Jehoiachin reigned as king of Judah for three months before the Babylonians conquered Jerusalem. More of Judah's wealth was plundered, and ten thousand Jews were taken to Babylon at that time, among whom were the prophet Ezekiel and his wife (2 Kgs. 24:14).

Sorrow and Comfort

Third Invasion: Nebuchadnezzar again returned to Jerusalem in 588 B.C. to suppress Zedekiah's rebellion. (He had also made an alliance with Egypt after pledging loyalty to Nebuchadnezzar.) Jerusalem fell in 586 B.C. after a long siege, and the city and temple were subsequently destroyed. There was a horrendous slaughter among the Jews and tens of thousands of survivors were taken as slaves to Babylon.

More than seventy years later between 605 and 586 B.C., every detail of Isaiah's prophecy to Hezekiah was fulfilled. How did the king respond to Isaiah's prophecy, which had been uttered as a rebuke against his foolish pride? The king said, *"'The word of the Lord which you have spoken is good!' For he said, 'At least there will be peace and truth in my days'"* (v. 8). Although the king accepted God's will, it does not seem that Hezekiah understood the prophet's reproof, nor was he grieved over knowing the appalling future that awaited his great-grandchildren. Rather, the king was just glad that the horrific events prophesied were not going to happen while he was on the throne. The lack of remorse over foolish behavior is a good indication of how much pride is harboring in the heart.

In previous chapters, Isaiah said that Assyria was God's disciplinary rod in the region, but from now on He will focus on how God will use the Babylonians for the same purpose.

Meditation

The Christian who has stopped repenting has stopped growing.

— A. W. Pink

Repentance is as much a mark of a Christian, as faith is. A very little sin, as the world calls it, is a very great sin to a true Christian.

— Charles Spurgeon

Comfort for the Suffering
Isaiah 40:1-11

The first main section of Isaiah, chapters 1-39, emphasizes God's anger over Israel's vain religiosity and rebellion, the sin of the nations, and His right, as the Holy One of Israel, to judge it. We move from the overthrow of Gentile antagonists that have troubled Israel to consider the controversy between Jehovah God and His people. The final section of the book, chapters 40-66, highlights God's work of grace to deliver and to restore Israel. As mentioned in the *Overview* section, the final twenty-seven books of Isaiah are divided into three nine-chapter groupings, separated by the phrase: *"There is no peace for the wicked"* (48:22, 57:21).

The first section (chps. 40-48) primarily deals with promises of future deliverance for Israel from Babylonian oppression and exile. These prophecies are mostly near-term in focus. The second division of nine chapters (chps. 49-57) contains prophecies relating to the humiliation and suffering of God's Messiah, Israel's Redeemer. Chapter 53, speaking of Messiah's planned crucifixion, is at the center of this section. The final nine chapters (chps. 58-66) foretell the glorious consummation of God's salvation to Israel and grace to repentant Gentiles through Christ. In this section, Isaiah prophesies much about the future Kingdom Age when Israel will be refined and restored to God, and Christ will rule the nations with a rod of iron.

Real Comfort

The first verse of this section sets the tone for the remainder of the book: *"'Comfort, yes, comfort My people!' says your God"* (v. 1). The sorrow resulting from the unbelief and rebellion which permeated the first portion of Isaiah's book is now overcome by God's mercy and comfort. The word "comfort" (in some form of speech) appears three times in this chapter and fifteen times in chapters 40-66; hence it is the most comfort-saturated portion of Scripture in our Bibles. Obviously, God wanted to console His people so they would not lose hope during

Sorrow and Comfort

their long exile in Babylon. Isaiah's prophecies would inspire Jews enduring harsh oppression in the following centuries to also wait for Messiah's liberation.

In the next nine chapters, Isaiah will uphold the majesty of God and provide prophetic details about how God will end the Babylonian exile. This was to encourage Jerusalem, the ruined capital city of Judah, to understand that their long trial, likened to warfare in verse 2, was almost over; God's retribution for the nation's past sins was almost complete.

As God's prophet, Isaiah was a voice crying in the spiritual wilderness of Israel's apostasy, *"Prepare the way of the Lord; make straight in the desert a highway for our God"* (v. 3). The Jewish nation needed to embrace the Lord in faith and in truth before *"the glory of the Lord shall be revealed, and all flesh shall see it together"* (v. 5). Exalting the valleys, removing mountains, and straightening crooked ways relate back to verse 3; the Jewish nation was to smooth out the way for Messiah's coming (v. 4). A flat and straight highway meant that faithful believers were morally and spiritually seeking the Lord and inviting others to join them. The process will commence when Israel exercises genuine faith in revealed truth and it will be completed in the Kingdom Age when Israel receives the Holy Spirit and is completely "smoothed out," spiritually speaking, forever.

All four of the Gospel writers apply verse 3 to John the baptizer (Matt. 3:1-4; Mark 1:1-4; Luke 1:76-78; John 1:23). Though John dwelled in the desert, his preaching made a highway for the Lord Jesus through the spiritual wilderness of Israel. As a result, many believed on Christ, and like His disciples, witnessed the glory of God. John said, *"And the Word became flesh and dwelt among us, and we beheld His glory, the glory as of the only begotten of the Father, full of grace and truth"* (John 1:14). But as in Isaiah's day, the majority of the Jewish nation rejected John's message concerning Christ's coming:

> *He was in the world, and the world was made through Him, and the world did not know Him. He came to His own, and His own did not receive Him. But as many as received Him, to them He gave the right to become children of God, to those who believe in His name* (John 1:10-12).

Indeed, many witnessed the glory of God in Christ during His first advent, but the entire world did not see it, for Christ was sent to find the

Devotions in Isaiah

lost sheep of Israel (Matt. 15:24). In the Kingdom Age, however, *"all flesh shall see it together; for the mouth of the Lord has spoken"* (v. 5).

A second voice speaks in verse 6, which is God's own voice directing His prophet to *"cry out."* Isaiah asks, *"What shall I cry?"* The Lord wanted Isaiah to remind the remnant that men are mutable, they fade quickly in the same way that grass and flowers appear and wither, but the Word of God stands forever (vv. 6-8). Everything in the world is decaying, corroding, rusting, or deteriorating in some fashion, but Bible prophecy is immutable and sure! Peter reminds suffering Christians in his day of the same truth:

> *And so we have the prophetic word confirmed, which you do well to heed as a light that shines in a dark place, until the day dawns and the morning star rises in your hearts; knowing this first, that no prophecy of Scripture is of any private interpretation, for prophecy never came by the will of man, but holy men of God spoke as they were moved by the Holy Spirit* (2 Pet. 1:19-21).

Isaiah would later prophetically speak of the suffering Savior, but initially he emphasizes an era in which Messiah's glory will permeate the world. No doubt the prophet wondered how what he was expressing would all come about, but such detail was not shown to him. He seems to indicate that Jews returning from Babylon in the future will be proclaiming the good tidings message, *"Behold your God"* throughout Israel, suggesting that Messiah would reign then (vv. 9-11). Indeed Messiah will reign over His covenant people when a refined remnant returns to Israel, but that would not be until after the Battle of Gog and Magog and the Battle of Armageddon, which Ezekiel will foretell about a century later (Ezek. 38-39). Shortly after these battles, Israel's repentance through God's word as effected by the Holy Spirit will occur – only then will the Jews accept their Messiah. Isaiah did not have the benefit of Jeremiah, Daniel, Ezekiel, and Zechariah's prophecies to put the pieces of the Second Advent puzzle together.

With the help of New Testament revelation, the Church has an even greater opportunity to understand how these Old Testament prophecies do fit together, though clearly much disagreement still exists today on particulars. With that said, like the suffering Jewish remnant of the sixth century B.C., the Church also has the light of Bible prophecy shining in a dark and evil world to direct our attention to the bright morning star in the eastern sky. The morning star provides evidence that a new and glorious day is about to dawn.

This is why Christ, in the closing passage of Scripture, likens Himself to *"the bright and morning star"* (Rev. 22:16). Focusing on Christ, instead of on the spiritual darkness we are living in, inspires hope for the glorious day which is to come. For this reason, John writes, *"For the testimony of Jesus is the spirit of prophecy"* (Rev. 19:10). Bible prophecy is centered in the person of Jesus Christ, the Bright and Morning Star. Scripture contains predawn events of His coming in order to encourage those who are watching and waiting for Him. Dark times will precede the curtain call of the Church Age, yet believers have the hope of their *Bright and Morning Star*. He shall come for His beloved bride at the dawning of the Day of the Lord, and then the *Sun of Righteousness* (Mal. 4:2) shall rise in His full fury and flood the earth with His glory! Then everywhere shouts of acclamation, "Behold your God," will be heard, and the darkness will be overcome by the full revelation of Jesus Christ.

> In hope we lift our wishful, longing eyes,
> Waiting to see the Morning Star arise;
> How bright, how gladsome will His advent be,
> Before the Sun shines forth in majesty!
>
> How will our eyes to see His face delight,
> Whose love has cheered us through the darksome night!
> How will our ears drink in His well-known voice,
> Whose faintest whispers make our soul rejoice!
>
> — James G. Deck

Behold Your God

In Isaiah 4, we investigated the four "Branch" declarations in the Old Testament which emphasize each of the four Gospel themes, that is, the four ways that the Father wants us to appreciate His Son. Likewise, the Old Testament contains four "behold" commands to convey the same message; one of these is in verse 9: *"Behold your God."*

The word "behold" means "to earnestly look upon with regard"; it may convey an element of surprise or wonder. These four "behold statements" are God the Father's invitation to Jews, and indeed to mankind, to gaze upon and admire His dear Son.

Rejoice greatly, O daughter of Zion! Shout, O daughter of Jerusalem! ***Behold, your King*** *is coming to you; He is just and having salvation, lowly and riding on a donkey, a colt, the foal of a donkey* (Zech. 9:9).

Behold! My Servant *whom I uphold, My Elect one in whom My soul delights! I have put My Spirit upon Him; He will bring forth justice to the Gentiles* (42:1).

Thus says the Lord of hosts, saying: "***Behold, the Man*** *whose name is the Branch! From His place He shall branch out, and He shall build the temple of the Lord"* (Zech. 6:12).

O Zion, you who bring good tidings, get up into the high mountain; O Jerusalem, you who bring good tidings, lift up your voice with strength, lift it up, be not afraid; say to the cities of Judah, "***Behold your God!****"* (40:9).

These four Messianic titles align with the four Gospel presentations of Christ:

> Behold your King – Gospel of Matthew
> Behold My Servant – Gospel of Mark
> Behold the Man – Gospel of Luke
> Behold your God – Gospel of John

The pattern of God's plan for human redemption was first revealed to us in Genesis 22. Abraham's saga is so traumatic, yet so awe-inspiring, that our finite minds are captivated to ponder Calvary from a perspective of divine anguish. God would judge His innocent and only begotten Son at Calvary, near Jerusalem, for our sin. Only by embracing the Savior's cross at Jerusalem would man find forgiveness and a solace to comfort his grieving soul.

The Lord Jesus declared the kingdom gospel message (the good tidings) to the lost house of Israel at His first advent: *"Zion, you who bring good tidings, get up into the high mountain; O Jerusalem, you who bring good tidings, lift up your voice with strength, lift it up, be not afraid; say to the cities of Judah, 'Behold your God!'"* (v. 9). The "you" in verse 9 is feminine, which connects with the feminine

Sorrow and Comfort

pronouns of verse 2, meaning the "you" is the Jews in Jerusalem. This is where the good tidings message carried by Jews throughout the land would originate.

First century Israel rejected Christ's good news, but Jewish witnesses will preach the same message again during the Tribulation Period, just prior to Christ's second advent (Matt. 24:9-14; Rev. 7:4-8). Angels will also preach the everlasting gospel message to the inhabitants of the earth. The content of this message is: do not follow the Antichrist, fear God and worship Him, for judgment of the wicked and Christ's kingdom are coming (Rev. 14:6-11). A multitude of Gentiles will believe this message and be saved, though many will be martyred for rejecting the Antichrist (Rev. 7:9-14, 20:4).

Because of Jewish rejection, good tidings are being heralded to the Gentiles during the Church Age. Those who trust in the death, burial and resurrection of Christ alone for redemption will be saved (1 Cor. 15:3-4). It was the Lord's will for evangelism to begin at Jerusalem with Jewish witnesses and then spread to the uttermost parts of the world (Matt. 28:19-20; Acts 1:8). During the Millennial Kingdom, the message to the world shall be, *"And it shall come to pass that everyone who is left of all the nations which came against Jerusalem shall go up from year to year to worship the King, the Lord of hosts, and to keep the Feast of Tabernacles"* (Zech. 14:16). The Lord ascended into heaven from Jerusalem, and He will return to Jerusalem to establish His earthly kingdom (Acts 1; Zech. 14).

From Isaiah 2:1-5 and 66:20 we learn that Jerusalem shall then be the religious center of the world. Christ will reign from there, and there all the nations will come to praise, worship, and learn (Zech. 14:16-21). There will be no war or violence, only peace. All the earth shall see the glory of the Lord Jesus. So great will be the glory of the Lord upon the earth that there will be no need for the sun or moon to illuminate it (60:18-20). Though due to Jewish disobedience God permitted its destruction several times in its history, Jerusalem is the location where God chose to place His name. The Lord wept over the city, suffered in the city, and chastened its inhabitants, but there is a day coming when it will be full of joy and will shine forth the glory of God to all nations!

To provide comfort to the surviving Jewish remnant in the future (i.e., returning from Babylon, or suffering during the Tribulation Period), Isaiah figuratively characterizes how Christ will rule in Jerusalem:

Devotions in Isaiah

Behold, the Lord God shall come with a strong hand, and His arm shall rule for Him; behold, His reward is with Him, and His work before Him. He will feed His flock like a shepherd; He will gather the lambs with His arm, and carry them in His bosom, and gently lead those who are with young (vv. 10-11).

Isaiah emphasizes both the Lord's power and tenderness in caring for His people. These are chief qualities of a true shepherd, which are often not found together in leadership today. Figuratively speaking, an arm is used to symbolize strength in Scripture. Isaiah uses the metaphor a dozen times in his writings (more than any other writer) to convey the concept of God's strength to deliver when no one else can (e.g. Isa. 59:16; see also Ex. 6:6). Men may arm wrestle to pit their strength against one another, but when God flexes His arm, none can compete with Him. It is with this same strong arm that the Good Shepherd feeds and leads His sheep and also carries His lambs (the helpless and weak) in His bosom. This strong, compassionate Messiah will be greatly appealing to the surviving Jewish remnant in the Millennial Kingdom, and is to us too.

Meditation

Come to the Savior now, He gently calls thee;
In true repentance bow, before Him bend the knee.
Come to the Savior now, you who have wandered far;
Renew your solemn vow, for His by right you are;
Come, like poor wandering sheep returning to His fold;
His arm will safely keep, His love will never grow cold.

— John Wigner

Alone In Majesty
Isaiah 40:12-31

After describing the Messiah's tender care of His flock (them), the prophet highlights various aspects of God's majesty in order to quell any lingering doubts as to their future security and also to affirm God's dependability to do all that He promised. Isaiah presents the Lord as the Creator and Controller of all things who has an intense desire to lavish on His people the greatest possible blessing.

Unlimited Knowledge

Isaiah begins by posing five rhetorical questions in verses 12-14 that affirm God's incomparable knowledge as the Creator. Only God can span the universe with His hand, scoop up and measure the oceans in the palms of His hands, and weigh out the mountains on His scales (v. 12). Only God has the infinite knowledge and understanding to fashion the heavens and the earth; no one provided counsel or instruction to "the Spirit of the Lord" during the creative process (vv. 13-14). "The Spirit of the Lord" refers to the Holy Spirit.

Throughout Scripture, the roles within the Godhead are consistently represented: God the Father declares the will of God (He directs), God the Son executes the will of God, and the Holy Spirit enables and ratifies the will of God to be done, usually through the Son. Each Person of the Godhead acts to the praise of God's glory (Eph. 1:6, 12, 14). The fact that the Father chooses does not imply that the Son and the Holy Spirit do not have individual wills – for They do – but they always align with the Father's (John 6:38; 1 Cor. 12:11). The fact that the Holy Spirit issues power to ratify God's will does not mean that the Son does not have power to invoke miracles – He does, for *"in Him all things consist"* (Col. 1:17). On some occasions the Son did miracles by His own power and apparently not through the direct power of the Holy Spirit (Luke 5:17, 8:46).

Comparing Isaiah's statement with the whole of Scripture, we can see all three Persons of the Godhead involved with creation: The Father directed (vv. 12-14; Acts 17:24), the Son created, perhaps spoke it into being (Heb. 1:2, 11:3; Jn. 1:3; 1 Cor. 8:6; Col. 1:16-17), and the power of the Spirit formed it (Gen. 1:2; Ps. 104:30; Job 26:13, 33:4).

It is by the Son that we know God, for *"He has spoken unto us by His Son"* (Heb. 1:2). One cannot constrain what is mysterious and beyond human comprehension into a formula of operation; yet, Scripture does portray the Trinity in a consistent way and with distinct roles. For what we do not understand, let us simply remove our shoes and not trespass upon holy ground.

God's creation is so immense and superb that all the people from all nations would be a mere particle of dust on His colossal scales (v. 15). Isaiah is not belittling man's importance, for Adam was made in the image and likeness of God, but rather how small mankind and all creation is in comparison to God. Therefore, even if man could offer all the wood and animals from lush Lebanon, these would be inadequate sacrifices to honor the Lord (v. 16).

Isaiah says: *"All nations before Him are as nothing, and they are counted by Him less than nothing and worthless"* (v. 17). The prophet is not saying that humanity is insignificant to God, but rather that man is nothing in comparison to God (i.e., the nations "before Him"). The only thing that elevates people over any other part of creation is their relationship with Almighty God.

Paul reminds us that, spiritually speaking, everyone is born estranged from God and is unprofitable to Him, and it is only justification in Christ that will change this (Rom. 3:10-12, 20-25). Hence, believers should remember that only their connection with Christ makes them valuable to God for we too, naturally speaking, are insignificant in comparison to His greatness. Those sanctified by Christ are His and are to live for Him (1 Cor. 1:2, 6:11; Eph. 5:25-27). Our gifts and abilities have value only when, through the power of the Holy Spirit, they are set apart for God's glory. Without Christ we would be nothing more than worthless dust on God's galactic balances, but in Christ, we are fully justified and blameless before God (1 Cor. 1:8).

Unrivaled Majesty

Isaiah then addresses a matter which provoked the Almighty Creator's hot jealousy – the idolatry of His people. Isaiah identifies two types of idols to showcase the majesty of God (vv. 18-20): First, there is the rich man's idol which is forged by a craftsman, then overlaid with gold and decorated with silver. Second, there is the poor man's idol which is constructed of wood so it will not fall over and is fashioned by his own hand. Isaiah's point is that all the materials used to create these idols, and even the people who manufactured them, were created by God. Thus the Creator and not what was created by Him, should be worshipped. Isaiah's rhetorical questions, *"To whom then will you liken God? Or what likeness will you compare to Him?"* (v. 18) suggest that God cannot be compared to creation and, in fact, is above it.

To further substantiate this meaning, the prophet supplies vivid imagery of God's sovereign position above creation (vv. 21-22). God is like a king enthroned in the highest heavens. His abode in the heavens is likened to a gigantic tent pitched above the earth. When He looks down on the round planet from this lofty dwelling place, the nations appear to Him as mere grasshoppers (i.e., they are insignificant). Though poetic in nature, Isaiah's statement is also scientific: *"He who sits above the circle of the Earth..."* (v. 22). The Hebrew word *chuwg* implies a continuous circle or circuit about the Earth. Some suggest this means the earth is spherical, but in any case, a circular shape is implied by the text.

Because of His high position of majesty, it is nothing for Him to establish or remove kingdoms from the earth (v. 23). God can uproot and remove political empires as easily as He can strip a planted field clean by a whirlwind (v. 24). This statement was meant to encourage suffering exiled Jews; God could effortlessly put down the Babylonian Empire at any time.

Isaiah wanted his audience to understand that there was no one like God. In fact, He cannot be compared to anything in His creation, because He is above it (v. 25). He is the all-powerful, all-knowing God who created and continues to sustain all celestial bodies, including an innumerable host of stars which God knows by name (v. 26).

Unlimited Power

If God is aware of and controls every star in the universe, the Jews should not think that God was somehow unaware of their plight and was not heeding their prayers (v. 27). Isaiah then brings his message to a climax:

Have you not known? Have you not heard? The Everlasting God, the Lord, the Creator of the ends of the earth, neither faints nor is weary. His understanding is unsearchable (v. 28).

El Olam is translated the "Everlasting God" in verse 28 and stresses the unchanging character of God (see Gen. 21:33). Isaiah declares that the eternal, immutable God is Lord, the Creator of all things. His knowledge is beyond measurement, and He never grows weary of controlling all that He has made. We read in Genesis 2:1-3 that after six days of creating the heaven and the earth (i.e., that portion of creation that pertains to man), He rested on the seventh day. Isaiah is telling us that it is impossible for the One in which all life exists to be wearied by His creative and controlling work. Rather, when God rests, it is in response to His satisfaction with His creative work, not to weariness. Hence, a strong correlation between satisfaction in God and enjoying His rest is conveyed throughout Scripture.

In Canaan, the Israelites, as empowered by God, engaged in faithful conflict to possess their inheritance. Although they initially entered into God's rest (Josh. 11:23), they failed to secure their inheritance in faith after receiving it – they did not go on with the Lord (Josh. 13:1). Consequently, the rest Jehovah had for them was never fully realized and, in time, was completely lost. The writer of Hebrews uses their failure as an exhortation, *"Let us therefore be diligent to enter that rest, lest anyone fall according to the same example of disobedience"* (Heb. 4:11). The matter of victorious living has not changed; continued faith and obedience ultimately translate into obtaining divine possessions and God's rest.

In the Church Age, believers do not labor for a *place* of rest; our rest and inheritance are in a *Person* – *"Christ in heavenly places"* (Eph. 1:3). Thus, Paul could pray for fellow believers, *"The Lord of peace Himself give you peace in every way"* (2 Thess. 3:16). Christ is the believer's satisfaction and resting place. In our world we may not forge images of gold and silver as the Jews did, but we can easily create imaginary idols that divert our affections and rob us of Christ's communion and blessing. Matthew Henry warns, "Whatever we esteem or love, fear or hope in, more than God, that creature we make equal with God, though we do not make images or worship them."[97] Christ must remain the believer's first love, and all other relationships and things must be a distant second in comparison. Otherwise we will provoke the Lord to jealousy, and He may invoke drastic means in an effort to regain our proper affection (1 Cor. 10:22, 11:30).

Isaiah was writing to a future remnant of discouraged Jews who would be exiled in Babylon. His message to them was, though you are weak and weary, trust and rest in the Lord (go on with Him) and He will strengthen you to endure. In fact, you will soar like eagles above your calamity (vv. 28-31). They would be depleted of strength, but if their confidence and satisfaction were in the Lord, He would uplift them emotionally and spiritually to triumph in the trial. In this way they would experience God's rest.

Paul learned through practical circumstances the truth affirmed by Isaiah: *"He [God] gives power to the weak, and to those who have no might He increases strength"* (v. 29). Paul asked the Lord to remove an ongoing infirmity, but was denied in order that he could experience God's grace in an abounding and persistent way: *"My grace is sufficient for you, for My strength is made perfect in weakness"* (2 Cor. 12:9). What was Paul's response to this declaration?

> *Therefore most gladly I will rather boast in my infirmities, that the power of Christ may rest upon me. Therefore I take pleasure in infirmities, in reproaches, in needs, in persecutions, in distresses, for Christ's sake. For when I am weak, then I am strong* (2 Cor. 12:9-10).

Paul was in agreement with the Lord on the matter. He knew that he would be more blessed by going on with the Lord in the trial and experience His abundant grace, than by having the difficulty removed and not knowing all that he missed.

The reason many of God's people today do not see the hand of God in their lives is that they are not practically dependent on Him. Hence, they do not pray, or cannot do so in genuine faith, or do so with impure motives (i.e., they lust for what is outside of God's will). Our sincere prayers not only move the hand of God to act on our behalf, but through them, the Lord also revives our parched souls: *"Those who wait on the Lord shall renew their strength; they shall mount up with wings like eagles, they shall run and not be weary, they shall walk and not faint"* (Isa. 40:31).

Meditation

You who dwell in the shelter of the Lord,
Who abide in His shadow for life,
Say to the Lord: "My Refuge,
My Rock in whom I trust!"

And He will lift you up on eagle's wings,
Bear you on the breath of dawn,
Make you to shine like the sun,
And hold you in the palm of His hand.

— Josh Groban

I AM and I Will
Isaiah 41

In this chapter, Isaiah summons all nations to consider God's special relationship with His covenant people. God loved Israel and was committed to protecting her; those who oppressed the Jewish nation had no hope of surviving God's wrath.

God Speaks

Isaiah addresses the islands (KJV) or coastlands (NJKV) to ensure that all peoples, even in remote locations of the world, should heed God's warning (v. 1). They were even invited to come near and *"renew their strength,"* that is, to put forth their best arguments to try to foil God's wisdom and purposes. Of course, no one can out-debate the Lord!

Speaking on God's behalf to the nations, Isaiah proclaims: *"I, the Lord, am the first; and with the last I am He"* (v. 4). The eternal God controls the destinies of the nations and therefore determines the events of human history. For example, God called a ruler in the east to establish a new kingdom which would subdue many nations (v. 2).

To whom is Isaiah referring? Some have suggested Abraham, but his battle with the Mesopotamians would hardly account for the international scale of conquest being described. Others cite Joshua, who did conquer many pagan people during the Canaan Conquest, but the Israelites were not being oppressed by a foreign power at the time – rather they were the aggressors. Furthermore, Joshua journeyed northward from the Sinai Peninsula, not from the Far East.

The purposely unnamed conqueror could not be the Assyrians to the northeast, as they had invaded Israel many times, and verse 3 implies that the vanquisher had not visited Israel previously. The invader might be Nebuchadnezzar and the Babylonians, whom, like the Assyrians, God used to carry out His righteous judgments on many nations. However, since Isaiah is trying to encourage a future remnant of Jews being oppressed in Babylon, we understand that the prophet is referring to Cyrus, the future king of the Medo-Persian Empire (who is identified in chapters 44 and 45). Cyrus would conquer the Babylonian Empire (13:17-19) and release Jewish captives, which Isaiah speaks more specifically about in chapters 44, 45, and 48.

Isaiah then mocks the behavior of the Gentile nations when God empowers Cyrus to overcome them. First, nations throughout the known world would intensely fear Cyrus (v. 5). Second, they would band together in an attempt to impede the Persian conquest (v. 6). Third, their craftsmen would respond by creating more idols which could be worshipped and petitioned for assistance (v. 7). Rather than turning to God and receiving mercy, these pagans will seek help from images created with their own hands. What sense did that make?

No doubt, Isaiah wanted his rebuke against paganism among the Gentiles to be heeded by the Jews also. Why would the Jews, who were chosen by God and who enjoyed a special relationship with Him, ever want to embrace the worthless false gods of the nations? God had called them out from the nations to be His special people and to have communion with Him:

But you, Israel, are My servant, Jacob whom I have chosen, the descendants of Abraham My friend. You whom I have taken from the ends of the earth, and called from its farthest regions, and said to you,"You are My servant, I have chosen you and have not cast you away" (vv. 8-9).

The reference to Abraham is not consequential given the context of Isaiah's message. Joshua commences his final address to the Jewish nation, who had secret idols among them, by mentioning that Abraham was previously a pagan in Mesopotamia (Josh. 24:2). For this reason, Moses described Abraham as *"a Syrian ready to perish"* (Deut. 26:5). Though Abraham was an idol-worshipper on the road to condemnation, Stephen declares that the *"God of Glory"* appeared to Abraham in Ur and called him to leave his home and journey to a land that God would show him (Acts 7:2-3). Why did God pick a man tainted by idol worship for His covenant? God had to choose somebody – He chose Abraham who responded in faith to God's invitation (51:1-2). God rules over His creation in whatever way He deems best.

God made a sovereign choice to establish Abraham's descendants as a privileged nation, from whom the Messiah would eventually come. Isaiah's point is that God had specifically chosen Abraham and his

Sorrow and Comfort

descendants to be a special people for Himself, meaning they must be free of idolatry. Abraham left the idols of his family in Ur to have communion with the God of Glory in the land promised to him; the Jewish nation must do the same. To highlight the blessings of such a relationship, Isaiah notes that, because of his faith and obedience, Abraham became God's friend (v. 8; Jas. 2:23)! He is also spoken of as the Father of all spiritual seed (Rom. 4:11-12, 9:6-7), a great man of faith (Heb. 11:8), and a stranger and pilgrim while on earth (Heb. 11:13).

There are so many wonderful outcomes when an individual or, even better, a nation is in fellowship with God. Unfortunately, the Jewish nation in Isaiah's time did not follow the example of their father Abraham. But although their hearts were not with Jehovah, Isaiah wanted his countrymen to know that God's heart was still with them and He was the One who controlled their future. Accordingly, there is a strong link between "I AM" and "I will" throughout the remainder of this chapter (there are fourteen occurrences of these phrases):

> *Fear not, for **I am** with you; be not dismayed, for **I am** your God. **I will** strengthen you, yes, **I will** help you, **I will** uphold you with My righteous right hand* (v. 10).

This is tender and personal language from the Creator to His chosen people. The implication was, "Israel, wake up! Has any idol ever expressed such offered devotion and sacrificial help to ensure your welfare?" Even in Israel's rebellious state, the Lord says, *"I am with you."* The Jews had turned their backs on Him, but He had not turned away from them.

About a century later, the prophets Jeremiah (Jer. 3) and Ezekiel (Ezek. 16) affirmed God's spiritual relationship with Israel in terms of a marital union. This reminded the Jews of their acceptance with God, though their sinful practices had severed their fellowship and intimacy with God. The Jewish nation was like an adulterous wife that God had divorced, but would later receive again after she was restored to purity. God was committed to upholding, strengthening, and refining those He had chosen to express His love to – He was with them no matter what. God had extended many unconditional promises to Abraham and later to the nation of Israel which He had to keep. This meant that Israel was secure in God's love, though the outworking extremes of that love might be quite painful.

Devotions in Isaiah

For believers in the Church Age, it is relatively easy for us to think or speak condescendingly of Israel's stubborn and foolish behavior. But would not the Lord feel the pain of misplaced devotion and allegiance within the Church, which is spiritually one with Him, even more keenly than He did centuries ago with Israel? Having seen God's stern dealings with Israel for idolatry and with Judah for religious fraud, this author wonders how much longer the Lord will tolerate the same in Christendom today.

The Lord Jesus once encountered a group of self-righteous, religious zealots who were demanding the death of a woman caught in the act of adultery. Their demands were hypocritical; the fact that the guilty man had been set free demonstrated their lack of reverence for God's Law (Deut. 22:22-24). The Lord told them, *"He who is without sin among you, let him throw a stone at her first"* (John 8:7). He successfully appealed to their consciences, and they all departed from the guilty woman. It would be pharisaical for us in the Church Age to fling a stone at adulterous Judah and ignore the application of the illustration. Do we allow idols in our hearts to displace our love for the Lord Jesus? Do we flirt with the world and feast on immoral things, and then draw near to our Lord with vile filth still on our breath as we pray sweet nothings into His ear? Are we superficially pretending to be a chaste virgin awaiting her wedding day? Is our bridal attire stained with unconfessed sin and religious pride?

Although we live in a different dispensation of God's working, the application of Israel's error is still pertinent today. In Christ, all true Christians enjoy security, though the enjoyment of our relationship with Christ is dependent on good behavior and uncontaminated thought-life. Sometimes it seems as if the Lord is far away, but when we come to our senses and turn back to Him, we find that He was right there with us all along. The abiding presence of the Lord Jesus Christ is a great defense against entering into sin. His nearness repels evil from our minds and strengthens us to overcome the lusts of our flesh. Frustration, edginess, weakness, and anxiety are warning signs that we have lost the sense of His presence, and that we need to realign our thinking with His in order to gain His peace again.

In contrast with God's choosing Israel, there was no such promise to the nations. Therefore any nation oppressing His covenant people should expect to be overcome by God in His timing (vv. 11-12). Twice, Isaiah says such nations *"shall be as nothing."* Though Israel was as weak and vulnerable as a worm, they should not fear their attackers, for "the Holy One of Israel," their "Redeemer," would help them (vv. 13-14). Only God is holy and only God can redeem sinners. In a future day, the Jews would thrash their enemies in the same way that a threshing cart passes over sheaves of grain to separate the chaff and grain, and then the former is carried away by the wind (v. 15). After experiencing God's powerful deliverance from all their enemies, Isaiah says that Israel will *"rejoice in the Lord, and glory in the Holy One of Israel"* (v. 16).

Given the context of verses 17-20, verses 11-16 also likely refer to Israel's final deliverance from Gentile oppression to commence the Kingdom Age. When Israel is restored to the Lord, no Jew will suffer thirst, for there will be an abundance of springs, rivers, and pools even in arid regions (vv. 17-18). Furthermore, God will plant a variety of trees in these desert areas to provide ample shade from those passing through (v. 19).

As summarized by J. M. Riddle, verse 20 represents the culmination of the prophet's argument:

> God has made specific promises in connection with the future, both near and far. He has stated this beforehand, so that "they may see, and know, and consider and understand together, that the hand of the Lord hath done this, and the Holy One of Israel hath created it." The mark of a true prophet was the accuracy of his predictions (Deut. 18:20-22; Jer. 28:9), and the accuracy of His word proves that the Lord is the true God. Idols are incapable of predicting anything, and this follows.[98]

Because the Holy One of Israel is omniscient and omnipotent, He alone is able to control the future of the nations and to write their history. He has promised to bless and protect His covenant people and to make those who oppress them as nothing.

Silent Idols

Having stated God's argument to the nations, Isaiah now challenges them to consult their numerous idols to control the future in some specific way that would cause others to revere them (vv. 21-23). Of course, Isaiah's point is that the inability of the idols to govern future events, as the God of the Jews does, means that they are worthless and those who worship them are an abomination to God (v. 24). Only stubborn pride or utter foolishness would explain why someone would continue worshipping a bogus idol. God detests both!

In contrast with helpless and worthless idols, the God of the Jews did control the outcome of the future. Through Isaiah, God had foretold that a strong deliverer would come from the north and the east to conquer nations and to end the Jewish exile in Babylon (vv. 25-26, 45:1). There was a coming day in which a messenger would deliver news to Jerusalem that the exiled captives had been released by Cyrus (44:28) and that they were coming back to Judah (v. 27). Isaiah's conclusion is that idols only confuse people and provide them no more meaningful counsel than would the wind (vv. 28-29). Accordingly, it would be wise for the nations to turn from their worthless idols to the Holy One of Israel who does control every aspect of the future for all that He has created.

In our modern culture we shy away from the whole subject of idols because sophisticated people do not waste money on such things, or do we? The second of the Ten Commandments says: *"You shall not make for yourself a carved image – any likeness of anything that is in heaven above, or that is in the Earth beneath, or that is in the water under the Earth; you shall not bow down to them nor serve them. For I, the Lord your God, am a jealous God"* (Ex. 20:4-5). Have you ever heard someone say, "God to me is ..."? The individual is revealing his or her self-concocted god, an imaginary god which fits his or her liking and, therefore, will condone that person's moral standard and the frivolous ways in which he or she squanders resources. In this way, holiness becomes relative; a self-manufactured god will not judge sin, but rather will promote it. This idol may not be a golden calf, but neither is it the Lord as revealed in the Bible.

> Pure morality points you to the purest one of all. When impure, it points you to yourself. The purer your habits, the closer to God you will come. Moralizing from impure motives takes you away from God.
>
> — Ravi Zacharias

God does not have varying degrees of holiness and righteousness; His very character defines moral integrity, and all that does not measure up to it will be judged. When an individual replaces the true God of Scripture with a created image (whether visible or imaginary),

Sorrow and Comfort

he or she has violated the second of the Ten Commandments. Creating an imaginary god that approves of sin and endorses a future that we desire is never a good idea.

Isaiah's message reminds us that we cannot draw near to God except in spirit and in truth (John 4:23). To reverence anything but the only true God as represented in Scripture is idolatry, and idolatry in any form corrupts good morals, ruins our lives, and angers the Lord.

Meditation

> To have a faith, therefore, or a trust in anything, where God hath not promised, is plain idolatry, and a worshipping of thine own imagination instead of God.
>
> — William Tyndale

> The essence of idolatry is the entertainment of thoughts about God that are unworthy of Him.
>
> — A. W. Tozer

Two Advents
Isaiah 42

Rather than addressing seemingly unconnected or even contrasting subjects separately, Scripture often presents them in tandem to draw out their deeper spiritual meaning. For example, God called upon *prophets* to represent Himself to the people but used *priests* to represent the people to Himself. Moreover, it may seem that Paul and James disagree regarding how salvation is received, yet their teachings are merely two bookends for the whole truth: man is saved by grace through faith, but faith never stands alone; it will be evidenced by good works. Similarly, many have been confused concerning the two advents of Christ, but both are absolutely necessary. The purpose of Christ's first advent was for Him to be a sacrifice for sin and to offer grace to whoever will accept it, but His second advent to earth will be to judge the wicked, to comfort the oppressed, and to rule the world in righteousness.

Isaiah identifies accomplishments of Christ's two advents in this chapter. His first coming is discussed in verses 1-7 (although some aspects of this prophecy will not be fulfilled until His second advent), while Christ's second coming is addressed in verses 10-17.

Christ's First Advent

Isaiah begins by expressing one of the four "behold" statements contained in the Old Testament which form God the Father's invitation to the Jews, and, indeed, to mankind, to gaze upon and admire His dear Son: *"****Behold! My Servant*** *whom I uphold, My Elect One in whom My soul delights! I have put My Spirit upon Him; He will bring forth justice to the Gentiles"* (v. 1). As discussed in chapter 40, the *"Behold! My Servant"* statement reflects the Gospel of Mark's presentation of the lowly Servant of Jehovah.

Isaiah ascribes the title "servant" primarily to the Messiah, as in verse 1 (and 49:3-7, 52:13), but also to the faithful remnant of Israel (41:8, 43:10, 44:21, 48:20), and to Cyrus (44:26). The context of the related passage permits us to determine who is being referred to.

Sorrow and Comfort

Verse 1 contains one of several references to the Trinity in the book of Isaiah. The Father delights in the Son and the Father gives the Son the Holy Spirit to complete His earthly mission, which is simply stated, *"He will bring forth justice to the Gentiles."* Given the four "behold" Old Testament statements, the roles within the Godhead presented throughout Scripture, and the work of the servant described in verse 1, we can confidently conclude that the servant is the Son of God, Israel's Messiah, and not Israel herself (Isa. 53:1). At times, the Jewish nation is referred to as God's servant (v. 19), but the ministry and character of God's Servant in verses 1-7 describes Christ's first sojourn on the earth.

The Hebrew word rendered "judgment" is *mishpat*. Strong's Hebrew Dictionary indicates that this word means "a verdict (favorable or unfavorable) pronounced judicially, especially a sentence or formal decree."[99] "He will bring forth" is translated from the multi-faceted verb *yatsa'* which here implies "He will declare or show."[100] Matthew, quoting this verse, renders it "He will declare" (Matt. 12:18). Adam Clarke suggests that the phrase should be rendered as "He shall publish judgment to the nations."[101] Jamieson, Fausset, and Brown describe what Christ was declaring to all men during His first advent:

> Judgment speaks of the gospel dispensation, founded on justice, the canon of the divine rule and principle of judgment called "the law" (Isa. 2:3; compare Isa. 42:4, 51:4, 49:6). The Gospel has a discriminating judicial effect: saving to penitents; condemnatory to Satan, the enemy (John 12:31, 16:11), and the willfully impenitent (John 9:39). Matthew 12:18 has, "He shall show," for "He shall bring forth," or "cause to go forth." Christ both produced and announced His "judgment." The Hebrew dwells most on His producing it; Matthew on His announcement of it: the two are joined in Him.[102]

Isaiah foretold Israel's rejection of Christ during His first advent (6:10; 53:1), which John later acknowledges (John 12:37-41). Regardless of Israel's denunciation of God's Servant, Isaiah prophesied that Christ's ministry would be so effective that even Gentiles could believe in Him and be saved. Paul, referring to Isaiah's prophecies (8:14, 28:16), writes: *"Behold, I lay in Zion a stumbling stone and rock of offense, and whoever believes on Him will not be put to shame"* (Rom. 9:33). Christ successfully published the counsel and will of God concerning salvation to not only the Jews, but also to Gentiles.

Devotions in Isaiah

Christ will execute justice, end Gentile oppression, and will restore the Jewish nation to Himself at His second advent, but this is not the main focus of verse 1. God's judicial decree offering salvation to whosoever will believe is. This is why the angel, speaking to the shepherds on the night of Christ's birth, could say: *"Do not be afraid, for behold, I bring you good tidings of great joy which will be to all people."* And shortly after Christ's birth, Simeon prophesied what Isaiah wrote in verse 6: *"For my eyes have seen Your salvation which You have prepared before the face **of all peoples, a light to bring revelation to the Gentiles**, and the glory of Your people Israel"* (Luke 2:30-32). The Jewish Messiah was not merely bringing good news to the Jews. The New Covenant, sealed by His own blood, permitted an offer of salvation to all men.

Until the Jewish nation receives the benefits of the New Covenant during the Tribulation Period, the Lord Jesus Christ is building His Church, which, although including both Jews and Gentiles, is chiefly composed of Gentiles. Moreover, God is bestowing blessings on Gentile believers to provoke the Jews to jealousy; this will ultimately result in their return to Him (Rom. 11:11-15). The Jews stumbled over Christ at His First Advent, and the blessing He offered them instead fell into the laps of the Gentiles, who were not expecting it (Luke 20:9-16; Rom. 9:32). This permitted God to righteously call a people that were not His covenant people to be His children also. God would bring the Gentiles into the good of the New Covenant (Hos. 1:10, 2:23; Rom. 9:25-26).

During His first advent, Christ would be known for being soft-spoken (v. 2) and gentle (e.g., He will not even break a bruised reed which has no strength, though most people would; v. 3). God's Servant would be faithful to declare truth (v. 3), and would not be discouraged, but would complete the work God had given Him to do, that is to declare God's message of peace to the nations (v. 4). Obviously, this was not the Messiah that Israel was looking for; the Jewish nation wanted immediate and complete deliverance from Gentile oppression. Hence, Matthew quotes verses 1-4 to affirm that the demeanor of Jesus Christ was exactly what Isaiah had prophesied the Messiah would exhibit (i.e., during His first earthly sojourn; Matt. 12:18-21).

The ministry of the Messiah would prosper, because the One who created all things would uphold His Servant, whom He appointed, to complete the mission of establishing a New Covenant that would benefit all men (vv. 5-6). Isaiah's message agrees with what other prophets foretold of God's New Covenant. Ezekiel promised that God would be able to establish a *Covenant of Peace* with the Jewish nation in a coming day through His Shepherd (Ezek. 34:25). Jeremiah says that this would be an everlasting covenant resulting in eternal blessing to the Jews (Jer. 32:40). This promise is understood to be literal, for God will erect an eternal city where the Jewish remnant will dwell (48:2, 52:1). Isaiah proclaimed that through this covenant, *"Israel shall be saved in the Lord with an everlasting salvation"* (45:17). Why was the New Covenant needed and how did it secure such blessing for Israel?

The writer of Hebrews informs us that this covenant was sealed by Christ's blood and would accomplish what the Old Covenant could not – propitiation for sins (Heb. 8:8). The Old Covenant was conditional in nature; the Jews had to keep God's Law to receive God's blessing (Ex. 19:5-8; Heb. 8:9). The New Covenant would be unconditional in nature and would be the means by which God would honor His covenant with Abraham, which was instituted by two immutable things – God's word and His oath (Heb. 6:13-18), neither of which can fail. Thankfully, as Paul explains in Ephesians chapters 2 and 3 and Romans 11, Gentiles become a second benefactor of this covenant and in Christ receive all the blessings promised to Israel. Consequently, Christ, in performing God's righteous will, is able to give spiritual sight to those (Jews and Gentiles) blinded by sin and to release those imprisoned in darkness from their eternal doom (v. 7).

Christ's Second Advent

When matched with New Testament Scripture, many of Isaiah's prophecies affirm the deity of Christ. For example in verse 5, we read, *"Thus says God the Lord, who created the heavens and stretched them out."* But in the New Testament, the Lord Jesus is identified as the Creator. John proclaims of Christ, *"All things were made through Him, and without Him nothing was made that was made"* (John 1:3). Paul states that He is the Creator and Sustainer of all things (Col. 1:16-18). The writer of Hebrews repeats God the Father's own declaration that His Son laid the foundations of the earth (Heb. 1:8-10). We can conclude that there was nothing created that the Son did not accomplish; therefore, it would be impossible to create Himself! He therefore must be God.

Furthermore, notice that verse 8 declares there is only one God and He will not share His glory with another (i.e., God alone is to be revered and worshipped). This upholds the commands of God committed to Moses to relay to the Israelites (Ex. 20:1; Deut. 5:7). The Lord Jesus confirmed this truth when He was tested by Satan (Matt. 4:10). Isaiah's point is that no idol can control the future. God is foretelling "a new thing" to ensure that His people know He is the one true God and they will glory in Him (vv. 8-9). Only the Lord directs history, past and future, to accomplish His high purposes for the benefit of His people.

Isaiah states that only God is to be worshipped and that He will not share His glory with anyone else. Yet, in the New Testament we witness God's Son repeatedly worshipped by men. The Magi from the East worshipped the Lord Jesus, when He was a child (Matt. 2:11). The healed blind man worshipped the Lord Jesus after understanding that He was the Son of God (John 9:38). Mary anointed Him with expensive ointment as an act of worship (John 12:3). The hosts of heaven will worship the Lamb, the Lord Jesus Christ (Rev. 5:12-14, 19:10). Indeed, only God is to be worshipped, and God the Father is pleased when His Son is worshipped and appreciated by men as God. Wise men agree with Paul, *"Christ came, who is over all, the eternally blessed God"* (Rom. 9:5).

Thankfully, after His second advent, Isaiah says that Christ will be worshipped by those dwelling in cities and villages, on islands and on far away mountain peaks (implying that all men everywhere will honor him; vv. 10-12). The mention of Kedar and Sela implies that Arab voices will be among those singing praises to God.

In contrast with the gentle and soft-spoken disposition of His first advent, Isaiah states the Christ will be the bold Conqueror in His second: *"The Lord shall go forth like a mighty man; He shall stir up His zeal like a man of war. He shall cry out, yes, shout aloud; He shall prevail against His enemies"* (v. 13). Christ has waited two thousand years to vindicate Himself. He has been patient and longsuffering, but, when He appears on earth again, He will be forthright in executing judgment and His voice will have the intensity of a woman in painful labor (v. 14). We know that the Lord takes no pleasure in punishing the wicked; however, His righteous character demands that justice be upheld on the earth, despite how much it agonizes Him to do so (Ezek. 33:11).

Sorrow and Comfort

Those who will not revere Him will be ashamed and will perish, for Messiah will dry up their lands (vv. 15, 17). However, for those who will trust Christ, He will give them light and will guide them in the ways of God (v. 16). This revelation would later encourage those Jews returning from their Babylonian exile.

God's Unfaithful Servant

If, after reading Isaiah's writings, the Jewish nation wondered why the Lord did not lead and protect them, they would have their answer: They were acting like a blind and deaf servant (vv. 18-19). God's indictment against His people is candid: *"Seeing many things, but you do not observe; opening the ears, but he does not hear"* (v. 20). It is interesting that Matthew quotes verse 1 to ensure that we identify Jesus Christ as God's Servant (Matt. 12:18), and then a few verses later he records the Lord performing a miracle:

> *Then one was brought to Him who was demon-possessed, blind and mute; and He healed him, so that the blind and mute man both spoke and saw. And all the multitudes were amazed and said, "Could this be the Son of David?"* (Matt. 12:22-23).

In a coming day, the Lord's Servant will heal the unfaithful servant, the Jewish nation, of their spiritual blindness and then all they will want to do is talk about the Son of David. All their questions will be answered and they will praise their Messiah – the Lord Jesus Christ. However, until that time, their willful disobedience to God's expressed word (the Word incarnate) will result in dire consequences.

In the infancy of the Jewish nation, Joshua rehearsed the Mosaic Law to the twelve tribes of Israel situated in the natural amphitheater between Mount Gerizim and Mount Ebal. The Law posed conditional terms: God's blessings for obedience and His judgment for disobedience (such as being conquered and plundered by a foreign nation; v. 22). Isaiah states that the Law reflects the righteousness of God and should therefore be esteemed and honored (v. 21). Paul tells us that the Law reflects God's holy character and therefore is *"holy, and the commandment holy and just and good"* (Rom. 7:12). The problem the Law poses for humanity is that no one could keep it and so no one could be holy before God. Paul says that this was the purpose of the Law, to show man his sin (Rom. 3:20) and that no one could approach God through a system of good works, but rather that man needs a Savior (Gal. 3:24). No amount of good deeds can pay for even one infraction against the Law – a person is a law-breaker through disobedience. No amount of obedience can change that fact.

Unfortunately, Judah did not heed God's warnings; they continued disobeying God's Law (v. 23). Sadly, even after experiencing God's intense anger in response to their rebellion (i.e., He was the One who would cause the Babylonians to plunder and destroy Jerusalem by fire; v. 24) the Jewish nation still did not seek the Lord (v. 25). This is why God needed to send His Servant, in whom He delights, to the earth to deliver and guide Israel in righteousness. Left to ourselves, we will always go our own way and disappoint God (53:6). We too need Immanuel, God with us, to have any hope of escaping God's wrath over sin and of living a life pleasing to God.

Meditation

All hail to Thee, Immanuel, the ransomed hosts surround Thee;
And earthly monarchs clamor forth their sovereign King to crown Thee.
While those redeemed in ages gone, assembled round the great white throne,
Break forth into immortal song: All hail! All hail! All hail Immanuel!

All hail to Thee, Immanuel, our risen King and Savior!
Thy foes are vanquished, and Thou art omnipotent forever.
Death, sin and hell no longer reign, and Satan's power is burst in twain;
Eternal glory to Thy Name: All hail! All hail! All hail Immanuel!

— D. R. Van Sickle

I Am the Lord, Your God
Isaiah 43:1-7

In chapter 40, Isaiah began a new section to address God's restoration of Israel. Chapters 40 and 41 would encourage future Jews exiled in Babylon to be looking for a leader from the east to release them. Using this future liberation as a backdrop, the prophet now tells his countrymen that God was also going to raise up His Servant, their Messiah, to deliver them from spiritual captivity. The work of the Messiah at His first coming made this possible, but the nation would remain enslaved by spiritual darkness and rebellion until His second advent.

Given the pitiful state of the nation at the end of chapter 42, one might anticipate a harsh pronouncement of judgment to initiate this chapter, yet, nothing but God's goodwill is declared to His people. W. E. Vine suggests this transition serves an important message to Israel:

> The change from righteous indignation to loving consolation and comforting promises and assurances is deeply significant. It is designed to demonstrate that restoration could not be accomplished by any meritorious efforts on the part of His erring people. Their dire need must be met by divine grace.[103]

So how will God demonstrate His grace and mercy to wayward Israel? Despite the nation's present unworthiness, the prophet instructs future exiled Jews not to fear (vv. 1-7), for Jehovah will prove to all nations that He is their God (vv. 8-13) by bringing them back home from Babylon (vv. 14-28).

Do Not Fear – You Are Mine!

Future exiled Jews (referred to as "Jacob," the father of "Israel") were not to fear because the Lord had created, formed, redeemed, and called the nation to be His (v. 1). God's expression of love to them, *"You are Mine,"* is both tender and emphatic. At Mount Sinai, Jehovah wanted the Israelites to understand that He wanted to enter into a personal covenant with them and commune with them. The Psalmist is joyfully aware of this truth: *"Know that the Lord, He is God; it is He who has made us, and not we ourselves; we are His people and the sheep of His pasture"* (Ps. 100:3). Not only did God want the Jews to understand that they *were* His people, He also wanted them to know that He *wanted* them for His people. It was not just the reality of the relationship that was to be understood, but that God's love had instigated it (see also Ezek. 16:1-14).

Israel was the Lord's and they could count on Him, but Israel would not be able to enjoy this relationship unless they maintained holiness, for Jehovah is holy. Thus, the Israelites had to agree to keep God's Law as a condition of maintaining fellowship within the relationship that God had secured by redemption (i.e., through the Passover lamb). The main stipulation of fellowship was stated clearly by God in Exodus 19:5, *"If you will indeed obey My voice and keep My covenant, then you shall be a special treasure to Me above all people; for all the earth is Mine."* If the Jews obeyed the Word of God and kept His Law, then they would be blessed by God and be His highly esteemed people. Jehovah considered them to be a peculiar treasure upon the earth and they were to act accordingly.

Isaiah then reminds the displaced remnant that, just as Jehovah had redeemed them in Egypt and had miraculously brought them out of slavery in their infancy, He also promised them an Exodus from Babylon in which no one would be able to harm or impede them (v. 2). Despite arduous trials, as depicted by the references to floodwaters and fire, God would be with them and would protect them. His love for them was so immense that He promised to give Egypt, Cush, and Seba (Sheba) as a ransom to deliver them from Babylon (v. 3). Why would God permit these regions to be conquered by Cyrus? Because Israel was precious to God and these victories would lead to the ultimate overthrow of the Babylonian Empire and the release of those God loved: *"Since you were precious in My sight, you have been honored, and I have loved you; therefore I will give men for you, and people for your life"* (v. 4).

J. A. Motyer notes that the verbs used to express God's regard for His people in verse 4 are all in the perfect tense: *"you were precious," "you have been honorable,"* and *"have loved you."* God's love for them in the past continued into the present and would continue into

Sorrow and Comfort

eternity.[104] They have been, still are, and will always be loved of God. Thank the Lord that His love is not *imperfect* (i.e., incomplete or not enduring). Despite all His people's shortcomings, the Lord was ever watching over them and would bring them home from Babylon.

This meant the Jews returning to the holy land would be under the protection of God's servant, Cyrus. The Lord told His people, *"Fear not, for I am with you; I will bring your descendants from the east ...west...north...south... and from the ends of the earth"* (vv. 5-6). While the return of exiled Jews from Babylon is the main focus of Isaiah's statements, the language of verses 5-7 highlights an even greater return of Jews to Israel at the end of the Tribulation Period (Matt. 24:31; Ezek. 39:28-29). Those gathered back to Israel then will be called by God's name. They were created for His glory and will reflect His holiness to the nations (v. 7).

The Lord Jesus has affirmed similar words of love and security to His Church and in a coming day He will return to gather believers into heaven to be with Him:

Christ also has loved us and given Himself for us, an offering and a sacrifice to God for a sweet-smelling aroma (Eph. 5:2).

Christ also loved the church and gave Himself for her, that He might sanctify and cleanse her with the washing of water by the word, that He might present her to Himself a glorious church, not having spot or wrinkle or any such thing, but that she should be holy and without blemish (Eph. 5:25-27).

What then shall we say to these things? If God is for us, who can be against us? He who did not spare His own Son, but delivered Him up for us all, how shall He not with Him also freely give us all things? Who shall bring a charge against God's elect? It is God who justifies. Who is he who condemns? It is Christ who died, and furthermore is also risen, who is even at the right hand of God, who also makes intercession for us. Who shall separate us from the love of Christ? Shall tribulation, or distress, or persecution, or famine, or nakedness, or peril, or sword? (Rom. 8:31-35).

For if we believe that Jesus died and rose again, even so God will bring with Him those who sleep in Jesus. For this we say to you by the word of the Lord, that we who are alive and remain until the coming of the Lord will by no means precede those who are asleep.

For the Lord Himself will descend from heaven with a shout, with the voice of an archangel, and with the trumpet of God. And the dead in Christ will rise first. Then we who are alive and remain shall be caught up together with them in the clouds to meet the Lord in the air. And thus we shall always be with the Lord (1 Thess. 4:14-17).

Whether the nation of Israel or the Church, those whom Christ loves never need to worry about being separated from His love, concern, or protection. Paul told the Christians at Corinth to eagerly wait *"for the revelation of our Lord Jesus Christ, who will also confirm you to the end, that you may be blameless in the day of our Lord Jesus Christ"* (1 Cor. 1:8). Israel's promises in Christ are earthly; the Church's inheritance in Christ is heavenly, but all will be fulfilled for God's glory: *"For all the promises of God in Him [Christ] are Yes, and in Him Amen, to the glory of God through us"* (2 Cor. 1:20).

Only One God and Savior

As we compare New Testament Scripture with God's own proclamations recorded by Isaiah we understand that the Redeemer of Israel is also the Savior of believers in the Church Age. There is none like Him for He is the Holy God who created all things:

For I am the Lord your God, the Holy One of Israel, your Savior (v. 3).

I, even I, am the Lord, and beside Me there is no Savior (v. 11).

Thus says the Lord, the King of Israel, and his Redeemer, the Lord of Hosts: "I am the First and I am the Last; besides Me there is no God" (44:6).

I am the Lord, and there is no other; there is no God besides Me (45:5).

For I am God, and there is none else; I am God, and there is none like Me (46:9).

Only God is perfect, self-sufficient, and self-existing. Nothing created can be compared to Him. He is holy! The prophet Ezekiel tells us that God's intervention to defend Israel from Gog and Magog (who will invade Israel during the middle of the Tribulation Period) will prove to the nations that Jehovah is present in Israel and will also awaken the slumbering Jewish nation to exalt Him: *"So I will make My holy name known in the midst of My people Israel, and I will not let them profane My holy name anymore. Then the nations shall know that I am the Lord, the Holy One in Israel"* (Ezek. 39:7-8). God Himself, *the Holy One of Israel,* shall reign over the nations from the midst of His people.

The New Testament reveals this same truth when speaking of the Lord Jesus Christ, the God-man, and the holy One of Israel. He was acknowledged as being holy in the womb by the angel Gabriel (Luke 1:35). Demons, while fearing premature judgment, asserted: *"Let us alone! What have we to do with You, Jesus of Nazareth? Did You come to destroy us? I know who You are – the Holy One of God!"* (Mark 1:24). Peter proclaimed why Christ was holy: *"We have come to believe and know that You are the Christ, the Son of the living God"* (John 6:69). The early church recognized the intrinsic holiness of Christ (Acts 4:27, 30) and that He was the only Savior (Acts 4:12; John 14:6).

"I Am" Statements

As discussed in the *Overview* section, the book of Isaiah reads topically like a mini-Bible. In several ways, the 66 chapters of Isaiah correspond thematically with the 66 books of the Bible. Another example of this association is seen in the seven "I am" statements in Isaiah 43, as compared to the seven "I am" statements of the 43rd book of the Bible – John:

"I am" statements from Isaiah 43:
"I am the Lord, your God" (v. 3).
"That you may know and believe Me, and understand that I am He" (v. 10).
"I, even I, am the Lord" (v. 11).
"I am God" (v. 12).
"Indeed before the day was, I am He" (v. 13).
"I am the Lord" (v. 15).
"I, even I, am He who blots out your transgressions" (v. 25).

"I am" sayings in John Gospel (the 43rd book of the Bible) pertaining to the Lord Jesus:
"I am the bread of life" (John 6:35).
"I am the light of the world" (John 8:12).

> *"I am the door of the sheep"* (John 10:7).
> *"I am the good shepherd"* (John 10:11).
> *"I am the resurrection and the life"* (John 11:25).
> *"I am the way, the truth and the life"* (John 14:6).
> *"I am the true vine"* (John 15:1).

In this chapter, Isaiah refers to the *I AM* of the Bible; He alone is Israel's Redeemer, Lord, and God. The Gospel of John introduces the same *I AM* to the entire world – He alone is the giver of light, love, and life (key expressions in John). The Lord Jesus acknowledges the importance of believing that He is the I AM of the Bible in order to be saved: *"Therefore I said to you that you will die in your sins; for if you do not believe that I am* [He]*, you will die in your sins"* (John 8:24; the implied "He" after "I AM" is not in the Greek text).

At the burning bush, God answered Moses's question, *"What is Your name?"* with this response: *"I AM that I AM."* In preparation for their deliverance from Egypt and the wilderness experience to follow, God wanted His covenant people to know Him as "I AM." The Hebrew word *hayah* is used here to mean "I will be," and is a wordplay on *Yahweh* (Jehovah) in Exodus 3:15, which means "to be." Moses was to tell the children of Israel that I AM (the self-existing One) had sent him to them. Both Isaiah and John tell us that this same "I AM" is the eternal, holy God who possesses life in Himself and is the only One who can save sinners. Whether Old Testament or New Testament – there is only one Redeemer, one Savior, one Lord, and one God – the I AM of the Bible.

Meditation

> Blessed be God, our God,
> Who gave for us His well-beloved Son,
> The gift of gifts, all other gifts in one;
> Blessed be God, our God.
>
> What will He not bestow!
> Who freely gave this mighty gift unbought,
> Unmerited, unheeded, and unsought,
> What will He not bestow?
>
> Who shall condemn us now?
> Since Christ has died, and risen, and gone above,

Sorry and Comfort

For us to plead at the right hand of Love;
Who shall condemn us now?

— Horatius Bonar

The Witness to Be Delivered
Isaiah 43:8-28

In the previous seven verses, Isaiah declares that the Great I AM of Scripture is the eternal God, the Holy One of Israel, the Creator, the Redeemer, and Israel's only Savior. God now summons the nations to His courtroom and sets before them afflicted and spiritually blind Israel as evidence to consider. The nations were to ponder the state of dispersed Israel under the Babylonian Empire. They were to verify that what God had said He would do against the Jewish nation, He had done (v. 8). Then the Lord challenges the nations to foretell the future and then bring it about in such a way that genuine witnesses can confirm the feat (v. 9).

Turning to distressed and despondent Israel, the Lord states what He desires to accomplish in them and indeed will accomplish:

"You are My witnesses," says the Lord, "and My servant whom I have chosen, that you may know and believe Me, and understand that I am He. Before Me there was no God formed, nor shall there be after Me. I, even I, am the Lord, and besides Me there is no savior" (vv. 10-11).

God's deliverance of Israel will demonstrate to the nations, and to Israel, that He is God and their Savior. "Savior" is a title of God found eight times in Isaiah, which is more than any another book in the Bible. The prophet is emphasizing that only God can deliver Israel out of such a desperate situation, and furthermore only God can save man from the destructive outcome of sin. What God reveals about what He will do for the Jewish nation and then how He will bring it about will clearly be something no idol could ever accomplish (vv. 12-13). To all this, the Jews were to be God's witnesses to the nations (vv. 10, 12, 44:8).

We pause to consider an application of verses 10-13. Have not believers in the Church Age also witnessed such a great deliverance from death that there should be no question in our minds as to who the

Sorrow and Comfort

Savior is – the Lord Jesus Christ? Like Israel, the Church is to be a light and a testimony of Christ to the nations – we are His witnesses. Not long after the Lord Jesus chose His disciples, He told them of His light-bearing ministry to the world and that they would be responsible to continue it: *"I am the light of the world. He who follows Me shall not walk in darkness, but have the light of life"* (John 8:12). *"You are the light of the world ... Let your light so shine before men, that they may see your good works and glorify your Father in heaven"* (Matt. 5:14-16). The light of Christ (i.e., His truth) was to shine out of them wherever they went. After His resurrection, the Lord formally commissioned His disciples to do just that: *"You will receive power when the Holy Spirit comes on you; and **you will be My witnesses** in Jerusalem, and in all Judea and Samaria, and to the ends of the earth"* (Acts 1:8). They were to preach the gospel message and to teach those responding to it all they knew to be true concerning Christ. That work has continued to the present day and will continue until the end of the Church Age (Matt. 28:19-20).

Every Christian is to be a witness for Christ – an instrument of God to illuminate the way of salvation for the lost. Those who respond to the gospel message are then to receive the teachings of Christ, so that they too can share the good news with others. Paul engaged in this important work while at Ephesus and those who received the truth from him passed it on to others (Eph. 4:20-21). True followers of Christ are willing to be witnesses for Christ wherever He has them, and whenever the opportunity arises to share the gospel message with the lost.

"Thus says the Lord" (v. 14) is a frequent phrase in the latter portion of Isaiah's book; here it is used to clarify the previous verses – what the Lord will do for the Jewish nation: *"For your sake I will send to Babylon, and bring them all down as fugitives – the Chaldeans, who rejoice in their ships. I am the Lord, your Holy One, the Creator of Israel, your King"* (v. 15). The Babylonian conquerors who would inflict so much devastation on Israel would be conquered by the Medes and the Persians; their ships would become sunken wrecks. Then God would accomplish an even greater exodus from Babylon for His people than what He had accomplished in Egypt centuries earlier when He drowned Pharaoh's army in the Red Sea (vv. 16-17).

Given the certainty of this great deliverance, God tells His people, *"Do not remember the former things, nor consider the things of old. Behold, I will do a new thing"* (vv. 18-19). God had previously

Devotions in Isaiah

delivered His people out of Egypt by sending ten plagues on that nation and then decimated her army in the Red Sea. However, God's deliverance of His people from Babylon would be so spectacular in comparison that they were not to ponder the previous exploit, but to consider the "new thing" that God would accomplish for them. The Jews would not need to worry about surviving the long trip back to Israel from Babylon. The Lord would provide a secure highway through the desert with plenty of water to drink, and no wild beasts would threaten them (vv. 19-20). God's gracious provisions and protection for His homeward-bound people would cause them, whom God had reserved for Himself, to praise Him (v. 21).

Although the context of the passage is focused on the Jews' return from Babylon, this chapter challenges the nations to consider the evidence of an even greater future feat: How God will gather Jews throughout the world back to Israel in the Kingdom Age, and how He will bless them so abundantly that they will become the envy of all nations (Zech. 8:23). Much Bible prophecy centers in this great achievement, which, when fulfilled, will again prove that Israel's Jehovah is the only true God. He completely controls the future.

Isaiah wanted the Jewish nation to realize that their future deliverance from Babylon would not be based on religious doings such as offerings, sacrifices, or burning sweet incense to the Lord (vv. 22-23). Why would such offerings be unaccepted by God? There are at least two answers to this question. First, because their attitude towards the Lord was wrong; consequently, they were not honoring Him with their sacrifices (v. 23). Second, because Babylon would destroy the temple and there would be no means for Jews to offer God anything in accordance with the Law. This meant that no sin or trespass offerings could be presented by a priest on behalf of the guilty sinner, nor could the High Priest atone for the nation's sins on the Day of Atonement. As we saw in Isaiah's opening message, these things wearied the Lord anyway, because the Jews were pursuing religious form and not acting out of genuine conviction or devotion (1:11-15).

All this meant that Israel's offenses were piling up, and the Lord wanted His people to realize how wearisome their sin was to Him: *"But you have burdened Me with your sins, you have wearied Me with your iniquities"* (v. 24). The psalmist earlier wrote that God was *grieved* by sin (Ps. 95:10), but Israel's present situation was beyond mere grief; it was a heavy burden to Him.

Sorrow and Comfort

Scripture employs a variety of allegories to help us understand how wearisome willful sin, rebellion, and misplaced devotions are to God. The prophet Amos (speaking for the Lord) informs idolatrous Israel: *"Behold, I am pressed under you, as a cart is pressed that is full of sheaves"* (Amos 2:13). Amos describes the injury to God in terms that we can identify – Israel's idolatry was crushing His heart under a cart fully loaded with grain. The wonder of the gospel is that a heavy-hearted God caused the object of His love – His sinless Son – to be sin for us, that we might have our burden of sin removed (2 Cor. 5:21). Thankfully, in a coming day, God will no longer be wearied and grieved by our sin. Nor shall we!

There was no means for Israel to make herself righteous before God and she had no basis to argue her innocence before God (v. 26). Rather, the Lord's case against Israel was air-tight: Their "first father," which referred to Adam (Hos. 6:7) or to Abraham (Gen. 12:18), had sinned against God and then Israel's prophets and priests had also transgressed against the Lord and led the nation into sin (v. 27).

How could sinful and exiled Israel, being dead in trespasses and sins, be reconciled with God when there was no legitimate means of accomplishing that? The only solution for this hopeless situation is God's grace and mercy: *"I, even I, am He who blots out your transgressions for My own sake; and I will not remember your sins. Put Me in remembrance"* (vv. 25-26). But how could God righteously forgive Israel's sin? The answer to this question is that Christ would later pay the judicial price for all of Israel's offenses at Calvary; this would permit God to offer mercy to His people for His own sake. As a result, the God of Israel who is burdened by His people's sins (v. 24) is also quite eager to blot those sins from His memory (v. 25). Praise the Lord for His long-suffering and forgiving nature!

Although the judicial aspects of Israel's offenses could be absolved in Christ through grace, God still needed to make them righteous in the practical sense. The only way to purge them of their idols was through severe chastening: *"Therefore I will profane the princes of the sanctuary; I will give Jacob to the curse, and Israel to reproaches"* (v. 28). God would lift up Nebuchadnezzar to overcome the Assyrian Empire, to punish the wicked nations in the region, and to disgrace His own people through the destruction of Jerusalem, the temple, and Jewish society. God loves His people – He must act for their betterment and for the honor of His own name which His people had shamed.

Devotions in Isaiah

Although this chapter ends on a dismal note, Isaiah will tell his countrymen in the next chapter *"not to fear"* what the Lord will do, but rather to trust in His promises during the strenuous trial ahead. This is good counsel for God's people in every age – stand on God's promise and He will demonstrate His goodness.

Meditation

>Standing on the promises of Christ my King,
>Through eternal ages let His praises ring,
>Glory in the highest, I will shout and sing,
>Standing on the promises of God.
>
>Standing on the promises that cannot fail,
>When the howling storms of doubt and fear assail,
>By the living Word of God I shall prevail,
>Standing on the promises of God.
>
>Standing on the promises I cannot fall,
>Listening every moment to the Spirit's call
>Resting in my Savior as my all in all,
>Standing on the promises of God.

— R. Kelso Carter

Israel's Recovery Without Idols
Isaiah 44

As already previewed, God's refining and restoring of Israel, displaced during the Babylonian captivity, foreshadows God's final work in the Jewish nation during the Tribulation Period. By the end of the Tribulation Period, the Jewish nation will receive a new heart and be indwelt by the Holy Spirit (vv. 1-6; Ezek. 36:17-26; Joel 2:18-28). This will begin with the sealing of the 144,000 Jews in the early days of the Tribulation Period (Rev. 7).

The Jews in Babylon were not to despair. They were to trust the Lord to better them spiritually, morally, and politically through their hardship. They were the ones God had chosen to form a nation for His glory; therefore, they could count on God's help, for He is always faithful (vv. 1-2). Consequently, God consoles the suffering remnant: *"Fear not, O Jacob My servant; and you, Jeshurun, whom I have chosen"* (v. 2). Jacob was renamed "Israel" by the Lord and through his twelve sons, the nation promised to Abraham greatly expanded. "Jeshurun" means "upright one" and is another name for Israel, but this name reflects the holiness God desired to be in His people (Deut. 32:15, 33:5).

The refreshing times to be enjoyed in Judah (after the Babylonian captivity ended) included the abundance of rain which would ensure agricultural prosperity (vv. 3-4). However, this outpouring of water from heaven would only be a foretaste of all that Israel will experience in the Kingdom Age when God will pour out the Holy Spirit on His people. Then the Jews will flourish like well-watered grass and trees and each one will gladly proclaim: *"I am the Lord's"* (v. 5).

Altogether Unique

The thought of Israel being richly blessed and restored to God forever caused Isaiah to launch into a lengthy section emphasizing the fallacy of idols – Jehovah was alone in majesty (vv. 6-23). Jehovah was "Israel's King," "Redeemer," "the First and the Last," and "the

Almighty" God who alone controls the future (v. 6). Hence, the Lord again challenges any idol (false god) to prove that it can arrange the future and make it history (v. 7). This implied that there were no others like Him, a fact which the Lord affirms: *"Is there a God besides Me? Indeed there is no other Rock; I know not one"* (v. 8).

Given this understanding then, it would be pointless to trust in idols. Rather, Israel would be wise to trust in the only self-existing, omniscient God who foretells and commands the future. Accordingly, the only true God, their God, has commanded His people not to fear the future because He governs it completely (v. 8).

Altogether Foolish

The prophet concludes that, since idols are totally worthless and bring shame on their worshippers, only the spiritually blind and ignorant would expect something made with their own hands to know more than they do or do something they cannot (v. 9). So the Lord asks the obvious question: *"Who would form a god or mold an image that profits him nothing?"* (v. 10).

Besides the irrationality of creating one's own god, Isaiah points out that these supposed deities were created by men who themselves are not deity: *"The workmen, they are mere men"* (v. 11). It is unreasonable to suggest that men could create something more powerful than themselves. The ontological term we use today to express this principle is *existential causality*. A blacksmith gets hungry and thirsty, and must eat and drink to have the strength required to forge his idol out of metal and then to hammer it into shape – so how can he create a god more powerful than himself (v. 12)? Likewise, a carpenter must chop down a tree, saw and plane it smooth, and then outline the image of his idol on the wood before constructing it. How then can he create something with divine power (vv. 13-14)? How does being a man who tires while fabricating his god inspire confidence in it? Anyone stooping to such incongruity will suffer shame in the future – an idol has no life and no power.

Furthermore, what sense did it make to bow down to a piece of carved wood, when the idol-maker used the chips and shavings from the same tree for firewood to cook over or for warmth (vv. 15-16)? "What a good day this has been – I have warmed myself at a fire and have a god to worship, all out of the same tree." Then, when trouble comes, the idolater says to the part of the tree that he did not burn,

Sorrow and Comfort

"*Deliver me, for you are my god*" (v. 17)! We add, "How dumb is that?" to express contempt for such foolish thinking.

Paul tells us that those who choose to worship the creature instead of the Creator are given over to a reprobate mind (Rom. 1:24-28). "*For the wrath of God is revealed from heaven against all ungodliness and unrighteousness of men, who suppress the truth in unrighteousness*" (Rom. 1:18). Instead of discerning the design and sophistication of creation and looking for the Designer, these pagans are content to glory in what they see (vv. 18-19; Rom. 1:21-23). Consequently, without the Holy Spirit's work of conviction and enlightenment, such idolaters will remain in their depraved condition and the worst that is in man will be evident in their behavior (Rom. 1:27-31).

Speaking of the idolater, Isaiah colorfully expresses the irony of this sad fact: "*He feeds on ashes; a deceived heart has turned him aside; and he cannot deliver his soul, nor say, 'Is there not a lie in my right hand?'*" (v. 20). Without God, the darkened conscience of the pagan will never understand the truth – idols are nothing but a lie. An idolater will never obtain the spiritual nutrition that they seek from an idol. As Albert Barnes concludes, he will "be like a man who sought for food, and found it to be dust or ashes."[105] Similarly, Peter warns that false teachers are empty wells and clouds without rain (2 Pet. 2:17). Like putrid idols, these workers of iniquity provide nothing to enhance and energize the believer for service.

Remember Your Omnipotent God

In contrast to the lowly craftsman constructing something he hopes will have divine power, Isaiah reminds Israel that the One with highest power formed them. Therefore, they should worship their Creator, the only One who could forgive their sins. Consequently, he warns his countrymen not to forget the Lord:

> *Remember these, O Jacob, and Israel, for you are My servant; I have formed you, you are My servant; O Israel, you will not be forgotten by Me! I have blotted out, like a thick cloud, your transgressions, and like a cloud, your sins. Return to Me, for I have redeemed you* (vv. 21-22).

Furthermore, there was a day coming in which all creation would praise God for what He had accomplished in restoring and exalting the Jewish nation:

Sing, O heavens, for the Lord has done it! Shout, you lower parts of the earth; break forth into singing, you mountains, O forest, and every tree in it! For the Lord has redeemed Jacob, and glorified Himself in Israel (v. 23).

If all creation was to the praise of God's glory, what sense did it make to take a minute portion of it and worship it as a god? Rather, Israel should listen to and honor the Creator of all things who formed the nation according to His good pleasure and redeemed it in His mercy (v. 24). No part of creation could accomplish that!

Therefore, God was determined to frustrate the words of false prophets and diviners alike (v. 25). He would be careful to fulfill every word spoken by His prophets concerning the return of His people from Babylon to Judah (v. 26). As an example, if His prophets said to the water "dry up," then God would dry up the rivers (v. 27).

Isaiah then introduced Cyrus well over a century prior to his birth, who would be king of Persia. Cyrus was to be, and indeed was, God's instrument to topple the Babylonian empire, to release the Jews from captivity, and to rebuild the temple in Jerusalem (44:28-45:1; Ezra 1:1-2). And, incredibly, neither the Babylonian, nor the Persian empires existed at the time of this prophecy. Isaiah writes:

Who says of Cyrus, "He is My shepherd, and he shall perform all My pleasure, saying to Jerusalem, 'You shall be built,' and to the temple, 'Your foundation shall be laid.'" Thus says the Lord to His anointed, to Cyrus, whose right hand I have held – to subdue nations before him and loose the armor of kings, to open before him the double doors, so that the gates will not be shut (44:28-45:1).

The Cyrus Cylinder, which was discovered in 1879 A.D., records King Cyrus' overthrow of Babylon and his subsequent release of Jewish captives. According to the Nabonidus Chronicle, Ugbaru (the governor of Gutium, perhaps Darius) entered the city during the time of the annual Babylonian feast on October 12, 539 B.C. Then Cyrus entered the city a little over two weeks later to seal the victory; he was now the uncontested king of the entire, previously Babylonian Empire. He would punish the Babylonians, end the Jewish exile, and initiate the rebuilding of the temple in Jerusalem which Isaiah will foretell in the next chapter (45:1-4).

Sorrow and Comfort

This is an incredible prophesy in that it names both the individual and the feats he will accomplish but at a time when Solomon's Temple was still standing, and while Israel was still an autonomous Jewish state, and when Assyria was the dominant world power.

Clearly, Jehovah, through the prophets of old, has declared His future plans for the Jewish nation. There are still hundreds of prophecies indicating that the Messiah is coming again and that Jehovah is not finished with His covenant people. In this chapter, Isaiah has told us that, in a future day, once idolatrous Israel will be restored to Jehovah in purity, and that the wealth and honor of the nations will be hers. At that time, the Jews' relation with the Messiah will serve as a beacon to draw all men to praise the blessed Savior – the Lord Jesus Christ.

Meditation

> Jehovah reigns in majesty,
> Let all the nations quake;
> He dwells between the cherubim,
> Let earth's foundations shake.
> Supreme in Zion is the Lord,
> Exalted gloriously,
> Ye nations, praise His Name with awe,
> The Holy One is He.
>
> The mighty King loves justice well,
> And equity ordains;
> He rules His people righteously,
> And faithfulness maintains.
> O magnify the Lord our God,
> Let Him exalted be;
> In worship at His footstool bow,
> The Holy One is He.

— Paraphrase of Psalm 99;
Author Unknown

None Else
Isaiah 45

In this chapter, Isaiah uses Israel's future deliverance from Babylon through Cyrus to further contrast the impotence of idols with the only true God who controls human history and is able to save. J. M. Riddle suggests that the chapter may be divided in the following way:

> God and history (vv. 1-14); and, God and salvation (vv. 15-25). The phrases "none else" (vv. 5, 6, 14, 18, 22) and "no God else" (v. 21) emphasize that the Lord is incomparable, and the references can be summarized as follows: there is "none else" in history" (vv. 5, 6, 14), in creation (v. 8), in prophecy (v. 21), and in salvation (v. 22).[106]

None Else Controls History

In the previous chapter, Isaiah named the future Persian king, Cyrus, whom God would use to collapse the Babylonian empire, to release the Jews from captivity, and to rebuild the temple in Jerusalem (v. 1). This prophecy was spoken 150 to 180 years before it occurred, and Cyrus' name is recorded in Scripture twice to ensure there is no confusion about whom God would use to accomplish these feats:

> *Who says of Cyrus, "He is My shepherd, and he shall perform all My pleasure, saying to Jerusalem, 'You shall be built,' and to the temple, 'Your foundation shall be laid.'" Thus says the Lord to His anointed, to Cyrus, whose right hand I have held – to subdue nations before him and loose the armor of kings, to open before him the double doors, so that the gates will not be shut* (44:28-45:1).

This is an incredible prophecy, for it names both the individual and his future feats at a time when Solomon's Temple was still standing and when Israel was still an autonomous Jewish state. It is joined by several others in fulfilment. For example, just prior to the time of the exile, Jeremiah prophesied that the Jewish captivity in Babylon would last only seventy years (Jer. 25:11-12, 29:10) and with the overthrow of

Sorrow and Comfort

the Babylonian empire, the Jews would be liberated and permitted to return to their homeland. The prophet Daniel, as an elderly man who had lived through the seventy-year exile, understood that Jeremiah's prophecy was fulfilled by the Persian victory (Dan. 9:2). God had severely chastened the Jews for their idolatry, but He had also kept His promise to *"not make an end of them"* (Jer. 30:11) and He would bring them home again.

What facilitated the fulfillment of this prophecy? First, God moved in the spirit of Cyrus not only to release the Jews, but also to rebuild God's temple in Jerusalem. Second, the Jewish historian Josephus wrote that Cyrus was shown the prophecy of Isaiah and wanted to fulfill it (*The Antiquities of the Jews* 11.1.1). Both the Word of God and the Spirit of God had an effect on Cyrus to accomplish the will of God.

How would you react if you read portions of a nearly two-hundred-year-old document that called you by name and stated that you would conquer the Babylonian Empire, be king of Persia, release the Jews from slavery, and then help them rebuild their temple in Jerusalem? And furthermore the God of the Jews who foretold these things promised to go before your army and decimate any opposition and permit you to despoil the nations you conquered (vv. 2-3). And then you were told why the God of the Jews would do all this for you:

> *That you may know that I, the Lord, who call you by your name, am the God of Israel. ... I have even called you by your name; I have named you, though you have not known Me. I am the Lord, and there is no other; there is no God besides Me. I will gird you, though you have not known Me, that they may know from the rising of the sun to its setting that there is none besides Me. I am the Lord, and there is no other* (vv. 3-6).

If you were told all this, you would do exactly what Cyrus did. He fulfilled the predetermined counsel of God by granting the Jews throughout His kingdom liberty to go back to Jerusalem and to rebuild their God's temple.

Does this mean Cyrus believed that Jehovah, the God of the Jews, was the one true God? Not likely. The Cyrus Cylinder (538 B.C.) records Persian King Cyrus' conquest of Babylon and his subsequent release of Jewish captives. The Cylinder includes this statement: "May all the gods whom I have resettled in their sacred cities daily ask Bel and Nebo for a long life for me." Cyrus worshiped Bel and Nebo, the gods of Persia. By releasing those who had been in Babylonian captivity and honoring their gods, Cyrus hoped to establish loyal buffer nations on the perimeter of his empire and to ingratiate himself with the gods of these nations, including Jehovah of the Jews. Cyrus thought that by being in good standing with all proclaimed deities of the surrounding nations, it would certainly be well with him. Yet, Jehovah is no man's debtor; in fact, He was acting on behalf of His covenant people to orchestrate the entire matter (v. 4). Cyrus was merely God's "anointed," or chosen vessel, to accomplish His will (v. 1).

The Lord concluded His message to Cyrus by saying that *"I am the Lord, and there is no other; I form the light and create darkness, I make peace and create calamity; I, the Lord, do all these things"* (vv. 6-7). H. A. Ironside remarks that this is a striking statement by God to Cyrus in light of Persian beliefs:

> In Persian sacred writings such as the Zend-Avesta, the Persians gave the primary place to Ormazd, the one true living God. They gave Ahriman a very large place as the supernatural foe of God, who is in constant conflict with Him. One was the God of light; the other was the spirit of darkness. One was the God of peace; the other was the spirit of war. One was the God of goodness; the other was the spirit of evil.[107]

Light and darkness cannot exist together – darkness is defined by the absence of light. Wickedness is defined by what is not declared holy by God's very character. God did not create sin, but He did bestow upon angels and humans the capacity of choice to willingly reflect His righteous glory or to oppose it. In this design – not of sin, but of opportunity – the concept of love is forged. Love and obedience are intimately tied together throughout Scripture. If Cyrus would respond to the light shown him, then he could enjoy peace, but if he chose to walk in darkness, there would be calamity. So regardless of what Cyrus did, God was sovereign over His creation.

A sovereign God is ultimately responsible for all calamities that occur, though He may not be the one doing the work (sometimes he permits others to do the work, e.g., Satan). He may also choose not to interfere within the natural order to prevent disasters, which occur as the fallout of original sin (Amos 3:6).

Although many in Cyrus' day did not know the sovereign God of the universe, there is coming a time in which He will be known by everyone (i.e., during the Millennial Kingdom). Then, His righteousness (i.e., all of His self-determined purposes matching His righteous nature) will shower down on the entire earth and His salvation will spring up everywhere (v. 8). Having prophesied of a coming era when God's glory will fill the earth and all men will acknowledge Him, Isaiah is prompted to issue the final woes of his book. Since these are the only woes within the final section of Isaiah (chps. 39-66), his warning carries added weight:

> *Woe to him who strives with his Maker! Let the potsherd strive with the potsherds of the earth! Shall the clay say to him who forms it, "What are you making?" Or shall your handiwork say, "He has no hands?" Woe to him who says to his father, "What are you begetting?" Or to the woman, "What have you brought forth?"* (vv. 9-10).

Because the Lord created all things, He alone has the right to govern what He has created. Any created thing voicing disapproval of God's self-determining ways was in danger of being destroyed. What right does a broken vessel have to accuse the potter of wrongdoing? Is it appropriate for a child to question his parents as to why they brought him or her into the world? The obvious answer to both questions is "no." Therefore, Israel, whom God created, should not question God's corrective discipline of the nation or His using Cyrus to end their Babylonian exile (vv. 11-13).

None Else Can Save

Thinking about God's sovereignty promoted the prophet to foretell what God would ultimately accomplish in His purposes: All Gentile nations would recognize Him alone as God and would be subservient to Israel (v. 13). Because much of what the Savior of Israel does is covert or not fully explained, it might seem to some Jews that He is hiding (v. 14): *"Truly You are God, who hide Yourself, O God of Israel, the Savior"* (v. 15)! F. B. Hole explains why the remnant might think God hides Himself as He accomplishes His purposes for them:

> A servant of God has very truly and aptly remarked, "God's ways are behind the scenes, but He moves all the scenes which He is behind." Men may act to achieve their own purposes without any thought of

God and yet God may be behind their doings, overruling them to serve His own ends.[108]

God's ways are so far above ours that often we really have no idea what He is doing for His glory and our good. However, during the Kingdom Age, the Lord will be fully revealed as Israel's Deliverer and all will witness His glory. This revelation will be so clear that anyone who embraced idols before will be ashamed and those having faith in Jehovah will never be embarrassed to identify with Him (vv. 16-17).

Isaiah proclaimed that *"Israel shall be saved in the Lord with an everlasting salvation"* (v. 17). The only way that would be possible would be through an everlasting covenant which ensured salvation, but the Law was not such a covenant. As noted in chapter 42, the prophet Ezekiel foretold that God's coming Shepherd would be able to gather up the lost sheep of Israel and feed, protect, and care for them because He would establish a *Covenant of Peace* with the Jewish nation (Ezek. 34:25). Jeremiah says that this would be an everlasting covenant resulting in eternal blessing to the Jews (Jer. 32:40).

As prophesied by Isaiah and the other Old Testament prophets, God did institute a New Covenant with His people that would give them eternal salvation, a new and clean heart, and allow the Holy Spirit to indwell them forever (Jer. 31:31-40). Christ, as High Priest, sealed this covenant with both Judah and Israel with His own blood (Luke 22:20; Heb. 8:8). Hence, there is only one individual who can be Israel's Shepherd and King-Priest forever, the Lord Jesus Christ.

Isaiah concludes his warning against rebelling against the Creator's will by stating that God's creative power gives validity to His future use of Cyrus in His plans to liberate the Jews. The fact that God can only speak the truth further verifies that it will happen (vv. 18-19).

Seeing the God of the Jews controlling the Gentiles to accomplish His plans for His people should cause the Gentiles to turn from their idols to the one true God – the Creator of all things (vv. 20-21). God's gracious invitation in verse 22 proves that He is not the God of the Jews only, but of all men, and He desires that none should perish, but receive salvation in Him: *"Look to Me, and be saved, all you ends of the earth! For I am God, and there is no other."* Whether men choose Him or not, God will receive glory from His creation: *"I have sworn by Myself; the word has gone out of My mouth in righteousness, and shall not return, that to Me every knee shall bow, every tongue shall take an oath"* (v. 23). When will this ultimately occur? Certainly, those living

Sorrow and Comfort

on the earth will give the Lord homage during the Millennial Kingdom (v. 24). But when will those who have already died honor the Lord?

In a future day, all the wicked will be resurrected and positioned before Jesus Christ at the Great White Throne of God (Rev. 20:11). Their agonized response will be immediate; they shall bow the knee to Him. Though their mouths will be stopped because of the convicting evidence against them (Rom. 3:19; Rev. 20:12), their tongues when loosened will confess *that Jesus Christ is Lord.*

> *Wherefore God also hath highly exalted Him, and given Him a name which is above every name: That at the name of Jesus every knee should bow, of things in heaven, and things in earth, and things under the earth; and that every tongue should confess that Jesus Christ is Lord, to the glory of God the Father* (Phil. 2:9-11, KJV).

At that moment of reckoning, Jesus Christ will be far more than a man to them; He will be known as their Lord and Supreme Judge! Those who chose not to honor Him in life, who chose not to receive His gift of eternal life, will honor His judgment and will receive eternal death. During the Kingdom Age those living on earth will honor the Lord Jesus and the nation of Israel will be found righteous (i.e. be justified) in Him and they will rejoice in that: *"In the Lord all the descendants of Israel shall be justified, and shall glory"* (v. 25). Paul, quoting Isaiah, affirmed that God would refine and save a future remnant of the Jewish nation: *"Though the number of the children of Israel be as the sand of the sea, the remnant will be saved"* (Rom. 9:27). Seeing that God always does what He says He will do – Oh Israel, why would you ever put your trust in a lifeless idol or question the ways of a God who loves you forever?

Meditation

> Judge not the Lord by feeble sense,
> But trust Him for His grace;
> Behind a frowning providence
> He hides a smiling face.
>
> His purposes will ripen fast,
> Unfolding every hour;

The bud may have a bitter taste,
But sweet will be the flower.

Blind unbelief is sure to err
And scan His work in vain;
God is His own Interpreter,
And He will make it plain.

— William Cowper

The Unique God
Isaiah 46

Isaiah commenced the latter section of his book with two important questions for idolatrous Israel – questions that highlight the uniqueness of God: *"To whom then will you liken God? Or what likeness will you compare to Him?"* (40:18). God cannot be fully illustrated or explained by what is seen in nature. God is beyond nature. Therefore it is impossible to understand Him from a naturalistic point of view; we must have supernatural revelation (1 Cor. 2:10-12). If man had only the natural world to testify to God's existence, we might be aware of His presence without ever knowing Him personally.

However, God desires not just that the nation of Israel should know Him, but that all men would seek Him out and have fellowship with Him. For that reason, He declares in Scripture who He is and the means by which condemned sinners can be forgiven and enjoy communion with a Holy God. The God of the Bible reveals Himself as the eternal Creator and Sustainer of all things. He is unique in character and attributes – He is holy! Isaiah tells us that God is eternal (44:6), He is the Creator of all things (44:24) and again in this chapter that He is unique; there is none like Him (v. 9). The point is that God alone is sovereign over His creation and He reveals Himself in what He does and foretells in Scripture. This is how we know the God of the Jews is the one true Creator.

Accordingly, God is justified in using Cyrus to deliver His people from Babylon (the focus of chapter 45). He is also righteous in using Babylon to chasten Judah, and then crushing Babylon, with her putrid gods, after serving His purposes. J. A. Motyer provides the following outline to better understand the contrast in this chapter between dumb burdensome idols and the true creating, saving, burden-bearing God:

The burdening gods (vv. 1-2)
The burden-bearing God (vv. 3-4)
The made gods, burdens without saving power (vv. 5-7)

The making God (vv. 8-11)
The saving God (vv. 12-13)[109]

The prophet commences his arguments by stating that the huge metal idols of Bel and Nebo would not be able to save Babylon from God's judgment to come. John A. Martin describes the pagan scene for us:

> Bel, not to be confused with the Canaanite Baal, was another name for Marduk (Jer. 50:2), god of the sun. Nebo, son of Marduk, was a god of learning, writing, and astronomy. Large images of those gods, carried about on Babylon's New Year's Day festival, were heavy and burdensome.[110]

Since these idols were themselves heavy and cumbersome, how could they relieve Babylon's burden of judgment? In contrast, the God of the Jews would sustain and carry His people through their season of chastening and refining (vv. 3-4). In fact, God wanted His people to know that He had watched over them and cared for them since their conception (Ps. 139:14) and birth (v. 3), and into their autumn years (v. 4). In their infancy, the enemy had tried to eradicate them, but God had protected the nation.

The Lord Jesus affirmed God's concern for children, and He threatened with dire consequences those who abuse them (Matt. 18:6). Children have guardian angels to provide a certain level of protection against the forces of evil which work to prevent them from understanding divine truth and turning to God (Matt. 18:10). Just as a shepherd with one hundred sheep is concerned about one lamb that strays from the fold, God is concerned about each child and desires that none be lost (Matt. 18:14).

In comparison, manmade gods of silver and gold often appear beautiful, but they do not possess compassion, or the ability to protect anyone (vv. 5-6). In fact, they are dependent on men to care for them. Idols must be carried around, cleaned, and then propped up so they do not fall over. They cannot even care for themselves, let alone anyone else (v. 7).

Since Isaiah is speaking about Babylon in this chapter, the context of the passage would suggest that the "transgressors" (v. 8) and "stubborn-hearted" (v. 12) refer to the Babylonians – they were to remember that the God of the Jews is the only true God (v. 9).

Sorrow and Comfort

On a practical note, Isaiah's instruction to recall what is important is a good admonition for believers also: *"**Remember this**, and show yourselves men; **recall to mind**, O you transgressors. **Remember the former things** of old, for I am God, and there is no other; I am God, and there is none like Me"* (vv. 8-9). The mental exercise of "recalling" requires the mind to focus on the past faithfulness of God or His promises and directives. We tend to forget the Lord, our past mistakes, and His past faithfulness. Thus, there is much exhortation in Scripture to remember the Lord, His goodness and His commands (Deut. 6:12, 8:11, 9:7; Luke 22:19). What is the benefit of refocusing the mind backward upon historical events or divine statements? We reacquaint ourselves with God's promises of deliverance and we recall His past faithfulness through the storms of life.

Unlike lifeless inarticulate idols, God proves that He is the unique Creator who predetermines and controls the future (v. 10). For example, He will raise up Cyrus from the east to execute vengeance on Babylon. Cyrus will be like a swift ravenous bird (e.g., an eagle) that sweeps down on its unsuspecting prey; God will use him to devour Babylon (v. 11).

Then, through His evangelical prophet, the merciful, omnipotent God of the universe graciously extends to the stubborn-hearted worshippers in Babylon the offer of salvation:

> *Listen to Me, you stubborn-hearted, who are far from righteousness: I bring My righteousness near, it shall not be far off; My salvation shall not linger. And I will place salvation in Zion, for Israel My glory* (vv. 12-13).

Commenting to verse 13, W. E. Vine observes, "On the basis of His righteousness, established for Israel, as for us, on the ground of the death of Christ, God will 'place salvation in Zion for Israel my glory.'"[111] Salvation for Jews and Gentiles would be secured in Israel. The Babylonians needed righteousness but they were not going to obtain divine justification in their homeland – they would have to leave their idols in Babylon and venture to Israel to worship God in Zion. That was the place and those were the people whom God called His own. Abram received a similar invitation from the Lord centuries earlier (Gen. 12:1-3). He was to leave his idols in Ur and journey to a land that the "God of Glory" would show him. Abram put his trust in a God that he did not know and obeyed His word by faith.

Faith is the ability of the soul to reach beyond what can be verified by the human senses and to trust what he cannot confirm by his or her own understanding. Hebrews 11:3 reminds us that it is only by faith that we know that the visible things we see did not happen by chance from visible realms, but from the hand of the invisible Creator. This is why one must have faith to please God, *"for without faith it is impossible to please Him"* (Heb. 11:6).

God performed no signs and wonders for Abraham. He simply reconfirmed His word to Abraham. That was good enough for him – he simply trusted God and believed. God responded by accrediting a standing of righteousness to Abraham's account. This accrediting, or accounting, of divine righteousness to a sinner who exercises faith is seen throughout the Bible and is thoroughly explained by the Apostle Paul in Romans 4 and 5. Obviously, God wanted no confusion on this matter, for the words "believe," "counted," and "righteousness" all occur for the first time in the Bible in one verse (Gen. 15:6) and in one Divine declaration just after the first reference to "the word of the Lord" in the Bible (Gen. 15:1).

Genesis 15:6 again appears three times in the New Testament: Romans 4:3, Galatians 3:6, and James 2:23. In Abraham's case, what preceded imputed righteousness? His faith. In Noah's case, what preceded imputed righteousness? God's grace. Combining these two important truths we have: *"For by grace you have been saved through faith, and that not of yourselves; it is the gift of God, not of works, lest anyone should boast"* (Eph. 2:8-9). Both God's means of salvation through grace and man's responsibility to lay hold of this gift by personal faith are clearly presented in Genesis, as throughout the Bible. Isaiah was offering the pagans in Babylon an opportunity to be justified by grace through trusting in God's invitation. Then they, like the Jews, would have a relationship with the God of Israel.

Meditation

> May we read these Scriptures, and their truths believe,
> Own our need as sinners, and God's Son receive;
> In assurance resting, His commands obey,
> And in His grace growing, live for Him each day.
>
> — A. P. Gibbs

Babylon Shall Fall
Isaiah 47

In the last chapter, Isaiah pronounced judgment on Babylon's gods and offered Babylon's pagans an opportunity to worship the one true God. The prophet now concludes God's message to Babylon by promising her doom.

Isaiah poetically describes Babylon's condition after the Persians conquer Babylon. Speaking of the once thought impenetrable capital city, he says: *"Come down and sit in the dust, O virgin daughter of Babylon; sit on the ground without a throne"* (v. 1). Babylon's inhabitants would no longer be treated delicately like a young virgin, but rather they would be stripped of their clothing, abused, and forced to grind flour (vv. 2-3). A few would escape across the river, but most would become captives weeping and wallowing in humiliation.

Verse 4 records Israel's response to the fall and shame of their captors: *"As for our Redeemer, the Lord of hosts is His name, the Holy One of Israel."* Exiled Jews were completely helpless in effecting their own release from captivity. So, when they witness the impossible happen, they will realize that the Holy One of Israel had kept His word, as spoken by the prophets: God will redeem His people out of Babylon.

The Lord had chosen pagan Babylon as the rod of correction for His people Israel (God's inheritance; v. 6). However, like the Assyrians before them, the ruthless empire had gone too far in abusing God's people. They would be severely punished for their cruel attitude and behavior towards the Jews. Babylon would no longer be "the Lady of Kingdoms," but would be brought down into silence and darkness (v. 5). This passage describes the pride and self-confidence of Babylon. She was confident in her wealth, her massive, fortified capital, and her resources sufficient to sustain a long siege if required. Because Babylon thought she would rule over the nations forever and because she showed no mercy to her captives, the Lord would give her something to think about through the Persians (v. 7).

Babylon thought she was invincible and secure. She happily continued in her indulgences and enchantments. She proudly believed that *"I am, and there is no one else besides me; I shall not sit as a widow, nor shall I know the loss of children"* (v. 8). But she was destined to be fully conquered, meaning that not only would she lose all her children, but she would also become a destitute widow (v. 9). Babylon did not believe she answered to anyone: *"I am, and there is no one else besides me"* (v. 10). She was blinded by the delusion that her knowledge obtained through demonic means (sorceries, astrology, etc.) would guide her safely through the future, but she would soon learn that only God is unique (v. 11).

In a mocking satire, the Lord urges the Babylonians to use all their sorceries and stargazers in an attempt to save themselves from the destruction He would bring upon them (vv. 12-13). This would prove that all the efforts of all Babylon's soothsayers and counselors were like worthless stubble that should be burned (v. 14). Neither could the collective efforts of Babylon's commercial partners save her from doom (v. 15). Isaiah concludes his message to proud Babylon by stating the inescapable outcome of God's Word: "No one shall save you" (v. 15). While individuals could still repent and turn to the Lord, the empire itself was doomed and nothing could change that.

Twice in this chapter Babylon claimed to be unique, that is, nothing in creation could be compared to her achievements and glory (vv. 8, 10). However, the Bible declares that only God is perfect, self-sufficient, and self-existing – there is none like Him, for He is holy! Isaiah tells us that these same divine attributes will be found in God's Messiah, the Savior of the world: *"For I am the Lord your God, the Holy One of Israel, your Savior"* (43:3). *"I, even I, am the Lord, and besides Me there is no savior"* (43:11). *"Remember the former things of old, for I am God, and there is no other; I am God, and there is none like Me"* (46:9). These prophecies foretell that the coming Savior of mankind would be, and is, none other than the unique Holy God of the universe.

The New Testament uses plain language to speak of the deity of Christ, while the Old Testament often uses types, symbols, and numerical imagery to proclaim the same truth. John especially and emphatically introduces the Lord Jesus in the opening verses of his gospel account as being truly God, the Creator:

Sorrow and Comfort

> *In the beginning was the Word, and the Word was with God, and the Word was God. He was in the beginning with God. All things were made through Him, and without Him nothing was made that was made. In Him was life, and the life was the light of men. And the light shines in the darkness, and the darkness did not comprehend it* (John 1:1-5).

There is one unique God who created all things and He is also the unique Savior who redeems what was defiled by sin. The Lord Jesus Christ is our loving Savior and the eternal Son of God.

Meditation

>Eternal Son, eternal Love,
>Take to Thyself Thy mighty power;
>Let all earth's sons Thy mercy prove;
>Let all Thy saving grace adore.
>
>The triumphs of Thy love display;
>In every heart reign Thou alone;
>Till all Thy foes confess Thy sway,
>And glory ends what grace began.
>
>— Charles Wesley

Come Near to Me
Isaiah 48

Isaiah 48 is the prophetic crescendo for the previous eight chapters. The prophet has foretold the fall of Babylon and the judgment of her gods, and the climax of Israel's chastening and exile. The entire chapter forms a strong exhortation to Jewish captives in Babylon. (Many of them were apostate, but God had maintained a faithful remnant there also.) The Jews were to remember God's promises (vv. 1-11), and His sovereignty in dealing with them (vv. 12-19). And, after Cyrus crushed the Babylonian Empire and granted their emancipation (vv. 20-22), they were to return to Israel.

Deliverance Unmerited

Isaiah commences his closing remarks of this nine-chapter section by reminding Israel of their past hypocrisy. They took oaths in God's name, but then did not reverence His name by honoring their promises (v. 1). They thought they would receive God's favor because they were associated with Jerusalem (though they lived in Babylon) and because they said they trusted in Jehovah (v. 2).

How silly are the things men think will make them spiritual or will somehow earn God's favor, when in fact these facades have no value to God. God appreciates sincerity, devotion, and obedience, but Israel's profession (vv. 1-2) did not match their practices (vv. 3-8). Even after hearing all that Isaiah had foretold about their forthcoming punishment, they were still unwilling to yield to God or to change their ways (vv. 3-4). Isaiah foretold that his future audience would also remain stubborn and proud.

Foreknowledge of the nation's disposition made it necessary for the prophet to reveal God's detailed plans for them. Hopefully, when these events unfolded in time, the Jews would recognize that Jehovah and not some idol, was responsible: *"Even from the beginning I have declared it to you; before it came to pass I proclaimed it to you, lest you should say, 'My idol has done them, and my carved image and my molded image have commanded them'"* (v. 5). Although Satan often mimics God's handiwork and deceives mankind through supernatural signs, he cannot explicitly control future events or create life (Ex. 8:16-19), nor is he omniscient, knowing the end from the beginning. Only God can forecast and govern forthcoming events with accuracy.

Isaiah says that this is why many of God's messages to Israel were prophetic. God wanted them to know He was the one true God so they would reject the many false gods of their day. For this reason, one-fourth of the Bible is prophetic in nature, with the greatest majority of this content relating to God's covenant people. Only the true Creator and Sustainer of all things could possibly know what will transpire in the future. Jehovah was proving to His people that He was the omnipotent, omniscient, immutable, and eternal God. Jehovah wanted the Jews to flee idolatry and embrace Him, the one true God.

Unfortunately, false prophets have plagued the Jews throughout their history. The problem is compounded by the fact that God's prophets always seemed to be greatly outnumbered by their counterparts. The ministries of Elijah (1 Kings 18), Micaiah (1 Kings 22), and Jeremiah (Jer. 20) serve as good examples. Time and again, God's prophets have suffered greatly for their faithfulness to be one voice for God among a throng of dissident and often hostile people. The standard of a true prophet of God is one hundred percent accuracy (Deut. 18:20-22). This provides confirmation that the message is indeed from God, and history has shown Isaiah to be a true prophet of God.

But, in general, Israel had rejected Isaiah's previous prophecies (v. 8), so God now provided them new predictions (v. 6). This did not mean that God had just thought of something new and was developing His plans for Israel on the fly. Rather, God divulges information to men incrementally based on their response to previous revelation. Israel was unyielding, so Isaiah foretells how God would bring Israel out of captivity. Moses promised the infant Jewish nation that if they embraced idols God would expel them from the Promised Land; however, they also knew that God's covenant with Abraham meant that He would bring them back home (Gen. 15:18-21; Deut. 30:1-5). Isaiah tells his countrymen where they were being exiled to and how God would bring them back – long before it happened. When Israel witnessed the specifics of this revelation occur, they would know that Jehovah had done it (v. 7). No false god had had any part in their deliverance, nor had the Jews accomplished their release through their own knowledge or efforts.

Deliverance Promised

Furthermore, Isaiah tells Judah that God's wrath against them would be deferred for a while to permit exiled Jews to return to their homeland (v. 9). While they were in Babylon, He would be refining them through affliction, but after seventy years in Babylon there would be a reprieve which would permit their departure (v. 10; Jer. 25:11). The type of refinement spoken of in verse 10 is difficult to determine: *"I have refined you, but not as silver; I have tested you in the furnace of affliction."* In his opening message Isaiah rebuked Judah's moral and spiritual impurities, *"Your silver has become dross,"* which was worthless to God (1:22). But then the Lord promises *"I will turn My hand against you, and thoroughly purge away your dross"* (1:25). Evidently, the furnace of Babylon would purge many impurities from the Jewish nation, but God's overall anger, as related to their impurities, would be tempered with mercy, lest Israel be consumed by His wrath. More purifying would still be required afterwards to make them refined silver.

A few decades later, the prophet Jeremiah likened himself to a tester of metals, and Judah to unrefinable ore (Jer. 6:27-28). He knew the hearts of his rebellious countrymen; they were hardened and had not been softened by the refining efforts of his prophecies. The people of Judah were corrupt through and through; the desired precious metal could scarcely be found in them. So far, God's attempts through prophesies to remove the stubborn components of bronze, iron, and lead from their makeup were unsuccessful. God wanted purified silver, but His people were so full of impurities, that He must utterly reject them (Jer. 6:29-30). Refuse silver has no value; it must either be cast away or exposed to intense heat to remove its dross. God knew how to remove the wicked dross from Judah: Babylon would be the flame, Jerusalem the chaff, and God's prophetic word the catalyst for the Refiner's fire. Any living soul emerging from that great conflagration would assuredly be genuine silver.

Jeremiah seems to be describing what God wanted to accomplish through the Babylonian exile, but Isaiah highlights the reality of the situation. God wanted pure silver in Judah, that is, an undefiled and uncorrupted people that fully trusted and loved Him. Although the Jews

Sorrow and Comfort

would be purged of their idolatry while in Babylon, the perfection that God longs for in all His people would be impossible to achieve then. Likewise, in the Church Age, we understand that believers should sin less because of their sinless position in Christ (Rom. 6:1); however, sinless perfection is not possible until glorification occurs (1 Jn. 3:2-3). By drawing near to and being sustained by Christ, we will be conformed to His image and thus sin less (Rom. 8:29). Children of God are marked by righteous living (i.e., they do not practice sin; 1 Jn. 3:8-9). Those who have not been born again habitually practice sin without remorse – the fallen nature within them rules their behavior (1 Jn. 3:10).

Through Isaiah, the Lord had foretold how, when, and why He would cause Babylon's fall. He did this that His people especially would realize that no idol could foreknow or accomplish such things and that He alone was the true God: *"For My own sake, for My own sake, I will do it; for how should My name be profaned? And **I will not give My glory to another"*** (v. 11). God's dealings with Israel and His desire to honor His own name should prompt all believers to consider what we do and say. In this matter Paul admonishes us:

> *But God has chosen the foolish things of the world to put to shame the wise, and God has chosen the weak things of the world to put to shame the things which are mighty; and the base things of the world and the things which are despised God has chosen, and the things which are not, to bring to nothing the things that are, that no flesh should glory in His presence. But of Him you are in Christ Jesus, who became for us wisdom from God -- and righteousness and sanctification and redemption – that, as it is written, "He who glories, let him glory in the Lord"* (1 Cor. 1:27-31).

God continues to prompt our admiration and worship by using weak and foolish things/people to confound the profound, secularly speaking. Understanding that without Christ we can do nothing (John 15:5), but in Christ we can do all things (Phil. 4:12) should keep believers from glorying in themselves. Any and all praise must be the Lord's. When we glory in ourselves, we follow the example of proud Babylon, which God was determined to bring to nothing. Scripture is full of timeless reminders of who should always be the One to receive glory:

Be exalted, O God, above the heavens; **let Your glory be above all the earth** (Ps. 57:5).

Give to the Lord, O families of the peoples, give to the Lord glory and strength. **Give to the Lord the glory** due His name; bring an offering, and come into His courts (Ps. 96:7-8).

Not unto us, O Lord, not unto us, but to Your name **give glory**, because of Your mercy, because of Your truth (Ps. 115:1).

I am the Lord, that is My name; and **My glory I will not give to another**, nor My praise to carved images (42:8).

Everyone who is called by My name, **whom I have created for My glory**; I have formed him, yes, I have made him (43:7).

Therefore, whether you eat or drink, or whatever you do, **do all to the glory of God** (1 Cor. 10:31).

But he who glories, **let him glory in the Lord** (2 Cor. 10:17).

But **God forbid that I should glory, save in the cross of our Lord Jesus Christ**, by whom the world is crucified to me, and I unto the world (Gal. 6:14; KJV).

It is man's highest occupation to worship and to praise God! God does not permit others to intrude upon His supreme position and authority or to diminish the outshining of His glory. Babylon had intruded upon God's glory by proclaiming: *"I am, and there is no one else besides me"* (47:8, 10). God alone is unique – He is alone in majesty.

Regardless of what is meant by *"I have refined you, but not as silver,"* God would accomplish His plans for testing and restoring Israel for the honor of His own name. The exact fulfillment of foretold events would cause Israel and the nations to know that Jehovah alone is God and that He is a God who honors His covenants.

It is at verse 12 that Isaiah transitions from speaking of Cyrus the deliverer, to his Antitype, the Lord Jesus, who will ultimately deliver the Jewish nation forever from oppression at the conclusion of the Tribulation Period. Hence, the prophet exhorts the Jewish nation to remember that the One who is the First and the Last has chosen them as

Sorrow and Comfort

a special people (v. 12). He is the Creator of all things (v. 13) and is the only One who controls the future (v. 14). The latter fact would be proven when God executed His judgment on Babylon through his called servant Cyrus (v. 15).

Deliverance for the Obedient

What was the intent of all this information? God wanted His people to draw near to Him now in faith (v. 16)! Verses 16-17 contain probably the clearest reference to the trinity in the entire Old Testament (with Isaiah 61:1-2 a near second). Notice that the One speaking (the Creator of all things and Controller of the future; vv. 13-14) is the second person of the Godhead, as He refers to God the Father and God the Spirit as equals:

> "**Come near to Me**, *hear this: I have not spoken in secret from the beginning; from the time that it was, I was there. And now the Lord God* [God the Father] *and His Spirit* [the Holy Spirit] *have sent Me* [God the Son]." *Thus says the Lord, your Redeemer, the Holy One of Israel*: "*I am the Lord your God, who teaches you to profit, who leads you by the way you should go*" (vv. 16-17).

The three persons of the Godhead are clearly seen in verse 16. As God often speaks of Himself as the Redeemer and Holy One of Israel, the specific focus of personage(s) in verse 17 is not as distinct, although clearly the second person of the Godhead continues to speak. Given what He says about Himself later, it seems likely that verse 17 is referring to Him personally: *"The Spirit of the Lord God is upon Me, because the Lord has anointed Me to preach good tidings..."* (Isa. 61:1). He, the Son of God, the eternal Word, became flesh (John 1:18) to teach God's way of salvation to humanity.

This passage unfolds to us God's great plan of salvation for humanity: God the Father and the Holy Spirit sent the Son to earth to become the Redeemer, the Holy One of Israel. "The Holy One" was a title the demons used to refer to Christ while speaking with Him during His earthly sojourn (Mark 1:24; Luke 4:34). Moreover, the Redeemer, the Person speaking, clearly identifies Himself as the Lord, the God of Israel. New Testament Scripture further explains the meaning of this verse: The Lord Jesus stated that He had come to the earth to do the Father's will (Luke 22:42; John 10:18, 14:31). The angel Gabriel announced to Mary that she would conceive and give birth to the Lord

Devotions in Isaiah

Jesus through the overshadowing power of the Holy Spirit (Luke 1:35). The Father sent the Son, and the Holy Spirit enabled the incarnation so the Son of God could come.

God's tri-unity is distinctly seen early in Scripture as the pronouns "Us," "Our," and "Their" are employed to describe God's actions in the creation of man (Gen. 1:26), after the fall of mankind (Gen. 3:22), and again when God confounded mankind's language (Gen. 11:4-7). God introduces Himself to us as *Elohim* in Genesis 1:1 and continues to refer to Himself as such throughout the chapter. *Elohim* speaks of God's majesty, power, and omnipotence as the Creator. The *-im* suffix is the Hebrew ending that denotes a plurality of three or more. *Elohim* is the plural form of *Eloah*. *Elohim* may be translated literally as *gods*, but in the context of this passage it is clearly used in the singular – the name of the mighty Creator. Thus, *Elohim* is a plural name with a singular meaning. The word *"Elohim"* accounts for nearly ninety percent of the references to *"God"* in the English Old Testament. (*Elohim* is employed in the Hebrew text approximately 2700 times.)

Obviously, the Bible teaches the existence of only one true God; yet, God refers to Himself as being plural in personage, as indicated both by the use of pronouns such as "Us" and "Our" and the Hebrew noun form *Elohim*. Scripture further identifies the persons of the Godhead: Father, Son, and Holy Spirit. To be a person means to possess individual personality, that is, an intellect to reason, a sensibility to ensure an emotional response (i.e. feelings), and a will to make choices. Thus, all three persons of the Godhead have individual personalities, but exist as one Being.

There is one unique God consisting of three individual Persons, each having the same divine attributes and characteristics. Each is perfect in grace, mercy, and love and is all-powerful, all-knowing, and all-present (dwelling everywhere).

Unfortunately, the One who had shown Israel the right way of salvation had been ignored; therefore the nation would experience exile and the death of their children, rather than the peace and righteousness He wanted them to enjoy (vv. 18-19). Disobedience to God's revealed will always has painful consequences.

The same One who was here speaking through Isaiah would, centuries later, personally deliver a message of peace to Israel: *"I am the way, the truth, and the life. No one comes to the Father except through Me"* (John 14:6). Yet, Israel would reject His message and

Sorrow and Comfort

demand that its Messenger, the Lord Jesus Christ, be crucified. Consequently, the Jewish nation would again suffer God's wrath, but this time through the Roman Empire. Jerusalem and the temple were again destroyed in 70 A.D.

This nine-chapter dissertation on how God would end the Babylonian exile of His people concludes with God urging His people to leave Babylon after Cyrus permitted them to come home (v. 20). God promised to protect and care for those Jewish pilgrims who would obey this command, just as He protected the nation during the Egyptian Exodus centuries earlier (v. 21). But, if His people preferred to live in pagan Babylon rather than to commune with Him in Israel, they should know: *"There is no peace for the wicked"* (v. 22). Commenting on this verse, Albert Barnes writes:

> To the transgressor of the laws of God there can be no permanent peace, enjoyment, or prosperity. The word "peace" is used in the Scriptures in all these senses. There may be the appearance of joy, and there may be temporary prosperity. But there is no abiding, substantial, permanent happiness, such as is enjoyed by those who fear and love God.[112]

To this summary all true believers should be able to add their "amen." The dispersed Jews in Babylon were immersed in a pagan culture that was ruled by sensuality, materialism, and luxury. Having freed His people from their idolatry, God wanted them out of Babylon (the world) to be with Him in Israel. Sadly, when Cyrus did grant the Jews liberty, most chose to disobey the Lord and remain in Babylon. Then, as it is today, when the affections of His people become entangled with the cares, the amenities, and the moral corruption of this world, God is grieved.

> Worldliness is excluding God from our lives and, therefore, consciously or unconsciously accepting the values of a man-centered society. ...Worldliness is not only doing what is forbidden but also wishing it were possible to do it. One of its distinctives is mental slavery to illegitimate pleasure. Worldliness twists values by rearranging their price tags.
>
> — Erwin W. Lutzer

God was offering full redemption and complete deliverance to Israel, but it hinged on whether His people were willing to part from Babylon to have fellowship with Him. Today, worldliness is any sphere in which the Lord Jesus is excluded. The Lord Jesus told His disciples the night before He was crucified, *"If the world hates you, you know that it hated Me before it hated you. If you were of the world, the world would love its own. Yet because you are not of the world, but I chose you out of the world, therefore the world hates you"* (John 15:18-19). James likened worldliness to the sin of spiritual adultery. *"Adulterers and adulteresses! Do you not know that friendship with the world is enmity with God? Whoever therefore wants to be a friend of the world makes himself an enemy of God"* (Jas. 4:4). Worldliness is the love of passing things, and things have no eternal value, except in how they are used to please God. The Lord's people of all ages should understand that worldliness opposes God, and God hates it. He is still pleading with His people today, "Come near to Me."

Meditation

> Fear not, I am with thee, O be not dismayed,
> For I am thy God and will still give thee aid;
> I'll strengthen and help thee, and cause thee to stand
> Upheld by My righteous, omnipotent hand.
>
> When through fiery trials thy pathways shall lie,
> My grace, all sufficient, shall be thy supply;
> The flame shall not hurt thee; I only design
> Thy dross to consume, and thy gold to refine.
>
> — John Rippon

God's Faithful Servant
Isaiah 49

This chapter commences the second of three nine-chapter subdivisions in the latter section of Isaiah (chps. 40-66). The first division dealt with the judgment of Israel's idolatry, the fall of Babylon, and the release of enslaved Jews by God's servant, the Persian Cyrus (chps. 40-48). The second division pertains to the ministry of God's suffering Servant, the Messiah, in restoring His covenant people to Himself and to a place of blessing (chps. 49-57). The third division reveals the blessings to Israel through Messiah's completed work and presents visions of His coming glory in the Kingdom Age (chps. 58-66). As previously mentioned, these three sections are separated by the statement, *"There is no peace for the wicked."*

Chapters 49-57 may be further divided into four main subjects:

49:1-50:11	Being rejected by the Jewish nation, Messiah offers salvation to the Gentiles.
51:1-52:12	The refined, believing remnant of Israel will be exalted with Messiah.
52:13-53:12	The Messiah will suffer as humanity's Sin-bearer before being exalted.
54:1-57:21	In the Millennial Kingdom, both Jew and Gentiles will experience Messiah's salvation.

Isaiah organized his book to show a remarkable correlation between the revelation of Cyrus as Israel's future deliverer from Babylon (44:24-48:22) and the future Messiah, who will deliver the Jewish remnant from worldwide oppression (49:1-53:12). Accordingly, this second of the three nine-chapter sections might well be entitled: "The Greater Deliverer and Deliverance." Chapter 49 is the threshold by which we enter into the innermost sentiment of the book entitled Isaiah – "God's Salvation." There should be no surprise then that the One who most delights God's heart is at the center of His attention and purposes throughout this nine-chapter oracle of grace.

The Servant's Work

In the first six verses, God's chosen Servant, the Messiah, is speaking to Israel and the nations. God the Father addresses His Son, the Messiah, beginning in verse 7. The Servant-Messiah called on the islands and the nations to heed His message, for He had been called by God from His mother's womb for a special assignment (vv. 1, 5). The Messiah says that His mouth was like a sharpened sword, and that He was a sharp arrow in God's quiver (v. 2). This meant that He had God's full endorsement and endowment of power to enforce His message and to punish rebels. The Servant-Messiah then recounts God's words to Him: *"You are My servant, O Israel, in whom I will be glorified"* (v. 3). J. M. Riddle observes:

> While there is clearly a distinction between the speaker and the nation of Israel (this is particularly obvious in vv. 5-6), the speaker does say, "And he said unto me, Thou art my servant, *O Israel*, in whom I will be glorified" (v. 3). W. E. Vine points to the explanation in saying, "Christ identified Himself with His people Israel, for it is in close association with Him that the restored nation is to become His servant, and it is in Israel that the Lord will yet be glorified on the earth." M. C. Unger also understands the passage as referring to Israel's Messiah: "He in whom the vocation of Israel as the Savior of the world is consummated."[113]

The nation of Israel had been created to honor Jehovah, but had been unfaithful. In contrast, the Messiah, drawn from the Jewish nation, would behave as the nation should have – God would be glorified through the excellence of His Person and the splendor of His doings.

A few days before His crucifixion, the Lord Jesus was considering the agonizing, redemptive work before Him at Calvary: *"'Now My soul is troubled, and what shall I say? "Father, save Me from this hour?" But for this purpose I came to this hour. Father, glorify Your name.' Then a voice came from heaven, saying, 'I have both glorified it and will glorify it again'"* (John 12:28). The Servant-Messiah's highest occupation was to do the will of His Father and to honor His name. The Lord explained this to His disciples who were concerned that their Master needed to eat: *"I have food to eat of which you do not know"*

Sorrow and Comfort

(John 4:32). They were confused by this statement and wondering if He had already eaten, so the Lord further explained: *"My food is to do the will of Him who sent Me, and to finish His work"* (John 4:34). Unlike the nation of Israel that was supposed to be God's loyal servant, the Messiah would be – He desired only to do that which pleased His Father!

This must be the ambition of any servant of the Lord, for often we do not see, at the time, the benefit of our ministry, nor are we rewarded immediately for fulfilling our calling. This was the experience of the Messiah during His first advent. There was little evidence that His ministry had been effective, and, in fact, He suffered much rejection and ultimately death to accomplish it. Yet, this did not discourage Him, because He was delighted to do the Father's will and He also knew that in due time, He would be rewarded for His faithful ministry (v. 4). The Lord Jesus shows us that ministry precedes reward and suffering precedes glory.

The nation of Israel is clearly not the "servant" spoken of in verses 1-5, for the Messiah says that God formed Him in His mother's womb (speaking of His incarnation) and called Him to a specific ministry: *"To bring Jacob back to Him, so that Israel is gathered to Him"* (v. 5). Obviously, the One speaking is not Jacob (the Jewish nation) and furthermore, Israel cannot bring itself back to God. Only God can accomplish that feat. Not only would the Servant-Messiah accomplish the work of restoring the tribes of Israel to God in righteousness, but God told Him that He would also be *"a light to the Gentiles, that You should be My salvation to the ends of the earth"* (v. 6). Paul reveals that it was God's plan to use believing and blessed Gentiles to provoke Israel to jealousy and to draw them back to Himself (Rom. 11:11). By quoting several Old Testament prophets, the apostle further explains that it was always God's intention to offer salvation to both Jews and Gentiles:

> *That He might make known the riches of His glory on the vessels of mercy, which He had prepared beforehand for glory, even us whom He called, not of the Jews only, but also of the Gentiles? As He says also in Hosea: "I will call them My people, who were not My people, and her beloved, who was not beloved." And it shall come to pass in the place where it was said to them, 'You are not My people,' There they shall be called sons of the living God"* (Rom. 9:23-26).

While in earnest prayer, the prophet Daniel acknowledged the sins of the Jewish nation, which had resulted in their *"shame of face"* (Dan. 9:8). God had chosen the Jews to stand forth as *"a light to the nations"* (Dan. 9:6), that is, as a great witness to the entire world of God's holiness, faithfulness, mercy, and longsuffering nature. However, in their rebellious condition, the Jews did not represent God as a holy people – the outcome of which was shame. The Jewish nation was supposed to be God's light to the nations, but failed. So God called His Servant (His Son) to be that light (Luke 1:79) – He did not fail.

God the Father assured His Servant, that though He would be despised and rejected by His own people (John 1:10-11), His ministry would be effective in reaching the nations (v. 7). There was a day coming when the kings and princes of all nations would worship the Servant-Messiah, because He was faithful to His divine calling. F. B. Hole summarizes verses 6 and 7:

> But if we can see the fulfilment of verse 6 today, we wait to see verse 7 fulfilled in a future day, which, we trust, is approaching. Jehovah is truly the Redeemer of Israel, though the One whom He sent is despised and abhorred in the servant's place. The hour draws near when, in the presence of this Servant, kings shall rise from their seats and princes shall do homage before Him. Men refused Him but God has chosen Him.[114]

The Work of Regathering

In the Millennial Kingdom, that is *"in an acceptable time"* and *"in the day of salvation,"* God will fulfill all His promises to His covenant people through the Messiah and will restore Israel to Himself (v. 8). The entire land of Israel will be well supplied with fresh water and will be marked by vigorous fertility. This will ensure that the returning Jewish captives, coming from any direction, will have plenty to eat and drink, and find shade from the sun during their pilgrimage home (vv. 8-10). God would remove all obstacles that might impede pilgrims journeying home from faraway places (vv. 11-12).

Isaiah has been declaring the words of the Servant-Messiah (vv. 1-5) and the decrees of God concerning His Servant and the outcome of His ministry (vv. 6-12), but in verse 13 he implores creation to rejoice and praise the Lord. Why? *"For the Lord has comforted His people, and will have mercy on His afflicted"* (v. 13). The prophet was elated

Sorrow and Comfort

by God's immense comfort and compassion available to all those who need help, including the Gentiles.

The Work Depreciated

Isaiah then records a dialogue between God and the Jewish nation (i.e., the people of Zion; vv. 14-16). Given the profound promise and lovely description of Israel's regathering in the previous verses, the melancholy attitude of the Jews is quite anti-climactic. They felt that God had forgotten and abandoned them (v. 14). However, God responded by saying that was impossible because the name of the nation was inscribed on the palms of His hands (v. 16). This meant that anytime God raised His hands, poetically speaking, He would be reminded of the nation He had created and dearly loved. Consequently, though it might be possible for a nursing mother to forget or ignore her child, He could not forget, nor neglect His people (v. 15).

Surviving Jews will be able to return to Israel because all of her destroyers will be removed from the land – they will be "far away" (vv. 17, 19). The Millennial Kingdom of Christ will begin directly after *The Judgment of Nations* at the conclusion of the Tribulation Period. The Lord Jesus taught about this judgment in the seventh of the Kingdom Parables found in Matthew 13:47-50. In that parable, the Lord casts a net into the sea (depicting the nations – Rev. 17:1, 15) and then sorts through His catch. Those who did not follow the Antichrist are separated from those who did. The "good" are permitted into His kingdom; the "bad" are committed to eternal judgment. The net represents the influence of the kingdom gospel message that will be preached worldwide during the Tribulation Period (Matt. 24:14). This message consists of a warning not to worship the Antichrist and a declaration that judgment of the wicked and Christ's kingdom are coming soon (Rev. 14:6-12). The fish represent the living Gentiles who are saved during the Tribulation Period.

The Judgment of Nations is more specifically spoken of in Matthew 25:31-46 when the Lord separates the sheep (i.e., those who are allowed into the kingdom) and the goats (those who are eternally judged). Christ will punish all those who followed the Antichrist and persecuted the Jews during the Tribulation Period (Matt. 25:40). This judgment will occur just after Christ's return to the earth at the end of the Great Tribulation (Matt. 24:21, 29, 36-41) and will not be expected by the general populace. The Judgment of Nations is done suddenly, and those unfit for the kingdom will be abruptly removed from the earth. The Judgment of Nations is also pictured in Daniel 2:35, 44-45 and described in Revelation 19:20.

Daniel informs us that there will be a 75-day interval between the destruction of the Antichrist at the battle of Armageddon and the beginning of the blessings of the Kingdom Age (Dan. 12:7-13; Rev. 17-21). This time period is necessary to cleanse the earth of the defilement and the devastation which occurred in the previous seven years. Daniel illustrates this truth through his interpretation of Nebuchadnezzar's dream in which the stone from heaven (Christ) falls to the earth and smashes an image representing all Gentile dominion throughout the ages. The debris is then blown away by the wind and, afterwards, the stone grows into a great mountain. The Spirit of God is pictured in the wind (John 3:8), and mountains in Scripture are used to symbolize kingdoms (Isa. 2:2-3; Mic. 4:1; Rev. 17:9-10). After all wickedness has been purged from the planet and it has been supernaturally rejuvenated to nullify the effects of sin, Jerusalem will be the seat of God's glory on the earth.

When Israel sees all that God has accomplished for her and that all her oppressors have been smitten by her Messiah, the nation will be in jubilation, like a bride enjoying her ornaments (v. 18). As intended in the days of Joshua, the Promised Land will once again be full of her children and God will dwell with them in peace (vv. 20-21).

The Gentiles at Work

Isaiah says that the Lord will also lift up His hand to the Gentiles and with a beckoning gesture invite them to partake of the blessings of knowing the Messiah (v. 22). The result of this invitation will be that Gentiles (even those of high society) will worship the Lord in Jerusalem and will be favorable towards the Jews and assist them during the Kingdom Age (v. 23).

The conquered seldom experience deliverance from their captors, but God promised to deliver *"the captives of the righteous"* (v. 24). *"I will contend with him who contends with you, and I will save your children"* (v. 25). God will punish those who oppose His people by causing their aggressors to attack and kill each other: *"I will feed those who oppress you with their own flesh, and they shall be drunk with their own blood as with sweet wine"* (v. 26). When the nations witness all that God has accomplished on behalf of Israel through their

Sorrow and Comfort

Messiah, then they will know: *"That I, the Lord, am your Savior, and your Redeemer, the Mighty One of Jacob"* (v. 26). Through the Lord Jesus Christ the entire planet will be immersed in God's glory and all men will be in awe of Him!

No doubt, the above prophecies would encourage Jews who would be one day exiled in Babylon, but the entire passage speaks of a greater deliverance than Cyrus could ever accomplish. When the Kingdom Age commences, the Jews will look back over centuries ruined and stained with blood and tarnished by rebellion and idolatry, and they will gladly declare of their Messiah, *"The Lord shall be King over all the earth. In that day it shall be – 'The Lord is One,' and His name One"* (Zech. 14:9).

Meditation

> Hail, mighty Victor! Behold He comes from out the grave.
> Shout, shout His triumph! Oh, tell abroad His power to save.
> Sing, sing with gladness, proclaim the news over land and sea:
> He reigns forever, great Ruler over all is He.
>
> Glory, laud, and honor unto Christ the Lord be given.
> Praise Him! All ye people, mighty Ruler of earth and Heav'n.
> Praise Him! All ye stars of night.
> Praise Him! All ye shining hosts of light.
> Oh! That men would bless and praise His holy Name,
> Would praise His holy Name.
>
> — Isaac H. Meredith

The Suffering Servant
Isaiah 50

In introducing this chapter, J. M. Riddle reminds us that God is a master jeweler:

> His brightest gems are displayed against a dark background. Attention has already been drawn to the fact that it is in the setting of a failed servant [pictured here as an unfaithful wife] that God displays the beauty of His unfailing Servant. ... It is against the dark background of national failure that the perfect service of the Lord Jesus is described in this chapter.[115]

The Unfaithful Wife

God challenges His covenant people (the descendants of idolaters who were still idolaters) to find their mother's bill of divorce or to identify any creditors that He had sold them to (to settle a debt so to speak). The Lord's questions are in response to the complaint stated in the last chapter by some in Zion (Jerusalem): *"The Lord has forsaken me, and my Lord has forgotten me"* (49:14). Regrettably, they had failed to realize that their sensed estrangement from Jehovah did not result from an interruption of His love for them, but from their own iniquities: *"For your iniquities you have sold yourselves, and for your transgressions your mother has been put away"* (v. 1). God had not yet formally "put them away;" they (the Southern Kingdom) had pulled away from Him. The Lord did not want to be estranged from His wife, figuratively speaking. Isaiah was ensuring that his countrymen knew that God did not want to discard them or sell them into slavery. Rather, they had chosen this outcome for themselves.

Although it was not God's original design for marriage, the Law permitted a husband to give his wife a divorce certificate detailing her fault(s) and then she would be required to leave the home (Deut. 24:1). Israel (speaking of the Northern Kingdom) had played the harlot by embracing other gods, and would not repent and return to Jehovah. Jeremiah confirmed later that Jehovah had finalized a *"bill of divorce"* which had put Jews in the Northern Kingdom out of the land (Jer. 2:26-29, 3:8). This occurred in 722 B.C. when Assyria conquered Israel and then enslaved and exiled much of the Jewish population.

Yet several prophets foretold that the repentant wife (Israel – speaking of the entire Jewish nation) would be restored to her Husband (Jehovah) in a future day (Hos. 2:14, 19-20; Ezek. 16). Would not the One who dries up the seas, creates rivers in the wilderness, and clothes the heavens with blackness be able to redeem and rescue Israel (vv. 2-3)? The answer to God's four rhetorical questions on this point is "yes" – God is able to restore His once adulterous wife in purity.

Paul confirms the same truth in the New Testament: *"They* [the natural branches – Israel] *also, if they do not continue in unbelief, will be grafted in, for God is able to graft them in again"* (Rom. 11:23). But this grafting back into the olive tree, picturing all the blessings in Christ through the fulfillment of the Abrahamic covenant (the root), will not be accomplished until Israel receives the Holy Spirit at the conclusion of the Tribulation Period (Rom. 11:25; Joel 2:26-32). The Lord wanted His people to know that they were not put away forever; He had a plan to fully restore them to Himself and even to exalt them among the nations. Hence this chapter is speaking of a future day when Israel has been fully restored to God. Then, the Jewish nation will no longer be able to produce a bill of divorce when asked – it will have been absolved. Today, Israel is still under a divorce decree, but in the Kingdom Age this will not be the case.

The first three verses describe the dark background (a rebellious people estranged from God and unresponsive to His Word), which permits the voice of God's faithful Servant to be heard more clearly. He is always responsive to God's Word, is innocent in all His ways, and is completely devoted to God.

The Faithful Servant

Some commentators see the Servant (Christ) as the speaker in the first three verses, instead of God the Father. If that is the case, Christ's deity (as Creator and Governor of the Universe) introduces His humiliation, as One who humbly takes the Learner's place, but is yet rejected. However, it is normally God (not specifically the Son) who speaks to Israel about the covenant of marriage and the bill of divorce for infidelity (i.e., their idolatry; see Ezek. 16:38 with Jer. 3:8). Regardless of the Speaker, Isaiah often asserts that the Servant-Messiah would be fully God and fully man.

The prophet next notes two aspects of the Servant's ministry: learning through experience and teaching through example. The Sovereign Lord God taught His lowly Servant daily how to care for the weary:

> *The Lord God has given Me the tongue of the learned, that I should know how to speak a word in season to him who is weary. He awakens Me morning by morning, He awakens My ear to hear as the learned. The Lord God has opened My ear; and I was not rebellious, nor did I turn away* (vv. 4-5).

The context of the passage confirms that the Father did not open His Son's ear with an awl to mark Him as a perpetual bond-servant (Ex. 21:6). Rather, opening the ear refers to diligently listening with the intent to obey what is heard. As F. B. Hole explains, this is why the Lord Jesus' ministry was so effective – He knew and always did the Father's will:

> The word "learned" in verse 4 really means a disciple or one who is instructed, and our Lord took that humble and subject place when He came as the Servant of the will of God. He had indeed the opened ear, as was also predicted in Psalm 40, and He took that place that He might be man's true neighbor, and speak the word in season to him that is weary. Morning by morning He heard the words He was to speak to others; hence His own statement to His disciples, "the words that I speak unto you I speak not of Myself (John 14:10).[116]

When one speaks only the words God would want him to speak, then the greatest benefit of those words is enjoyed. Words fitly spoken are powerful to heal, to sooth, to correct, to exhort, and to do all that God desires His word to accomplish. When we speak our own words, our troubles begin.

Job challenged his three companions to abandon vague insinuations and to supply detailed allegations that he could consider; to this end he noted, *"How forceful are right words!"* (Job 6:25). Right words have force, but inappropriate words dig a pit for the innocent. It is our nature to jump to conclusions without all the facts and then to deliberately and ungraciously share these presumptuous verdicts with others. Such behavior distorts the truth concerning the guilty and even worse, defames and defrauds the innocent. God is not honored in either case. Solomon reminds us that *"there is one who speaks like the piercings of a sword, but the tongue of the wise promotes health"* (Prov. 12:18). This was the example of the Servant-Messiah: All His words were "right words" to encourage, to strengthen, or to convict. Words can heal or hurt; let us be wise in how we use them, especially when conversing with those who have locked themselves into a cell of despair.

God's Servant was faithful to live out what He was told no matter the cost to Himself personally (v. 5). The Servant then conveys His determination to expend Himself on Israel's behalf (and on ours too) despite the human brutality and divine judgment He knew He would suffer:

> *I gave My back to those who struck Me, and My cheeks to those who plucked out the beard; I did not hide My face from shame and spitting. For the Lord God will help Me; therefore I will not be disgraced; therefore I have set My face like a flint, and I know that I will not be ashamed* (vv. 6-7).

Verse 6 tells us that Christ, during His first advent, would be scourged, beaten in the face, and spat on. Matthew records the direct fulfillment of these prophesies in his gospel account (Matt. 26:67, 27:26, 30). Thankfully, two thousand years ago, the Lord Jesus did not enter into His rest until He had secured ours, through the shedding of His own blood.

Although Christ's face was set as a flint towards Jerusalem (v. 7), He also had an intense focus beyond the cross. The Lord Jesus shows us that trusting in God's future promises results in present joy. He had God's promise that He would not be left in the grave, but would be exalted to His right hand of majesty on high:

> *Therefore my heart is glad, and my glory rejoices; My flesh also will rest in hope. For You will not leave my soul in Sheol, nor will You allow Your Holy One to see corruption. You will show me the path of life; in Your presence is fullness of joy; at Your right hand are pleasures forevermore* (Ps. 16:9-11).

Looking unto Jesus the author and finisher of our faith; **who for the joy that was set before Him endured the cross***, despising the shame, and is set down at the right hand of the throne of God* (Heb. 12:2; KJV).

The assurance of God's Word brought Christ hope for the future and an infusion of joy while bearing tremendous pain and suffering. His disciples faced death with the same hope and endured tremendous suffering for the joy set before them. History records that Aegeas crucified Andrew, Peter's brother, for his faith in Christ. Seeing his cross before him, Andrew bravely spoke, "O cross, most welcome and longed for! With a willing mind, joyfully and desirously, I come to thee, being the scholar of Him which did hang on thee: because I have always been thy lover, and have coveted to embrace thee."[117] Why could Andrew approach his cross with joy and determination? He watched the Lord approach His cross in the same manner.

Assuming personal ownership of God's promises will infuse joy into any situation. *"For we were saved in this hope, but hope that is seen is not hope; for why does one still hope for what he sees? But if we hope for what we do not see, we eagerly wait for it with perseverance"* (Rom. 8:24-25). During the deepest trials of life, it is possible to have present joy in God's future promises.

So while the Servant-Messiah understood that He would suffer much to convey God's message of love and life to Israel, He also knew that the Lord God would also vindicate Him:

For the Lord God will help Me; therefore I will not be disgraced ... I will not be ashamed (v. 7).

He is near who justifies Me (v. 8)

Surely the Lord God will help Me; who is he who will condemn Me? (v. 9)

The suffering Savior knew God's word (v. 4), obeyed God's expressed will (vv. 5-6), and trusted in God's promised help (vv. 7-9). He had every confidence that those who would reject and oppress Him during His first advent would stand before Him to be judged in a coming day. They would become nothing, like an old garment that moths have feasted on (v. 9). God will completely vindicate His Son!

Sorrow and Comfort

The chapter closes with an exhortation to those who fear the Lord (speaking to Israel) to obey the word of God's Servant. It is likely that the Holy Spirit is speaking first person in verses 10-11, rather than Isaiah, as the speaker commands the people *"to trust in the name of the Lord and rely upon His God,"* *"obey the voice of His Servant,"* or they will suffer judgment from *"My hand."* Obviously, Isaiah would not be able to inflict retribution on all his countrymen with his own fists.

An Example to Follow

The instruction to trust and rely on the Lord would be especially needful during the intense darkness associated with Messiah's rejection and suffering. God's plan of justifying sinners through the substitutionary death of Christ would not be a plan man would naturally understand. Therefore those who fear the Lord would have an opportunity to exercise faith: *"Let him trust in the name of the Lord and rely upon his God"* (v. 10). However, those who want to walk according to their own light of understanding (as pictured in a self-kindled fire) will *"lie down in torment"* – suffer God's eternal condemnation (v. 11).

A central message of the Bible is that there is no hope for those who die without being justified (i.e. receiving forgiveness of sins and obtaining a righteous standing in Christ; Heb. 9:27). Contrary to what some teach, there is no purgatory. The lost will spend eternity in hell. Christ has already done everything necessary to purge our sins (Heb. 1:3), and to rescue us from eternal judgment, but He will not force anyone to go to heaven – it is our choice (2 Pet. 3:9). The Bible vividly describes the ultimate fate of those who reject God's truth. The following are terms used in association with hell:

- *"Shame and everlasting contempt"* (Dan. 12:2)
- *"Everlasting punishment"* (Matt. 25:46)
- *"Weeping and gnashing of teeth"* (Matt. 24:51)
- *"Unquenchable fire"* (Luke 3:17)
- *"Indignation and wrath, tribulation and anguish"* (Rom. 2:8-9)
- *"Their worm does not die* [putrid endless agony]*"* (Mark 9:44)
- *"Everlasting destruction"* (2 Thess. 1:9)
- *"Eternal fire ... the blackness of darkness forever"* (Jude 7, 13)
- *"Fire is not quenched"* (Mark 9:46)

Devotions in Isaiah

Revelation 14:10-11 tells us the final, eternal destiny of the sinner: *"He shall be tormented with fire and brimstone ... the smoke of their torment ascended up forever and ever: and they have no rest day or night."* The Bible's teaching of eternal punishment for unforgiven sinners offends people; therefore, many are watering down the truth, teaching that hell is a state of non-existence or quick annihilation. However, misrepresenting the truth to avoid its consequence is never a good idea.

God does not enjoy punishing rebels, but His holy character demands it. He longs for all men to repent and to turn to Him by faith, as He has said, *"I have no pleasure in the death of the wicked, but that the wicked turn from his way and live"* (Ezek. 33:11). Everlasting "hell fire" was not originally prepared for mankind but, rather, for Satan and rebellious angels (Matt. 25:41). However, God will use this domain of torment to also punish those who reject His only solution for sin – the substitutionary death of His Son, the Lord Jesus Christ.

Isaiah's message to those who genuinely fear God is to trust in Christ alone for salvation and then follow His faithful example of obedience and devotion. This is the path of faith that leads to salvation and pleasing God, but Isaiah also speaks of another path leading to death and destruction. Those who ignore God and put their faith in human methods and traditions or trust in themselves for salvation will suffer a horrible end. God's salvation is completely beyond human achievement; it is a gift of God completely founded in grace: **G**od's **R**iches **A**t **C**hrist's **E**xpense!

Meditation

People do not have to do something to go to hell; they just have to do nothing to go to hell.

— John MacArthur

The national anthem of hell is, "I Did It My Way."

— Assorted Authors

Comfort for the Remnant
Isaiah 51

The last chapter concluded with a challenge to follow the faithful Servant's example of obedience to experience all God's goodness; those who do not will suffer forever. The Lord now speaks to those who did choose the path of righteousness, no matter the cost of doing so.

God begins by consoling the faithful remnant of Israel who were waiting for His salvation: *"you who follow after righteousness, you who seek the Lord"* (v. 1). To these seeking saints He says three times, *"Listen to Me"* (vv. 1, 4, 7). Correspondently, there will be three times God calls on His people to *"awake,"* for He is taking action on their behalf (vv. 9, 17, 52:1). J. M. Riddle summarizes these three "awake" messages as follows: God's ability to deliver (vv. 9-16); God's anger transferred (vv. 17-23); God's announcement of deliverance (52:1-12).[118]

This chapter is a solace for the faithful remnant: complete fulfillment of God's promises will occur in the Kingdom Age (vv. 1-16), and comfort to Jewish survivors under Babylon's rule will also be provided (vv. 17-23).

Encouragement for the Righteous

The allegorical commands of verse 1, *"Look to the rock from which you were hewn and to the hole of the pit from which you were dug"* are explained by the following verse. God called Abraham alone into a covenant and promised to make him the father of nations. Although well on in years, God blessed Abraham and his wife with a son from whom came many descendants, including the nation of Israel (v. 2).

In the same way that God accomplished the impossible (bringing Israel into existence), He would also work to restore the Jews to their homeland and make it a paradise (like Eden) for them. Then the entire region will be full of joy, gladness, thanksgiving and singing (v. 3). However, during the long interim, the righteous were to follow the example of Abraham and Sarah (i.e., Israel's founders), who had to wait many years before they experienced the joy of Isaac's birth as promised by God.

When unjust suffering continues day after day without any sign that relief is forthcoming, the child of God is likely to cry out to the Lord as David did, *"How long, O God?"* (Ps. 13:1-2). David's heart was filled with sorrow as he wrestled inwardly with his thoughts and outwardly against his adversary. Had God forgotten him? Why was God ignoring him? Yet, as he continued to ponder God's unfailing mercy and faithfulness to His Word, David knew his enemies were fighting a losing battle. Waiting on the Lord can often feel like a heavy weight, but be encouraged, dear believer. God is utterly faithful to do what He says He will do. Isaiah did not want the believing remnant to be discouraged, but to keep trusting in the Lord during the long years of waiting.

There was a day coming when the Messiah, God's arm, would reveal God's Law to all nations, and justice and righteousness would be established worldwide (vv. 4-5). Accordingly, there will be blessing, not only for those whom God calls *"My people"* and *"My nation,"* but also for *"the peoples"* ("the peoples" is plural in both verse 4 and 5). *"My arms"* who will judge *"the peoples"* are likely glorified saints who return to the earth from heaven to rule and reign with Christ in His kingdom (Matt. 19:28; Rev. 5.10, 19:14).

Although *"the earth will grow old like a garment, and those who dwell in it will die in like manner,"* God's *"salvation will be forever"* (v. 6). Isaiah repeats a similar statement in verse 8 and sandwiches the application between these two verses: The remnant, having God's Law in them now and the eternal hope of God's salvation before them, should not be discouraged by the insults and reproaches of their enemies (v. 7). They were to follow the example of the Servant-Messiah who willingly suffered for the joy before Him (50:6-7); ultimately all their enemies would perish in divine judgment.

Deliverance of the Ransomed

Given this reality, verses 9-11 then record the prayer of the righteous remnant, or perhaps a prayer offered by the prophet on their behalf. They request that God would again rise up in power as He did in delivering Israel from Egypt centuries earlier (v. 9). Egypt is depicted as the mythical havoc-causing serpent Rahab (see comments

Sorrow and Comfort

on 30:7). These faithful believers were asking God to deliver them from their oppressors with the same extreme power by which He dried up the Red Sea and then drowned Pharaoh's army in it (v. 10). The waiting remnant wanted to witness another great exodus which would bring them joyfully back to Zion.

The Lord responds to their prayer:

So the ransomed of the Lord shall return, and come to Zion with singing, with everlasting joy on their heads. They shall obtain joy and gladness; sorrow and sighing shall flee away. "I, even I, am He who comforts you. Who are you that you should be afraid of a man who will die, and of the son of a man who will be made like grass? (vv. 11-12).

W. E. Vine observes that the Lord's response here "is scarcely exceeded anywhere in Scripture in the beauty of its language, and in the sweetness of the assurance given to God's people as to their future."[119] Indeed, with tender language the Lord reminded His people that He is the Creator, the Sustainer of all things, and their Comforter. Then He consoled them – those they feared would perish like grass.

Furthermore, He promised to free the exiled captives in a new exodus: They would not perish in foreign lands, and they would have plenty of provisions on their homeward journey (v. 14). The Lord then confirms why He will accomplish the restoration of the Jewish people to their homeland: *"I am the Lord your God ... I have covered you with the shadow of My hand ... You are My people"* (vv. 15-16). Such a personal message from the almighty Creator affirming His love and care for His people would certainly encourage the suffering remnant to remain faithful until deliverance came.

Isaiah declares several times that Jerusalem will be the religious center of the World and Christ shall reign from that city in His kingdom (v. 16, 2:1-5, 66:10-18). All the earth shall see God's glory at this time. Usually when Isaiah speaks of a new heaven and new earth, he is referring to all that happens starting with the Kingdom Age (65:17); however, the prophet in this chapter does indicate that it will be necessary for God to lay new foundations for heaven and earth (vv. 6, 16). The Lord Jesus Himself pledged this: *"Heaven and earth will pass away, but My words will by no means pass away"* (Luke 21:33).

Isaiah did not have the further revelation we have in the New Testament concerning the distinction between the Millennial Kingdom (the Day of the Lord; Rev. 20) and the Eternal State (the Day of God; Rev. 21-22). Before John describes the New Jerusalem coming down out of heaven in Revelation 21, he records the destruction of the earth, including the Old Jerusalem: *"Now I saw a new heaven and a new earth, for the first heaven and the first earth had passed away. Also there was no more sea"* (Rev. 21:1).

Turning from this boundless future emancipation which would free Jerusalem from Gentile rule forever, the prophet seeks to encourage the faithful remnant in the sixth century oppressed by Babylon (vv. 17-23). God desires the inhabitants of Jerusalem to understand that they have drunk up to the dregs the fullness of His fury (i.e., the cup of trembling) and that He would soon deliver them through Cyrus (v. 17). The city had suffered much death, famine, and destruction, but this would end and God would comfort the survivors (vv. 18-21). Those who had oppressed the Jews, even walked on their dead bodies in the streets of Jerusalem, would in turn experience His wrath (vv. 22-23).

Meditation

    Jerusalem, lift up thy voice!
    Daughter of Zion, now rejoice!
    Thy King is come, whose mighty hand
    Henceforth shall reign o'er every land

    He comes to every tribe and race,
    A Messenger of truth and grace:
    With peace He comes from Heaven above
    On earth to found His realm of love.

    Let all the world with one accord
    Now hail the coming of the Lord:
    Praise to the Prince of heavenly birth
    Who brings peace to all the earth.

                      — Johan O. Wallin

Awake and Behold
Isaiah 52

Whereas the message of the last chapter would encourage surviving Jews during the Babylonian occupation, Isaiah now inspires Jerusalem's inhabitants to hope for the city's final deliverance from Gentile oppression in the Kingdom Age.

Jerusalem Restored to Rule

This is the third of the three connected "awake" messages, two of which were in the previous chapter:

Awake, awake! Put on your strength, O Zion; put on your beautiful garments, O Jerusalem, the holy city! For the uncircumcised and the unclean shall no longer come to you (v. 1).

Figuratively speaking, Jerusalem would again put on strength and garments when she was rebuilt under Cyrus' decree; however, the promise that Gentiles would no longer control and pollute the city will not be fulfilled until the Millennial Kingdom (48:2). At that time, Jerusalem will be able to remove the shackles of her slavery and shake off the dust of her mourning; she would never be enslaved again (v. 2).

Previously, Isaiah had told his countrymen that they had sold themselves into slavery because of their stubborn sin (50:1). Now God promised to redeem them out of servitude without them paying anything – God, at Calvary, would pay for their final redemption (v. 3). This was good news indeed, because the Jews had nothing with which to pay for their release or to satisfy God's righteous anger over their sin.

The Lord provides a brief history of His people's enslavement to highlight His means of making Himself known to them. To emphasize the personal nature of this message, the Lord speaks of the Jews as *"My people"* three times in verses 4-6. His people were enslaved in Egypt and He powerfully released them through great feats of His glory. Then

Assyria conquered the Northern Kingdom and exiled many Jews; they also put the Southern Kingdom under tribute (v. 4). Soon another power, Babylon, would invade the land and relocate many Jewish captives from Judah and would blaspheme the God of the Jews while doing so (v. 5).

But each of these estrangements/enslavements would end because God was faithful to His word. By foretelling and then accomplishing what seemed impossible (restoring His people to their homeland), Israel would know that it was He who did it: *"Therefore My people shall know My name; therefore they shall know in that day that I am He who speaks: 'Behold, it is I'"* (v. 6). It is a great solace to understand that God often permits grievous trials in our lives to draw us back into His strong, open arms. These hardships usually permit us to experience the wonder of God in ways we would not have otherwise. God makes Himself known through His deliverance – the best example being Calvary, where the Lord Jesus conquered sin and death to offer us the gift of eternal life in Him.

Although the Jewish captives returning from Babylon in the days of Zerubbabel greatly rejoiced in their deliverance, that event was only a foretaste of the worldwide liberation that would occur during the Kingdom Age. Surviving Jews returning to Zion from distant lands will herald the good news of their emancipation (v. 7). The Gentile nations will know that Israel's God reigns when He regathers His people in Zion (v. 8). The Jewish remnant will sing and rejoice over the comfort and redemption extended to them by their God. This incredible work of grace will awaken the nations to just how strong God's Holy Arm is (vv. 9-10).

God's Holy Arm

How will God's strength to save be shown to all nations? The power of God's outstretched arm would be demonstrated through His redeeming Lamb (v. 10). The prophet Isaiah uses the term "arm" a dozen times in his book to speak of God's strength to deliver and redeem His people: *"The Lord has sworn by His right hand and by the arm of His strength"* (62:8).

Isaiah acknowledged Israel's moral deficiency and their need for God's arm of salvation, saying, *"But your iniquities have separated you from your God; and your sins have hidden His face from you so that He will not hear"* (59:2). They were in the bondage of sin and thus separated from God without, naturally speaking, any hope of restoration.

But the prophet continues: *"And He [God] saw that there was no man, and wondered that there was no intercessor; therefore His arm brought salvation unto Him; and His righteousness, it sustained Him"* (59:16). When it came to finding someone to stand in the gap for the Jews, and for all humanity, no one was found who could righteously plead man's case because all of humanity had fallen below God's minimum requirement to come into His presence – sinless perfection. Therefore, God sent His own Arm (His Son) to be an intercessor for us: *"The Lord has made bare His holy arm in the eyes of all the nations; and all the ends of the earth shall see the salvation of our God"* (v. 10). The intercessor had to be God Himself (His own Arm) to be the perfect sacrifice and to sustain the judgment of a Holy God for all man's sin. To properly demonstrate God's power, His Holy Arm was stripped bare for all to see.

The Hebrew word for "the salvation" in Isaiah 52:10 is *yeshuw`ah*, which is composed from the compounding of these two words. The name "Jesus" is derived from the Hebrew words *Yehovah* (Jehovah) and *Yasha* (salvation). Jesus literally means "Jehovah saves," a fact many Old Testament passages repeat when the New Testament equivalent "Jesus" is substituted for the Hebrew word *Yeshuw`ah*: *"The Lord has made bare His holy arm in the eyes of all the nations; and all the ends of the earth shall see the [Jesus] of our God"* (52:10), *"Truly my soul silently waits for God; from Him comes my [Jesus]. He only is my rock and my [Jesus]; He is my defense; I shall not be greatly moved* (Ps. 62:1-2). *"That Your way may be known on earth, Your [Jesus] among all nations"* (Ps. 67:2). All Scripture declares the Lord Jesus as the divine Savior – God's Salvation.

All Captives to Return

When God's Holy Arm brought deliverance, the Jews were not to stay in foreign lands, but to return to Zion in holiness: *"Depart! Depart! Go out from there, touch no unclean thing; **go out from the midst of her, be clean,** you who bear the vessels of the Lord"* (v. 11). For those who say the latter half of Isaiah was not written by him, but later by a Babylonian exiled Jew, the words *"Go out from there"* pose a difficulty. How could this supposed author write "from there" when he really meant "from here"? When deliverance did come, the Jews were to return to their homeland purged of all filthiness and were to be holy vessels fit to worship Jehovah.

While this section would greatly encourage purified Jews returning to their homeland in the sixth century B.C., the Lord's command purposely does not name Babylon. "Her" is a general term speaking of wherever the Jews might be in the future – they should never be defiled by Babylonian-type philosophies and corruption. So while the end of the Babylonian captivity is clearly alluded to, there is also an application of verse 11 which foretells the spiritual renewal of Israel at the end of the Tribulation Period (not specifically Cyrus' deliverance).

> In the present passage, Babylon is not specifically named. "They are bidden to go out from the scene of their captivity. The language of the command bears reference to Babylon, but Babylon here stands for more than the city itself, it speaks of world conditions, as the preceding context shows" (W. E. Vine). M. C. Unger links the past with the future in his comment: "The exiles are emphatically commanded to speedily leave Babylon. To the worldly-minded, long residence had made many loathe to leave it, as will also be the case with the Lord's people in mystical Babylon (the satanic world system) just prior to Messiah's destruction of it at His second advent (Rev. 18:4)." There can be no doubt that "coming events cast their shadow before them," and that the return from Babylon resulting from the decree of Cyrus (Ezra 1:1-3) foreshadowed the coming repatriation of God's people by divine power. Two important things should be noted: the purity required (v. 11) and the protection provided (v. 12).[120]

God desired His people to remain pure vessels fit for His use (i.e., like the consecrated temple vessels being returned by Cyrus). The Lord would ensure their safety and provisions for traveling home, so they did not need to embark on a breakneck journey; rather, they were to enjoy their homeward trek (v. 12).

God's Servant Recognized and Exalted

The Lord Jesus Christ is the powerful, redeeming Arm of God! He willingly stretched forth His own arms to receive Roman nails and in so doing nailed our death sentence to His cross (Col. 2:14) – He is God's Salvation available for all humanity and for all time! Verses 10 and 13 connect God's strong, bare Arm with His lowly wise Servant.

Sorrow and Comfort

> **Behold, My Servant** *shall deal prudently; He shall be exalted and extolled and be very high. Just as many were astonished at you, so His visage was marred more than any man, and His form more than the sons of men; so shall He sprinkle many nations. Kings shall shut their mouths at Him; for what had not been told them they shall see, and what they had not heard they shall consider* (vv. 13-15).

Within the New Testament, we find two "behold" exhortations that frame the beginning and ending moments of the Lord's ministry on earth. John the Baptist, who prepared the way for the Lord's coming, proclaimed in reference to the Lord Jesus, *"Behold the Lamb of God, who takes away the sin of the world"* (John 1:29). Just hours before the death of our Lord, after He had been mocked, buffeted, scourged, and spit upon, Pilate presented Jesus to the Jews, saying, *"**Behold, your King!***" (John 19:14). It was a gruesome presentation. Thorns had broken the Lord's brow. His beard had been wrenched from His face as an undesired weed is uprooted and discarded from a garden. Roman fists had pulverized His comely visage in vicious sport.

In Scripture, when the Lord is presented in a position of authority (as King and as God), the possessive pronoun "your" precedes the title, but when the position of a lowly servant is in view, the pronoun "My" appears; Christ is man's King and Jehovah's Servant. In the latter case, Christ is in accordance with the will of the Father. He humbly lowered Himself (not in essence, but in the sense of position) below His rightful station of divinity and took on the form of a Servant – a bare Arm. This characterized Christ's first advent, as seen when Pilate presented a badly beaten Jesus to a mocking crowd: "Behold your King."

The point of verse 13 is that God's Servant acted "prudently" (did the will of God) during His first earthly sojourn and will therefore be highly exalted when He returns. Until that time, the Lord Jesus sits on His Father's throne in heaven (Rev. 3:21). Then Christ's character and work will be vindicated and all His enemies will know that He is the eternal Son of God. He, who has already been highly exalted to the right hand of God and has a name above all others, will be honored by all who remain on the earth (Phil. 2:9; Heb. 1:3)!

What King is this that the entire world will exalt? Isaiah foretold that Christ would be so physically marred by human brutality that He would cease to resemble a man (v. 14). Any movie's portrayal of these events or any artist's conception of this scene will be incredibly sanitized from the gory reality. Isaiah also declared what the Jewish attitude towards their God-sent Messiah would be upon that hallowed day: *"When we see Him, there is no beauty that we should desire Him"* (53:2). So, when presented with their king, the Jews emphatically shouted, *"We have no king but Caesar"* (John 19:15). In accordance with God's sovereign plan, their King was crucified, but would be raised up from the dead to reign over them in a future day.

Given the meaning of verse 14 the statement *"so shall He sprinkle many nations"* in verse 15, probably speaks of the spiritual work of redemption Christ accomplished at Calvary. This would reflect a literal meaning of the Hebrew verb translated "sprinkle." However, it is worth noting that the verb also has an uncommon meaning of "causing to leap (i.e. in joyful surprise or startle)"[121] Some Bible translations apply this meaning because the latter portion of verse 15 relates to Christ's second advent:

"As many were astonished at him ... so shall he startle many nations" (RSV).

"So shall many nations regard him with admiration" (Septuagint).

"Just as many were astonished at Him, so shall He startle many nations" (AV).

Isaiah closes this chapter by emphasizing the prudent behavior of the Messiah and His divine exaltation by Gentile "kings" and "nations" who "had not been told" and "had not heard" about Him previously (v. 15). Righteous suffering (v. 13) before exaltation and glory (vv. 14-15) is a principle we find throughout Scripture (Rom. 8:18-19).

During Christ's first advent, worldlings saw nothing special about the Lord Jesus; however, in His second advent, the nations will be astounded at His appearance (v. 14). What was there to esteem in a supposed criminal, a condemned man who had been brutally beaten and nailed to a cross? However, in a coming day the entire world will understand what God accomplished at Calvary through the suffering Jewish Messiah. They previously misjudged Christ; they did not esteem Him. But at His next appearing their jaws will drop in amazement. The Son of God, the King of kings, will be before them in all His glory and His visage will be astounding.

Sorrow and Comfort

Meditation

Great Jehovah, mighty Lord, vast and boundless is Thy Word;
King of kings, from shore to shore Thou shalt reign forevermore.
Jew and Gentile, bond and free, all shall yet be one in Thee;
All confess Messiah's Name, all His wondrous love proclaim.

— Fanny Crosby

The Suffering Servant
Isaiah 53:1-9

Notice the presentation of the Messiah in the previous verses as contrasted to this chapter. The humiliation and glory of God's perfect Servant is presented in Isaiah 52:13-15 to all Gentiles, who, generally speaking, did not know what God said He would accomplish through Him (52:10, 15). However, in this chapter, Christ's sufferings and exaltation are described in respect to Israel, who had previously heard, but chose not to believe (v. 1). In a future day, the faithful remnant will reflect deeply on the dreadful reality of that decision, yet they will rejoice that God did not cast the Jewish nation aside forever.

The Validity of Isaiah 53

In all the Old Testament, there is not another text that so plainly and fully foretells the sufferings of Christ as God's chosen sin-bearer and the glory He obtained afterwards (Ps. 22 being a close second). For that reason, skeptics have often attacked the authenticity and validity of this text. However, the evidence is overwhelming that God has preserved His word down through the ages that we might know what He has and will accomplish through His beloved Son – our Redeemer and Savior.

From 1946 through 1956 a collection of nearly a thousand biblical documents dating between 300 B.C. and 70 A.D. were found in eleven Qumran Caves located about a mile northwest of the Dead Sea. This collection is referred to as *The Dead Sea Scrolls* (DSS). The entire book of Isaiah was recovered, as were portions of all thirty-nine Old Testament books, except Esther. The oldest Masoretic Text of Isaiah in existence (dating back to about 800 AD) was compared to the DSS Isaiah scroll (dated 200 to 300 B.C.). After a thousand years of copying, how much would the two documents agree? The answer was: extremely well.

For example, of 166 Hebrew words in Isaiah 53, only 17 letters were different; 10 were spelling variations; 4 pertain to minor stylistic changes. The remaining 3 were found in the additional word "light" in verse 11.¹²² None of these minor changes altered the meaning of the passage in the slightest. This proves that God has preserved an accurate prophetic portrait of His Son for us to appreciate.

An angel directed Philip, the evangelist, southward into the desert. Then the Holy Spirit told him to overtake the chariot of the Ethiopian Treasurer who was returning to his homeland from Jerusalem (Acts 8:26-29). The Ethiopian was reading this portion of Isaiah, but he did not understand it. After reading verses 7 and 8, aloud he asked Philip, *"I ask you, of whom does the prophet say this, of himself or of some other man?"* Philip then, *"beginning at this Scripture, preached Jesus to him"* (Acts 8:34-35). Indeed, the entire chapter pertains to the Lord Jesus Christ and is therefore widely quoted or referred to by the apostles in the New Testament:

Verse 1: John 12:38; Romans 10:16
Verse 4: Matthew 8:17
Verses 5-6: 1 Peter 2:22-25
Verses 7-8: Acts 8:32-33
Verses 12: Mark 15:28; Luke 22:37

Besides direct quotations there are another dozen allusions to terms and phrases found in this chapter in the New Testament (e.g. John 1:29, 36; Rom. 4:25; 1 Cor. 15:3-4; 2 Cor. 5:21; 1 Pet. 1:19; 1 John 3:5; Rev. 5:6, 7:14). This chapter prophetically describes the rejection and suffering of the Lord Jesus as God's Sin-bearer for humanity and His subsequent death, resurrection, and exaltation into the presence of God.

The Servant's Regard

Isaiah commences with the voices of the Jewish remnant (perhaps including the apostles and Jewish believers in the Church Age) mournful that only a few of their countrymen considered the message of God's arm of salvation significant. J. M. Riddle observes three negative acknowledgments by the lamenting remnant: "there was no faith in Him (v. 1); no desire for Him (v. 2); no sympathy for Him (v. 3)."¹²³ They acknowledged that there was nothing about the Servant-Messiah's appearance or His message that would naturally lead to an immense following (v. 2). He looked no different than other men and He had no flamboyant appeal or zealous plans against Rome; rather, His focus was mainly on the spiritual needs of the people.

Devotions in Isaiah

The Jews wanted political deliverance from Gentile rule and oppression, as promised to Abraham; they were not interested in spiritual revival or being reconciled to God in righteousness. So Isaiah says, God's Servant was a tender plant before Him (i.e., His visible life was full of spiritual vitality and fully approved of God). But regrettably, He was rooted in dry ground (describing the spiritual deadness of the Jewish nation at that time). Accordingly, God's Messiah was not what Israel wanted and the nation flatly rejected Him without pity:

He is despised and rejected by men, a Man of sorrows and acquainted with grief. And we hid, as it were, our faces from Him; He was despised, and we did not esteem Him (v. 3).

However, in a coming day the entire nation scattered throughout the world will realize that the substitutionary death of the Servant-Messiah was for the consequences of their own sin, not His.

Surely He has borne our griefs and carried our sorrows; yet we esteemed Him stricken, smitten by God, and afflicted. But He was wounded for our transgressions, He was bruised for our iniquities; the chastisement for our peace was upon Him, and by His stripes we are healed (vv. 4-5).

At Christ's return the refined remnant of Israel will realize that they rejected their Messiah, the One who entered into their adversity and dealt with their affliction. Previously, they thought He was in league with Beelzebub the prince of demons (Mark 2:10), was the son of a fornicator (John 8:41), and was a sinner (John 9:24). Surely this man who was outspoken against the religiosity of the Jewish leaders (Matt. 23:2-36; Luke 20:46-47) got exactly what He deserved – He was *smitten by God, and afflicted*. At that time, the nation regarded Christ's crucifixion as a divinely-inflicted judgment that He deserved, but at His second advent Israel will recognize the true nature of His ministry during His first advent.

Commentators disagree as to what exactly bearing our griefs and carrying our sorrows refers to – the cause of sin or merely the effect of sin. Yet, it seems reasonable that if the Lord dealt with the root cause and offense of sin, then that would remove sin's sting (e.g., disease, death, etc.). On this point F. C. Jennings writes:

Sorrow and Comfort

> Christ sees on all sides the sorrowful consequences of sin ... and He removes them all. But He who had the power and authority on earth (Mark 2:10) to remove the *effect*, or penalty, *thus made Himself responsible for the cause*. And who could do that save He who was to bear the sin that caused those sufferings, in His own body on the tree?[124]

Indeed, the Lord Jesus healed many of their infirmities during His earthly sojourn and He grieved with the grieving, but did that cause him to be judged at Calvary by God? He suffered for the judicial offense of sin, not the damage it caused, though He will repair all of that as well in a future day. Christ dealt with the sum total heartache and pain that sin causes rather than just physical consequences of sin (i.e., not just physical healings).

Having the essence of life within Himself, the Lord inherently had the power to heal the blind, the deaf, the sick, and to raise the dead to life. But without the work of the cross, all those who had received such blessings would still experience both physical and spiritual death. Commenting on the above verses, Norman Anderson writes:

> This will be the language of Israel in the coming day of their conviction and repentance, for the nation shall yet learn the truth of the sympathetic as well as the sacrificial and redemptive sufferings of the holy Sin-Bearer. Verse 4 certainly teaches us – as quoted in Matthew 8:17 – that He first bore in His spirit that which he removed by His power. He entered, in the deep and holy feelings of His heart, into all that His people suffered. *He* suffered sympathetically in the acuteness of His sinless perfection; *they* for their sins under the governmental hand of God. The day will assuredly come when the sufferings of the holy Sin-Bearer shall be rightly apprehended; then shall Israel say in deep contrition, "He was wounded for our transgressions."[125]

Transgressions are one form of sin which relates to offenses against God's revealed will. Israel had willingly violated God's Law given them through Moses and had rejected God's solution – salvation in Christ. As mentioned previously, death means "separation" in the Bible and is the result of sin. Death, then, would describe Israel's communion with God as His covenant people. At this juncture, the nation of Israel is spiritually dead, separated from God and headed for misery. Christ's healings recorded in the Gospels would be only a temporary blessing to the condemned, unless He bore God's wrath for human sin.

This is why Paul declares, *"For He made Him who knew no sin to be sin for us, that we might become the righteousness of God in Him"* (2 Cor. 5:21). Because Christ was judged on our behalf, the way to God is now open through Him: *"For there is one God and one Mediator between God and men, the Man Christ Jesus, who gave Himself a ransom for all, to be testified in due time"* (1 Tim. 2:5-6). Because of Christ's suffering and death, we can experience forgiveness and God's peace. In the future, restored Israel will realize what Christ accomplished for them and that He alone could righteously bear the chastisement for their "transgressions" and "iniquities."

The prophet twice employs the imagery of a sheep in this chapter to convey two distinct points. First, he likens Israel's disposition (representing humanity's fallen condition) to that of sheep which go their own way and become lost: *"All we like sheep have gone astray; we have turned, every one, to his own way and the Lord has laid on Him the iniquity of us all"* (v. 6). Man, left to himself, will always go his own way; he will turn away from God. Sadly, when one sheep goes astray, others often follow – this is what happened with the nation of Israel; her many false prophets led her away from the Lord. Thankfully, this verse which begins sadly with "all," also ends with the solution for "all" – the substitutionary death of Christ. He bore the judgment for "all" our iniquities, so that whoever would receive His forgiveness by faith could be righteously forgiven by a Holy God!

Thankfully, the Lord is about the work of seeking, calling, and saving lost sheep! Isaiah tells us what our response should be to His calling: *"Seek the Lord while He may be found, call upon Him while He is near* (55:6). But, to seek the Lord one must repent (turn from going his or her own way and agree with God about the matter of sin). Then, a seeking Savior and a seeking sinner will find each other. This reality will occur nationally for Israel at the end of the Tribulation Period. They will see Christ in all His glory and realize that He was smitten, wounded, bruised, chastised, and pierced for them. He willingly suffered unfathomable agony so that they could be forgiven and restored to God.

The Servant's Righteousness

With this understanding Isaiah applies a second sheep motif in verse 7 to the Lord Jesus. Although sheep tend to go their own way, sheep are also inclined to remain silent and to not resist being sheared. This meek and submissive disposition reflects Christ's meek attitude towards His own death. He did not argue against the Jews or defend himself before the Romans in order to preserve His own life, but rather He silently and submissively faced the cross (Mark 14:61; John 19:9). Christ willingly endured the blasphemy and afflictions of men, and the wrath of God for sin not His own. Then He readily laid down His life.

John said of the Lord Jesus, *"Behold! The Lamb of God who takes away the sin of the world!"* (John 1:29). The Lord was not a possible lamb, but the only Lamb whom God could righteously judge for our sin. The Lord was a spotless Lamb; He was thoroughly tested for some thirty-three years to prove His sinless perfection. The Lord Jesus lived His entire life without sin – He was without blemish, a fact that His enemies could not deny. We understand that Christ, as *holy humanity* (Luke 1:35), could not sin. There was nothing in Him that could respond to sin; He was and is *"sin apart"* (Heb. 4:15, Darby). The Lord's holy essence repulsed sin and loathed its working; hence Christ was the only Lamb who could be offered to God as a suitable sin offering.

Furthermore, Christ was not surprised by the cross; He knew fully what His ministry would cost Him – His life (John 12:27-22). The Lord Jesus laid aside His glory and position in heaven to become a man in order to be our sin-substitute at Calvary:

> *Who, being in the form of God, thought it not robbery to be equal with God: but made Himself of no reputation, and took upon Him the form of a servant, and was made in the likeness of men: and being found in fashion as a man, He humbled Himself, and became obedient unto death, even the death of the cross* (Phil. 2:6-8; KJV).

The incredible meekness of the Lamb of God is observed in this action; He willingly stooped to humanity and was fashioned in the *likeness* of sinful flesh (John 1:14; Rom. 8:3). Through the incarnation, the Lamb of God completely identified with the wandering sheep He came to save. Hence, the Lord *"was taken from prison"* (i.e., He was arrested, bound, and interrogated) and led away to be judged without legal representation or due process. God permitted it all, the result of

Devotions in Isaiah

which was His Son's death: *"cut Him off from the land of the living"* (v. 8). God declares that the judgment of His Servant was not for any crime that He committed, but *"for the transgressions of My people He was stricken"* (v. 8). Sadly, many orthodox Jews believe that the "He" in this passage is "Israel," but verse 8 clearly states that the "He" (God's Servant – the Messiah) suffered for the punishment of Israel's sin. No amount of divine affliction upon a guilty nation could ever judicially compensate for their sins.

Isaiah prophesied that God's Servant would suffer and die with transgressors (v. 12). The Roman soldiers were going to bury Christ with the criminals that He had been crucified with, but Isaiah says He would have an honorable burial in a rich man's tomb. Isaiah explains why: *"Because He had done no violence, nor was any deceit in His mouth"* (v. 9). The Lord Jesus had done nothing wrong; He was suffering for all those who had. Matthew records the fulfillment of this prophecy; Christ was crucified with two malefactors and later buried in the new tomb of *"a rich man from Arimathea, named Joseph"* (Matt. 27:38, 57-60). The Lord was righteous at His trial (v. 7), at His cross (v. 8), and at His burial (v. 9).

Meditation

>Man of Sorrows! What a name,
>For the Son of God, who came,
>Ruined sinners to reclaim.
>Hallelujah! What a Savior!
>
>Bearing shame and scoffing rude,
>In my place condemned He stood;
>Sealed my pardon with His blood.
>Hallelujah! What a Savior!
>
>Guilty, vile, and helpless we;
>Spotless Lamb of God was He;
>"Full atonement!" can it be?
>Hallelujah! What a Savior!
>
>Lifted up was He to die;
>"It is finished!" was His cry;
>Now in Heav'n exalted high.
>Hallelujah! What a Savior!

Sorrow and Comfort

> When He comes, our glorious King,
> All His ransomed home to bring,
> Then anew this song we'll sing:
> Hallelujah! What a Savior!
>
> — P. P. Bliss

The Exalted Servant
Isaiah 53:10-12

Pleased to Bruise?

If it were not for verse 11, the full ramifications of verse 10 would be completely baffling: How could the Father be pleased to bruise His Son and then prosper Him afterwards?

Yet it pleased the Lord to bruise Him; He has put Him to grief. When You make His soul an offering for sin, He shall see His seed, He shall prolong His days, and the pleasure of the Lord shall prosper in His hand (v. 10).

In some of Isaiah's messages, determining who is speaking is challenging at times. The extensive use of pronouns, while aiding the poetry also causes difficulties in determining the fuller ramifications of the passage. It is suggested that "Lord" or Jehovah (v. 10) refers to God the Father as does "He" (v. 10), "You" (v. 10), and "My" (v. 11), while "Him" and "His" refer to the Lord Jesus, the "Righteous Servant" (v. 11) who is submitting to His Father for the benefit of others. J. G. Bellett discusses how the remnant reflects on this statement as pertaining to the threefold benefits of Christ's suffering:

> The remnant again rehearses Messiah's sufferings, as He endured them at the hand of Jehovah. The passage reads as if the saints had just caught the preceding words of Jehovah, wherein He had vindicated His holy One and righteous servant, and wondered therefore that in spite of this, "it pleased the Lord to bruise Him," but soon recovering, as it were, from their surprise, through a fresh apprehension of the purpose and necessity of these sufferings, they anticipate and celebrate that threefold blessed fruit of them which in due time the Lord was to gather.
>
> First, "He shall see His seed" – that He should have His household about Him like a flock of sheep, should gather the great congregation,

should be encircled by the ten thousand times ten thousand, and the thousands of thousands who should understand and magnify the grace of these His sufferings, and say, "Worthy is the Lamb that was slain" (Rev. 5:11-12).

Second, "He shall prolong His days" – that He should enter manifestly upon the power of an endless life, that "having died unto sin once, He should live unto God," that "He that was dead should be alive forevermore." And here we observe that this promise embraces all the seed which He was to see and gather, according to the first promise; for He should take them with Himself into this life: having Him, the Son, they were with Him to have life eternal (1 Jn. 5:12); death, as touching them, was to be swallowed up in victory.

Third, "The pleasure of the Lord shall prosper in His hand" – that He should have dominion; and that in His hand dominion should not again be abused and forfeited as it had been of old, but that the pleasure of Jehovah should be fully answered, and a scepter of righteousness order in peace all things throughout the reconciled heavens and earth.[126]

Isaiah explains that God the Father would bruise His own Son and cause Him to suffer deep grief as an *asham* (a sin offering; Jer. 51:5) for His people. This is why Christ, while nailed to the cross and veiled in darkness, cried out: *"Eli, Eli, lama sabachthani?"* that is, *"My God, My God, why have You forsaken Me?"* (Matt. 27:46). Through His acceptable sin sacrifice, God would be able to extend the offer of forgiveness to Israel and to all of humanity. Those who respond in faith will be eternally redeemed by the blood of Christ. Thus, a spiritual race of redeemed people, after His own kind, would be brought into being as His seed.

However, Isaiah also says that God will prolong His Servant's days and prosper Him. This would be possible only through His resurrection after His death and burial. The cross was not His end, but a new beginning for us to be able to love and honor Him. Christ would come forth from the grave a mighty Victor over death and Satan, in fact, over all the principalities and powers (Eph. 1:19-21). David prophesied that Christ would be resurrected and exalted to the highest position of prominence after completing His redemptive work (Ps. 2:7); Luke references this prophesy and explains its fulfillment (Acts 13:22-35). Both Peter and Paul quote David (Ps. 16:9-10) to confirm that there

Devotions in Isaiah

was a prophetic meaning to his statement relating to the future resurrection of Christ, the Holy One of Israel (Acts 2:25-28, 13:35-37).

The exalted Christ will then establish the will of God universally. He will establish a kingdom on earth that will honor God in every way. Then *"the pleasure of the Lord shall prosper in His hand."* Isaiah continues to discuss the fruitfulness of the Son's selfless sacrifice for humanity in verse 11:

> *He shall see the labor of His soul, and be satisfied. By His knowledge My righteous Servant shall justify many, for He shall bear their iniquities* (v. 11).

Following the pronoun key previously established, this verse would mean that "He" (the Father, as confirmed by the "My" as the One speaking) was completely satisfied with the propitiation His Son provided at Calvary on behalf of humanity. While this understanding may be correct, F. B. Hole takes the position that the "He" refers to the Son's own satisfaction in the beneficial results of His finished work:

> Not only is the risen Servant to fulfil all the pleasure of Jehovah, but He Himself is to be satisfied as He sees the full result established as the fruit of "the travail of His soul." We are little creatures of small capacity, so that a very little will satisfy us. His capacity is infinite; yet the fruit of His soul's travail will be so immeasurable as to satisfy Him. Do not our hearts greatly rejoice that so it is to be?[127]

Whether or not the "He" identifies the Son as the speaker, or the Father, both thoughts are certainly true. The latter portion of the verse speaks of the Son's knowledge and understanding of the Father's will for Him, which led Him to the cross. While this meaning (of the second sentence in verse 11) is preferred, it is also true that "by the knowledge of Him" men will be justified (John 17:3). The Lord could also rejoice in knowing that many souls would be justified through the knowledge of His finished redemptive work.

J. N. Darby translates verse 11 as follows: *"He shall see of the fruit of the travail of His soul, and shall be satisfied: by His knowledge shall My righteous servant instruct many in righteousness; and He shall bear their iniquities."* The Hebrew word *tsadaq* is rendered "shall justify" in the NKJV and KJV, but is translated "instruct ... in righteousness" by Darby. This is a fair rendering of *tsadaq* which means "to cleanse" or

Sorrow and Comfort

"to be turned to righteousness." If Darby's translation is more correct, then the thought would be this: The basis of righteous blessing has been obtained by Christ's finished work at Calvary, and all who are brought into God's blessing through Christ shall be instructed in the righteousness of their standing in Him. This means that Christ does not merely justify those He suffered for, but desires to fully equip them in understanding matters of positional and practical righteousness. Being born again in Christ means there is a responsibility of living out the righteous standing that we have received by grace.

This means that believers should never get over the immensity of Christ's redemptive work at Calvary. Two thousand years ago Jesus Christ tasted death for every man (Heb. 2:9) and was the propitiation for all human sin ever to be committed (1 Jn. 2:2). While the Son was hanging between heaven and earth upon a Roman cross, God the Father judicially punished Him for all human sin. *"There is no more offering for sin"* (Heb. 10:18). It cannot be said, however, that sin is no longer present in the world or that the consequences for sins committed no longer exist – it is, and they do. But from God's point of view, Christ has done all that is necessary for individuals to receive forgiveness for their sins. A person must simply trust Christ as Savior and receive God's forgiveness. God would be unjust to judge mankind a second time for all their crimes, but an individual must trust Christ alone to receive the imputed righteousness of God to his personal account. Only then does an individual have an acceptable standing with God.

The greatest blessing of life is to be justified by the Just One – in Him all believers have a righteous standing and are thus called "saints." God's holy character ensures that He must judge sin. God would be unjust if He did not prosecute that which opposes His nature, as a lack of action against sin endorses wickedness. Although justice is guaranteed, the timing in which God chooses to vindicate His holiness will occur in accordance with His sovereign purposes. A forgiven sinner need never worry about suffering God's judicial wrath for his sins: *"But God demonstrates His own love toward us, in that while we were still sinners, Christ died for us. Much more then, having now been justified by His blood, we shall be saved from wrath through Him"* (Rom. 5:8-10). Because the Lord Jesus was judged in the place of the sinner, all those who trust in Christ as Savior are declared right (justified) by God in Him. Because God is a just God, we can be assured that the offense of our sin was fully judged in His Son (vv. 10-11; Rom. 3:25).

> God's compassion flows out of His goodness, and goodness without justice is not goodness. God spares us because He is good, but He could not be good if He were not just.
>
> — A. W. Tozer

The Servant's Reward

This rich chapter concludes with the rightful exaltation and recompense of God's faithful Servant and a reference to His priestly intercession on behalf of those who are His. The One who was numbered with the transgressors to bear the full judgment for human sin (necessitating His death) will permit those who trust in Him to share in the benefits of His victory:

Therefore I will divide Him a portion with the great, and He shall divide the spoil with the strong, because He poured out His soul unto death, and He was numbered with the transgressors, and He bore the sin of many, and made intercession for the transgressors (v. 12).

Commentators have differing views on what *"I will divide Him a portion with the great, and He shall divide the spoil with the strong"* actually means. What seems to be central is the ancient idea that a victor would normally share with his fellows the spoils of those he conquered. Several verses in the New Testament convey this meaning.

The Lord Jesus taught that *"no one can enter a strong man's house and plunder his goods, unless he first binds the strong man. And then he will plunder his house"* (Mark 3:27). On the night before His crucifixion the Lord also foretold that He would conquer Satan to accomplish the release of those in his death grip: *"Now is the judgment of this world; now the ruler of this world will be cast out"* (John 12:31). By securing a means of salvation for humanity, the triumphant Savior despoiled Satan of many souls that were following him into the Lake of Fire. Christ is now leading "captivity captive" (those who were once in Satan's clutches) heavenward and bestowing on them the wealth of heaven – which was not available to them previously (Eph. 1:3, 4:8).

Sorrow and Comfort

Christ is the Victor, and God has given Him the plunder of the defeated, but how do "the great" and "the strong" in verse 12 convey this understanding? Some commentators favor the Septuagint's rendering of the verse: "I will give him the mighty for a portion" and "He shall divide the spoils of the mighty." The idea is that those Christ died to make righteous will be His inheritance and He will share the spoils of the defeated with them. God will certainly ensure that the rewards His Son receives will be worthy of the death He died.

This meaning seems likely, but there is also a practical application in the text, if we understand "the great" to refer to those made righteous by Christ and then remain "strong" in Him. Then the verse would speak of Christ rewarding proportionally those who have borne reproach for His Name in the world which hated and crucified the Lord. Those who share in His rejection on earth now will also share in His glory later. The Lord Jesus put the matter this way:

> *To him who overcomes I will give to eat from the tree of life, which is in the midst of the Paradise of God* (Rev. 2:7).
>
> *He who overcomes shall not be hurt by the second death* (Rev. 2:11).
>
> *To him who overcomes I will give some of the hidden manna to eat. And I will give him a white stone, and on the stone a new name written which no one knows except him who receives it* (Rev. 2:17).

Overcomers, true believers, in faith lay hold of what is available to them in heavenly places (Eph. 1:3) in differing degrees, as shown in the parable of the pounds (Luke 19:12-27), but Christ will honor faithfulness. He values those who follow His example of faithfulness – persistence will be rewarded appropriately at the Judgment Seat of Christ.

The same Hebrew verb *paga* concludes verses 6 and 12. In verse 6 we read that God the Father *"made"* His Servant to be the sin-bearer, but in verse 12, Christ interposed Himself *"and made intercession for"* – on behalf of – those whose sins He would bear. In the latter action, Christ willingly became the great mediator between God and man: *"For there is one God and one Mediator between God and men, the Man Christ Jesus, who gave Himself a ransom for all"* (1 Tim. 2:5-6).

While it is true that on the cross Christ did make intercession to God for those who blasphemed and oppressed Him (Luke 23:34), the intercession He accomplished as humanity's Sin-bearer was much wider in scope (Heb. 2:9). He asked His Father only to *suffer with* (literally "to let be") His accusers at Calvary, but through His propitiation transgressors are fully accepted by God.

Thankfully, all those who truly trust in the benefits of Christ's sin-bearing and intercession will be *"heirs of God and joint heirs with Christ"* (Rom. 8:17) and shall *"reign with Him"* (2 Tim. 2:12). When we trust in the gospel message of Jesus Christ, God rewards us with Christ and all the riches that are in Him (Eph. 1:3). By God's mercy, the believer escapes hell, and by His grace, he or she inherits heaven and all that Christ has (Rev. 21:7). After the great Chicago fire, Moody was meditating on the Lord's declaration of Revelation 21:7 when questioned about his losses:

> After the Chicago Fire I met a man who said, "Moody, I hear you lost everything in the Chicago fire." "Well," I said, "you understood it wrong; I didn't." He said, "How much have you left?" I can't tell you; I have got a good deal more left than I lost." "You can't tell how much you have?" "No." "I didn't know that you were ever that rich. What do you mean?" "I mean just what I say. I got my old Bible out of the fire; that is about the only thing. One promise came to me that illuminated the city a great deal more than the fire did. *'He that overcometh shall inherit all things; and I will be his God and he shall be My son.'* You ask me how much I am worth. I don't know. You may go and find out how much the Vanderbilts are worth, and the Astors, and the Rothschilds, but you can't find out how much a child of God is worth. Why? Because he is a joint-heir with Jesus Christ!"[128]

How much does Christ own? Some scientists suggest that our universe is 20 billion light-years across – what is the value of 200 million galaxies? Who can tell, but as believers it is all ours because it is all His. And the Lord Jesus is intent on sharing it with us. For that reason He continues as our High Priest to intercede on our behalf until we receive our inheritance with Him. The Lord Jesus offered intercession to God on our behalf at Calvary to reconcile us with God, but His priestly work for His people will continue until the last believer is with Him (Heb. 7:24-27). Not only did the Man of Sorrows save from the horror of Hell those who will trust Him, He freely bestows on them the vast riches of Heaven also. What a Savior!

Sorrow and Comfort

Meditation

Crown Him! Crown Him! Crown the Savior King of kings;
In your hearts enthrone Him, Lord and Master own Him;
Crown Him! Crown Him! While heaven exultant rings;
Crown the blessed Savior King of kings.

Soon He is coming back again, a thousand years on earth to reign;
We'll see Him by and by, we'll see Him by and by;
All the redeemed with Him He'll bring,
Who in their hearts have crowned Him King,
And they shall live and reign with Him on high.

— Leila N. Morris

Forever Salvation
Isaiah 54

The theme of this chapter is expressed in the concluding statement of the final verse: *"'This is the heritage of the servants of the Lord, and their righteousness is from Me,' says the Lord"* (v. 17). The servants of the Lord have a divinely imputed *position* of righteousness because of the propitiation achieved in the last chapter by His righteous Servant (53:11). Those justified in Christ also have a great heritage (rewards and possessions) in Him. In this chapter we learn more about Israel's future salvation and blessings in Christ.

Isaiah speaks of Israel's regathering to the land, her numerical growth, and the nation's peaceful future under Christ's protection. The nations will oppose Israel during the Tribulation Period, but God will use that tumultuous seven-year period to restore the Jewish nation, His adulterous wife, to Himself (Jer. 30:7; Rev. 12:13-17). As we see in this chapter, those Jews surviving this terrible holocaust will enter Christ's kingdom (also 4:2).

Growth and Assurance

During the Kingdom Age, the Jewish nation will experience numerical growth. In the Jewish culture a barren woman was scorned, as children were considered a measure of God's blessing on a family and were needed to aid the family and assist aging parents. While spiritually estranged from God for centuries, Israel had been like a childless wife in mourning. However, after Israel's spiritual revival at the end of the Tribulation Period, God will bless her with many children, which will prompt her joyful singing (v. 1). She will have so many children, in fact, that homes (tents) will have to be enlarged to accommodate them (v. 2). This bursting posterity will ensure that all the cities in Israel, desolated during the Tribulation Period, will be inhabited again (v. 3).

No longer will Israel bear the shame and remorse of her childless widowhood, spiritually speaking (v. 4). To this end, God will call His once-adulterous wife back home. That is, He will gather all surviving Jews worldwide back to Himself and to the land He promised Abraham and the patriarchs long ago:

> *For your Maker is your husband, the Lord of hosts is His name; and your Redeemer is the Holy One of Israel; He is called the God of the whole earth. For the Lord has called you like a woman forsaken and grieved in spirit, like a youthful wife when you were refused* (vv. 5-6).

The titles Isaiah employs are chosen to arouse a sense of security and significance: "your Maker," "your Husband," "the Lord of Hosts," and "your Redeemer." As God's restored wife who has received the Holy Spirit, Israel will be more faithful and fruitful in the Kingdom Age than she ever was before. The Hebrew noun translated "Maker" in verse 5 is plural, literally "Makers." This is consistent with other passages in Scripture. For example, "Creator" in Ecclesiastes 12:1 is also plural – "Creators." Though the Son is the visible representative of the Godhead in this blissful restoration, the Father and the Holy Spirit rejoice in their communion with Israel also.

Psalm 45 is a royal psalm which celebrates the wedding day of the mighty king and prophetically captures the scene that Isaiah is describing to us. The king's surpassing character and gracious words indicate he was blessed of God (Ps. 45:2). The psalmist anticipated that this mighty king would demonstrate his valor by upholding truth, humility, and righteousness as he rode into battle; he would therefore achieve stunning victories among the nations (Ps. 45:3-5). The regal attire of the king on his wedding day was perfumed with myrrh, aloes, and cassia. (The Lord Jesus was buried with these spices.) The festive ceremony would take place in the King's palace (Ps. 45:15).

The closing scene is described: the king's queen, adorned with gold, stands with him at his right side; the kings' daughters, also present, receive honor on this merry occasion (Ps. 45:9). The psalmist then reminisces on a moment just prior to the bride's appearance for the ceremony. Knowing the king's desire and delight in his new queen, the poet counsels her to faithfully honor and adore him (Ps. 45:10-11). In doing so, she would be blessed and would have the praise and blessing of the people (Ps. 45:12). The writer then describes the moment of her presentation to the king; she is escorted by bridesmaids, and is adorned with gold and a beautifully embroidered gown (Ps. 45:13-15). The song closes with the prediction that the marriage union will be blessed with many sons who will be princes in the land, thus ensuring the king will be remembered throughout the nations and for generations to come.

This glorious wedding panorama relates to Christ's Second Advent to earth – then the Lord will again be spiritually unified with the nation of Israel and both will be honored by the nations. This commences directly after the conclusion of the marriage supper of the Lamb in heaven (Rev. 19:7-16), which is enjoyed by Christ with glorified believers (the Church, and perhaps Old Testament saints). Certainly, the Lord told parables that present the Church as His heavenly bride, as taught by Paul in the fifth chapter of Ephesians, but Psalm 45 is Jewish in focus, and thus the prophetic emphasis is on the future restoration of Israel, the once-adulterous wife of Jehovah. With this understanding, the nations ruled by Christ during the Kingdom Age are the *"Kings' daughters,"* who will do homage to the King, and the new Queen is the revived nation of Israel.

Isaiah then offers us a sense of God's delight in His once-disloyal wife being restored to Him:

For a mere moment I have forsaken you, but with great mercies I will gather you. With a little wrath I hid My face from you for a moment; but with everlasting kindness I will have mercy on you," says the Lord, your Redeemer (vv. 7-8).

The immutable and eternal attributes of God are evident in the expression "a mere moment." From a human perspective, what the Jewish people have suffered since the sixth century B.C. to this present day can hardly be characterized as *"a little wrath"* for *"a mere moment."* But time has no hold on God or on His purposes, and, though His wrath is momentarily provoked because of rebellion, it is His everlasting kindness and great mercy that reveal His fuller nature. God, who is eternal, longs to demonstrate His grace and mercy on an ongoing basis.

Speaking of God's eternal nature, the psalmist wrote: *"a thousand years in Your sight are like yesterday when it is past"* (Ps. 90:4). To God, the events unfolding on earth are over in the blink of an eye. What is obvious from the passage is that God never stopped loving Israel; it was Israel who deserted Him. So from God's perspective, there had been only a short interruption in the communion He would eventually enjoy with His people forever.

Sorrow and Comfort

In Christ, Gentiles also enjoy a special relationship with God. Hence, those in the Church will also be in God's presence and will be learning of His grace throughout eternity:

> *But God, who is rich in mercy, because of His great love with which He loved us, even when we were dead in trespasses, made us alive together with Christ (by grace you have been saved), and raised us up together, and made us sit together in the heavenly places in Christ Jesus, that in the ages to come He might show the exceeding riches of His grace in His kindness toward us in Christ Jesus* (Eph. 2:4-7).

Once Israel is restored to God in the Kingdom Age, God promises that He will never need to rebuke or punish them again – the days of His wrath will be past, just as one might sigh (Ps. 90:9). Isaiah refers to God's covenant with Noah, when God promised never to destroy the earth again by a flood (v. 9). History has shown that God has honored His covenant with Noah. Therefore, Isaiah says that Israel can trust the Lord to keep His promise to never chasten them again. Even if the mountains and the hills of the earth are removed (and someday they will be), God will not renege on His covenant: *"My kindness shall not depart from you, nor shall My covenant of peace be removed"* (v. 10).

Why can God establish this unconditional covenant with restored Israel? Sustained spiritual fruitfulness can be produced only through spiritual rebirth which coincides with the Holy Spirit being poured out upon the Jewish nation at the end of the Tribulation Period. At that time, they will know and worship Jesus Christ as Messiah (Joel 2:25-3:21; Zech. 12:10-13:1). At the end of the Tribulation Period, the refined Jewish nation will receive the Holy Spirit and will obtain spiritual life in Christ. A people completely controlled by the Holy Spirit will never disappoint the Lord; thus there will be no need for His correction!

Beauty and Protection

Jerusalem was *"the afflicted one,"* who suffered many Gentile invasions through the centuries, and without comforters (v. 11). That would never occur again. In fact, God promised to rebuild the city's foundation and walls with precious gems, and to mount gates of crystal with rubies for capstones (v. 12). This is a poetic expression of His promised care and esteem for Jerusalem. Not only did the Lord promise to supply and protect the Jews, but He also promised to teach their children the ways of righteousness so that they would enjoy His peace and prosperity also (vv. 13-14).

During "the time of the Gentiles" God permitted nations, such as Assyria, and Babylon, to overrun and defeat Israel to accomplish His sovereign purposes. However, that would never happen again. Any nation daring to assemble itself against Israel will fail because God had not decreed that activity: "Indeed they shall surely assemble, but not because of Me. Whoever assembles against you shall fall for your sake" (v. 15). The nations gathering might refer to the Battle of Gog and Magog during the mid-portion of the Tribulation Period (Ezek. 38-39), or to the Battle of Armageddon at the end of the Tribulation Period (Zech. 14; Rev. 19), or to the battle with nations summoned by Satan at the end of the Kingdom Age (Rev. 20).

Continuing to assure the restored remnant of God's forever protection, Isaiah reminds them that God created and controls the blacksmith who forges weapons of war in the fire (v. 16). Therefore:

"No weapon formed against you shall prosper, and every tongue which rises against you in judgment you shall condemn. This is the heritage of the servants of the Lord, and their righteousness is from Me," says the Lord (v. 17).

Although this verse specifically applies to Israel, the same truth is confirmed in the New Testament for the Church: A believer's righteous standing is imputed from God alone. The believer's union with Him ensures that no opposition can overcome His servants until their warring days are done!

Who shall separate us from the love of Christ? Shall tribulation, or distress, or persecution, or famine, or nakedness, or peril, or sword? As it is written: "For Your sake we are killed all day long; we are accounted as sheep for the slaughter." Yet in all these things we are more than conquerors through Him who loved us. For I am persuaded that neither death nor life, nor angels nor principalities nor powers, nor things present nor things to come, nor height nor depth, nor any other created thing, shall be able to separate us from the love of God which is in Christ Jesus our Lord (Rom. 8:35-39).

God's promise to preserve Israel serves as a reminder to every servant of God that while on earth we are immortal and invincible until the Lord's work in us and through us is complete. On this point, Paul wrote: *"For we are His workmanship, created in Christ Jesus for good works, which God prepared beforehand that we should walk in them"* (Eph. 2:10). May each believer be faithful to walk the course to which he or she is called, so that at the end of our sojourn on earth each one may be able to echo the words Paul spoke just before his death, *"I have fought the good fight, I have finished the race, I have kept the faith"* (2 Tim. 4:7).

Meditation

> O tempted one, look up, be strong; the promise of the Lord is sure,
> That they shall sing the victor's song, who faithful to the end endure;
> God's Holy Spirit comes to thee, of His abiding love to tell;
> To blissful port, over stormy sea, calls Heaven's inviting harbor bell.
>
> — John Yates

All May Come
Isaiah 55

Having addressed, in the previous chapter, Israel's eternal salvation, Isaiah highlights the fact that God is merciful. He invites all in need to "come" to Him to be satisfied.

Summoning the Unsatisfied

The unsatisfied were invited to come to God to receive provisions which cannot be bought with money. The invitation to "come" is repeated three times in the first verse: *"Everyone who thirsts, come to the waters; and you who have no money, come, buy and eat. Yes, come, buy wine and milk without money and without price"* (v. 1). While God does supply the physical needs of those who trust in Him, the primary focus of Isaiah's invitation is the spiritual satisfaction of individuals in the Jewish nation. Why spend money on bread which cannot satisfy one's true need? It would be wise to receive from God that which abundantly delights the soul forever (v. 2).

God promises to satisfy our spirit's deepest need without any human compensation (i.e., no one can buy or earn His forgiveness through payment or doing "good works"). Peter reminds believers that their God counted only one thing precious enough to redeem their souls – the blood of Christ: *"Knowing that you were not redeemed with corruptible things, like silver or gold, from your aimless conduct received by tradition from your fathers, but with the precious blood of Christ"* (1 Pet. 1:18-19). Both the Old Testament and the New Testament state that material wealth, regardless of its value, cannot purchase the redemption of one sinner.

Gentiles who respond to God's invitation to come will be brought under His New Covenant with Israel, as a second benefactor. Gentiles who had not been God's people could become His, and receive His blessing which was previously promised only to Israel (Hos. 1:10, 2:23; Rom. 9:25-26; Eph. 2:12-16, 3:6). As explained in Isaiah 42, the New Covenant, sealed by Christ's blood, would accomplish what the Old

Covenant could not – propitiation for sins (Heb. 8:8). The Old Covenant with Israel was conditional in nature; the Jews had to keep God's Law to receive God's blessing (Ex. 19:5-8; Heb. 8:9). The New Covenant would be unconditional in nature and would be the means by which God would honor His covenant with Abraham.

The reference in verse 3 to *"the sure mercies of David"* refers to the subsequent unconditional covenant God established with David, namely that one of his descendants would sit on his throne and rule in righteousness and power forever (2 Sam. 7:15). Because of the everlasting covenant secured by Christ (Luke 22:20), God was able to keep His covenant with David. Therefore, the rightful heir to the throne of David, the Lord Jesus Christ, *"a leader and commander for the people,"* will rule the world in the Kingdom Age; He is God's *"Witness"* to all people (v. 4).

When speaking to Joshua on the eve of confronting Jericho, the Lord referred to Himself as the *"Captain of the Host of the Lord"* (Josh. 5:14; KJV). Terminology associated with high rank clings to the Lord throughout Scripture. The Hebrew word *sar* is rendered "commander" in Joshua 5:14, but translated as "prince" in Isaiah 9:6; the Lord is *"the Prince of Peace."* In the New Testament, the Greek word *archegos* is found only four times and each time speaks of the Lord Jesus: He is the *Prince* of Life (Acts 3:15), a *Prince* (Acts 5:31), the *Captain* of our salvation (Heb. 2:10), and the *Author* of our faith (Heb. 12:2). Without question, the Lord is the highest ranking authority over all His saints and, indeed, the armies of heaven. This descendant of David will rule so magnificently that the nations, seeing God's splendor in Israel, will journey there to worship Him also (v. 5). Verse 5 clearly shows that God intended to extended mercy to the Gentiles, as well as to Israel, through the work of His Son. This event does not speak of individual Gentiles being saved during the Church Age, but rather when all nations on earth will be blessed, which will not occur until after Israel's conversion.

Imploring the Wicked

Because God's offer of salvation is available for all men, not just for Israel, the prophet implores the wicked to repent of their evil deeds and turn to the Lord:

Seek the Lord while He may be found, call upon Him while He is near. Let the wicked forsake his way, and the unrighteous man his thoughts; let him return to the Lord, and He will have mercy on him; and to our God, for He will abundantly pardon (vv. 6-7).

Verse 6 advises the sinner what to do and verse 7 supplies the assurance of God's mercy if the sinner complies. This will be the message proclaimed to the nations during the Tribulation Period by Jewish evangelists and angels alike: Do not worship the beast or take his mark – worship God, for judgment is coming (Rev. 14:6-12). God's abundant mercy being extended freely to repentant sinners (who have done nothing previously to please God) seems illogical. What does God get out of such a proposition? The answer is redeemed souls. God judged His only Son in order to bless His vile enemies:

But God demonstrates His own love toward us, in that while we were still sinners, Christ died for us. Much more then, having now been justified by His blood, we shall be saved from wrath through Him. For if when we were enemies we were reconciled to God through the death of His Son, much more, having been reconciled, we shall be saved by His life (Rom. 5:8-10).

Our sense of fairness cannot reconcile why God would demonstrate such love, especially when it cost Him the death of His Son. And that is where we must rest. We cannot rationalize God's love or His ways and thankfully He does not expect us to:

For My thoughts are not your thoughts, nor are your ways My ways. For as the heavens are higher than the Earth, so are My ways higher than your ways, and My thoughts than your thoughts (vv. 8-9).

Lord, we are so thankful that your thoughts and ways are so far above ours; otherwise we would still be condemned sinners with no hope. Amen.

Skeptics often use the argument that apparent contradictions within Scripture prove that the Bible is fallible and, therefore, not the Word of God. Sometimes this supposition is used to prove that the God of the Bible Himself is fallible. While a few scribal errors will be found within the Bible as it exists today, no contradictions of context will be found in the Bible. If we think we have found a contradiction, it is because we have not properly discerned God's meaning of Scripture –

Sorrow and Comfort

for His ways are higher than our ways. Man is to search all of Scripture for an understanding which is upheld by all of Scripture – the truth is in the whole, and Scripture interprets Scripture.

Therefore, believers are not to ignore, doubt, subtract, or add to God's Word because they do not understand what it means or cannot fathom how God could possibly do what He says He will do. Isaiah illustrates this truth by likening God's Word to the rain and snow He causes to fall on the earth (v. 10). The moisture does not return directly to the clouds, but rather benefits the ground producing vegetation and grain, which then supplies man with basic staples. Likewise, God's word always has a benefit to man. It does not return to Him void (v. 11).

The Lord Jesus conveyed the same truth in the New Testament: *"For assuredly, I say to you, till heaven and earth pass away, one jot or one tittle will by no means pass from the law till all is fulfilled"* (Matt. 5:18). Paul says even if every man in the world testified against one of God's decrees, you would be wise to trust God (Rom. 3:4). His Word is sure; it is the majority opinions and the philosophies of men that lead us astray.

> God moves in a mysterious way His wonders to perform;
> He plants His footsteps in the sea and rides upon the storm.
>
> Deep in unfathomable mines of never failing skill
> He treasures up His bright designs and works His sovereign will.
>
> Blind unbelief is sure to err and scan His work in vain;
> God is His own interpreter, and He will make it plain.
>
> — William Cowper

Isaiah closes his invitation to Gentiles to be saved by highlighting the blessings of joy and peace under the Messiah in the Kingdom Age (v. 12). As already discussed, in chapters 11, 35, 41, and 44, the curses that God placed on the earth will be removed and the entire planet will be an agricultural wonder. Instead of thorn bushes and briers, every kind of tree will grow, some for shade and others for fruit. In poetic personification, the tree branches rocking in the wind are likened to hands clapping for joy (v. 13). Paul reminds us that creation groans for the time when the curses levied upon the earth for sin in Eden will be lifted:

For the earnest expectation of the creation eagerly waits for the revealing of the sons of God. For the creation was subjected to futility, not willingly, but because of Him who subjected it in hope; because the creation itself also will be delivered from the bondage of corruption into the glorious liberty of the children of God. For we know that the whole creation groans and labors with birth pangs together until now (Rom. 8:19-22).

Christ will remove these curses shortly after His second advent to earth. Isaiah's point in this chapter is that under Messiah's rule the entire planet will be joyful, peaceful, and fruitful. You would be a fool not to take advantage of such a great salvation. Come to God through Christ while you still can.

Meditation

Hear the blessed Savior calling the oppressed:
O ye heavy laden, come to Me and rest.
Come, no longer tarry, I your load will bear,
Bring Me every burden, bring Me every care.

Come unto Me, I will give you rest;
Take My yoke upon you, hear Me and be blessed.
I am meek and lowly, come and trust My might.
Come: "My yoke is easy, and My burden's light."

— Charles P. Jones

Salvation for Gentiles Also
Isaiah 56

Having discussed the wonderful aspects of God's future salvation offered freely to anyone in need, the Lord urges His people to live appropriately now: *"Keep justice, and do righteousness, for My salvation is about to come, and My righteousness to be revealed"* (v. 1). Isaiah commends those who will live in daily awareness of their coming blessings in Christ (vv. 1-8), and condemns those who do not (vv. 9-12).

Living for the Future

It is one thing to know about a future spiritual and physical deliverance, but an entirely different matter to live now in the light of Bible prophecy. Believing that God's salvation will come has a sanctifying effect on a believer's life, no matter what dispensation he lives in. For the Jews, this meant obeying God's Law, which included honoring the Sabbath Day and refraining from doing evil (v. 2).

However, Gentiles should never think that God has not offered them salvation with His people also (v. 3). All were welcome to be satisfied by God's goodness, even eunuchs who were excluded from congregational worship under the Law (Deut. 23:1). The Law declared a righteous standard of living for God's covenant people; He wanted them to learn about holiness and uncleanness. The Jews were to be a called out company to God from among the nations and to live separate from them. So any Gentile, or eunuch (by implication – anyone), who wanted to identify with Jehovah, and His people, and honor His Law would be accepted.

> *To the eunuchs who keep My Sabbaths, and choose what pleases Me, and hold fast My covenant, even to them I will give in My house and within My walls a place and a name better than that of sons and daughters; I will give them an everlasting name that shall not be cut off* (vv. 4-5).

This promise was extraordinary. Since a eunuch was unable to father children and so pass his name to the next generation, God promised to remember his name forever. Isaiah's point is that God did not limit His eternal salvation to the Jews only; anyone could receive deliverance by exercising faith in His Word, which would be evident by a changed life.

No Jew or Gentile in the Church Age is under the Law, though the Law is still holy, for it continues to reflect the character of God (Rom. 7:4-6, 12). The purpose of the Law was to show sin (Rom. 3:20) and its only solution – Christ (Gal. 3:24). However, the application of what Isaiah is saying is fully valid today: our salvation in Christ, though not yet fully received, should inspire us to holy living now.

Salvation means to deliver, to rescue, to pardon, to secure, to make safe. As Paul explains to the Corinthians, believers in the Church Age enjoy the benefits of a three-tense salvation:

Yes, we had the sentence of death in ourselves, that we should not trust in ourselves but in God who raises the dead, who delivered us from so great a death, and does deliver us; in whom we trust that He will still deliver us (2 Cor. 1:9-10).

Christians, through the gospel message, can rejoice that their souls are saved from the **penalty of sin**, and through the Holy Spirit they now have **power over sin**. Furthermore, they are to anticipate a future day when they will be saved from **the presence of sin**. At that moment a believer's body will be transformed into holy humanity. Nothing of the flesh nature inherited from Adam will remain, and we will be removed from the presence of sin (i.e., from the corruption of the world) to ever be with the Lord (1 Thess. 4:17). So a Christian has been saved (John 5:24; Eph. 2:8), is being saved (Phil. 2:12; Rom. 8:24), and will be saved (Rom. 13:11; 1 Thess. 5:9). Through trusting the gospel message, we are born again and receive eternal salvation, just as promised to the eunuch. However, those in the dispensation of the Law were not indwelt by the Holy Spirit as are believers today; therefore, they did not have the power to overcome the sinful impulses from within (Rom. 7:9-19). Yet, all believers have the hope of being with the Lord forever and that should have a sanctifying effect on the way we live. John puts the matter this way:

> *Beloved, now we are children of God; and it has not yet been revealed what we shall be, but we know that when He is revealed, we shall be like Him, for we shall see Him as He is. And everyone who has this hope in Him purifies himself, just as He is pure* (1 Jn. 3:2-3).

Those in Isaiah's day who loved the Lord's name and longed to serve Him by endeavoring to follow God's Law and be holy would be accepted with believing Israel before the Lord (v. 6). No one would be excluded from worshipping the Lord or from being in His presence at the temple, for God said, *"My house shall be called a house of prayer for all nations"* (v. 7). This benefit for all was a fulfillment of God's covenant with Abraham, which is made possible through Christ: *"In you all the families of the earth shall be blessed"* (Gen. 12:3). God wants to gather "whosoever will" to Him (v. 8). The invitation that Isaiah is extending to the Gentiles to know and experience God's goodness is similar to the way John closes the canon of Scripture by giving us a view of God's throne room in the New Jerusalem:

> *And he showed me a pure river of water of life, clear as crystal, proceeding from the throne of God and of the Lamb ... And the Spirit and the bride say, "Come!" And let him who hears say, "Come!" And let him who thirsts come. Whoever desires, let him take the water of life freely* (Rev. 22:1, 17).

Only those who want to be there will be. God forces no one to commune with Him and enjoy His salvation; however, those who do will experientially know the words of David to be true: *"Oh, taste and see that the Lord is good; blessed is the man who trusts in Him"* (Ps. 34:8)! And thankfully, those from *"every kindred, and tongue, and people, and nation"* (Rev. 5:9) will be there drinking the water of life. Salvation is not exclusive, except to those who reject God's gift of grace.

Unfortunately, in Isaiah's day there was not a mass turning to the Lord among Gentiles to be saved, nor was the nation of Israel, who enjoyed so many special privileges, taking advantage of His goodness. This realization prompted the prophet to conclude his second nine-chapter section (chps. 49-57) by shifting his focus from the wonderful salvation that the redeemed will enjoy in Messiah's future kingdom to the wicked who will not have any part in it – they will be condemned (56:9-57:21).

Living for the Moment

As a prelude to this final judgment, Isaiah summons the beasts (representing Gentile powers – probably Babylon's army) to devour (punish) Israel for her spiritual callousness (v. 9). Israel's watchmen (spiritual leadership) were blind and oblivious to God's ways; they were like watchdogs who want only to sleep and eat, rather than bark and warn of danger (vv. 10-11). Israel's priests and Levites were to guide the people Godward as good shepherds, but instead their own lust for gain and pleasure had blinded them to God's coming judgment. They thought, *"Tomorrow will be as today, and much more abundant"* (v. 12). We see the same type of foolish mentality in the New Testament; no matter the age, self-seeking, self-sufficient, and self-exalting people do not discern that God's judgment is coming.

Three days before Christ's crucifixion, His disciples asked Him, *"What will be the sign of Your coming, and of the end of the age?"* (Matt. 24:3). The Lord responded to their question by describing several escalating signs of the coming Tribulation Period and detailing chronologically events that will occur during those seven years. The Lord concluded by giving the following warning:

> *But of that day and hour knows no man ... but as the days of Noah were so shall also the coming of the Son of Man be. For as in the days that were before the flood they were eating and drinking, marrying and giving in marriage, until the day that Noah entered into the ark. And knew not until the flood came, and took them all away, so shall also the coming of the Son of Man be* (Matt. 24:36-39).

Prior to the Lord's Second Coming the behavior of man will be similar to that in Noah's day and in Isaiah's day. Sexual perversion and unceasing wickedness will characterize men just prior to judgment. Man will be living for all the pleasure life can offer and have no remorse for the Creator's grieving heart. Noah's contemporaries lived as if they had flood insurance, but the only insurance was the ark. Likewise today, in our post-Christian society, man lives for the day, not realizing that judgment is coming and that the good news of Jesus Christ is the only means of escape.

This is why the Lord did not tell His disciples to be looking for the Antichrist, but rather to be intently watching and waiting for His unannounced return to the air to rapture the Church (1 Cor. 1:7-8; Phil.

Sorrow and Comfort

1:6, 10; 1 Thess. 5:9; 2 Thess. 1:10). His coming will precede God's wrath upon the wicked, which is known as "the Day of the Lord." This day will come upon the wicked as an unexpected thief in the night (also see 1 Thess. 5:2; 2 Pet. 3:10). Israel's religious leaders were living for the moment, not for eternity; God would rouse them from their spiritual slumber with a wakeup call – the Babylonians.

Meditation

> It may be at morn, when the day is awaking,
> When sunlight through darkness and shadow is breaking
> That Jesus will come in the fullness of glory
> To receive from the world "His own."
>
> It may be at midday, it may be at twilight,
> It may be, perchance, that the blackness of midnight
> Will burst into light in the blaze of His glory,
> When Jesus receives "His own."
>
> Oh, joy! oh, delight! should we go without dying,
> No sickness, no sadness, no dread and no crying.
> Caught up through the clouds with our Lord into glory,
> When Jesus receives "His own."
>
> — Ira Sankey

Reviving the Wayward
Isaiah 57

The last chapter concluded with Isaiah's censure of Israel's ignorant watchmen, and her spiritual blindness and self-indulgent leaders. It is to be expected that where there are foolishness, deficiencies, and corruption in a governing body, the people in their care will be affected adversely. Isaiah confirms that the entire nation was suffering from deep-seated spiritual blindness and a lack of sensitivity for the things of God.

When Isaiah penned these words, *"The righteous perishes, and no man takes it to heart"* (v. 1), there were few righteous and merciful Jews in Israel, and those who were walking with the Lord were being persecuted by those who were not (v. 1). To witness God's people estranged from Him and going their own way vexed the souls of the faithful; it seemed to them the only way to escape this tragedy and to find peace was through death (v. 2). Many righteous people were "taken away," implying that they were selectively massacred. Perhaps Isaiah was alluding to the slaughter of the innocent under wicked King Manasseh towards the end of the prophet's life (2 Kgs. 21:16).

Spiritual Adultery

Regrettably, many Jews were engaging in pagan practices such as sorcery, astrology, and religious prostitution (v. 3, 2:6, 47:11). These rebels were committing hideous sins against God and at the same time were mocking and oppressing the righteous (v. 4). God bemoans their idol worship in high places and under oak trees and especially the sacrifice of their own children in heathen rituals (vv. 5-6). Spiritually speaking, the Jews were in bed with and engaging in lascivious practices with false gods; they were not in communion with Him (vv. 7-8).

God cites the utter stupidity of Israel's paganism: *"You went to the king with ointment, and increased your perfumes; you sent your messengers far off, and even descended to Sheol"* (v. 9). The Hebrew

Sorrow and Comfort

word for "king" is *melek*. As the Jews were traveling a distance to sacrifice, *melek* probably refers to *Molek*, the Ammon god (i.e., "Molech"). The Jews were so enamored with heathen practices that they ventured into Ammon to worship Molech, knowing that human deaths often occurred during such rituals. William MacDonald summarizes Israel's adulterous relationship with idols at the mountain shrines:

> Instead of writing the law of God on the posts... of the doors (Deut. 6:9, 11:20), they hang idolatrous symbols behind the doors, and engage in sex orgies. They bring gifts and offerings to the king (Molech means king) and send messengers to Sheol in search of new abominations. Even when they become exhausted by their dissipation, they do not give up, but seem to get their second wind and press on to further wickedness.[129]

Despite the personal cost, Israel somehow found renewed fortitude through these vain religious activities (v. 10).

Because God had seemingly been silent for a long time, most Jews no longer feared Him, nor even remembered Him (v. 11). Therefore God promises to get their attention through exposing and judging the unrighteousness of their works (v. 12). In a sarcastic tone, the Lord told His people to cry out to their idols for help when He judge them; then, He promised to blow their powerless images away with one puff of wind (v. 13). In contrast, those who put their trust in the Lord *"shall possess the land, and shall inherit My holy mountain."* This meant that the faithful would enjoy not only physical blessings, but also spiritual communion with the Lord in His kingdom.

Yearning for the Wayward

In the remainder of the chapter, Isaiah declares God's immense longing for the wayward to return to Him through brokenness and repentance. This re-echoes the main theme of the latter portion of Isaiah (chps. 40-66): God offers comfort, spiritual renewal, security, and blessings to repentant sinners through Messiah's New Covenant.

In chapter 40, Isaiah was a voice crying in the spiritual wilderness of Israel's apostasy, *"Prepare the way of the Lord; make straight in the desert a highway for our God"* (40:3). The faithful were now walking on that highway and wanted the way prepared for all Israel to come to the Lord, *"Prepare the way, take the stumbling block out of the way of*

My people" (v. 14). But the highway to the Lord is the same for all; yet those who do not want to get right with God find some reason to stumble over themselves. Genuine humility and a contrite spirit require a work of God in the hearts of those who truly want Him. The Jewish nation needed to embrace the Lord through genuine repentance and a willingness to go on with God by obeying His Word (walking in truth).

Jehovah yearned to commune with (live with) His backsliding people – but they needed to understand His sorrow over their spiritual infidelity. The situation was bleak and swift judgment was coming unless Israel experienced utter brokenness over her sin and returned to the Lord. He, in turn, promised to revive them:

> *For thus says the High and Lofty One who inhabits eternity, whose name is Holy: "I dwell in the high and holy place, with him who has a contrite and humble spirit,* **to revive** *the spirit of the humble, and* **to revive** *the heart of the contrite ones"* (Isa. 57:15).

The One who is over all ages to come forever, even after time ceases to matter (Rev. 10:6), offers the humble and contrite the opportunity to experience full and continual revival in His presence! Spiritual revival is what Israel needed then, and what the Church desperately needs today.

Less than two centuries after Isaiah penned these words a great revival broke out in Jerusalem (in front of the Water Gate) and spread throughout Israel. It was the comprehension of Scripture, through Ezra's teaching, that caused the people to weep bitterly and to turn to the Lord (Neh. 8:9). The Jews were grieved over their personal conduct, knowing it was not what God expected or demanded of them. The people began by confessing their sins, beginning with those in leadership, followed by the men, the women, and the children. This same kind of contriteness was observed during the revival some thirteen years earlier, after a brokenhearted Ezra publicly prayed and confessed the sins of the nation as his own (Ezra 9:10); this, in turn, prompted the people to be grieved over their own sins as well (Ezra 10:1-2). The Jewish nation desperately needed to be broken before the Lord and for Him to reanimate them spiritually.

Most, if not all, of the great revivals of the Church Age have begun with two fundamental realities: First, God's people were spiritually lethargic and pathetically settled in the world, and second, a remnant of consecrated, God-fearing, Christ-loving, Bible-believing Christians earnestly sought the Lord for a miraculous solution – revival. With this being the case, the modern Church is ripe for revival. What is needed now is for the latter condition to be satisfied. In 1740, when God began to move through New England, it was called "The Great Awakening." Before The Great Awakening, Christianity had sadly declined. Unitarianism had gained much ground, and pagan philosophy was poisoning the minds of millions of people; there was much indifference to the things of God. J.C. Ryle writes, speaking of England prior to the Methodist Revival, "These times were the darkest age that England has passed through in the last 300 years. Anything more deplorable than the condition of the country, as to religion, morality, and high principle, it is very difficult to conceive."[130]

The Church today is in much the same condition as it was when The Great Awakening took place over two centuries ago. Christians today know the Word of God better than those before them, but few know the God of the Word. Our pulpits are filled with more highly-degreed men than ever before, yet we have little knowledge of the true God. We study rather than pray, plan rather than trust, boast rather than weep. The modern Church has gone from experiencing and expecting the supernatural to being choked to death by the superficial.

As in the days of Isaiah, we desperately need revival and the conditions are ripe for it in the Church. What would happen if a few believers desperate for change would separate themselves from the world and consecrate themselves to God in prayer? Might God again shake and shift the earth for His glory? Might the Spirit of God again wring out the arrogance and tawdriness from our calloused hearts and cause them to beat spontaneously for Him? Might the masses be converted to Christ as in past times?

> Revival is that strange and sovereign work of God in which He visits His own people – restoring, reanimating, and releasing them into the fullness of His blessing.
>
> — Stephen Olford

Chastening for Peace

The Jews obviously did not understand God's immense love for them, nor did they realize the consequences of prompting the jealousy of their all-powerful God by persistent spiritual adultery. God is longsuffering; slow to anger, but His chastening rod (i.e., the

Babylonians) would fall against His perpetually backsliding people (v. 17). However, God did not want the godly remnant to be overcome with despair, hence He promises not to contend forever with the souls that He created, otherwise they would perish in His wrath (v. 16). William MacDonald observes:

> God did send forth His wrath against His covetous, backsliding people, but His anger has a limit. He will restore those who turn from their idolatry, causing them to bring Him the fruit of their lips.[131]

Sadly, history had shown that Jehovah had to continually and aggressively chasten His people to keep them abiding with Him, otherwise they would revert to their backsliding ways. Yet, it is God's nature to be patient and forgiving with His erring children! He longs to guide, to heal, and to comfort those He loves (v. 18). God offers peace to those who desire fellowship with Him and the opportunity to receive peace for those who are not (v. 19). Those who enjoy the Lord will be equipped to praise and serve Him, but those who desire to continue in wickedness will be judged by God – they will never know God's peace (v. 20): *"'There is no peace,' says my God, 'for the wicked'"* (v. 21).

With this solemn warning, Isaiah concludes his second nine-chapter section on the rich blessings that God will convey to the faithful (both Jew and Gentile) through Israel's Servant-Messiah. Isaiah's message, and that of the entire Bible is concisely summarized by John: *"He who has the Son has life; he who does not have the Son of God does not have life"* (1 Jn. 5:12). He who trusts God's Son, Israel's Messiah, shall have abundant life forever, and those who will not receive Him shall never experience peace.

Meditation

> Peace, troubled soul, thou need not fear;
> Thy great Provider still is near;
> Who fed thee last, will feed thee still:
> Be calm, and sink into His will.
>
> The Lord, who built the earth and sky,
> In mercy stoops to hear thy cry;
> His promise all may freely claim;
> Ask and receive in Jesus' Name.

Sorrow and Comfort

>Thus shall the soul be truly blest,
>That seeks in God his only rest;
>May I that happy person be,
>In time and in eternity.

>— Samuel Ecking

A Pitiful Spiritual Condition
Isaiah 58

In his third nine-chapter section of the latter portion of his book (chps. 58-66), Isaiah first summarizes Israel's present spiritual condition in this chapter and then God's glorious future for her once restored. The primary focus of the two previous nine-chapter sections has been to call to repentance. The theme of this last section is the promise of eventual deliverance and blessings.

Admonishing the Wayward

Since Isaiah has been warning Israel for decades about lawlessness, it would seem that God is summoning new heralds in the work of restoring Israel, rather than exhorting Isaiah on his preaching style or to have more fervency. They were to journey throughout Israel and lift up their voices like a trumpet to declare their transgressions and sins: *"Cry aloud, spare not; lift up your voice like a trumpet; tell My people their transgression, and the house of Jacob their sins"* (v. 1).

Whether the command was to Isaiah or to other faithful saints in his day, it is a good admonition for us to consider also. Matthew Henry urges Christians today to *"cry aloud, spare not"* from telling those identifying with Christ of their sin:

> The Holy Spirit had hypocrites of every age in view. Self-love and timid Christians may say, "Spare thyself"; dislike to the cross and other motives will say, "Spare the rich and powerful"; but God says, "Spare not": and we must obey God, not men. We all need earnestly to pray for God's assistance in examining ourselves. Men may go far toward heaven, yet come short; and they may go to hell with a good reputation.[132]

David realized that every aspect of his life was searched out, planned, and meticulously controlled by the Lord; hence, it would be wrong for him not to act when required to uphold God's righteousness

Sorrow and Comfort

(Ps. 139:17-22). Accordingly, Paul exhorted believers to *"have no fellowship with the unfruitful works of darkness, but rather **expose them**"* (Eph. 5:11). A mature believer wants what God wants. Today, we might hear a Christian say, "I will pray about that" in order to shun his or her responsibility to confront obvious sin. But silent neutrality condones sin – it is a sin not to reprove what one knows is morally wrong. Civil edicts that disdain the name of Christ and the moral failure of His Church should cause us to do more than to sorrow privately. Believers should be willing to expose the unfruitful works of darkness and beseech the Lord openly to act against what is known to be corrupt.

God again summoned faithful witnesses in Israel during Christ's ministry and then again in the Apostolic Era of the Church Age. This evangelistic activity will occur again during the first part of the Tribulation Period. God will have an angel count and seal 144,000 Jews (12,000 Jews from each tribe) to be His witnesses (Rev. 7:4). These Jewish witnesses will be protected by God as they preach the kingdom gospel message throughout the entire world during the Tribulation Period (Matt. 24:14; Rev. 7:4-8; 14:1-5).

Avoid Vain Fasting

The spiritual problem in Israel during the Tribulation Period will be the same one that Isaiah had been confronting since his first message (chp. 1): God's covenant people were engaged in religiosity in which He had no part (v. 2). They were engaged in mindless religious sacrifices, feasts, and vows as an outward means to somehow leverage God's blessing to them. For example, the Jews wondered if God was noticing how much they were fasting, that is, afflicting their souls through self-abasing religious activities (v. 3). But it was obvious that their fasting was not founded in genuine contriteness because they were unconcerned for the welfare of others. They were striving with each other, employers were exploiting their employees, and many were seeking their own pleasure instead of the needs of others (v. 4). Because their motives for their religious humility were corrupt, their prayers would not be heard and their worship would be rejected (v. 5). They did not yearn to know God or to obey Him; hence there was no inward reality of faith in what they were doing – God was unimpressed.

This sorrowful affliction infests much of the Church today. Religious people, ignorant of who God is and what He says, are trying to impress Him through good deeds, instead of through devotion settled in truth. As Paul puts it, this is *"having a form of godliness but denying its power"*; he then exhorts sound believers, *"from such people turn away"* (2 Tim 3:5). Believers should not be rubbing religious shoulders with those whom God detests.

Believers will not value what they do not understand, nor will they sacrifice for what they do not appreciate. The entire focus of discipleship is summed up in "being," not "doing." The Lord Jesus did not say to His followers, "you cannot *become* My disciples...." He stressed "you cannot *be* My disciples ...." Discipleship is a lifelong pursuit of Christ; it is not something you suddenly arrive at one morning. A true disciple of Christ is compelled to learn of Christ (Matt. 11:29) and to be like Christ (Matt. 10:25). Before we can contemplate honoring the Lord, we must first know Him and what He desires of us.

Why did the Jews in Isaiah's time think that fasting would somehow prompt God's favor, when He had required them to corporately fast only one day per year? The Law did not require the Jews to *"afflict their souls,"* except on the Day of Atonement (Lev. 16:31). Because of this unique distinction, the Jews in New Testament times commonly referred to the Day of Atonement as *"the fast"* (Acts 27:9). In the Old Testament, the Day of Atonement was sometimes referred to as "that Day" or "the Day" (Lev. 16:30). Because of its significance, it would be a day of rest (as a Sabbath day), a day of fasting and of serious reflection and repentance before the Lord.

As *"afflicting your souls"* (Lev. 23:27) is a vague term, the rabbinical writings set forth how the Jews were to observe the Day of Atonement. These call for a twenty-five-hour fast (from food and fluids), and a cessation of work, bathing, and marital relationships. The Day of Atonement was to be a day devoted to prayer and confession and, there was no other day like it on the Jewish calendar.

Clearly, "the afflicting of the soul" in Isaiah's day (v. 5) was just religious fluff and was void of the inner reflection and repentance prompted by "the Day of Atonement." God's commanded fast was to cause His people to pause and consider whether or not they were obeying His Law. So the Lord pointed out the futility of their present fasting. H. A. Ironside writes:

> Israel fasted "for strife and debate," but in His fasts God called on the Jews to recognize the importance of self-judgment. The fasts gave them opportunity to come before Him, to meditate on His dealings with them, to meditate on their own failures and sins, to confess them,

Sorrow and Comfort

and then to demonstrate the compassion of God by giving practical assistance to those who were needy. In other words, what God had in mind was not simply that they should deny themselves a little food, but that they should be constantly living lives of self-denial, dividing what God gave them with others, and sharing with the poor.[133]

The Jews in Isaiah's day were not the only ones who were adopting wrong attitudes concerning fasting. Believers in the Church Age would do well to heed his rebuke also. The Lord told His disciples:

When you fast, do not be like the hypocrites, with a sad countenance. For they disfigure their faces that they may appear to men to be fasting. Assuredly, I say to you, they have their reward. But you, when you fast, anoint your head and wash your face, so that you do not appear to men to be fasting, but to your Father who is in the secret place; and your Father who sees in secret will reward you openly (Matt. 6:16-18).

First, notice that the Lord said, *"when you fast."* This affirms that fasting should be a normal part of the believer's life. Second, fasting is not simply debasing one's self or appearing sad to appear spiritual to others, but rather a time of intense inner reflection and focused listening. Fasting for public display is contrary to its purpose and therefore negates its benefit. Hunger pangs remind us of our dependence on the Lord and lengthy times of introspection result in mental clarity to see things as God does. Third, Isaiah reminds us that heartfelt affliction of the soul would result in just and good conduct: the oppressed would be freed, those who were hungry would be fed, and the poor would be clothed (vv. 6-7). So, in verse 6, the prophet asks, *"Is your fasting what God has chosen?"* And then Isaiah indicates in verse 7 the type of fasting that would be acceptable to God, that which emphasizes moral transformation rather than ceremonial fanfare.

The Lord Jesus declared a similar message to hypocritical and ceremonial Israel during His first advent when He quoted Hosea 6:6 (on two different occasions): *"I desire mercy and not sacrifice"* (Matt. 9:13, 12:7). Fasting should result in a greater awareness of God's will and in a moral transformation. If our fasting does not lead to changed attitudes and behavior, then it did not achieve God's intended outcome.

Lastly, let us remember that vain, especially non-commanded, religious activities do not prompt God's blessing, but humble acts of righteousness do, because such actions reflect His glory to others (v. 8).

The Jews were to be a hospitable people, especially to their destitute brethren. Moses exhorted the nation: *"You shall not oppress one another, but you shall fear your God; for I am the Lord your God"* (Lev. 25:17). Besides our care for fellow believers in need, Solomon reminds us to also attend to the necessities of the poor in general: *"He who has pity on the poor lends to the Lord, and He will pay back what he has given"* (Prov. 19:17). *"He who gives to the poor will not lack, but he who hides his eyes will have many curses"* (Prov. 28:27). The Lord rewards those who attend to the needy, not those who fast but ignore the needy while seeking pleasure. In summary, God promised to heal His people, bless their fertility, answer their prayers, and to guide and satisfy them, if they ceased from neglecting and speaking evil of each other (vv. 9-12).

The Church would be wise to consider the Lord's rebuke of Israel's futile practices. As previously mentioned, God is not impressed by religious ritual, developed church tradition, sanctimonious form, and denominational smugness, but rather with personal living that conforms to divine truth (Col. 2:20-23). Isaiah's contemporaries were engaged in Judaism, not God-honoring, faith-produced biblical religion.

Avoid Vain Observances

Besides debasing the spiritual purposes for fasting, the Jews were also vainly honoring the Sabbath day. How one observed the Sabbath was a direct indication of a Jew's faithfulness to the Mosaic Law. Although the pattern of sanctifying the seventh day for the Lord was set up at the time of creation by God Himself (Gen. 2:1-3), it was not commanded until the Israelites were alone with God at Sinai. The fourth of the Ten Commandments issued by Moses at Sinai relates to the Sabbath day:

> *Remember the Sabbath day, to keep it holy. Six days you shall labor and do all your work, but the seventh day is the Sabbath of the Lord your God. In it you shall do no work: you, nor your son, nor your daughter, nor your male servant, nor your female servant, nor your cattle, nor your stranger who is within your gates. For in six days the Lord made the heavens and the earth, the sea, and all that is in them, and rested the seventh day. Therefore the Lord blessed the Sabbath day and hallowed it* (Ex. 20:8-11).

Sorrow and Comfort

The first four of the Ten Commandments were decreed to enable the Jews to remain loyal and devoted to Jehovah by preventing misplaced affections. Isaiah explains why honoring the Sabbath day was important to the Lord and why the Jews would be blessed if they did so:

> *If you turn away your foot from the Sabbath, from doing your pleasure on My holy day, and call the Sabbath a delight, the holy day of the Lord honorable, and shall honor Him, not doing your own ways, nor finding your own pleasure, nor speaking your own words, then you shall delight yourself in the Lord; and I will cause you to ride on the high hills of the earth, and feed you with the heritage of Jacob your father. The mouth of the Lord has spoken* (Isa. 58:13-14).

The Sabbath day, Saturday, was set aside to rest and to honor God. The Jews, their slaves, and their beasts of burden were all to rest on the Sabbath. Albert Barnes notes that the Jews were rewarded in three ways for keeping the Sabbath day holy: "(1) in great national prosperity, (2) in the lasting welfare of Jerusalem, and (3) in the wealth and piety of the people generally, indicated by their numerous sacrifices."[134] God's commands for us are always right, but sometimes what we are to do is right only because He commands it. Keeping the Sabbath day falls into the latter group, but regardless of why the commandment was issued, man is always blessed by doing what God commands. Isaiah says that those who keep the Sabbath show their delight in the Lord and will be blessed by Him. They will *"ride on the high hills of the earth"* (experience spiritual blessing) and *"feed* [on] *the heritage of Jacob"* (and enjoy earthly prosperity).

God honors those who obey His commandments. Consequently, the Sabbath day ordinance provided a simple test as to what God's people really valued – their own private affairs or what the Lord deemed important. The Lord is honored when His people remember and honor Him as requested, instead of doing what they are inclined to do for themselves on the day set aside for God. Today, the Church is not under the Law (Gal. 4:19-5:1 Rom. 7:4); in fact, the Jews are no longer under the Law either (2 Cor. 3:6-18; Heb. 8:13, 13:12-13), but the Ten Commandments still reflect God's moral standard to be lived out in His people (Rom. 3:20; Rom. 7:12-14). The Law is not dead, but we are dead to it; that is, it has no judicial hold on Christians (Rom. 7:4-6). Christians are not commanded to keep the Sabbath, but there is a principle throughout Scripture of setting aside one day in seven to honor God, and the early Church set a precedent for gathering on Sunday for this purpose.

To draw a distinction between Christianity and the Law (and, more importantly, the humanized system of Judaism derived from it), the early Church met on Sunday, rather than on Saturday. Christians continued to gather corporately on one day out of seven to worship the Lord, but they did so on the first day of the week, the day of Christ's resurrection (Acts 20:7; 1 Cor. 16:2). This day is also referred to as "the Lord's Day" by the apostle John (Rev. 1:10). Let us seek to make the Lord's Day a special day for the Lord. Saints should put aside their own personal ambitions and should gather to hear the preaching of the Word, to break bread, to pray, to encourage each other, and to engage in ministry which would draw people to Christ. The Lord's Day should be a special day for all spiritually-minded Christians – a day set aside to remember and honor the Lord with other believers. We are not under law in this matter, but we are bound by love to show our appreciation for the Lord.

Meditation

>Years I spent in vanity and pride,
>Caring not my Lord was crucified,
>Knowing not it was for me He died on Calvary.
>
>By God's Word at last my sin I learned;
>Then I trembled at the law I'd spurned,
>Till my guilty soul imploring turned to Calvary.
>
>Oh, the love that drew salvation's plan!
>Oh, the grace that brought it down to man!
>Oh, the mighty gulf that God did span at Calvary!
>
>— William Newell

God's Arm Saves
Isaiah 59

As witnessed in the previous chapter, Israel's spiritual condition was pitiful. Many were ensnared by paganism, while others were doing vain religious practices without devotion to Jehovah. Isaiah closed the last chapter with a wonderful promise of exaltation and reward for those who will delight in the Lord by walking with Him in truth (58:14). Sadly, there were few in Israel who would respond to this invitation. Because of Israel's stubborn, depraved state, it was evident that national rejuvenation and prosperity could only be obtained if God saved the nation. Subsequently, Isaiah informs his audience that God would send His arm (the Messiah) to accomplish Israel's deliverance – He would fulfill the Abrahamic Covenant.

Separated by Iniquities

It was important for the Jews to know that their God was aware of their situation, *"Nor His ear heavy, that it cannot hear"* and was able to save them – *"the Lord's hand is not shortened that it cannot save"* (v. 1). It was equally imperative for them to acknowledge their moral deficiency and their need for God to save them: *"But your iniquities have separated you from your God; and your sins have hidden His face from you so that He will not hear"* (v. 2). The prophet summarizes their depravity: they shed innocent blood, spoke lies and various perversities (v. 3); they did not pursue justice, but rather conceived how to do evil (v. 4); and they were harming each other like venomous snakes (v. 5). Just as wearing cobwebs for clothes does not adequately cover a person, God was completely aware of all their wickedness; He sees the secret things and knows the heart (v. 6). The Jews did not know the path of righteousness to experience God's peace; rather, they were rushing down evil paths to harm each other (vv. 7-8).

Paul quotes from this passage in Romans 3 when he provides a similar description of humanity's putrid and depraved state before God:

There is none righteous, no, not one; there is none who understands; there is none who seeks after God. They have all turned aside; they have together become unprofitable; there is none who does good, no, not one. Their throat is an open tomb; with their tongues they have practiced deceit. The poison of asps is under their lips. Whose mouth is full of cursing and bitterness. Their feet are swift to shed blood; destruction and misery are in their ways; and the way of peace they have not known. There is no fear of God before their eyes (Rom. 3:10-18).

The Jewish nation was in the bondage of sin and thus was separated from God without, naturally speaking, any hope of restoration (v. 2). The only solution was grace bestowed from God's own hand (v. 1) through the strength of His righteous arm (v. 16).

This imagery and the concepts it represents would not be new to Isaiah's audience. In Exodus 6, God spoke of using His outstretched arm to redeem the Hebrews and to work judgments which would deliver them from bondage (Ex. 6:6). God said He would deliver the Jews from their Egyptian captors. Yet, when Moses informed the people of God's plan, they did not believe him because of their anguish of spirit and cruel bondage (Ex. 6:9). Perhaps their rejection of Moses's message is the reason God permitted them to suffer with the Egyptians during the first three plagues, for God did not distinguish between the Hebrews and the Egyptians in His judgments until the fourth plague (Ex. 8:22). Only God can chasten His people and punish the wicked by the same rod of power.

To deliver His people from Egypt, God would redeem Israel by a Passover Lamb, which pictured the ultimate sacrifice of God's own Son, the Lamb of God, who would be judicially punished for the sins of the world (John 1:29). It would be through this redeeming Lamb that the power of God's outstretched arm would be demonstrated. As already mentioned, Isaiah uses the term "arm" a dozen times in his book to speak of God's strength to deliver and redeem His people: *"The Lord has sworn by His right hand and by the arm of His strength"* (62:8).

The Humble Confession

Though grieved over his fellow countrymen's sin, Isaiah does not assume a demeanor of superiority in order to look down his nose at them. Rather, he humbly applies the pronouns "we," "us," and "our" to

Sorrow and Comfort

identify himself with his corrupt nation deserving divine judgment (vv. 9-12).

Like Daniel and Ezra after him, Isaiah, the righteous prophet, did not hold back from confessing the sins of the nation as his own. Justice and righteousness evaded them because they were choosing to walk in darkness. Spiritually speaking, they had made themselves blind and deaf (vv. 9-10). As a result, the oppressed were growling like bears and lamenting like doves (v. 11). They longed for justice and deliverance but received none. The sins of the nation were numerous (e.g., coveting, lying, injustice, dishonesty), but Isaiah notes the worst part of their offense: *"departing from our God"* (vv. 12-15). To willfully reject God's light and to venture into darkness will always lead to our stumbling and harm.

To walk out of God's will is to step into *nowhere*.

— C. S. Lewis

God's Solution

Thankfully, God's solution for human degeneracy was not to morally reform the old nature, which will always yearn for its own way, but to impart His nature and life to deliver the afflicted from its ills. God foreknew that no condemned child of Adam could ever accomplish salvation for other sinners. Therefore, God Himself would be required to accomplish this feat: *"And He [God] saw that there was no man, and wondered that there was no intercessor; therefore, His arm brought salvation unto Him, and His righteousness it sustained Him"* (59:16). When someone was needed to stand in the gap for the Jews and for all humanity, no one was found who could righteously plead man's case because all of humanity had fallen below God's minimum requirement to come into His presence – sinless perfection. Therefore, God sent His own Arm (His Son) to be the intercessor for us: *"The Lord has made bare His holy arm in the eyes of all the nations; and all the ends of the earth shall see the salvation of our God"* (52:10).

The intercessor had to be God Himself (His own Arm). He would be the perfect sacrifice and would bear the judgment of a Holy God for all man's sin. To properly demonstrate God's power, His Holy Arm was stripped bare for all to see. Through His powerful Arm, God was

Devotions in Isaiah

promising to assist His people. This would be twofold: Spiritual salvation through His Arm's victory at Calvary, and physical deliverance from Gentile oppression at His second advent.

Verses 17-20 relate better to the latter deliverance. Like a warrior, God would charge the enemy and He would vanquish the devil, and break his hold on His people. God would flex His Arm, clothed with vengeance and zeal, and clad with righteousness for His breastplate and salvation for His helmet (v. 17). He would be victorious and would rightly recompense His enemies, those who opposed God and oppressed Israel (v. 18). What will be the outcome of God's Arm delivering Israel?

> *So shall they fear the name of the Lord from the west, and His glory from the rising of the sun; when the enemy comes in like a flood, the Spirit of the Lord will lift up a standard against him. The Redeemer will come to Zion, and to those who turn from transgression in Jacob* (vv. 19-20).

At His second coming, the Messiah will protect Israel and will execute justice on His enemies, who will be pouring into Jerusalem like a flood:

> *Behold, the day of the Lord is coming, and your spoil will be divided in your midst. For I will gather all the nations to battle against Jerusalem; the city shall be taken, the houses rifled, and the women ravished. Half of the city shall go into captivity, but the remnant of the people shall not be cut off from the city. Then the Lord will go forth and fight against those nations, as He fights in the day of battle. And in that day His feet will stand on the Mount of Olives, which faces Jerusalem on the east. And the Mount of Olives shall be split in two, from east to west, making a very large valley; half of the mountain shall move toward the north* (Zech. 14:1-4).

The Messiah will deliver and redeem the remnant of Israel who will turn to Him in repentance (v. 20). Such repentance and understanding could never be accomplished under the Law, but only through the New Covenant which will be accepted by the entire nation at Christ's Second Advent at the close of the Tribulation Period. The prophet Zechariah foretells this specific event:

Sorrow and Comfort

> *And I will pour on the house of David and on the inhabitants of Jerusalem the Spirit of grace and supplication; then they will look on Me whom they pierced. Yes, they will mourn for Him as one mourns for his only son, and grieve for Him as one grieves for a firstborn. In that day there shall be a great mourning in Jerusalem, like the mourning at Hadad Rimmon in the plain of Megiddo* (Zech. 12:10-11).

When Christ returns, the spiritual blindness of the Jewish nation will end. They will trust in the Lord Jesus Christ, their Messiah, the One they pierced two thousand years earlier and they will receive the Holy Spirit. Although individual Jews in the Old Testament were filled by the Holy Spirit in order to speak for the Lord or to serve Him effectively (e.g., Ex. 35:30-35; 1 Sam. 10:10), the nation as a whole has never been indwelt by the Spirit of God (Zech. 4:4-7). This indwelling will occur at Christ's second coming to the earth (v. 21). All this to say that God is a covenant-keeping God and His marvelous plan for the Jewish nation is still unfolding and will be completed according to His sovereign plan. A day is coming in which the Jewish nation will be restored to God and will provide a testimony of His goodness to the entire world (Hos. 14:6; Rom. 11:17-24). Then everyone will understand just how powerful God's Arm is!

Meditation

> O Christ, what burdens bowed Thy head! Our load was laid on Thee;
> Thou stoodest in the sinner's stead – to bear all ill for me.
> A victim led, Thy blood was shed, now there's no load for me.
> Jehovah lifted up His rod – O Christ, it fell on Thee!
> Thou wast sore stricken of Thy God; there's not one stroke for me.
> Thy blood beneath that rod has flowed: Thy bruising healeth me.
>
> — Ann Ross Cousin

Your Light Shall Shine
Isaiah 60

This chapter is the culmination of a unit of prophecy that began in chapter 58. J. M. Riddle observes the following outline, as pertaining to "light" in these three chapters:

> In chapter 58, darkness would give place to light, if God's people were obedient: *"Then* shall thy light break forth as the morning ... *then* shall thy light rise in obscurity, and thy darkness shall be as the noon day" (58:8, 10). In chapter 59, because of disobedience, there was no light: "we wait for light, *but* behold obscurity; for brightness, *but* we walk in darkness ... we stumble at noon day as in the night" (59:9-10). But in chapter 60, there is light in place of darkness:[135]

> *Arise, shine; for your light has come! And the glory of the Lord is risen upon you. For behold, the darkness shall cover the earth, and deep darkness the people; but the Lord will arise over you, and His glory will be seen upon you* (vv. 1-2).

The Kingdom Dawns

As noted in Isaiah 11, there are several clear distinctions between the Kingdom Age and the Eternal State which those holding an amillennial viewpoint ignore. For example, the seas and oceans we know today will still be present during the Kingdom Age (Isa. 11:9; Ezek. 47:18; Zech. 14:8), but there will be no seas in the new earth (Rev. 21:1). Furthermore, Israel is not in the land specified and the millennial tribal allotments have not been delegated yet (Ezek. 47:13-23). Likewise, geographic locations on earth today will exist in the Millennial Kingdom (Joel 3:18-19; Zech. 14:16-21), but obviously will not in the new earth. The new heaven and earth will not be created until after the Kingdom Age is concluded, Satan's last rebellion on earth is quelled (Rev. 20:7-10), and the planet we live on is destroyed (Rev. 20:11).

Sorrow and Comfort

As stated before, Peter further identifies the Kingdom Age as the Day of the Lord (2 Pet. 3:10), and the Eternal State as the Day of God (2 Pet. 3:12). At the end of the Day of the Lord (i.e., at the end of Christ's Millennial Kingdom), the heavens and the earth shall pass away with a great noise and their elements shall melt with fervent heat and be burned up (2 Pet. 3:10). Isaiah foretold that, after the Millennial Kingdom, God will create a new heaven and new earth (65:17).

Following this creative feat, Paul asserts that there will be a divine audit to confirm that Christ has completely dealt with all the negative repercussions of sin and has restored creation to perfection and to its proper association with God. All the damage caused by sin will be corrected and then God will be all in all (1 Cor. 15:26-28). It is the writer's opinion that in the eternal state, previous distinctions such as Old Testament saints, the Church, Tribulation saints, the nation of Israel, etc. will be remembered, but not emphasized. These distinctions served God's purposes in time while He was unfolding His great plan of salvation to man in various stages, but will not be significant in eternity (John 10:16; 1 Cor. 15:26-28; Rev. 21:24-27; 22:1-5).

Paul describes the future, earthly reality of this stewardship (i.e., the final dispensation) in this way: *"That in the dispensation of the fullness of the times He* [God] *might gather together in one all things in Christ, both which are in heaven and which are on earth – in Him"* (Eph. 1:10). During this thousand-year period, Christ will reign over the nations with a rod of iron (Rev. 12:5, 20:6) and, as Isaiah informs us, His glory will shine out from Jerusalem and will fill the earth (vv. 1-2; Ezek. 42:3). The nations, seeing what God has accomplished for Israel, will be attracted to this glorious light (thus, they will be drawn from spiritual darkness into the blessings of God's salvation also; v. 3).

Responding to Light

Not only will all Jews be brought back to Israel ("sons from afar") at the onset of the Kingdom Age, but redeemed Gentiles responding to God's light will also come to Israel and will bring their wealth loaded on camel caravans (vv. 4-5). The riches the Gentiles will bestow on Israel include: gold, silver, incense, and flocks and rams for sacrifices (vv. 6-7).

It is noteworthy that at Christ's first advent Gentile Magi from the east presented Him with gold, frankincense, and myrrh (Matt. 2:11). Myrrh was a burial spice and is associated with Christ's suffering and death (Mark 15:23; John 19:39). The Gentiles coming to see Christ after His second advent bring gold and incense, which symbolize His divine glory and His fragrant character, respectively, but no myrrh, which is associated with suffering, is presented. As the writer of Hebrews tells us, *"Christ was offered once to bear the sins of many. To those who eagerly wait for Him He will appear a second time, apart from sin, for salvation"* (Heb. 9:28). In His kingdom, our righteous Lord will not be associated with sin or with suffering, but rather with blessing and joy.

Some nations bringing their gifts and offerings to Jerusalem are named: Midian, Ephah, Sheba, Kedar, Nebaioth, and Tarshish (a nation known for their lucrative sea commerce; vv. 6-9). The nations will assist the Jews in rebuilding Jerusalem, as much of it will have been destroyed by the Antichrist during the Tribulation Period (v. 10). In the Millennial Kingdom, the city's gates will not need to be closed at night to secure the city, but will remain open at all times (v. 11). This is because the Lord is Jerusalem's security, and Gentile proselytes will not be hindered from coming to the temple and worshipping God.

In the Kingdom Age, the Jews will be highly esteemed by all Gentiles (vv. 12-15; Zech. 8:20-23). This worldwide favor for the Jewish people has never been realized at any time in human history. Rather, they have been displaced, conquered, and oppressed for most of their existence. Any nation not showing favor to Israel will perish in Christ's kingdom (v. 12). Rather, the nations, who once despised, hated, and afflicted the Jewish people, will come to Jerusalem to honor and support them as God's special treasure (vv. 13-15). God's covenant people will experience only joy forever once they are restored to God. Then, as Isaiah foretells, *"You shall know that I, the Lord, am your Savior and your Redeemer, the Mighty one of Jacob"* (v. 16).

From Isaiah 2:1-5 and 66:20, we learn that Jerusalem shall be the religious center of the world. The nations will bring their wealth to Jerusalem in honor of the Jews' God; Isaiah includes bronze and iron in addition to the gold and silver previously mentioned (v. 17). Christ will reign from Jerusalem and all the nations will come to praise, worship, and learn of Him and from Him. There will be no war or violence, only worldwide peace (v. 18). So great will be the glory of the Lord upon the earth that there will be no need for the sun or the moon to illuminate it (vv. 19-20). Then Israel will be righteous and will accurately display

Sorrow and Comfort

God's glory as a light to the nations, and He shall prosper them numerically and with great wealth (vv. 21-22).

Meditation

> O let your light, though little, shine out,
> Our Lord's command fulfilling,
> To live for Him wherever we go,
> And seek His will to do.
>
> O let your light shine steadily on,
> That all the world, beholding,
> May glorify your Father above,
> And praise His boundless love.
>
> O let your light shine peacefully on
> Till earthly cares are ended,
> And night and gloom shall vanish away
> In joy's eternal day.

— Fanny Crosby

Tidings of Good News
Isaiah 61

As mentioned in verse 1, it was through the ministry of the Holy Spirit that the Old Testament prophets were able to reveal the glories of the coming age (also, Ezek. 43:5; Zech. 12:10). Isaiah described the wonderful blessings of the Millennial Kingdom in the previous chapter, but in this chapter he points us to the One who will bring it all about – the anointed Servant of the Lord. His coming to Israel involved all three persons of the Godhead:

> *The Spirit of the Lord God is upon Me, because the Lord has anointed Me to preach good tidings to the poor; He has sent Me to heal the brokenhearted, to proclaim liberty to the captives, and the opening of the prison to those who are bound* (v. 1).

There have been several references by Isaiah to various persons of the Godhead and their involvement in bringing redemption and restoration to Israel (e.g. 48:16-17, 50:10-11). The person (identified as *"Me"*) speaking initially and throughout most of the chapter is Messiah Himself. He was sent by the Father to preach tidings of good news to the lost sheep of Israel. Matthew confirms that this was the mission of Jesus Christ:

> *From that time Jesus began to preach and to say, "Repent, for the kingdom of heaven is at hand." ... And Jesus went about all Galilee, teaching in their synagogues, preaching the gospel of the kingdom, and healing all kinds of sickness and all kinds of disease among the people* (Matt. 4:17, 23).

The Father anointed the Lord Jesus with the Holy Spirit to enable His work to be effectual, a matter that Matthew again verifies:

> *When He had been baptized, Jesus came up immediately from the water; and behold, the heavens were opened to Him, and He saw the*

Sorrow and Comfort

> *Spirit of God descending like a dove and alighting upon Him. And suddenly a voice came from heaven, saying, "This is My beloved Son, in whom I am well pleased"* (Matt. 3:16-17).

Two Days

However, the most compelling evidence that Messiah is speaking in this chapter is that the Lord Jesus read verse 1 and the first half of verse 2 while in a synagogue in Nazareth. Then He publicly confirmed that the passage was in reference to Himself:

> *And He was handed the book of the prophet Isaiah. And when He had opened the book, He found the place where it was written: "The Spirit of the Lord is upon Me, because He has anointed Me to preach the gospel to the poor; He has sent Me to heal the brokenhearted, to proclaim liberty to the captives and recovery of sight to the blind, to set at liberty those who are oppressed; to proclaim the acceptable year of the Lord." Then He closed the book, and gave it back to the attendant and sat down. And the eyes of all who were in the synagogue were fixed on Him. And He began to say to them, "Today this Scripture is fulfilled in your hearing"* (Luke 4:17-21).

The Jews understood that the Lord was claiming to be the One Isaiah was prophesying of (v. 22); however, they became enraged and sought to push Him over a cliff when afterwards He spoke of going to the Gentiles. The Lord did not read the remaining portion of verse 2 or verse 3, as that content pertained to His second advent, when He will return to judge the nations and restore Israel to a proper place of honor:

> *And the day of vengeance of our God; to comfort all who mourn, to console those who mourn in Zion, to give them beauty for ashes, the oil of joy for mourning, the garment of praise for the spirit of heaviness; that they may be called trees of righteousness, the planting of the Lord, that He may be glorified* (vv. 2-3).

Verses 1-3 again unfold to us God's great plan of salvation for Israel and for humanity. Thankfully, Christ did not come two thousand years ago to invoke *"the day of God's vengeance."* Rather, He came to seek and to save the lost (Luke 19:10). Nor would it be the appropriate time to console and restore Israel, for the nation would reject Him. *"Beauty for ashes, the oil of joy for mourning, the garment of praise for the spirit of heaviness"* foretells the end of Israel's suffering forever, and the joy and comfort they will receive when Messiah sets up His kingdom. Until then, the lost sheep of Israel will continue to wander in faraway places, but the Jews are destined to be planted as trees of righteousness in the Promised Land for God's glory. By referring to only the first part of this passage, the Lord shows us that He fully understood that God's plan of salvation would require two advents to the earth to complete.

Much of Israel's infrastructure will have been destroyed by the end of the Tribulation Period. With the dawning of the Kingdom Age, the nations will gladly assist the rebuilding of Israel and her cities (v. 4). Ezekiel foretold that many of these destroyed cities would, in fact, be rebuilt and resettled in exactly the same locations after God gathers His covenant people back to their homeland. Today, there are many cities in Israel that bear the ancient names of previous biblical cities: Cana, Nazareth, Jericho, Nain, Bethany, Bethlehem, Hebron, Gaza, etc. This is a testimony that God has honored part of Ezekiel's prophecy:

And I will multiply upon you man and beast; and they shall increase and bring fruit: and I will settle you after your old estates, and will do better [unto you] than at your beginnings: and ye shall know that I [am] the Lord.... For I will take you from among the heathen, and gather you out of all countries, and will bring you into your own land (Ezek. 36:11, 24).

Notice that the Lord Jesus put a curse on some Jewish cities, such as Capernaum, Bethsaida, and Chorazin, for their rejection of His message (Luke 10:13-16). Only a few ruins remain of those ancient Jewish cities today. According to God's prophetic word, several cities in Israel today are called by their ancient names; however, those specifically cursed by Christ do not exist.

Not only will Gentiles assist the Jewish nation to rebuild her cities and infrastructure, they will also work to reestablish Israel's agricultural prosperity (v. 5). Additionally, the wealth of the nations shall flow into Israel, and the Jews shall reflect the glory of God back to the nations. This was God's intention for them all along: *"But you shall be named the priests of the Lord, they shall call you the servants of our God"* (v. 6). However, this does not mean that every Jew can offer animal sacrifices on the Bronze Altar in the temple courtyard or sweet incense on the Golden Altar in the temple. Ezekiel tells us that only the Levitical priests who were descendants of Zadok could enter

Sorrow and Comfort

God's sanctuary and offer sacrifices to Him on behalf of the people (Ezek. 40:15-16).

Zadok was a faithful priest and loyal both to King David and then to King Solomon (1 Kgs. 1:26-27; 1 Chron. 29:33). Zadok was the first high priest to oversee Solomon's temple and now his descendants would have an honored position of authority within God's Millennial Temple. The Lord indeed rewards faithfulness. There will actually be two rooms on either side of the inner courtyard in the Millennial Temple set aside for these ministering priests (Ezek. 40:44-46). Prophets represent God to the people, while priests represent the people to God. It is this latter ministry that the Jewish nation will engage in on behalf of the nations. Israel will reflect the character of God to all people and because the Jews will enjoy such a wonderful, close association with God, everyone will seek to be blessed by honoring them.

In the Jewish culture, the firstborn son would receive a double portion of his deceased father's estate and would be honored as the new family/clan leader (Deut. 21:17). During the Kingdom Age, the nation of Israel will no longer suffer shame and confusion, but will have the "double honor" place of blessing and esteem among the nations (v. 7). When the nations see all that God has done for Israel and understand that He has conferred on her an "everlasting covenant," all the nations will agree that the Jews are a special people to the Lord (vv. 8-9; Zech. 8:23).

The Bridegroom Rejoices

Commentators see either the Messiah, or the redeemed remnant, or Isaiah as the speaker in verses 10-11.

> *I will greatly rejoice in the Lord, my soul shall be joyful in my God; for He has clothed me with the garments of salvation, He has covered me with the robe of righteousness, as a bridegroom decks himself with ornaments, and as a bride adorns herself with her jewels. For as the earth brings forth its bud, as the garden causes the things that are sown in it to spring forth, so the Lord God will cause righteousness and praise to spring forth before all the nations* (vv. 10-11).

If the speaker is Christ, then the idea is that the Victor, who is adorned in garments of righteous vengeance (59:17), is leading the redeemed remnant in joyful praise to God. This understanding reflects the fulfillment of David's messianic prophecy: *"I will declare Your name to My brethren; in the midst of the assembly I will praise You"* (Ps. 22:22).

Another possibility is that the redeemed, who have experienced God's full salvation, are interjecting their joyful praise in verses 10-11. Their excitement is likened to that of a bride and groom on their wedding day. But the difference is that the attire the remnant is adorned with was provided by the Lord. In springtime, a sown garden sprouts up with new life, likewise *"the Lord God will cause righteousness and praise to spring forth before all the nations"* because the Jewish people will promptly lead the effort (v. 11).

Regardless of who the speaker is in verses 10-11, both the above ideas are scripturally correct: Christ, the Victor, will lead the Jewish remnant (all of whom are clothed in righteous garments which He provided) in praise to God and they, in turn, will be an example that the nations will follow. There is a practical lesson that believers today can learn from Israel's past and prophetically foretold future: God prefers us to wear garments of salvation and righteousness now which reflect experiencing God in a tangible way, rather than being clothed with worthless deeds and shameful doings.

On this point, the rebuke of the Lord Jesus to the Church at Laodicea is most pertinent: *"You are wretched, miserable, poor, blind, and naked – I counsel you to buy from Me gold refined in the fire, that you may be rich; and white garments, that you may be clothed, that the shame of your nakedness may not be revealed; and anoint your eyes with eye salve, that you may see"* (Rev. 3:17-18). Those in the Church at Laodicea were not living for Christ; consequently, God's righteousness was not displayed in their lives. Though all believers in the Church have been declared positionally righteous in Christ, each believer has the opportunity to labor in righteous acts for Christ. Those things which are done in accordance with revealed truth and in the power of the Spirit have eternal value; these righteous acts are what the believer is adorned with throughout eternity. In heaven, the bride of Christ must have righteous attire; she is *"arrayed in fine linen, clean and bright, for the fine linen is the righteous acts of the saints"* (Rev. 19:8).

Paul explains in 1 Corinthians 15:40-42 that after the resurrection, some saints will shine forth the glory of God more brightly than others, just as some stars in the nighttime sky are more luminous than other stars. This acquired glory will directly reflect the good works that were done for Christ by His strength in this present life. Eternal glory, evidently, has a weight to it (2 Cor. 4:17); in other words, its quality is measurable and can be earned by believers through selfless service for Christ now. At the judgment seat of Christ, everyone worthy of God's praise shall receive it (1 Cor. 4:5). While the church at Laodicea was spiritually naked (i.e. they had no righteous acts for clothing), the Holy Spirit does bear fruit in the life of the individual "overcomer" (Rev. 3:18, 21). Though believers will suffer varying degrees of loss at the judgment seat of Christ, all will have the praise of God and are thus guaranteed righteous attire for eternity (1 Cor. 4:5).

The appropriate clothing for eternity is obtained through righteous acts; may all believers work now to secure for themselves a covering of eternal glory. Acts of righteousness done now will endow believers with a corresponding measure of glory in heaven (1 Cor. 15:41-42; 2 Cor. 4:17). Endeavoring to worship God through any means or method other than what His Word authorizes does not contribute to one's eternal attire. Israel has shown us that religious doings do not impress God, nor do they have any eternal value. The garments of praise, salvation, and righteousness are fitting attire for all saints of every age (vv. 3, 10).

Meditation

>We shall walk with Him in white,
>In that country pure and bright,
>Where shall enter naught that may defile;
>Where the day-beam never declines,
>For the blessed light that shines
>Is the glory of a Savior's smile.
>
>We shall walk with Him in white,
>Where faith yields to blissful sight,
>When the beauty of the King we see;
>Holding converse full and sweet,
>In a fellowship complete;
>Waking songs of holy melody.

— Eliza Hewitt

Beulah Land
Isaiah 62

Much of this chapter expresses the Lord's anticipation of and preparation for reestablishing Israel at His second coming. Messiah's resolve in this matter is wonderfully expressed in verses 1-7. He commences with a petition to God: *"For Zion's sake I will not hold My peace, and for Jerusalem's sake I will not rest, until her righteousness goes forth as brightness, and her salvation as a lamp that burns"* (v. 1). He concludes with instruction to the Jewish remnant: *"And give Him no rest till He establishes and till He makes Jerusalem a praise in the earth"* (v. 7).

Messiah's Appeal

Messiah's requests and instructions in verses 1-7 adamantly refute the *Replacement Theology* held by some Christians. In summary, this idea denies the Jews any opportunity of divine restoration as God's covenant people, or a peaceful residence in the Promised Land, or a status of honor in Christ's future kingdom. This view claims that since the Jews rejected their Messiah, God is finished with them. Thus, all God's covenant promises to the Jews have been fully transferred to those who would later be redeemed by Christ (mainly Gentiles), effectively leaving the nation of Israel with only God's curses. Yet, God declares that He will not rest until the above blessings have been accomplished for the Jewish nation.

The reference to Israel as a bright lamp shining forth righteousness and salvation is reminiscent of the scene in Genesis 15 when God instituted an unconditional covenant with Abraham. God passed through the midst of the animal pieces alone: *"A smoking furnace and a burning lamp that passed between those pieces"* (Gen. 15:17; KJV). The story of Israel from the time of Abraham can be summed up in these two figures – the "smoking furnace" and the "burning lamp." The *smoking furnace* represents those dark periods of time when Israel was being refined through suffering and fiery trials (Jer. 11:4). The *lamp*

Sorrow and Comfort

pictures those bright spots in Israel's history when Jehovah directly intervened to deliver a repentant Israel from aggression, captivity, and evil, which is how Isaiah is portraying Israel in verse 1. The thicker and darker the smoke, the brighter the lamp would seem during times of restoration. Certainly this would characterize Israel's awesome deliverance by Christ at the end of the Tribulation Period.

Jerusalem's glory will be so brilliant, by contrast, that the Gentiles will be astounded (v. 2). The city will be so different in demeanor that God will give it a new name. In ancient times, names were often given in association with an individual's character; hence, the meaning here is that Jerusalem will be so changed that it will required a new name to reflect the city's holy and royal glory: *"You shall also be a crown of glory in the hand of the Lord, and a royal diadem in the hand of your God"* (v. 3).

Man was originally created to rule over the world and to reflect the glory of God's likeness and image. For this reason, the writer of Hebrews affirms that God crowned humanity with glory and honor and set him over what God had created (Heb. 2:7). While the Church today represents the glory of the Lord, our citizenship is heavenly, but in a coming day, Israel will regain the glory and honor set aside for them on earth. Thus, Jerusalem will be *"a crown of glory"* and *"a royal diadem"* in the hand of God. What was lost in Eden will be restored and bettered in the Kingdom Age.

Although "Israel" is not specifically named, the people associated with Jerusalem are clearly at the center of this prophetic prayer. They will no longer be called "Forsaken" and "Desolate" but *"Hephzibah, and your land Beulah"* (v. 4). *Hephzibah* means "my delight is in her" and *Beulah* means "married one." Both names speak of God's enjoyment in the Jewish nation being fully restored to Him: His once adulterous wife (whom He had divorced and forsaken) is now cleansed of her impurities and will remain faithful to Him forever. In that day, Jerusalem will be rebuilt and filled with the restored remnant who are excited to be there. This is poetically conveyed by the phrase *"So shall your sons marry you* [Jerusalem]*"* (v. 5).

Some have difficulty reconciling Israel being Jehovah's restored wife with the teaching that the Church is the Bride of Christ (2 Cor. 11:2; Eph. 5:25-32) and the Lamb's wife, as seen in the New Jerusalem (Rev. 19:21-22). Two explanations are possible: First, the Bride coming down from heaven in the New Jerusalem probably includes other redeemed believers besides just those from the Church Age – as certainly Old Testament saints and Tribulation saints will have already experienced the First Resurrection by that time (Heb. 11:40; Rev. 20:4). This is not to say that these believers compose the Church, but rather they are part of the general congregation of the redeemed, called the *Bride,* which are all those adorning the New Jerusalem with the grace of God:

> *But you have come to Mount Zion and to the city of the living God, the heavenly Jerusalem, to an innumerable company of angels, to the general assembly and church of the firstborn who are registered in heaven, to God the Judge of all, to the spirits of just men made perfect, to Jesus the Mediator of the new covenant* (Heb. 12:22-23).

William Kelly offers a second explanation to the distinction between the restored wife of Jehovah (the Jewish nation) and the Bride of Christ:

> One speaks of what is for heaven, the other for the earth. And what hinders there being an object especially dear on high and another here below in that day? But there is no confusion of the two in Scripture. … Both are true, but their spheres are as distinct as the objects themselves, as the character of the relation which Christ bears to each, and even as the languages in which they are respectively revealed. To confound them is to deny the future hopes of Israel, and to lose the heavenly place of the church. The church has never been forsaken of God; while Zion unquestionably has; nor have we as members of the glorified Christ another fatherland but heaven, which cannot be termed desolate. Apply the language to Israel, and all is clear and unequivocal, without doing violence to a single expression.[136]

Whether the heavenly Bride associated with the New Jerusalem can be the Church exclusively is doubtful in the writer's opinion, as the scene likely relates to the Eternal State where distinctions among the redeemed appear not to be emphasized. However, the spiritual distinction between Israel (which has an earthly sphere of blessing) and the Church (which enjoys a heavenly sphere of blessing, including reigning with Christ on earth) is observed throughout Scripture. In the Kingdom Age, Jerusalem and Israel shall have a position under their King beyond every other place and people on earth. But the glorified Church will have a higher and nearer relationship to Christ, as shown

Sorrow and Comfort

through the limitations placed on Israel's approach to Jehovah in the Millennial Temple, described by Ezekiel (Ezek. 40-47).

This distinction between Israel and the Church can be traced all the way back to the call of Abraham, the spiritual father of all who will be redeemed (Rom. 4:16-17, 9:7-8). God spoke to Jacob in a dream and reconfirmed the covenant He had made with Abraham and Isaac (Gen. 28:14). Jacob was promised seed that would be as the *dust of the earth*. But when God spoke to Isaac, he was promised descendants as numerous as the *stars of heaven* (Gen. 26:4). Abraham, in whom the covenant was established, was promised both (Gen. 22:17). Why the difference? Because Isaac represents the resurrected Christ who has inherited a heavenly land and Jacob represents the expansion of the nation of Israel, which will inherit an earthly land during the Millennium.

Until the time of their restoration, the Jews are to be like watchmen stationed on the walls of a city (v. 6). Watchmen do not sleep, but are continually alert for approaching invaders. In other words, the faithful remnant was not to rest, or permit God to rest, by actively looking for and praying for the fulfillment of God's promises: *"Give Him no rest till He establishes and till He makes Jerusalem a praise in the earth"* (v. 7). Clear statements such as this in Scripture confer hope on the faithful Jewish remnant to bear up under centuries of oppression. The psalmist, for example, had great confidence that God would honor His covenant with David, which He reiterates and the congregation rejoices to hear (Ps. 132:11-18). Zion will again be filled with the glory of the Lord, Israel's enemies will be put to shame, and a descendant of David will occupy the throne in Jerusalem. This prayer has not been fully realized, as war and desolations are determined against the Jews until their previously "cut off" Messiah (Dan. 9:25-27) returns to crush the satanic rebellion that threatens their existence. Then, the prophesied Heir of David will rule in Zion over His people forever (vv. 6-7; Zech. 14:16-17).

God's Answer

Why can Israel be assured that the above blessings will come about? Because *"the Lord has sworn by His right hand and by the arm of His strength"* that there is a day coming in which the Jews will never again suffer loss or be oppressed (vv. 8-9). As previously mentioned, the prophet Isaiah uses the term "arm" frequently to speak of God's strength to deliver and redeem His people through His Servant, the Messiah. When God swears an oath by His own name and by His Son, there is nothing in the entire universe which will prevent Him from doing exactly what He says He will do!

This absolute assurance of things coming should prompt the urgency conveyed by the expressions in verse 10: "go through" (twice), "prepare the way," "build up" (twice), "take out," and "lift up." The Lord is on His way to set things right (speaking of the Kingdom Age), so the Jews should prepare themselves spiritually now and not wait for His physical coming: *"Say to the daughter of Zion, 'Surely your salvation is coming; behold, His reward is with Him, and His work before Him'"* (v. 11). The Lord's reward for faithfulness and His work of blessing and exalting Israel should excite the Jewish remnant to keep pressing on.

When Israel is restored to God, they will be known as *"The Holy People – the Redeemed of the Lord"* (v. 12). When Jerusalem is rebuilt and inhabited again, she will be called (besides the names mentioned in verse 4) *"Sought Out,"* and *"A City Not Forsaken"* (v. 12). All the future names for the Jewish people and for Jerusalem convey the certainty of what will be, and that God is moving, even now, to make it all happen. There is a day coming when all the saints of God will witness these events and will see God's glory in Beulah Land!

Meditation

Oh, my cup is overflowing
With the goodness of the Lord;
I am trusting in His mercy,
And rejoicing in His Word.

From the sighing and the longing,
That so oft my heart oppressed,
With my Savior and Redeemer
Now in perfect peace I rest.

I have climbed the rugged mountain,
On its summit now I stand;
Hallelujah! Hallelujah!
I have entered Beulah land.

— Fanny Crosby

The Day of Vengeance
Isaiah 63

The escalating anticipation of the Messiah's coming in the last chapter is now realized: *"For the day of vengeance is in My heart and the year of My redeemed has come"* (v. 4). Often people seek their own vengeance and do more harm to themselves than the person they wanted to harm. But when God executes vengeance, there can be only a terrible outcome for the recipient.

Notice that the order of days is reversed in verse 4 as compared to chapter 61, when the Lord Jesus came preaching tidings of peace during His first advent: *"To proclaim the acceptable year of the Lord, and the day of vengeance of our God"* (61:2). The opportunity to receive Christ and to be forgiven has passed. Now the Lord will judge the Antichrist and all the wicked on the earth, before establishing His kingdom for His redeemed.

So when the Lord does arrive in Israel, the remnant will ask Him two questions which Isaiah poses in synonymous parallelism: First, *"Who is this who comes from Edom, with dyed garments from Bozrah, this one who is glorious in His apparel, traveling in the greatness of His strength?"* (v. 1). Second, *"Why is Your apparel red, and Your garments like one who treads in the winepress?"* (v. 2). The answer to both questions is the same and is revealed in verses 3-6. Indeed, the Lord will have trodden down the grapes of His wrath in His winepress.

Edom and Bozrah, a city in Edom, are mentioned as being the grapes. Edom, as discussed in chapter 34 was a wicked nation southeast of the Dead Sea that often oppressed Israel throughout its early history. The Hebrew word *Edom* means "red." The father of the Edomites was Esau, who at birth *"came out red. He was like a hairy garment all over; so they called his name Esau"* (Gen. 25:25). Years later, he sold his birthright to Jacob for a bowl of "red stew," *"therefore his name was called Edom"* (Gen. 25:30). Prophetically speaking, Esau's descendants were destined to see red (i.e., their own blood) when God's Arm arrives to execute His wrath on the rebel nations (vv. 5-6). All who follow Esau's carnal example of living for selfish gain and for the moment, instead of for God's glory and eternity, will be judged.

Just as workers trample grapes in a winepress and get splashed with the juice, the Lord will be spattered with the blood of the wicked at the Battle of Armageddon, a scene that both Zechariah and John vividly describe (see discussion in chapter 29). When the Lord descends from heaven, His royal attire will already be stained with blood, which likely anticipates the bloodshed to occurring during the forthcoming confrontation (Rev. 19:13). As William Kelly explains this will be the day of the Lord's vengeance (61:2):

> Here it is Jehovah-Messiah executing unsparing judgement on earth, treading the peoples in His anger and trampling them in His wrath. Those who cavil at this as inconsistent with His holy goodness betray their own rebelliousness and the bad conscience which dreads His day at length, when He summarily puts down the iniquity which has so long destroyed the earth. When divine vengeance has done its necessary and righteous work with the peoples and enemies of Israel, the ways of God succeed in goodness, and the godly remnant, His people, testify to them with praise, as we shall next hear.[137]

When the Lord arrives in Israel, He will be wearing a fabulous royal robe stained red with the blood of the nations. This will visibly acknowledge His triumph over the Antichrist and his armies. He will be mighty and victorious in executing God's wrath on those who have afflicted His covenant people.

The Prayer of the Distraught Remnant

The first six verses describing Christ's victorious entrance into Jerusalem are the highpoint of this chapter. Knowing that Israel has such a glorious future should instill a sense of hopeful expectation in those suffering ongoing hardship. Isaiah had a particular interest in encouraging future exiled Jews in Babylon not to give up hope, but to wait for the Lord's deliverance through Cyrus. Some commentators, such as M. C. Unger, suggest that Isaiah is recording this prayer to inspire the Jewish remnant suffering during the Tribulation Period to wait patiently for Messiah to execute vengeance on their enemies. While this is possible, the language in verses 18-19, and at the close of the prayer (64:10-12), seems to better fit the nearer-term crisis in Babylon (about a hundred years into the future).

Sorrow and Comfort

Though the Jews, later in Babylon, would remember how God delivered their forefathers from Egypt, in general, they would not choose to rely on the Lord during their crisis. This is why, despite the presence of the faithful remnant, there is a hopeless tenor that often invades the prayer uttered by the exiled Jews in Babylon (63:7-64:12). The prayer is clearly prophetic in nature; Isaiah is writing what the Jews will be praying (or in some cases should be praying) while still under God's chastening hand in Babylon. The contents of this prayer should encourage Jews during future times of suffering, especially during the Tribulation Period, to evaluate their attitudes. While which Jewish remnant is actually uttering this prayer is debatable, the application of trusting in God's word and character is timeless.

The prayer commences by acknowledging God's tender mercies and loving-kindnesses shown to the Jewish nation by redeeming and delivering them from Egypt (vv. 7-9). God's arm, the Angel (or Messenger) of His presence was strong in Egypt to deliver His people. *The Angel of His presence* is the same as "the Angel (or Messenger) of the Lord" – a theophany of Christ, and thus the same Servant-Messiah that Isaiah has been speaking of throughout his book. Despite God's deliverance of His people from Egypt and His goodness to them in the wilderness, Israel rebelled against the Lord, which grieved the Holy Spirit (vv. 10-11). As a result, God fought against (chastened) His people through calamities, distresses, and invasion.

Isaiah's statement of rebelling against God and grieving the Holy Spirit is significant. First, clearly two Persons of the Godhead are in view, and second, the Spirit of God is not just a force or influence of God, but Someone who can be offended. The children of Israel will realize that grieving the Holy Spirit brings disastrous ramifications. The same truth is presented in the New Testament for believers in the Church Age.

On several occasions the Lord Jesus told His disciples that only good trees bear good fruit, and, likewise, that bad trees produce according to their nature (Matt. 7:17). His point was that a true believer is known by his or her fruit in the same way that *"a tree is known by its fruit"* (Matt. 12:33). Apple trees do not produce pears; they bear only apples. True Christians will be characterized by the fruit of the Spirit, not by works of the flesh. While it is true that not every Christian matures as he or she ought, every genuine child of God will grow and bear fruit to some extent; this is evidence of salvation (Jas. 2:17).

Devotions in Isaiah

Various reasons for a lack of maturity are possible. The sluggish believer may not be spending time in the Word of God as he or she ought, due to a preoccupation with temporal things and activities. They may not be serious about keeping short accounts with God by expediently confessing sin. All these carnal behaviors grieve and quench the Holy Spirit (Eph. 4:30; 1 Thess. 5:19). As believers, we do not want the Holy Spirit to oppose us, but rather to fill and control all that we do. Then we will be channels of grace streaming out to a world that desperately needs to see Christ.

Sadly, though Israel remembered God's strong deliverance from Egypt and how He provided them rest and daily guidance in the wilderness, the nation, for much of their history, chose to rebel against the Lord (vv. 11-14). Despite this fact, Isaiah, prophetically speaking, says that the nation (later in Babylon) will ask God why He has forgotten them and why He has restrained His compassion (v. 15). They will plead with God to be merciful to them as He was to their forefathers in Egypt – as if God had somehow forgotten about Israel and had to be reminded of His past mercy towards His covenant people (v. 16).

Verse 17 poses a startling appeal: *"O Lord, why have You made us stray from Your ways, and hardened our heart from Your fear?* (v. 17). Were the exiled remnant in such a spiritually despondent state that they accused God of leading them into sin, which resulted in their present hardship? Possibly, or they may be conveying a rhetorical question in regard to recognizing their past waywardness: "Given all that we, Your people, have suffered, why did You permit us to stray from Your ways?" Nonetheless, they knew that God was not responsible for their straying. Besides that, it is never a good idea to blame God for our difficulties – we choose our sin and He chooses the consequences for our sins. Sometimes, after we have learned a lesson in the school of hard knocks, God will extend mercy to alleviate the situation. But we must remember that the Lord is not obliged to show mercy. We should therefore be thankful when He does and we should not complain when He does not intervene at the exact moment we think He should.

Regardless of what the intended meaning of verse 17 is, the Jews in Babylon will ask the Lord to return them to their inheritance in Israel. They even cite the destruction of His temple as a legitimate cause for invoking God to take action on their behalf (v. 18). These exiled Jews realized that God established them as a people a long time ago, and also

Sorrow and Comfort

that it had been a long time since they were in a proper relationship with Him because they had not submitted to His rule (v. 19).

Meditation

> Wake, harp of Zion, wake again,
> Upon thine ancient hill,
> On Jordan's long deserted plain,
> By Kedron's lowly rill.
>
> The hymn shall yet in Zion swell,
> That sounds Messiah's praise,
> And thy loved Name, Emmanuel,
> As once in ancient days.
>
> For Israel yet shall own her King,
> For her salvation waits,
> And hill and dale shall sweetly sing,
> With praise in all her gates.
>
> O hasten, Lord, these promised days,
> When Israel shall rejoice,
> And Jew and Gentile join in praise,
> With one united voice!

— James Edmeston

A Second Request
Isaiah 64

The suffering Jewish remnant (those would suffer in Babylon) continue their prayer from the last chapter. Isaiah is declaring this prayer prophetically to encourage future generations and to reprove their possibly wrong attitudes. The remnant will plead with God for deliverance from oppression (vv. 1-4), they will acknowledge their own sinful disposition (vv. 5-7) and then confess their trust in the Lord (vv. 8-12). God will respond to this prayer in the next chapter (Isa. 65).

Intervention Sought

The remnant's bleak situation is evident by the extreme poetic language employed in their desperate plea. In the last chapter, they requested the Lord to:

> *Look down from heaven, and see from Your habitation, holy and glorious. Where are Your zeal and Your strength, the yearning of Your heart and Your mercies toward me? Are they restrained?* (63:15).

However, in utter desperation they now plead with God: *"Oh, that You would rend the heavens! That You would come down! That the mountains might shake at Your presence"* (v. 1). Albert Barnes describes what the phrase "rend the heaven" means:

> The phrase "rend the heavens," implies a sudden and sublime descent of Yahweh to execute vengeance on His foes, as if His heart was full of vengeance, and the firmament were violently rent asunder at His sudden appearance.[138]

Looking down to notice is much different than moving heaven and earth to deliver them from their enemies, which were also His enemies. The *"awesome things"* requested (i.e., supernatural intervention) would

Sorrow and Comfort

likely include overwhelming floods, fire from heaven, earthquakes, windstorms, etc. If God did make His presence known on the earth, then their enemies would be vanquished in a burning inferno, or a turbulent upheaval, as in a boiling pot (vv. 2-3).

Jehovah is a revealing God and the only true God. He acts on behalf of those who trust in Him, as evidenced by their obedience to Him: *"For since the beginning of the world men have not heard nor perceived by the ear, nor has the eye seen any God besides You, who acts for the one who waits for Him"* (v. 4). God has revealed Himself and His mysterious ways to humanity in a variety of ways through the ages (e.g. creation, conscience, miracles, etc.). Of special benefit is God's Word to us through the prophets of old and through the apostles in the infancy of the Church Age. Paul, quoting this portion of Isaiah, explains this wonderful fact:

> *But as it is written: "Eye has not seen, nor ear heard, nor have entered into the heart of man the things which God has prepared for those who love Him." But God has revealed them to us through His Spirit. For the Spirit searches all things, yes, the deep things of God. For what man knows the things of a man except the spirit of the man which is in him? Even so no one knows the things of God except the Spirit of God. Now we have received, not the spirit of the world, but the Spirit who is from God, that we might know the things that have been freely given to us by God* (1 Cor. 2:9-12).

These verses are often quoted in reference to the future, incomprehensible wonders of heaven, but that is not the context in which Paul uses it. Rather, as F. B. Hole explains, his focus is on what *"God has revealed"* to us.

> To this verse the Apostle Paul referred in 1 Corinthians 2:9, showing that though in ordinary matters men arrive at knowledge by the hearing of the ear – **tradition** – or by the eye – **observation** – or by what we may call **intuition**, these things can only reach us by **revelation** from God by His Spirit. Isaiah knew that there were things to be revealed. Paul tells us that they have been revealed, so that we may know them.[139]

What was not revealed to Israel concerning salvation has been disclosed to the Church, who, through the indwelling Holy Spirit, has the opportunity to understand the deeper things of God. At the time

Isaiah delivered God's messages, Israel knew that God loved them and was for them, but did not understand how or when He would demonstrate His power in delivering them from sorrow.

Unworthy of Help

With this understanding, the faithful remnant knew that God would not intervene for them until the nation confessed their sins, such as uncleanness, weakness, and lack of prayer (vv. 5-7). While aspects of the remnant's prayer are certainly self-focused, their confession of sin, that their suffering was because of their sin, and that they were unable to achieve any kind of spiritual remedy is refreshing. God honors such prayers of genuine humility. The suffering remnant had nowhere else to turn; they were desperate for God and for Him to faithfully act on His promises. The remnant declared their depravity to their Creator, and that the sum of all their good works was just filthiness to Him. As a result of understanding their condition, they call on God to save them.

The fallen nature of man enslaves him to sin (Rom. 6:19), and thus he will naturally endeavor to pull others under its influence and to enslave them too. As a result, natural man yearns to control and to use others for his advantage, rather than to serve and assist them. Even when natural man does assist others, it is still unacceptable to God because his motivation is impure; he either desires to gain something from his effort, to earn spiritual promotion, or to merit some reward. This is all humanized religion, but the fact remains that outside of Christ man can do nothing to please God: *"But to those who are defiled and unbelieving nothing is pure; but even their mind and conscience are defiled. They profess to know God, but in works they deny Him, being abominable, disobedient, and disqualified for every good work"* (Tit. 1:15-16).

Consequently, the sum of all the good works a sinner does in his lifetime is still counted as filthy rags to God. Understanding this truth, the remnant exclaims: *"But we are all like an unclean thing, and all our righteousnesses are like filthy rags; we all fade as a leaf, and our iniquities, like the wind, have taken us away"* (v. 6). Barnes comments, "No language could convey deeper abhorrence of their deeds of righteousness than this reference – it is undoubtedly to the *vestis menstruis polluta* [used menstruation rags]."[140] Just as a powerful storm blows away the leaves of trees, the remnant realized that they had been swept away by their own sins.

Sorrow and Comfort

Verse 6 illustrates just how offensive our sin is to God and also how putrid to Him are all our "good works" apart from His enablement and control. Today, people often minimize or excuse their sin with expressions such as: "I did my best, but that was not good enough," "I didn't mean to do anything wrong," "I just made a mistake" or "God made me this way." Sometimes, errors and failures are not sinful in nature, but it is morally wrong to label what is sin merely as "an error in judgment." Solomon tells us the danger of not being real with God about the matter of sin: *"He who covers his sins will not prosper, but whoever confesses and forsakes them will have mercy"* (Prov. 28:13). God's Word shows us what sin is and also how deceitful and offensive it is to God, that we might know that only He can establish a just means of forgiving sinners.

To this end, God's Law showed the depravity of man before man understood that he was depraved. It was the Law that caused Paul to realize that coveting was a sin and also that he lacked the wherewithal to stop coveting. He concludes, *"For I know that in me (that is, in my flesh) nothing good dwells; for to will is present with me, but how to perform what is good I do not find"* (Rom. 7:18). In our natural state, apart from God's salvation, we are hopelessly lost – like the destitute remnant, *"we need to be saved"* not only from the penalty of sin, but also from its power over us. Neither the unregenerate man in the flesh, nor the believer in the flesh can please God (Rom. 8:8)!

Consequently, all that man does apart from Christ (speaking of His propitiatory sacrifice and His enablement through the Holy Spirit; Rom. 8:9-14) has no value to God – in fact, it is insulting to Him. Every child of God must remember that, though we are saved by grace through the blood of Christ, we cannot worship or serve the Lord apart from the continual energizing power of the Holy Spirit (Phil. 3:3). Reliance on human wisdom, on the strength of the flesh, or on vain religiosity will be futile substitutes for that real spiritual power which has the capacity to fill the world with the aroma of Christ. We rest in Christ alone for salvation and all that matters during this life is that He be magnified in all things (Phil. 1:20-21).

The prophet grieves, on behalf of the faithful remnant, that so few Jews were moved to earnestly beseech the Lord to act on their behalf and to honor His name: *"There is no one who calls on Your name, who stirs himself up to take hold of You; for You have hidden Your face from us, and have consumed us because of our iniquities"* (v. 7). F. B.

Hole observes that the same lethargic attitude grips the Church today (referring to the Church in the first half of the 20th century):

> Further the prophet had to complain that no one was rightly moved by this state of things, so as to call upon the name of God; no one was found to take hold of God in supplication and prayer. The fact was that God had hid His face from them in His holy government. It was a sad state of affairs when no one was stirred to take the place of an intercessor.
>
> And without a doubt we may say the same as we look on the state of Christendom today. Bright spots there are, thank God! – spots where the Spirit of God is manifestly at work. But in spite of this, the picture over-all is a dark one. Evil abounds under the profession of Christ's name, and even where the Spirit of God is working, wholehearted servants of God are all too few. Who stirs himself up to take hold of God? Who prays to the Lord of the harvest, that He will send forth laborers into His harvest? – as the Lord Himself directed in Matthew 9:38. May God Himself stir us up, instead of hiding His face from us, if we fail to stir ourselves up in this matter.[141]

Indeed, may Christ awaken and revive His melancholy bride that she might act as if her Beloved really was the omnipotent, wonderful Savior that He is!

A Plea for Mercy

The remnant sought God's intervention (vv. 1-4), but knew that it was not merited (vv. 5-7). Therefore, they pleaded for mercy based solely on their covenant relationship with God, "their Father" (vv. 8-9). Although not every aspect of their prayer demonstrated perfect faith, the remnant concluded their petition with a confession of trust in the Lord. This prophetic prayer would assist the suffering remnant in Babylon to evaluate their disposition and situation and hopefully to respond to their hardship by turning to the Lord in faith.

The remnant addressed God as Father, suggesting that they had learned their lesson and were now obedient children, and as their Potter, to indicate that they were submitted to Him as pliable clay (v. 8). His obedient and submissive children were now asking their Father to restrain His anger against them and to assist them: *"Indeed, please look – we all are Your people"* (v. 9). Indeed, they were His people by covenant and the Lord had not forgotten that important detail.

Sorrow and Comfort

Lastly, the future exiled remnant reminds God that Israel's cities, including Jerusalem, were destroyed (v. 10). The beautiful temple in which their forefathers worshipped Him had been burnt (v. 11). The entire region was a wilderness; surely this was not a fitting place for them to reside with Him. Thus, the displaced remnant again asks God to no longer be silent or displeased with them, but to act on their behalf. Their prayer crescendos with their most pressing quandary: *"Will You restrain Yourself because of these things, O Lord? Will You hold Your peace, and afflict us very severely?"* (v. 12). In other words, "Lord, in view of how much we have already suffered and for the destruction to your temple, will You still refuse to help us?" God will respond to the remnant in the next chapter.

Meditation

> O Christ, He is the fountain, the deep, sweet well of love!
> The streams of earth I've tasted more deep I'll drink above:
> There to an ocean fullness His mercy doth expand,
> And glory, glory dwelleth in Immanuel's land.
>
> O I am my Beloved's and my Beloved's mine!
> He brings a poor, vile sinner into His house of wine.
> I stand upon His merit. I know no other stand,
> Not even where glory dwelleth in Immanuel's land.
>
> The Bride eyes not her garment, but her dear Bridegroom's face;
> I will not gaze at glory but on my King of grace.
> Not at the crown He giveth but on His pierced hand;
> The Lamb is all the glory of Immanuel's land.
>
> — Anne R. Cousin

God's Answer
Isaiah 65

In this chapter, Isaiah provides God's response to the long prayer of the exiled Jewish remnant (63:7-64:12), but not before rehearsing why they were being punished by Him. John A. Martin observes that the Lord's response in this chapter is a summary of Isaiah's entire book:

> In several ways the Lord's response to the remnant's prayers sums up the message of the entire Book of Isaiah. The Lord said that though He had constantly been presenting His love to Israel, they had rejected Him, which made judgment necessary (vv. 1-7). However, in that judgment, a remnant will be preserved (vv. 8-12). The consequences of righteous living differ from those of wicked living (vv. 13-17). The Lord will establish a glorious kingdom in which peace and righteousness will flourish (vv. 17-25).[142]

As in previous messages, Isaiah continues to plead with his countrymen to trust the Lord and to live righteously. God's response to the remnant's prayer commences with a review of Israel's deep-seated apostasy.

Apostasy Has Consequences

The Lord bemoans the fact that He has constantly reached out to Israel since the time He first called out to them, but, in general, the nation did not want Him or follow after Him. Israel did not ask for revelation about Him; rather, God says He revealed Himself to them, *"Here I am"*:

> *I was sought by those who did not ask for Me; I was found by those who did not seek Me. I said, "Here I am, here I am," to a nation that was not called by My name* (v. 1).

While the clear context of this passage is Israel's apostasy, Paul does quote this verse in Romans 10, but applies it to the Gentiles as an

Sorrow and Comfort

attempt to provoke the Jews to consider their present condition before the Lord: *"But Isaiah is very bold and says: 'I was found by those who did not seek Me; I was made manifest to those who did not ask for Me'"* (Rom. 10:20). W. E. Vine explains the Hebrew meaning of verse 1 which permitted Paul to also apply the verse to the Gentiles:

> The original has the past tenses, as in the RV margin: "I was inquired of (or rather, I was discernible) by them that asked not for Me (i.e., who refused to turn to God and seek Him); I was found (to be found) by them that sought Me not." God was ever ready to reveal Himself, had there been a heart to approach Him in humble desire to walk in His ways.[143]

No people group would know God, unless He first revealed Himself to them – God desires to show Himself to any humble person who will pursue Him. Paul's point was that in the Church Age, God was reaching out to the Gentiles (no longer to Israel primarily) through the worldwide proclamation of the gospel (Rom. 10:17-18).

Returning to the Jewish context of Isaiah 65, since the beginning, God has repeatedly held out His hand to guide and bless Israel, but they have been obstinate, independent, and rebellious: *"I have stretched out My hands all day long to a rebellious people, who walk in a way that is not good, according to their own thoughts"* (v. 2). Paul also quotes this verse (after applying the previous verse to the Gentiles) to validate that the same apostate spiritual condition existed in Israel in his day (Rom. 10:21). The Jews were religiously zealous, but not for God's righteousness through faith. Rather, they sought to establish their own righteousness through human traditions and legalistic rituals.

The Lord then lists the principal offenses that angered Him: First, His people sacrificed to false gods in pagan gardens (v. 3). Second, while sitting among the graves, they engaged in necromancy (v. 4). Necromancy involves supposedly speaking with departed souls, but the Bible calls these "familiar spirits" – fallen angels pretending to be what they are not. Third, they ate *"swine's flesh,"* which meant the Jews were violating their dietary laws (v. 4). Fourth, they had become religiously repugnant towards others: *"Keep to yourself, do not come near me, for I am holier than you"* (v. 5)!

These pompous zealots thought of themselves as superior to others because of their vain religious doings, but this behavior continually irritated God: *"These are smoke in My nostrils, a fire that burns all the*

Devotions in Isaiah

day." After the Babylonian exile, Israel never returned to idolatry, but rather became entrenched in legalism – self-promoting religion (Gal. 6:12-13). E. J. Young summarized the reality of their spiritual state: "Israel hated the holiness God had demanded"[144]; rather they sought to establish their own through zealous works (Rom. 10:1-3).

The conduct of His people was appalling and had to be judged in full. He would not keep silent – He loved them too much to permit them to continue plunging downward into self-destruction (v. 6). God had called Israel by His name, but their blasphemous behavior on the mountains of Israel was disgracing His name (v. 7). The situation could not be tolerated any longer. Through the Babylonians, God would do to Israel what He promised to do centuries earlier through Moses.

Moses warned the Israelites at that time that Jehovah would exile them if necessary to purge idolatry from the Promised Land. God had made good on His threat (Deut. 30:1-6). Moses also promised that if God did disperse them among the nations, He would indeed gather them back again into the land. This covenant with the Israelites was then conditional – they would be blessed if they obeyed God's commandments and punished if they did not (Jer. 29:9).

However, God's covenant with Abraham, which promised blessing and protection to a future refined nation of his descendants, was unconditional (Gen. 12:1-3). Eventually, there would be a nation from Abraham's lineage, which would inherit all of the Promised Land (Gen. 15:18-21) and be highly esteemed and blessed by all nations (Gen. 12:3). Until that time, the same Scripture that promised chastening, Moses's Law, also guaranteed restoration; this would encourage the Jews to flee from idolatry and seek God with all their heart. When they did, God would return them to Judah and commune with them again. Through Jeremiah, God promised Judah, *"You will seek me and find me when you seek me with all your heart"* (Jer. 29:13). The Jews knew about Jehovah, but they did not know Him intimately. In application, A. W. Tozer explains why it is important for those who have trusted Christ as Lord and Savior to keep seeking after God:

> Contemporary Christians have been caught in the spurious logic that those who have found Him need no longer seek Him. Come near to the holy men and women of the past and you will soon feel the heat of their desire after God. They mourned for Him, they prayed and wrestled and sought for Him day and night, in season and out, and

Sorrow and Comfort

when they found Him, the finding was all the sweeter for the long seeking.[145]

The great paradox of the Christian faith is that those who know the Lord Jesus Christ the best will be the ones who desire to seek Him more and to obey His Word.

Blessings and Curses

Though Isaiah warned that overwhelming judgment was coming against Israel, he also promised that God would not destroy all the clusters of grapes in the vineyard (v. 8). This meant that a remnant of Jews would return to Judah after the exile and through these clusters of grapes God would be refreshed as with new wine (v. 9). The Jews would then engage again in agriculture in the fertile coastal Plain of Sharon and tend their flocks again in the Valley of Achor, west of Jericho (v. 10).

However, those who would not trust in the Lord but chose to commit idolatry and to forsake His temple in Zion are marked for the sword (v. 11). Apparently, some Jews were worshipping the false gods *Gad* (meaning Fortune) and *Meni* (meaning Destiny) by putting food and drink before their images in an attempt to discern the future. Anyone willfully engaging in such sacrilegious practices could not claim ignorance and thus would perish: *"Because, when I called, you did not answer; when I spoke, you did not hear, but did evil before My eyes, and chose that in which I do not delight"* (v. 12).

Isaiah follows this stern warning with a comparison between the Lord's true servants and those who deserted Him (vv. 13-16). Those who trust and obey the Lord will eat, drink, rejoice, and sing joyfully in His presence because they are completely forgiven of past trespasses. In His Kingdom these faithful believers will receive another name befitting the new character they will exhibit after receiving the Holy Spirit: *"You shall leave your name as a curse to My chosen; for the Lord God will slay you, and call His servants by another name"* (v. 15). In contrast, those who abandon the Lord will suffer hunger, thirst, shame, grief, and death – they will not get a new name.

In heaven, believers will appreciate the Lord Jesus to the extent we have practically experienced Him in this life (2 Cor. 4:17). This may explain why each saint in glory will receive a white stone with a special name (presumably of the Lord Jesus) written on it – a name that no one else is aware of (Rev. 2:17). Among the throngs of heaven each person is guaranteed a special intimacy with the Lord Jesus which no one else can enjoy. Our lives are diverse, which means the Lord means something different to each of us. To the widow, He is "the Faithful Husband." To the orphan He is "the Caring Father." To the abused, He is "the Comforter of Sorrows."

In the Christian experience, the inheritance we each possess at present relates directly to how each believer has experienced the Lord's gracious and holy character. The Lord does not bestow such things as power and authority lightly; these are received in measure and in accordance with our capacity to retain each gift of grace in faith, love, and humility. To apprehend that which cannot be managed with wisdom would surely result in a worse outcome than not having a possession at all. Believers have different spiritual gifts, callings of ministry, talents to serve, and developed maturity in Christ. This means that each of us has different and varying capacities to receive and retain resurrection power as a spiritual possession.

The prophet's point here is that rebellion against God ultimately costs you everything and leaves you in hopeless despair. Why suffer such consequences when God offers you such a full and joyful alternative?

Israel's continued sin against the Lord had resulted in their confusion, shame and punishment: *"Righteousness exalts a nation, but sin is a reproach to any people"* (Prov. 14:34). They had more privilege than any nation and thus bore the reproach of their sin more than any nation. A nation that rebels against the Lord cannot expect His blessing, and a nation that does so under the guise of reverence should anticipate His condemnation. Yet, once the Jewish nation receives the Holy Spirit, she will forever be with the Lord in purity of blessed communion. Then the Lord says, *"They shall be My people, and I will be their God"* (Ezek. 27:23). He promises the faithful remnant that Israel's former failures will be forgotten because He has chosen to hide them from His eyes (v. 16). These and many more indescribable blessings will be realized in the Kingdom Age.

The Millennial Kingdom

The prophet wanted to inspire the faithful by telling them more about the new kingdom that God was preparing for them, one over which His Servant-Messiah would reign: *"For behold, I create new*

Sorrow and Comfort

heavens and a new earth; and the former shall not be remembered or come to mind" (v. 17). While this verse is often connected with the destruction of the earth, as described by John (Rev. 21:1), Isaiah is not referring to that event here, but rather to the new utopia that God will create during the Kingdom Age. In Isaiah's new heavens and new earth (the Kingdom Age), death and the opportunity for rebellion and sin still exist. This paradise will exist on the earth until what the Bible refers to as "the Day of the Lord" is fully realized.

As explained previously, "The Day of the Lord" is an Old Testament term that speaks of those times when Jehovah intervened in a visible and powerful way to judge the wicked on earth. This meaning continues into the New Testament and speaks specially of the Tribulation Period and the Millennial Kingdom of Christ. (Many of the Old Testament usages also speak of these future events.) The Day of the Lord concludes with the destruction of the earth and the subsequent Great White Throne judgment.

The Day of the Lord should not be confused with the Day of Christ. In Paul's first epistle to the Thessalonians, he spoke of Christ's imminent coming for His Church (1 Thess. 4:13-18), which is referred to as the Day of Christ with some variations, such as the Day of Jesus Christ (1 Cor. 1:8; Phil. 1:6, 10, 2:16). Paul also wrote the Thessalonians about the Day of the Lord which would follow (1 Thess. 5:1-5). Peter also speaks of the Day of the Lord (2 Pet. 3:10), and then introduces us to the Day of God, often referred to as the Eternal State (2 Pet. 3:12). Peter states that the Day of the Lord ends when the heavens and the earth pass away with a great noise and their elements melt with fervent heat and are burned up (2 Pet. 3:10). John tells us that this occurs directly after Christ's Millennial Kingdom and after the Great White Throne judgment of the wicked is complete (Rev. 20). Isaiah states that *"all the host of heaven shall be dissolved, and the heavens shall be rolled up like a scroll"* (34:4). John foretells that after the Millennial Kingdom, God will create a new heaven and new earth – this is the Day of God (Rev. 21:1).

Isaiah's description in verses 17-25 of God's new kingdom for the faithful clearly describes the Millennial Kingdom, not the eternal state, as building (v. 21), planting (v. 22), childbearing (v. 23), etc. are still occurring: *"My elect shall long enjoy the work of their hands. They shall not labor in vain, nor bring forth children for trouble; for they shall be the descendants of the blessed of the Lord"* (vv. 22-23).

During the Millennial Kingdom, Jerusalem will be the origin of joy for the entire earth:

But be glad and rejoice forever in what I create; for behold, I create Jerusalem as a rejoicing, and her people a joy. I will rejoice in Jerusalem, and joy in My people; the voice of weeping shall no longer be heard in her, nor the voice of crying (vv. 18-19).

During the Millennial Kingdom, death will be rare, mainly resulting from willful sin of those not yet in glorified bodies or controlled by the Holy Spirit (i.e., those surviving the Tribulation Period from the nations and their descendants):

No more shall an infant from there live but a few days, nor an old man who has not fulfilled his days; for the child shall die one hundred years old, but the sinner being one hundred years old shall be accursed (v. 20).

During the Millennial Kingdom, animals will no longer feed on each other or cause harm to one another or to any person. Peace and tranquility will characterize God's holy mountain, that is, His worldwide kingdom of justice, peace, and righteousness. Isaiah foretold:

"The wolf and the lamb shall feed together, the lion shall eat straw like the ox, and dust shall be the serpent's food. They shall not hurt nor destroy in all My holy mountain," says the Lord (v. 25).

What a blessing it will be when the curses that were put on the earth as a result of man's sin are lifted in the Kingdom Age (Rom. 8:21-22). A handful of seed casually scattered on a mountaintop will produce a great harvest (Ps. 72:16), longevity will be restored to humanity, weapons will be used as agricultural implements (Mic. 4:3), and a spirit of peace and tranquility will engulf the earth (11:9).

But the best part of all this is the oneness that the redeemed will enjoy with God. *"It shall come to pass that before they call, I will answer; and while they are still speaking, I will hear"* (v. 24). Previously Israel did not listen when God called to them, nor did they seek Him, but in the Kingdom Age, there will be no hindrances to full communion and fellowship with the Lord. All of this and more will be made possible by God's strong Arm – the Lord Jesus Christ – the King of Israel and the nations!

Meditation

> Come, gather, all tribes and all nations,
> To worship Jehovah our King;
> O, enter His presence with gladness,
> Your tribute of gratitude bring.
>
> O, sing of His power and glory,
> Great Ruler whose throne is the sky,
> Who giveth to men of His bounty
> In showers of grace from on high.
>
> O, sing of the wondrous redemption,
> The purchase of life for us all;
> O, give Him your song and your service
> For blessings that momently fall.
>
> — Adaline Hohf Beery

Devotions in Isaiah

God Keeps His Promises
Isaiah 66

Isaiah brings his literary work to its apex. First, he reiterates main themes he has often spoken of, and second, he acknowledges the complete fulfillment of God's promises to Abraham in the Millennial Kingdom. With great appropriateness, the prophet commences his closing remarks by affirming God's transcendence and Lordship over all things.

Isaiah employs poetic imagery to speak of God's majesty: God sitting on His lofty throne with the earth as His footstool (v. 1). God is the Creator and Sustainer of all things, so it would be impossible for man to construct a house for Him to reside and rest in (v. 2). Rather, Isaiah tells us what God does appreciate: *"But on this one will I look: On him who is poor and of a contrite spirit, and who trembles at My word"* (v. 2). Isaiah answers the question: "What type of man or woman bends the ear of God?" The answer is those who are in awe of Him and humbly submit to His Word. James puts the matter this way: *"The effective, fervent prayer of a righteous man avails much"* (Jas. 5:16). Thankfully, there were still such individuals in Israel, the remnant, and upon them the Lord would bestow His blessing.

Sadly, most of the Jewish nation in Isaiah's day suffered from murderous and idolatrous hearts; they engaged in vain religious rituals and rebelled against God's dietary laws (v. 3). It was obvious to God that their hearts were far from Him because they continued to do evil and they ignored His calls to repent and do what delighted Him (v. 4). These wandering religious nomads were going their own way and showed no remorse for oppressing faithful believers in the name of the Lord (v. 5). God promised to severely judge these rebels; they would all be ashamed when He destroyed the temple by the hands of the Babylonians (v. 6).

Sorrow and Comfort

Birth of a Son and Rebirth of a Nation

Isaiah then speaks of two births to the same woman, first "a male child," and then "her children": *"Before her pain came, she delivered **a male child**,"* (v. 7). *"Shall a nation be born at once? For as soon as Zion was in labor, she gave birth **to her children**"* (v. 8). That Israel was to give birth to the Messiah before the time of Jacob's trouble (the Tribulation Period; Jer. 30:6-7) is foretold in verse 7. John confirms the meaning of this prophecy (Rev. 12:5-6, 13) and Matthew and Luke note its fulfillment two thousand years ago in Bethlehem (Matt. 1:22; Luke 2:4-11). J. M. Riddle observes:

> The nation is described, not in all her moral and spiritual corruption, but as the center of divine administration and glory. Israel's future glory derives from the reign of her greatest Son. *"And she being with child cried, travailing in birth, and pained to be delivered ... And she brought forth a man child, who was to rule all nations with a rod of iron"* (vv. 2, 5). There can be no doubt about His identity: *"The Lord hath said unto me, Thou art my Son; this day have I begotten thee ... Thou shalt break them with a rod of iron"* (Ps. 2:7, 9). ... The birth of the "man child" is mentioned in Isaiah 66 to show that just as Christ was "brought forth" and preserved in adverse conditions, so, with equal certainty, the nation will travail, not with no result and to no purpose, but will bring forth "a nation ... her children."[146]

The first birth Isaiah spoke of was singular, a male child, but second birth will be plural – Israel's children. After Christ's second advent to the earth, the entire Jewish nation that survived the Tribulation Period will be endowed with the Holy Spirit and will experience spiritual rebirth.

Obviously, the Jewish remnant suddenly returning from Babylon under Cyrus's decree would be greatly encouraged by this prophecy. This event will be so abrupt and so unexpected (like a woman who delivers her baby after the first labor pain is felt; v. 8) that many Jews will think that Isaiah's prophecy had been fulfilled. Just as the newborn son delights in his mother, all Jerusalem will rejoice that God did not close the womb, but opened it to give Israel new life (vv. 9-11).

However, as we have already noticed, many of Isaiah's prophecies have a near-term and a far-reaching implication. Given the Millennial Kingdom context of the passage, the main focus of this prophecy is the future spiritual rebirth of Israel (not captives returning from Babylon),

Devotions in Isaiah

which will have full political ramifications. Both Isaiah and Jeremiah foretold Israel's future rebirth as a single nation, not as two kingdoms (Isa. 11:12; Jer. 3:18). However, only Ezekiel foretells that this united nation would be called "Israel." These prophecies refer to God's dealings with the Jews just prior to and then during the Millennial Kingdom when Christ will rule over them (Ezek. 37:22). Accordingly, as we approach the end of the Church Age, the initiation of these prophecies will be apparent, especially the regathering of Jews back into the land of Israel after centuries of global exile.

Recent events indicate that God has begun the process of bringing His covenant people home, hence setting the stage for what Isaiah is speaking of in this chapter. What is the far-reaching fulfillment of Isaiah's prophecy? That Israel and the nations will marvel that a Jewish nation, blessed and exalted by God, could come about "in one day" (vv. 7-9). Christ's Millennial Kingdom commences when every Jew on the planet is back in Israel under His protection and the entire nation has received the Holy Spirit (Ezek. 39:28-29).

During the Kingdom Age, Jerusalem will be the religious center of the world and the wealth of the nations shall flow into her (vv. 10-20). At this time, the Jewish nation will not only be restored to God, but will also be esteemed by all nations. In verses 12-13, Jerusalem is compared to a mother giving birth to a son, the new nation, but in verse 13, God is likened to a mother who comforts her adult children (His people). This latter thought captures the theme of Isaiah's book – Jehovah is a God of salvation and of immense comfort.

Isaiah foretold Israel's severe chastening and scattering, but he also foretold that God would restore His people to their homeland and would honor them before their enemies, on whom He promised to descend in judgment like fire and a whirlwind (vv. 14-16). The contrast is clear: God's faithful servants shall be comforted (v. 13), but their enemies shall receive His indignation (v. 14).

Idolaters and those who reject God's Law (e.g., eating swine) will perish (v. 17). This worldwide judgment, called "The Judgment of Nations" (Matt. 13:47-50, 25:31-47; Rev. 19:21), will occur at Christ's second advent, thus assuring that all the inhabitants of the earth see His glory (v. 18).

The broad implications of Isaiah's prophecy are obvious. When will Jewish evangelists travel to faraway countries to teach Gentiles about the Lord such that they respond by coming to Jerusalem to worship

Sorrow and Comfort

God (v. 19)? This did not happen in the sixth century B.C., but will happen during the latter days of the Tribulation Period and in the Millennial Kingdom. There will be 144,000 Jews sealed during the Tribulation Period to preach the kingdom gospel message throughout the earth (Matt. 24:14; Rev. 7:4-8, 14:1-5).

The result of this effort will be that all worshippers coming to the temple in Jerusalem will be blessed by Him who sits upon the *"mountain of holiness"* (vv. 20-21; Jer. 31:23). In this wonderful kingdom, denoted by the phrase "the new heavens and the new earth," Israel will enjoy fellowship with the Lord forever and all mankind will worship God in Jerusalem and be blessed by Him (vv. 22-23). However, those who rebel against God's Messiah will perish and the righteous shall watch the cremation of their corpses in the perpetual fires of the Hinnom Valley, Jerusalem's dump.

The final verse of this book is somber. Even after Israel is re-gathered, restored, and all the earth is being blessed by Christ, there will yet be a perpetual reminder of the awful result of rebellion and sin – Hell. Ultimately, all rebels will experience resurrection and after the Great White Throne judgment will join all the wicked in the Lake of Fire to suffer everlasting torment (Rev. 20:11-15). In Mark 9:44-48 the Lord Jesus quoted the last verse of Isaiah three times to solemnly warn unrepentant sinners of their eternal abode apart from Him: *"Their worm does not die, and their fire is not quenched"* (v. 24). As discussed in chapter 50, hell is a putrid, dark, agonizing, merciless eternal existence. Why would anyone choose to reject all the goodness offered to them in Christ to spend such a hopeless eternity apart from Him? The Lake of Fire will be an eternal witness to the appalling consequences of sin. In contrast, the Lord says that those who are *"poor and of a contrite spirit, and who trembles at My word"* (v. 2) will be eternally blessed in Christ!

The jubilation and blessing in Jerusalem after the Babylonian exile was short-lived because the Jews again disobeyed the Lord and were scattered among the nations. However, that brief festive event is a precursor to the future day when God will permanently restore His covenant people to Himself. They will then receive the Holy Spirit, will obtain a clean heart, and will never again rebel against their God. Then they will reap the full benefit of intimately knowing and being with their God.

W. E. Vine summarizes the tenor of Isaiah's messages with this brief application:

> All this brings home the folly, futility and sinfulness of pursuing our own way, carrying out our own designs and turning after that in which God cannot take pleasure, instead of waiting upon Him, listening to His voice and delighting in the fulfillment of His will. Through our walking with God He fulfills, and will fulfill, and the promises of His Word. He responds to delighted confidence in Him, by adding an Amen to His assurance. The peace of an obedient heart and a trusting spirit is that which enjoys the sunshine of His countenance and the calmness of holy communion with Him.[146]

Meditation

> O Christ, our God, who with Thine own hast been,
> Our spirits cleave to Thee, our unseen Friend.
> Make every heart that is Thy dwelling place
> A watered garden filled with fruits of grace.
>
> O grant us peace, that by Thy peace possessed,
> Thy life within us we may manifest.
> So shall we pass our days in holy fear,
> In joyful consciousness that Thou art near.
>
> — George Bourne

Endnotes

1. H. A. Ironside, *Isaiah* – Revised Edition (Loizeaux, Neptune, NJ; 2000), p. 255
2. J. G. Bellett, *An Introduction to Isaiah*, STEM Publishing: http://stempublishing.com/authors/bellett/Isaintro.html
3. William MacDonald, *Believer's Bible Commentary* (Thomas Nelson Publishers, Nashville, TN; 1989), Intro.
4. Alfred Martin, *Isaiah: The Salvation of Jehovah* (Moody Press, Chicago, IL; 1956), pp. 18-19
5. *The Greek New Testament* (the fourth edition), B. Aland, K. Aland, J. Karavidopoulos, C. M. Martini, and B. M. Metzger, editors (United Bible Society; 1993)
6. J. G. Bellett, op. cit.
7. William Kelly, *Isaiah - Exposition*, Part 2, STEM Publishing: http://stempublishing.com/authors/kelly/1Oldtest/ISA_PT2.html#a1
8. William MacDonald, *Believer's Bible Commentary* (Thomas Nelson Publishers, Nashville, TN; 1989), Isa. 1:18
9. F. B. Hole, *Isaiah*, STEM Publishing (chp. 1): http://stempublishing.com/authors/hole/Art/ISAIAH.htm
10. Albert Barnes, *Notes on the Old Testament – Isaiah* (Baker Book House, Grand Rapids, MI; reprinted 1851), 1:22
11. J. M. Riddle, *What the Bible Teaches – Song of Solomon and Isaiah* (John Ritchie LTD, Kilmarnock, Scotland; 2015) Isa. 2
12. Matthew Henry, *Matthew Henry's Concise Commentary on the Whole Bible* (e-Sword, electronic version); 2:1-9
13. J. A. Motyer, *The Prophecy of Isaiah* (InterVarsity Press, Downers Grove, IL; 1993), p. 55
14. Ibid., p. 56
15. William MacDonald, *Believer's Bible Commentary* (Thomas Nelson Publishers, Nashville, TN; 1989), p. 942
16. John A. Martin, *The Bible Knowledge Old Testament Commentary*, edited by J. F. Walvoord and Roy Zuck (Victor Books, Wheaton, IL; 1986), p. 1040
17. F. C. Jennings, *Studies in Isaiah* (Loizeaux Brothers, Neptune, NJ; 1935), Isa. 3
18. William Kelly, op. cit., chp. 3
19. E. J. Young, *The Book of Isaiah,* (Eerdmans Publishing Co., Grand Rapids, MI; 1965), Isa. 3
20. Albert Barnes, op. cit., 4:1
21. J. A. Motyer, op. cit., p. 59
22. F. B. Hole, op. cit., chp. 4

[23] Albert Barnes, op. cit., 5:10
[24] *The American Heritage Dictionary* (Houghton Mifflin Company, Boston, MA; 1978)
[25] F. B. Hole, op. cit., chp. 6
[26] Matthew Henry, *Commentary on the Whole Bible, Vol. 4*, (MacDonald Pub. Co., Mclean, VA; 1985), Isa. 6
[27] Albert Barnes, *Barnes Notes*, (Baker Book House, Grand Rapids, MI; reprinted from 1884 edition published by Blackie and Son, London), 1 Cor. 11:6
[28] William MacDonald, op. cit., p. 944
[29] J. A. Motyer, op. cit., p. 78
[30] W. E. Vine, *Isaiah: Prophecies, Promises, Warnings* (Oliphants, LTD, London, England; 1947), p. 32
[31] Ibid., p. 1047
[32] J. N. Darby, *Notes on Isaiah*, STEM Publishing (chp. 5): http://stempublishing.com/authors/darby/NOTESCOM/44005E.html
[33] Matthew Henry, op. cit., 7:10-16
[34] Bertrand Russell, *Skeptical Essays*; 1928
[35] Albert Barnes, op. cit., 7:22
[36] Albert Barnes, op. cit., 7:17
[37] Daniel D. Luckenbill, *Ancient Records of Assyria and Babylon* (Oriental Institute University of Chicago, Chicago, IL; 1926
[38] J. A. Motyer, op. cit., p. 92
[39] William Kelly, op. cit., chp. 8
[40] M. C. Unger, *Unger's Commentary on the Old Testament, Vol. 2: Isaiah to Malachi* (Moody Press, Chicago, IL; 1981), Isa. 8
[41] W. E. Vine, op. cit., p. 41
[42] H. A. Ironside, *Isaiah* – Revised Edition, op. cit., p. 57
[43] Albert Barnes, op. cit., 9:6
[44] Dr. R. P. Smith, *Authenticity and Messianic Interpretation of Isaiah* (University of Oxford, London; 1862), p. 63
[45] J. A. Motyer, op. cit., p. 121
[46] F. B. Hole, op. cit., chp. 11
[47] J. A. Motyer, op. cit., p. 132
[48] James B. Pritchard, *Ancient Near Eastern Texts Relating to the Old Testament* (Princeton University Press, Princeton, NJ; 1955), p. 306
[49] David Down, *Investigator 17, 1991* (March): Reprinted courtesy of SIGNS OF THE TIMES; 1983, Volume 98, Number 6)
[50] William Kelly, op. cit., chp. 13
[51] Ryrie, *Ryrie Study Bible* (NKJV), (Moody Press, Chicago, IL; 1986), p. 1054
[52] F. B. Hole, op. cit., chp. 17
[53] J. N. Darby, op. cit., chp. 18
[54] Albert Barnes, op. cit., 19:4
[55] Albert Barnes, op. cit., 20:2
[56] Matthew Henry, op. cit., 20:1-6

Endnotes

57 Ibid., 20:4
58 John A. Martin, op. cit., p. 1068
59 Josephus, *Antiquities* 13.9.1; 15:4
60 H. A. Ironside, *An Ironside Expository Commentary: Ezekiel*, op. cit., p. 269
61 Quintus Curtius Rufus, *History of Alexander the Great of Macedonia*; Section 4.4.10-21
62 H. A. Ironside, *Isaiah* – Revised Edition, op. cit., p. 108
63 J. A. Motyer, op. cit., p. 132
64 Matthew Henry, op. cit., 24:1-12
65 E. J. Young, op. cit., Isa. 25
66 J. M. Riddle, op. cit., Isa. 26
67 William Kelly, op. cit., chp. 26
68 Warren Wiersbe, *The Bible Exposition Commentary, Vol. 2* (Victor Books, Wheaton, IL: 1989), pp. 327-328
69 Dr. Howard Taylor, *Spiritual Secret of Hudson Taylor* (Whitaker House, New Kensington, PA: 1996), p. 351
70 H. A. Ironside, *Isaiah* – Revised Edition, op. cit., p. 125
71 F. C. Jennings, op. cit., Isa. 27
72 John A. Martin, op. cit., pp. 1075-1076
73 Jewish Virtual Library – Vital Statistic: Population of Israel [last accessed March 28, 2017]: http://www.jewishvirtuallibrary.org/jsource/Society_&_Culture/Population_of_Israel.html
74 John A. Martin, op. cit., p. 1078
75 Albert Barnes, op. cit., 28:20
76 Albert Barnes, op. clt., 30.1
77 H. A. Ironside, *Isaiah* – Revised Edition, op. cit., p. 144
78 John A. Martin, op. cit., p. 1080
79 F. B. Hole, op. cit., chp. 30
80 J. A. Motyer, op. cit., p. 262
81 J. M. Riddle, op. cit., Isa. 32
82 F. C. Jennings, op. cit., Isa. 32
83 James B. Pritchard, *Ancient Near Eastern Texts*, 2nd ed. (Princeton University Press, Princeton, NJ; 1955), p. 287
84 Albert Barnes, op. cit., 33:4
85 J. A. Motyer, op. cit., p. 264
86 J. A. Motyer, op. cit., p. 268
87 Edythe Draper, *Draper's Quotations from the Christian World* – Soul (Tyndale House Publishers Inc., Wheaton, Il. – electronic copy), Anger
88 Albert Barnes, op. cit., 34:4
89 Albert Barnes, op. cit., 34:5
90 J. A. Motyer, op. cit., p. 274-275
91 "The Siege of Lachish," *Odyssey Adventures in Archaeology* (Feb. 9, 2012): http://www.odysseyadventures.ca/articles/lachish_slides/lachish_text.htm
92 James B. Pritchard, op. cit.

Sorrow and Comfort

[93] John A. Martin, op. cit., p. 1089
[94] J. N. Darby, *Synopsis of the Books of the Bible Vol. 1*, op. cit., pp. 60-61
[95] John A. Martin, op. cit., p. 1090
[96] H. A. Ironside, *Isaiah – Revised Edition*, op. cit., p. 179
[97] Matthew Henry, op. cit., 40:18-26
[98] J. M. Riddle, op. cit., Isa. 41
[99] *New Exhaustive Strong's Numbers and Concordance with Expanded Greek-Hebrew Dictionary.* Copyright (c) 1994, Biblesoft and International Bible Translators, Inc.
[100] Ibid.
[101] *Adam Clarke's Commentary*, Electronic Database. Copyright (c) 1996 by Biblesoft
[102] *Jamieson, Fausset, and Brown Commentary*, Electronic Database. Copyright (c) 1997 by Biblesoft
[103] W. E. Vine, op. cit., Isa. 43
[104] J. A. Motyer, op. cit., p. 332
[105] Albert Barnes, op. cit., 44:20
[106] J. M. Riddle, op. cit., Isa. 45
[107] H. A. Ironside, *Isaiah – Revised Edition*, op. cit., p. 201
[108] F. B. Hole, op. cit., chp. 45
[109] J. A. Motyer, op. cit., p. 368
[110] John A. Martin, op. cit., p. 1100
[111] W. E. Vine, *Isaiah, Prophecies, Promises, Warnings* (Oliphants Ltd., London and Edinburgh; 1946), Isa. 43:13
[112] Albert Barnes, op. cit., 48:22
[113] J. M. Riddle, op. cit., Isa. 49
[114] F. B. Hole, op. cit., chp. 49
[115] J. M. Riddle, op. cit., Isa. 50
[116] F. B. Hole, op. cit., chp. 50
[117] W. Grinton Berry, *Foxe's Book of Martyrs* (Power Books, Old Tappen, New Jersey), p. 9
[118] J. M. Riddle, op. cit., Isa. 51
[119] W. E. Vine, op. cit., Isa. 51
[120] J. M. Riddle, op. cit., Isa. 52
[121] Brown-Driver-Briggs Hebrew and English Lexicon, Unabridged, Electronic Database. Copyright (c) 2002 by Biblesoft, Inc.)
[122] Ancient Hebrew Research Center/ Jeff A. Benner, *The Great Isaiah Scroll and the Masoretic Text* [Online] http://www.ancient-hebrew.org/bible_isaiahscroll.html [Accessed 21 June 2016]
[123] J. M. Riddle, op. cit., Isa. 53
[124] F. C. Jennings, op. cit., Isa. 53
[125] Norman Anderson, *Isaiah 53*, STEM Publishing: http://stempublishing.com/authors/anderson/ISAIAH53.html

Endnotes

[126] J. G. Bellett, *Musings on Scripture* (Vol. 3, Section 6), STEM Publishing: http://stempublishing.com/authors/bellett/ISA52_13.html
[127] F. B. Hole, op. cit., chp. 53
[128] Emma Moody Fitt, *Day by Day With D. L. Moody* (Moody Press, Chicago, IL; 1977), Oct. 9th
[129] William MacDonald, *Believer's Bible Commentary* (Thomas Nelson Publishers, Nashville, TN; 1989), Isa. 57:7-10
[130] William E. Allen, *The History of Revivals in Religion* (Revival Pub. Co, UK; 1951), chp. 1
[131] William MacDonald, *Believer's Bible Commentary* (Thomas Nelson Publishers, Nashville, TN; 1989), Isa. 57:14-19
[132] Matthew Henry, op. cit., 58:1-2
[133] H. A. Ironside, *Isaiah* – Revised Edition, op. cit., p. 247
[134] Albert Barnes, *The Bible Commentary Vol. 5* (Baker Book House, Grand Rapids, MI; reprinted 1879), p. 194
[135] J. M. Riddle, op. cit., Isa. 60
[136] William Kelly, op. cit., chp. 62
[137] William Kelly, op. cit., chp. 63
[138] Albert Barnes, op. cit., 64:1
[139] F. B. Hole, op. cit., chp. 64
[140] Albert Barnes, op. cit., 64:6
[141] F. B. Hole, op. cit., chp. 64
[142] John A. Martin, op. cit., p. 1119
[143] W. E. Vine, op. cit., Isa. 65
[144] E. J. Young, op. cit., Isa. 65
[145] A. W. Tozer, *The Pursuit of God* (Revell, Old Tappan, NJ; 1987), p. 16
[146] J. M. Riddle, op. cit., Isa. 66
[147] W. E. Vine, op. cit., Isa. 66 (p. 214-215)